Mathematics

Teacher's Book

Tony Gardiner

OXFORD
UNIVERSITY PRESS

Great Clarendon Street, Oxford OX2 6DP

Oxford University Press is a department of the University of Oxford.
It furthers the University's objective of excellence in research, scholarship,
and education by publishing worldwide in

Oxford   New York

Auckland   Cape Town   Dar es Salaam   Hong Kong   Karachi
Kuala Lumpur   Madrid   Melbourne   Mexico City   Nairobi
New Delhi   Shanghai   Taipei   Toronto

With offices in

Argentina   Austria   Brazil   Chile   Czech Republic   France   Greece
Guatemala   Hungary   Italy   Japan   Poland   Portugal   Singapore
South Korea   Switzerland   Thailand   Turkey   Ukraine   Vietnam

© Tony Gardiner 2007

The moral rights of the author have been asserted

Database right Oxford University Press (maker)

First published 2007

All rights reserved. No part of this publication may be reproduced,
stored in a retrieval system, or transmitted, in any form or by any means,
without the prior permission in writing of Oxford University Press,
or as expressly permitted by law, or under terms agreed with the appropriate
reprographics rights organization. Enquiries concerning reproduction
outside the scope of the above should be sent to the Rights Department,
Oxford University Press, at the address above

You must not circulate this book in any other binding or cover
and you must impose this same condition on any acquirer

British Library Cataloguing in Publication Data

Data available

ISBN-13: 978 01991 51530

20 19 18 17 16 15 14 13 12

Printed in Great Britain by Bell and Bain Ltd, Glasgow

Contents

Introduction — 1

Part 1
Background

1 Why an extension curriculum is needed — 9
2 The principles of elementary mathematics — 20

Part 2
The Works

3 Comments on and answers to the problems: book-by-book and section-by-section — 63

   Comments on the listing of sections in each book by topic — 63

3A *Alpha*
   Rough listing of sections by topic — 64
   Comments and answers — 65

3B *Beta*
   Rough listing of sections by topic — 97
   Comments and answers — 99

3C *Gamma*
   Rough listing of sections by topic — 152
   Comments and answers — 154

Glossary — 206

Introduction

This *Teachers' Book* accompanies a series of three books containing *extension* material designed for the top 25% or so of lower secondary pupils.

Apart from this introduction, the book has two parts.

◎ PART I contains an indication of why an extension curriculum is needed (Chapter 1) and an analysis of the character of elementary mathematics and its teaching (Chapter 2) – with particular reference to what matters most for those pupils who may need to study mathematics beyond age 16. This analysis is intended to provide food for thought and to give the user an insight into what lies behind the choice of material in Books *Alpha*, *Beta* and *Gamma*.

◎ Part II contains comments on, and answers to, the problems in each section of each of the first three pupil books (Chapter 3) and a Glossary indicating where standard terms first occur.

By its very nature any *extension* programme deviates from the standard curriculum path: teachers may therefore be relatively unfamiliar with its content and goals. However, the effectiveness of any teaching material (and especially extension material, with its long-term goals and higher expectations) depends to a large extent on whether the teacher understands and appreciates its goals, and so is more likely to use it in a manner that is consistent with its mathematical and educational intentions – even if their own style is significantly different. Hence those teachers who hesitate to adopt this series all at once may consider the following approach.

◎ Choose a number of linked sections (initially in Book *Alpha* or possibly Book *Beta*), and get to know them as well as you can. Then try using them to add spice to the standard diet you currently provide for top sets, always including **Problem 0**, but using your own judgement when to use a complete section, or when it is more appropriate to choose a *subset* of the problems listed.

◎ When in doubt, choose sections, problems and problem sequences that you yourself find appealing (remembering to include a sufficient number of each type of problem to ensure the necessary amount of practice, and taking care not to choose too many problems that are "interesting" but possibly too hard).

Good quality extension material is not specifically age-related: a good problem appeals to all ages – *as long as it is accessible*. Book *Alpha* is designed to be accessible to the top 25% or so of pupils in the first years of secondary school, limiting assumed prerequisite knowledge to what might be expected at some stage during Year 7 (age 11-12); *but it is in no way restricted to that age group*. Book *Beta* is designed to be accessible to pupils in Year 8 (age 12-13), in that prerequisite knowledge is limited to what might be routinely taught to the top 25% at some stage during Year 8; however, the material in book *Beta* is needed by, and can be used effectively with, any pupils in Years 8-10 who are not already familiar with its contents. Similarly Book *Gamma* is designed to be within reach of able pupils in Year 9 – though this statement should not be interpreted too narrowly. Year 9 pupils who have not worked through earlier books in the series are advised to attempt selected sections from Book *Alpha* and then to concentrate on Book *Beta* before attacking the material in Book *Gamma*. The material in Book *Gamma* will also be of value to many older pupils.

In schools with higher levels of expectation, some of the material in each book may seem accessible to younger age-groups. However, there are good reasons for hesitating to use the material prematurely, even if at first sight it looks accessible. The material seeks to encourage pupils not just to grind out answers, but to *think* and to talk about elementary techniques – which presumes a certain level of sophistication. Nevertheless, teachers are encouraged to adapt and to use sections in ways the author never imagined!

The material uses the current English *Frameworks* as a rough guide. But within this constraint, it seeks to capture and to convey *the essence of elementary mathematics* rather than to reflect current expectations and norms.

Forty years ago England had a worldwide reputation for the way its schools extended able young mathematicians. This past reputation needs to be interpreted with caution. However, there is no escaping the fact that the structures *currently* in place fail to lay appropriate foundations for the most able 25%. Mathematics retains its perennial appeal – as shown by the huge expansion in mathematics competitions and other extra-curricular opportunities. Yet very few English Year 9 students achieve at the expected level for able pupils (as indicated by international comparisons – see Chapter 1, Section 1.2).

Mathematics at all levels begins when two or three elementary ideas have to be selected and combined – often in slightly unexpected ways – to solve an elementary but unfamiliar problem. An extension curriculum that embodies this principle is urgently needed – and not just for a small minority of pupils. It should be designed to establish a stronger foundation for a large fraction (around 25%) of each cohort, providing material suitable for *whole classes*, so offering teachers and senior management something to enrich the daily diet of *at least one top set* in every secondary school.

The range of ability between the 75th percentile and the 99th percentile is staggering. Hence the items in books *Alpha*, *Beta* and *Gamma* have been classified into **three levels**:

- *Tasters* (numbered **T1** etc.) are meant to be accessible to all those in the target group in the sense that they should all be able to tackle the problems and to have a degree of success – though some pupils will inevitably begin to struggle with the later problems even on *Taster* sets.

- *Core* items (numbered **C1** etc.) cover curriculum topics relatively systematically, but may be appropriate only for a subset of those who engage with the *Tasters*. How big this subset is will inevitably depend on the school and how the pupils have been taught.

- *Extension* items (numbered **E1** etc.) push *Core* ideas slightly further, or venture a little beyond the official curriculum, whilst keeping their feet firmly on the ground.

Very roughly one might expect *Tasters* to be suitable for 25% of each cohort, *Core* to be suitable for 15-20%, and *Extensions* suitable for 5-10%; however, such figures are highly dependent on teachers' expectations.

Each *Taster* and *Core* section includes a set of problems that is designed to encourage pupils to *develop a specific conceptual insight*, using material that is *closely related to what one finds in most mathematics classrooms*. The problems are to be actively tackled, and thought about – not merely 'answered'. Much of the relevant prerequisite material for these sections should have been covered in ordinary classwork. However, as is natural in a 'series', some *Taster* and *Core* sections in the second and third books develop ideas introduced in the *Taster* and *Core* sections of earlier books in the series (but never depend on ideas from the *Extension* sections of earlier books). *Internal* prerequisites that might otherwise be overlooked are indicated at the top of the relevant section; obvious prerequisites (e.g. where the section title indicates a link with some earlier section – such as *Sequences B*, or **More angles**) are not mentioned explicitly. More general issues and connections are clarified in the present *Teachers' Book*. In general:

C2 C12

- Earlier sections tend to be easier (in some sense) than later sections, but there is nothing to stop teachers selecting sections to suit their needs.

- The purpose of each section may be missed if pupils are allowed to produce answers in a way that is not in the intended spirit. In particular, the label '**NC**' means 'No Calculators'.

- Each *Taster* or *Core* section is designed to be used with a complete class. Every such section begins with (i) a short introductory text and (ii) a **Problem 0**.
  (i) The short introductory text in each section must be understood before pupils begin, but teachers are encouraged to decide for themselves how best to structure any necessary review.
  (ii) Problem 0 is to be tackled by the whole class. Where this is done individually in the first instance, the results should subsequently be discussed as a group, with contributions and explanations orchestrated by the teacher *to bring out the intended spirit of the section*, and to emphasise the intended approach and the expected layout as indicated in the introductory text.

- Problem 0 is *not* meant to be solved by the teacher as a 'worked example'. Rather it is to be solved *by the class* and should be used to bring out – and to correct – misconceptions and errors, so that every member of the class understands how to approach such problems, and so that all pupils emerge from the discussion with a clear idea of what is expected in that section.

- Problem 0 often includes a harder part. This too is to be solved *by the class*, with explanations *from the class*, to ensure that everyone sees how the simple principles being developed can be used to solve harder problems.

- Each section requires one or more *specific* insights: any contributions during the preliminary class discussion that could obscure the intended focus need to be handled carefully. The *way* in which the problems are solved is crucial. Hence the initial class discussion needs to be handled in such a way as to ensure that pupils emerge with the tools they need to tackle the problems that follow in the intended spirit.

Roughly speaking, my goal has been to pursue important themes from the official curriculum in ways that make mathematics more attractive, exploring simple ideas *more deeply*, and bringing out *connections between these simple ideas*. The existing curriculum should thereby be mastered in greater depth, with *connections* between topics being established and exploited in a way that counteracts the trend in recent years towards

  (i) increasing fragmentation
  (ii) superficial coverage
  (iii) lack of fluency
  (iv) failure to develop a clear notion of mathematical proof

all of which contribute to a general failure to engage pupils' mathematical imagination.

Many able pupils are not used to tackling unfamiliar problems using only what they know. When they meet unfamiliar material, there may be pressure on the teacher to 'help' by giving rules that might reduce pupils' need to struggle. However, such premature rules prevent pupils from developing their own habit of 'sense making', and deprive them of both the satisfaction of achieving the relevant unexpected insight for themselves, and the experience of applying that insight to new problems.

Mathematical mastery requires a considerable amount of repetitive exercising of simple processes. Repetitive practice is needed in order to achieve the level of *fluency* and *accuracy* that will allow longer chains of calculation to be completed without introducing unanticipated errors due to 'overload'. Such repetition can be a source of considerable pleasure and satisfaction for the learner (and often involves a greater degree of challenge than we acknowledge). Most sections contain lots of exercises to provide this kind of *repetition-with-a-purpose*.

It is also important that basic techniques should be routinely used to solve more demanding problems. Thus most *Taster* and *Core* sections include a number of problems of a more demanding kind; such problems sometimes appear in a shaded box . These problems are not necessarily harder, or intended for a minority; the shaded box is simply an indication that these problems require a greater degree of thought or perseverance.

Extension sections provide additional (mostly harder) problems, mainly for those pupils who have already devoured the *Taster* and *Core* sections and who need something more demanding. The *Extension* sections differ slightly from the *Taster* and *Core* sections: whereas the *Taster* and *Core* sections are designed to be used with whole classes, and so have a clear structure, the *Extension* sections may be appropriate only for a minority of those in a top set; so it seems counterproductive to prescribe how they should be used. Each *Extension* section has a theme – but the focus is sometimes slightly blurred to keep pupils on their toes. Later problems in each section still tend to be harder than earlier problems, but more demanding problems are rarely included in a shaded box. *Extension* sections should be seen as an extra resource to be used as teachers and pupils see fit.

Elementary mathematics retains its unrivalled potential to appeal to young minds. But many essential techniques and attitudes have recently been downplayed or neglected. This neglect stems in part from pressure on schools to demonstrate 'success' in narrowly focused, and increasingly predictable, central assessments. Unfortunately, tests which are obliged to demonstrate success shy away from those aspects of elementary mathematics that appeal to young minds precisely because they are *accessible, but slightly elusive*. But as observed above, 'mathematics proper' begins when two or three elementary ideas need to be combined to solve an unfamiliar problem. **This series of** books provides problem sequences that aim to reinstate this experience on a very simple level.

- The material requires pupils who are willing to struggle, to experience discomfort, and who come to accept this as 'normal' (even tantalising).

- In each section **Problem 0** (tackled by the class under the guidance of the teacher) provides the opportunity for any necessary review and preparation.

Pupils may still feel uncomfortable when confronted with the need to work quickly and accurately, or to make sense of unfamiliar-looking problems; but this activity is quintessentially human, and – provided that the demands being made are not unrealistic – the result for ordinary pupils can only be positive. In particular, one can anticipate a fresh flexibility, self-criticism, and self-correction when the same pupils are faced with more straightforward tasks.

Part 1
Background

1 Why an extension curriculum is needed

1.1 If you want to build higher, you'd better first dig deeper

To lay a path or patio, it suffices to prepare a shallow base on which to lay the flagstones. When building a bungalow, one needs to dig footings of a metre or so and lay concrete foundations for the walls to sit upon. But when preparing to build a taller structure, it can take many months of digging and pile-driving to prepare the foundations before there is any visible progress 'above ground'.

In much the same way what constitute suitable foundations in school mathematics will depend on what a particular group of pupils might one day need to *build upon* those foundations. The higher one may ultimately need to build, the deeper and stronger the foundations one must be prepared to lay.

The series *Extension mathematics* deliberately avoids rushing ahead prematurely: it concentrates instead on laying strong foundations in basic technique, and on cultivating flexibility in selecting and combining simple methods. It should thereby serve *large numbers* of pupils, including all those who might one day need to make sense of mathematically based data, or who might find themselves studying a mildly numerate discipline at university. In the modern world, these groups constitute an increasingly large fraction of each age cohort – a fraction which we take to be of the order of 25%.

The 1999 national curriculum provides a fragmented set of headings; but the interpretation of such a list has to depend on the target audience. For example, the full-blooded arithmetic of fractions may be deemed a luxury for some pupils; but it is an inescapable rite of passage for those who may later need to use formulae or elementary algebra, to interpret graphs and functions, or to solve problems involving ratio and proportion, scale factors and enlargements.

The surprising power of elementary mathematics lies in recognising that one can often achieve more than one has a right to expect by combining the simplest tools in fairly standard ways. It should be a central goal of mathematics education *to allow as many pupils as possible to experience this as an integral part of their daily diet of school mathematics*. That is what this series seeks to achieve.

The challenge of helping more pupils to achieve this central goal is an important one. But it has been obscured by those who would like us to believe that one can somehow by-pass the mathematical 'nursery slopes', where beginners gain confidence by proceeding step-by-step, and head straight for the open mountain side – as if basic technique, appreciation of mathematical structure, and mastery of the subtle art of application could all be learned at the same time. They can't.

If we want more 18 year olds to have the confidence to use simple mathematical methods, their experience of mathematics at lower secondary level

- must bring out the fundamental principles on which elementary mathematics is based (some of which are discussed in Chapter 2);

- must achieve a robust fluency in using individual techniques;

- must underline the range of problems that elementary mathematics can help us to solve;
- must develop key links *between* topics (such as the use of number, measures, fractions, surds and algebra in geometry); and
- must routinely cultivate objective mathematical reasoning which allows pupils to test the correctness of any method or solution they wish to use.

Rather than exploring 'the open mountain side' directly, this series of books uses ordinary school mathematics and basic technique to weave a rich tapestry of exercises and problems that should ultimately equip many more pupils to appreciate the wonders of the mathematical wilderness. It is not our primary concern here to engage with the fascinating world of investigations, imaginative problem solving, and harder problems in elementary mathematics; however, those who wish to progress to this more ambitious realm will find plenty of relevant material in the author's other books (*Maths challenge 1, 2, 3*, Oxford University Press 2000; *Mathematical puzzling*, Dover Publications 1999; *Discovering mathematics: the art of investigation*, Dover Publications, 2007; *Mathematical challenge*, Cambridge University Press 1996; *More mathematical challenges*, Cambridge University Press 1997; *The mathematical olympiad handbook*, Oxford University Press 1997).

1.2 The context

Modern society is increasingly dependent on mathematics. Yet school mathematics is being routinely taught and assessed in a way that fails to provide what pupils – and future adults – need. Basic material is not being learned in a sufficiently rich way to provide a foundation for subsequent learning; and the typical school diet is not sufficiently stimulating to convince good students that they should continue their study of mathematics.

Many sections of government – at national and European level – are concerned about the current shortfall in technically qualified manpower. In the UK the Roberts' report *SET for success* (April 2002) highlighted the dramatic shortage of home-grown graduates in relevant disciplines. This report was primarily concerned with Science, Engineering and Technology (hence the acronym 'SET' in Roberts' title, rather than STEM); but it recognised the central importance of addressing weaknesses in school mathematics, and recommended the review which eventually produced the report *Making mathematics count* (2004).

However, the official response to shortages in qualified manpower, or to pupils' failure to engage with difficult subjects, often assumes that problems in education can be addressed in the spirit of naive economics – by simply 'dropping the price'. Politicians and bureaucrats think that the way to make mathematics more attractive is to *reduce the level of intellectual challenge* to a point where they imagine more students will be prepared to engage with the subject. What such an approach fails to recognise is that, **if the mathematical substance of a programme is diluted below some crucial threshold, the subject loses its coherence and appeal.**

The uncomfortable truth is that one cannot attract pupils to study 'hard' subjects by continually lowering the intellectual demand. To be sure, one needs *an administrative framework which offers suitable rewards for the amount of work required*. But one also has to ensure that pupils experience *the essence of the discipline* in an appropriate way, and at an appropriate age. They need a serious and memorable experience of school mathematics, that allows many more of them to achieve fluency in basic technique, and to grapple with the kind of challenging problems which should be completely standard. Only then will we begin to persuade more young minds to pursue studies in highly numerate disciplines.

What grounds are there for suggesting that we could be doing better? The number of 18-year-olds in the UK proceeding to university has grown substantially. But the number choosing to study mathematics has remained stagnant for decades (at around 4000). We clearly need more students to take their study of mathematics as far as they can; but the number of UK students choosing to proceed to study A level mathematics has been allowed to decline steadily and is now worryingly low and stubbornly stagnant. Numbers reached an all-time low of 53 000 or so in 2004 and 2005. Emergency moves to reduce what was expected of students after 2003 led to a slight recovery in numbers; but this in no way addressed the basic challenge, which is still to achieve a substantial increase in the number of those who emerge at 16 and at 18 with a satisfactory grasp of elementary mathematics.

Many of the changes during the last 30 years have been imposed or driven by external *bureaucratic* structures (a uniform exam system, a national curriculum, inspections, national tests, league tables, targets, politically driven national strategies, medium term plans, etc.). Opportunities for teacher-led curriculum development based on professional judgement have been stifled. In their place we have witnessed wave upon wave of official initiatives, programmes and strategies intended to meet official 'targets'. What impact have these initiatives had?

The amounts of money invested in these initiatives and the pressure exerted on those involved to produce evidence of 'improvement' could be interpreted as indicating that the underlying problems were being taken seriously. However, to assess their real impact, one must distinguish between *claims* of improvement based on *internal* measures (e.g. national tests at age 7, 11 and 14), and the evidence of *external* measures (such as the more reliable of the international comparisons: e.g. TIMSS – *Trends in International Mathematics and Science Study*).

- Internal tests (and hence test results) vary from year to year as a result of incidental drift. But they are also subject to political pressure to report 'improved' scores. For example, in 1999 the percentage of pupils achieving 'level 4' at age 11 leapt overnight from 59% to 69% – a jump which was politically convenient at the time, but which was clearly fabricated. Internal tests cannot in themselves provide evidence of improvement – though they can and do provide evidence of negative trends.

- External tests are certainly not immune to change; but they are largely free of the kind of local pressures referred to above that may distort longitudinal assessment in any one particular country.

Hence the marked improvement in the average scores of English Year 5 pupils in the TIMSS international comparisons between 1999 and 2003 is noteworthy. England's Year 5 TIMSS average score in 1995 and in 1999 was poor. The improvement registered in 2003 was greater than for any other country – which suggests that recent changes have had a marked impact. However, as we shall see, when interpreting this rise a degree of caution may be in order.

In any international comparison pupils in one particular country are bound to find some items less familiar than others. But certain TIMSS 2003 Year 5 items stand out as being 'just what the (English) doctor ordered'. For example, one item asked:

$15 \times 9 = \ldots$.

Improving the fluency of ordinary pupils in handling such basic tasks was one of the things the *Numeracy Strategy* was explicitly designed to address. The above task can be solved by a number of very natural strategies, all of which would appear to be well-known in English primary schools. Hence one could be forgiven for thinking that this is precisely the kind of question that would have been intensively practised, and that English Year 5 pupils should perform comparatively well on such an item.

If stated in isolation, the result – '59% of English pupils answered the above item correctly' – might strike many teachers as satisfactory, even creditable. But one should perhaps suspend judgement until it becomes clear what happened in comparable countries, where children often start school much later, and where arithmetic instruction is less tightly focused on 'numeracy'.

Many of the 46 countries that took part in TIMSS are far less 'developed' than England, and have few comparable advantages. Yet **the international *average* success rate on this item was 72%.** The USA achieved 73%. Russia (where primary school only begins at age 7) managed 90%. And many far eastern countries managed in excess of 90%. So one is forced to consider the twin possibilities:

- that we have got used to setting our sights too low, and
- that there may be ways of 'teaching for a more general understanding' that are more effective than the kind of tightly focused approach England has adopted in recent years.

Such thoughts may be strengthened by the observation that English Year 9 performance in TIMSS (2003) showed no improvement on the low levels of 1995 and 1999 (with a poor performance in the categories of 'Number', 'Algebra' and 'Geometry' being partially disguised by a significantly higher score in 'Data-Handling', which many countries do not see as part of the mathematics curriculum at this level).

All of which suggests the possibility that the improved scores in Year 5 may be superficial, and that the approach currently adopted in England may be too strongly focused on narrowly defined short-term goals that do little to develop pupils' mathematical ability in the long-term.

This possibility is dramatically underlined by the breathtaking (under-)performance of English Year 9 pupils at the TIMSS 'advanced benchmark' in 1995, 1999 and 2003 – a benchmark that is especially relevant to a series containing 'extension' material.

The average TIMSS score for the complete cohort (for those countries participating in 1995, 1999 and 2003) was set at 500, with a standard deviation of 100. But the body of mathematical items included specified subsets that were identified as being particularly appropriate diagnostics for those performing at specific levels – *low, intermediate, high,* and *advanced*. A score of 550+ (i.e. slightly above average) was chosen as the '*high* benchmark', and a score of 625+ was taken as the '*advanced* benchmark'.

Problems at the 'advanced benchmark' level are relatively standard, but are likely to require pupils to identify two or more basic steps in order to solve a routine task, to extract and use information presented in written form, or to use a standard procedure in a slightly more general setting than normal.

Though such scores are never predictive, the 'advanced benchmark' represents, roughly speaking, the level at which the top 20-25% of pupils in Year 9 should be working – a group that includes most of those who will one day need to use mathematics in a moderately serious way in their work, or who may become future undergraduates in mildly numerate disciplines. This is a group that England traditionally served rather well. Indeed, conventional wisdom still assumes this to be the case. But the reality is now very different, and has been so for some time.

Many of the 46 countries taking part in TIMSS 2003 at Year 9 have weak educational systems, and this tends to reduce the 'International Average' score. Recognising that the 'average' was an inappropriate measure of the strengths and weaknesses of England's performance, the agency which produced the 'English national report' used a *Comparison Group* of a dozen countries (including USA, Scotland, New Zealand, Italy, Hungary, Singapore), which was felt to provide a more appropriate yardstick for comparison purposes.

Among the very mixed collection of 46 participating countries, the *average* number of Year 9 pupils performing at or above the 'advanced benchmark' of 625 was just 6%. This average was clearly distorted by a relatively large number of low-performing countries. A more relevant statistic is the fact that **13%** of Year 9 pupils in the *Comparison Group* of countries scored at or above this level. So the fact that **just 5%** of the English cohort scored at this level should come as a considerable shock, and should oblige us to take a long hard look at where we have gone wrong.

Just as the early national curriculum overlooked the central importance of English and Mathematics at primary level, so we have lost sight of many of the key milestones in elementary mathematics at secondary level, the crucial links between them, and the amount of work that is needed to help large numbers of pupils achieve a robust mastery of this essential material. Too many peripheral topics have been added, and important multi-faceted themes have been reduced to isolated one-step routines – purely to satisfy the demands of short-term, superficial assessment. We have also forgotten to make sure that mathematics in primary and lower secondary school sets out in a spirit, and in a direction that might enable it to constitute (as it should) the important first steps on a much longer mathematical journey.

Instead of seeing school mathematics as part of an extended development, there is a serious danger that recent 'improvements' have been largely due to pupils being systematically trained to solve specific kinds of tasks *as though they were ends in themselves*.

1.3 The challenge

The situation summarised in the previous section cannot be shrugged off. There is an urgent need to develop and to implement

- an extension curriculum and associated assessment framework for able pupils aged 11-16;
- which will provide an appropriate challenge; and
- which will significantly increase the number of students proceeding with enthusiasm to a similarly challenging mathematical provision at age 16-19

The problem was neatly summarised in the 1995 report *Tackling the mathematics problem* (London Mathematical Society, Institute of Mathematics and its Applications, Royal Statistical Society):

> 'Mathematics, science and engineering departments appear unanimous in their perception of a *qualitative* change in the mathematical preparedness of incoming students.
>
> Their criticisms of students' preparedness concentrate on three main areas.
>
> 4A Students enrolling on courses making heavy mathematical demands are hampered by a serious lack of *essential technical fluency* - in particular, a lack of fluency and reliability in numerical and algebraic manipulation and simplification.
>
> 4B Compared with students in the early 1980s, there is a marked decline in students' analytical powers when faced with simple two-step or multi-step problems.
>
> 4C Most students entering higher education no longer understand that mathematics is a precise discipline in which exact, reliable calculation, logical exposition and proof play essential roles; yet it is these features which make mathematics important.
>
> These criticisms affect all those undergraduate courses which presuppose a basis of mathematical technique.'

The three domains highlighted in **4A**, **4B**, **4C** above have still not been addressed. There has been no debate about what should constitute 'essential technical fluency'; mathematics assessment has become so 'predictable' that most teachers see no need to cultivate students' 'analytical powers'; and the character of elementary mathematics as 'a precise discipline in which exact, reliable calculation, logical exposition and proof play essential roles' seems not to be understood by those responsible for either curriculum or assessment.

1.4 Why the target group should be around 20-25% of the cohort

The *Gifted and Talented* programme focused on 5-10% of each cohort – *across all subjects*. The figure was arrived at without wider consultation, and despite clear advice from many quarters that the chosen focus was too narrow to influence what happens day-to-day in ordinary classrooms.

After extensive debate in the wider mathematical community, it is now generally accepted that, to be effective, any systematic provision for able pupils needs first to target a group of around 20-25% of each cohort. Let me try to explain why.

It takes time and effort to lay the foundations on which elementary mathematics rests. Most pupils need time to absorb new ideas and methods, and to identify and overcome basic mistakes. So effective provision for able pupils cannot be based on occasional activities, talks, or visits – no matter how remarkable they may be. Long-term progress depends on consistent, day-by-day provision. Hence we need an appropriate curriculum and assessment structure which ordinary schools can implement relatively easily.

Such a curriculum should provide the necessary experience to enable pupils to make an intelligent choice whether to study mathematics moderately seriously at age 16-19. It should also lay a suitable foundation for those who may later go on to study university courses which require a basic mathematical competence (which now includes not only Engineering and Physics, but courses such as Business Studies, Computer Science, Economics, Biology, Chemistry, Psychology, Sport Science, and Geography), and should also serve others who might later need to use significant elementary mathematics in their work.

The simplest estimate of the size of this group indicates that one should target around 25% of each cohort. Focusing on such a substantial percentage has three important consequences.

First it serves to constrain those who might otherwise be tempted to set the demands of such an extension curriculum unrealistically high. An extension curriculum can then be designed in a way that fits naturally into the broader tapestry of provision for ages 11-16.

Second it means that there is no reason why (almost) all schools should not be expected to offer such a curriculum to at least one top set.

But there is a far more significant reason for targeting a substantial fraction of each cohort: namely that it *removes the need* to pretend that we know how *to identify* some small subset of each cohort for whom such provision is 'appropriate'.

The idea that one must first 'identify' and then 'provide' presumes the existence of something concrete that can be identified. This assumption is called the 'medical model', because it lay at the root of the revolution that occurred in medicine when 'being off colour' was routinely interpreted as having a simple cause that one should therefore try to identify and treat. The approach is stunningly effective *insofar as the body is a mechanical system*. The same is then obviously applicable to machines we have created: the response to mechanical malfunction is first to diagnose the fault, and then to 'treat' it.

Education is different. Where resources are limited (as with specialist music schools), one may see no alternative to first 'identifying', then 'providing'. But though considerable energy has been devoted to considering how this process is best conducted, its predictive success remains rather limited. The approach may also have some relevance in fields such as ballet, where a long specialised training is needed, and where much can apparently be inferred from the physique of the young child. It is also possible that particular schools with a very restricted intake may have developed ways of achieving something similar in mathematics. *But in most schools, and hence when formulating national policy, the approach is potentially damaging for educational, social, and mathematical reasons.*

First, we do not know how to 'identify' talent reliably on a large scale. And in those cases where we have reason to believe that we can identify genuine talent, those so identified have the annoying habit of reacting against 'having been identified' (to say nothing of the effect of such identification on those who are rejected along the way). Able children are not medical cases; and 'talent' is not a disease – which one first has to diagnose, and then treat.

Second, the myth of 'ability' and of our claim to be able to 'identify' those who possess it distracts us from the long term challenge of helping *all* pupils to achieve what they are capable of (a point that is convincingly illustrated in The myth of ability, by John Mighton (Anansi 2003)).

Third, although it is hard not to be impressed by mathematical flair when one meets it, mathematics is more of a marathon than a sprint. Thus, whether or not one demonstrates impressive flair at a young age, the most important mathematical, educational and social lessons are probably related to the need for perseverance and self-criticism, and for a dogged insistence that things should make sense.

Ability is *latent*, and develops in response to the provision made. It is a talent that has to be used and honed over many years. It can be cultivated. But it can also be destroyed.

The whole focus on 'identification' is a red herring; it is also potentially damaging. Adolescents may appreciate being challenged; but there are times when they need to remain relatively anonymous. An extension curriculum designed for a large fraction of each cohort can meet both requirements in a perfectly natural way, without the need to pretend that we know how to identify genuine talent.

Sound policy has to be based on statistics. Highways are planned and provided on the basis of 'models of predicted road usage', not on the pretence that we can identify in advance which individual motorists will choose to use any particular route. We use some proven model of road-usage to make an estimate of the likely demand for a particular route (with a specified range of error), and then leave policy-makers to provide accordingly.

For an effective extension curriculum, all that is needed is to decide what fraction of the cohort could benefit from such provision and then to provide a structure which serves that cohort, and which can be effectively implemented at the chalkface. It may still be helpful to provide guidance to help schools assess who this curriculum is intended for; but such pragmatic decisions are best made without engaging in the spurious charade of 'identification'.

1.5 What themes should an extension curriculum address?

The detailed answer to this question is given in the three accompanying pupil books. However, there are certain things that deserve to be said here. An extension curriculum

- must address the need to establish a more robust mastery of basic technique in core curriculum areas (as illustrated, for example, by the results of TIMSS)
- must routinely incorporate basic one-step techniques into an ability to solve simple multi-step exercises and harder problems
- must cultivate pupils' willingness and ability to deploy flexibly what they know when tackling and solving harder problems.

Initial work has to focus on the first two of these areas. These may seem relatively mundane; but the example below illustrates what goes wrong when work in this area is neglected, and one should never underestimate the quiet satisfaction many pupils gain from achieving mundane mastery. Adolescents may pretend to grumble when faced with the expectation that they should achieve 'robust mastery'; but they can be touchingly appreciative once they experience that sense of 'getting on top of' things, and discover – perhaps for the first time – that they can actually use what they have learned.

The extent of our current failure to achieve basic competence has been disguised by the assessment-driven practice of breaking down multi-step exercises into a sequence of 'one-piece jigsaws'. Consider the following example:

> *Two cyclists cycle towards each other along a road. At 8 am they are 42 km apart. They meet at 11 am. One cyclist pedals at 7.5 km/h. What is the speed of the other cyclist?*

There is nothing hard in this task – so we shall call it an *exercise* rather than a *problem* (see Section 2.2.16 for more on this distinction). Such multi-step exercises require students to extract simple information from the written statement (as in all *word problems*), and to implement three or four steps each of which requires little more than primary school arithmetic. Thus large numbers of students in Year 8 should be able to work with such material, and large numbers of Year 9 students should be able to solve them routinely.

Yet evidence from the last few years suggests that 30% or more of those *with a grade A in A level mathematics* cannot produce the correct answer to the above exercise.

Each ingredient step can certainly be handled *in isolation*. A difficulty arises only when these students are confronted by the need to coordinate and to perform (correctly!) three or four simple steps on the trot – at which point the typical student's 'operating system' regularly becomes unstable.

Such examples underline the urgent need to provide

- a stronger foundation of basic technique;
- a richer, more challenging, and more rewarding diet – including multi-step exercises and problems as a routine ingredient; and
- higher expectations

for at least the top 20-25% of each cohort. In particular, before engaging with 'harder problem solving in non-standard situations' (*Making mathematics count*, 2004, Recommendation 4.5) we need to address honestly weaknesses such as those illustrated by the above example, so that large numbers of 15 year olds have the basic equipment and experience to reliably solve such simple multi-step exercises.

1.6 What *kinds* of material should be included?

Each item in this series of books has been shaped by three complementary criteria:

- Pedagogical principles
- Core content
- Mathematical means

Pedagogical principles (general themes that are rooted in the way human beings learn elementary mathematics, and which therefore guide one's thinking in a strategic, broad brush manner) are explored in more detail in Chapter 2. They include such things as

- the role of standard procedures;
- the way in which 'atomic skills' are combined in solving more complex problems;
- the importance of repetition, memory, speed and accuracy;

- the way one-step routines need to be integrated to solve multi-step problems; and

- the way basic 'direct' procedures (such as addition, or multiplying out brackets) relate to the corresponding 'inverse' operations (such as subtraction, or factorising).

Core content refers to those mathematical milestones that serve as 'trig points' in the landscape of school mathematics: tables; standard measures; place value; standard written algorithms; angles in a triangle; equivalent fractions; length and perimeter; ratio; formulae; decimals; area and surface area; powers; inequalities; logic and contradiction; estimation; prime factorisation; isosceles triangles; coordinates; infinity; arithmetic of fractions; parallel lines; negative numbers; parallelograms; rates and averages; congruence; volume; scale factors; sequences; ruler and compass constructions; Pythagoras' theorem; the distributive law; right prisms; recurring decimals; circles; product rule for counting; surds; algebraic simplification; linear and quadratic equations; functions and graphs; similarity; trig functions. Figure 1 on page 19 presents a two-dimensional 'map' of this *core content* (up to age 14/15) in which the relative positions of items often indicate subtle dependencies.

The *pedagogical principles* and the *mathematical means* that give life to this core content are elaborated elsewhere in Chapter 1 and Chapter 2.

The *core content* specifies the mathematical hills that have to be climbed. The *pedagogical principles* outline the spirit in which these hills are to be climbed. All that remains is to choose the route – or the *mathematical means*.

There are many ways of reaching the summit of any particular mathematical hill. If all that was required was to reach the top of the relevant hill as quickly as possible, a direct route might suffice. But some of the surrounding foothills are bound to be more familiar than others, and a slight detour may make the overall ascent easier. An obscure route may make the climb more difficult, but may offer a better mathematical view, or develop skills that will be needed in a later tricky ascent. In elementary mathematics, the *implicit* lessons often have the most lasting impact! The most appropriate route, or *mathematical means*, is rarely the most obvious one. For example:

- to encourage pupils to show their working (and hence to allow the teacher to spot the source of any errors), it may make sense to design problem sequences so that they avoid use of a calculator (*Alpha* T1, T2, T4, T5, T6, etc.);

- to reinforce ideas of place value one may choose to set tasks which are considerably easier when place value is used flexibly (*Alpha* T1), or to use puzzles that stretch and extend understanding of place value (*Alpha* T10, T13, T25, C8, C16);

- to prepare for subsequent work with symbols, it may make sense to set ostensibly arithmetical exercises that become easy when algebraic structure is exploited (*Alpha* T4);

- to lay the groundwork for fractions, it may help to postpone a direct attack until a much more thorough grasp of *integer arithmetic* has been established (*Alpha* T12, C14, *Beta* T16); similarly, work with integers, fractions and surds may be used to prepare the way for elementary algebra;

- to cultivate familiarity with integer squares and cubes one may choose to embed the exercise in the form of crossnumbers (*Alpha* E9) or arithmetical surprises (*Beta* T10).

Figure 1

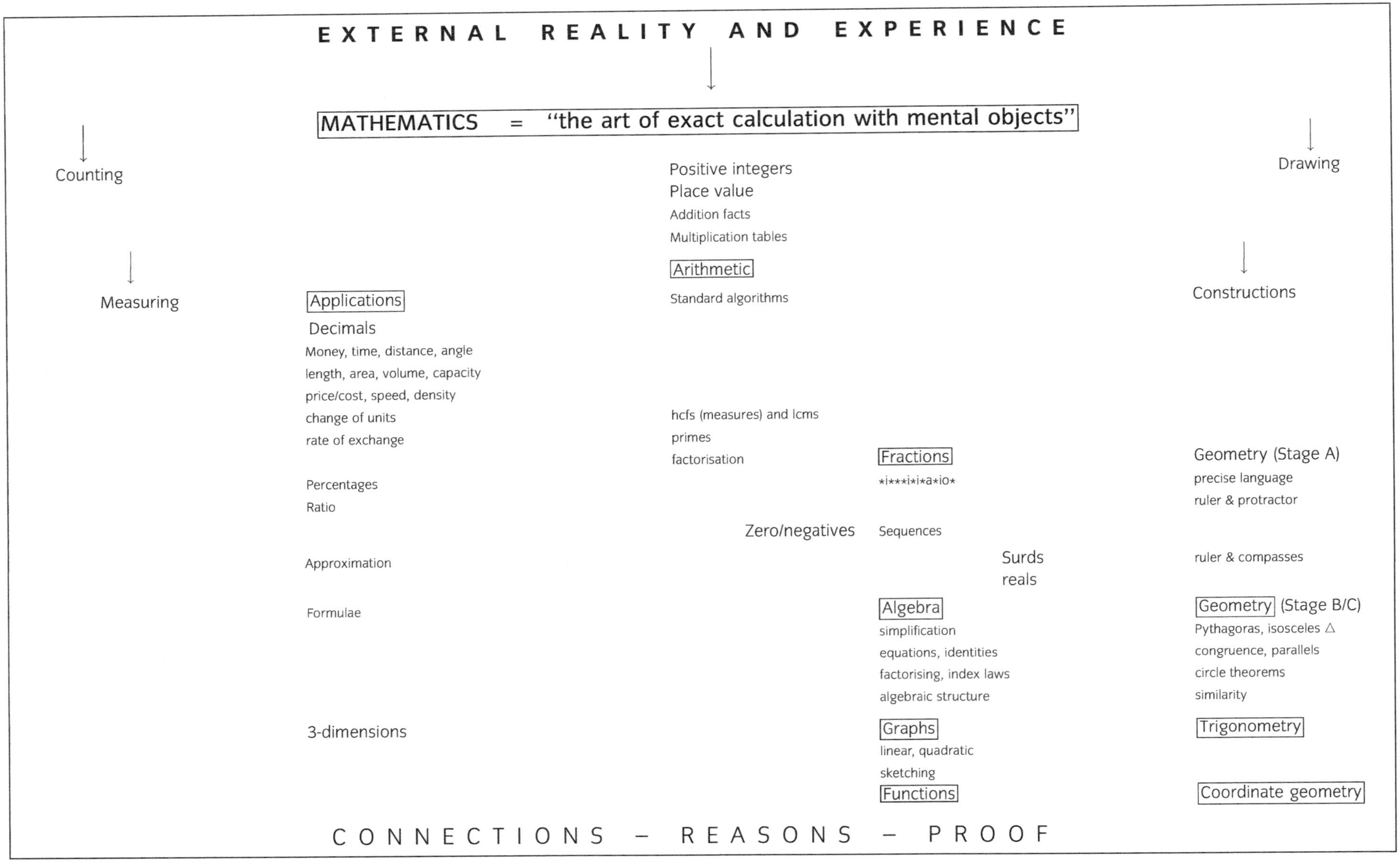

EXTERNAL REALITY AND EXPERIENCE

MATHEMATICS = "the art of exact calculation with mental objects"

→ Counting

→ Measuring

Positive integers
Place value
Addition facts
Multiplication tables

Arithmetic
Standard algorithms

Applications
Decimals
Money, time, distance, angle
length, area, volume, capacity
price/cost, speed, density
change of units
rate of exchange

Percentages
Ratio

hcfs (measures) and lcms
primes
factorisation

Approximation

Zero/negatives

Formulae

Fractions
*i****i*i*a*io*

Sequences

Surds
reals

Algebra
simplification
equations, identities
factorising, index laws
algebraic structure

3-dimensions

Graphs
linear, quadratic
sketching

Functions

→ Constructions → Drawing

Geometry (Stage A)
precise language
ruler & protractor

ruler & compasses

Geometry (Stage B/C)
Pythagoras, isosceles △
congruence, parallels
circle theorems
similarity

Trigonometry

Coordinate geometry

CONNECTIONS — REASONS — PROOF

2 The principles of elementary mathematics

2.1 Towards a common language

Extension material in England has often taken the form of collections of problems, starting points, or ideas presented in an endearingly anti-authoritarian spirit: 'these have worked for us; maybe you too will find them useful'. Teachers and pupils are welcome to use the sets of problems in *Extension mathematics* in this spirit. However, the series does not fit comfortably into this relaxed tradition: forty years work with pupils, students, and teachers have increasingly highlighted the need for a considerably more systematic approach.

The English are often said to be *pragmatic* rather than fundamentalist, philosophical or idealistic. Whatever this may mean, it has at times worked to our advantage. For example, in the 1960s, we were spared the worst excesses of 'new math' partly because curriculum development was controlled, or strongly influenced by experienced and mathematically competent teachers, whose reforming enthusiasm was tempered by their practical concern for real pupils. However, now that curriculum and assessment are centralised, and are controlled by bureaucrats with little or no insight into why elementary mathematics is important, we urgently need a 'common language' in terms of which one might express the principles that should underpin change and improvement – *knowing that they will be understood*.

A common language and a shared understanding is needed in three areas. The first and simplest of these three areas should be a shared understanding of what constitutes the *core content* of school mathematics – since much of this is determined *by mathematics itself*. For example, the central importance of ratio and proportion (both in everyday life and in the application of mathematics) implies the need to manipulate equations involving fractions, which in turn depends on a thorough grasp of integer arithmetic. Similarly, the ubiquity of graphs and functions highlights the need to handle formulae and algebraic expressions and to relate these to the behaviour of lines and curves; and the analysis of structures in three dimensions underlines the crucial role played by two-dimensional cross-sections and plane euclidean geometry. A consensus concerning core content would make it clear which topics play a central role for most pupils at lower secondary level.

In the absence of such a consensus, all one can say is that very few sections in the three pupil books owe their inclusion purely to the author's personal taste: most sections *forced* their way into the draft contents list – though the *form* in which topics have been treated is far from canonical!

Some important themes have received less attention than they deserve – and some have even been excluded: uncomfortable choices always have to be made. In general it was felt better to omit, or to postpone, a topic if its inclusion would have reduced the prospects of achieving an appropriate level of mastery in more important areas.

The second area in which a shared understanding is needed concerns the art, or craft, of *mathematics teaching*. This is scarcely an area where the author can claim expertise! It may nevertheless help if we distinguish two very different sub-domains.

The first subdomain is the *didactical analysis* of specific mathematical topics or processes (OED: '*didactics = the science or art of teaching*'). Didactical analysis is the process of taking a key topic, or strand within the curriculum (such as the arithmetic of fractions), analysing the inner structure of the material (including what it has to be based on and what will subsequently need to be based on it), identifying the main hurdles faced by the learner, and then assessing the relative merits of alternative approaches. Each linked grouping of sections in the pupil books, together with the accompanying text and the comments and answers in this book, could be viewed as offering a preliminary analysis of this kind. But for a serious didactical analysis of key themes in secondary mathematics the reader is referred to H. Freudenthal, *The didactical phenomenology of mathematical structures* (Reidel 1983).

The second subdomain concerns the question of whether there exist – independent of the mathematics one wishes to convey – general strategies that constitute useful guides for those who teach mathematics. At school level, most readers will have far more relevant experience than the author. So we shall merely highlight a number of areas where one does not have to be an expert to see that awkward questions need to be asked. For example:

- There may be good reasons why school inspectors decided to emphasise the need for lessons that exhibit 'pitch and pace'; but when teaching mathematics, one has to be ready (and free) to respond to the unexpected, to slow down, to back up, to go over things again. A mathematics lesson is not a floorshow.

- The official drive for 'pitch and pace' may exacerbate the very English habit of flitting from one topic to another, revisiting the same material year after year. Mathematics instruction at all levels requires one to regularly revisit familiar material, and to re-interpret what one thought one knew with a view to extending it in new ways. In such cases the ground needs to be carefully prepared so that pupils are in a position to embrace the relevant 're-interpretation and extension'. And given such preparation, sufficient time needs to be devoted to the topic to ensure that significant and lasting progress is made. This is quite different from the widespread current English practice of revisiting familiar material year after year (after year) with little cumulative progress, in the vain hope that repeated encounters will magically allow some pupils to overcome their difficulties.

- The ways in which technology and software can help ordinary pupils learn (or hinder them from learning) basic mathematics warrants more serious discussion. Too often software is used in precisely those situations where the teacher's judgement would allow a better choice of material suited to a particular group of pupils, or where pencil and paper calculation or drawing would be a far more effective way of embedding an idea in pupils' long-term memories.

- Whilst every pupil matters, they all need to access *the same mathematics*. Hence, if taken too seriously, much of the current rhetoric concerning 'learning styles' and 'individual learning programmes' threatens to undermine much good mathematics teaching.

- The limitations of introducing a topic exclusively via 'easy' worked examples is discussed at length in Section 2.2.17 under the heading *Problem solving Japanese-style* (and is directly related to the intended spirit of 'Problem 0').

- It is hard to see any justification for the kind of 'modular' structures which have become so widespread – except possibly for 'terminal' mathematics courses (on which nothing will ever try to build). Mathematics is inescapably *cumulative*, so any structure which compartmentalises the subject matter, or which conveys the impression that material is only learned for one particular piece of assessment, is likely to backfire – at least for those who subsequently need to use what they have been officially certificated as having learned. One consequence of the compartmentalisation resulting from modular assessment is that our best 18-year-olds increasingly think mathematics can be mastered by 'approximate mimicry', and no longer understand that its whole power and purpose is lost unless it is 'comprehended' with the mind.

The third area where a common language is urgently needed concerns broader *pedagogical* issues that arise directly out of *the character of elementary mathematics* itself. These are discussed in the next section. English pragmatism often by-passes such concerns; but when they have been publicly aired in recent years, these issues have been generally welcomed. They are addressed here because of the influence they have exerted on the choice and organisation of material in the pupil books.

2.2 Principles arising from the nature of elementary mathematics

2.2.1 Teaching and assessment: the fundamental distinction

For some years educational debate in England appeared to accept the idea that 'teaching and learning can be driven by assessment'. In mathematics there is now a clear consensus that this assumption, and the resulting assessment models, have completely distorted teaching and learning – especially for able pupils.

- The mathematics that able pupils most need to master demands a considerable investment of time and effort on the part of both teachers and students.

- This investment is only repaid *in the longer-term*, and is therefore routinely circumvented by those interested mainly in short-term success.

The essential content of this crucial long-term investment is elusive, and is therefore unlikely to be tested in modern public examinations, since these are increasingly obliged to be 'accessible' and to guarantee success to large numbers of students. In contrast, successful mathematics teaching routinely expects pupils to struggle with problems that are considerably harder than those on which they will one day be assessed.

In short, we have created a system that actively discourages good mathematics teaching.

To indicate the significance of these remarks, we look ahead for the moment and relate them to the two most relevant principles among those which feature later in this section – namely:

- the distinction between one-step routines and *multi-step* problems and exercises (2.2.4),

and

- the contrast between *direct and inverse operations* (2.2.5).

'One-step' routines versus 'two-step, or multi-step' tasks

One-step routines are important because they need to be instantly available when one is struggling to select and to combine simple steps into a solution to a possibly non-standard, but not too difficult, *multi-step problem*. (The simplest one-step routines are often *direct* operations, and so provide the raw material for the step discussed below – from *direct* to *inverse* operations.)

Unfortunately solutions to multi-step problems can be elusive. So those who are determined that public examinations should be 'fair' regularly press for any multi-step problem to be broken down (i.e. literally destroyed, or de-constructed!) into its component single steps – no doubt with any necessary answers to intermediate steps being given, as though completing a pre-structured sequence of separate steps were the same as solving the original *multi-step* problem.

Students and teachers then naturally conclude that all that is needed for success in (school) mathematics is

◉ to master the individual single steps, and

◉ to follow instructions.

One result is that teachers in English schools concentrate on training each cohort to become experts in completing the kind of 'one-piece jigsaw' that is likely to be assessed – and fail to notice that their charges cannot handle the simplest multi-step exercises (such as *The two cyclists*, Section 1.5).

In fact, one-step routines are as much (and as little) the essence of mathematics as individual notes are the essence of jazz! As in jazz, mathematics only begins when one achieves not only mastery of one-step routines, but a willingness to explore and to combine these basic units in unexpected ways to solve multi-step problems. An acceptable curriculum and assessment structure has to respect this key feature of elementary mathematics.

The art of solving simple two-step or multi-step problems demands flexibility and confidence. As with performing jazz in public, mastering the art of tackling two-step, or multi-step, problems in mathematics to the point where one can operate reliably under scrutiny requires extensive practice and experience *at a considerably higher level* than that which is ever likely to be scrutinised. Good mathematics teaching takes for granted this need for extensive practice and experience at a higher level than will ever be assessed in public exams. 'Assessment success' is never the primary goal of such teaching, but follows as a natural *by-product*.

'Direct' versus 'inverse' operations

Most operations in elementary mathematics come in linked pairs. One begins by introducing some *direct* operation (such as addition, or learning ones tables, or scaling-up both the numerator and the denominator of a given fraction to form fractions equivalent to a given simple fraction). Direct operations are *deterministic* – and lead to a guaranteed *output*.

Direct operations are important because they constitute the essential ingredient in the corresponding *inverse* operation (such as subtraction, or factorising 72, or reducing a given fraction to its simplest form). An inverse operation is generally far less mechanical than the associated direct operation, and its successful implementation presupposes complete mastery of the corresponding direct operation.

Direct operations need to be instantly and robustly available when one is struggling to implement the corresponding inverse operation. Carrying out a subtraction – whether tackled holistically and mentally, or done column by column via the usual layout – requires one to consider a number of possible additions in order to select the correct answer at each stage; and reducing a given fraction to its 'simplest terms' requires one to scan the numerator and denominator in search of possible common factors.

However, the search for common factors to simplify a fraction can be elusive $\left(\text{try } \frac{91}{143}, \text{ or } \frac{428\,571}{999\,999}, \text{ or Section T16 in Book } Beta \text{ on your pupils or your non-mathematical colleagues!}\right)$. So those devising mark schemes for public assessments are reluctant to insist on the routine 'simplification' of such fractions as $\frac{18}{36}$. And where simplification is essential to make sense of the rest of the problem, they may even be tempted to supply the required answer by formulating the question as: 'Show that the fraction … is equal to $\frac{1}{2}$.'

These trends lead textbook authors and teachers to conclude that in English school mathematics pupils are likely to be able to pass any assessment on the basis of approximate mastery of the corresponding 'direct' operation alone, and hence that they no longer need to master the more important (and harder) inverse operations.

At present everything is distorted by assessment which is too narrow, too frequent, and too 'high-stakes'. We need to work together to ensure that the timing and the form of official assessments (and the use made of any results) are designed to support high quality teaching and learning of elementary mathematics.

2.2.2 Structure: What does elementary mathematics lead on to (and why does it matter)?

What we teach at primary and lower secondary level is inevitably a succession of 'beginnings'. Pupils learn to count; they combine sets and add; they learn to apply number to basic measures; they learn their tables; they apply all this to calculating areas; and so on. There are evident dependencies between topics, but these are rarely clarified; instead, the overwhelming impression is of a mass of undifferentiated detail. There is a vague sense of cumulative progress, but these many 'beginnings' are not presented or experienced as the initial segments of extended 'developmental lines', lines which continue way beyond the age of 14.

It may be unrealistic to expect all teachers to have a profound insight into 'what school mathematics leads on to'. However, it is essential that we should all appreciate

◎ that we are *laying foundations* on which others will subsequently have to build.

In particular, we need to look behind the given programme of study, or the succession of chapters in the textbook, and work to develop a 'professional map', which highlights the most obvious 'lines of dependency' that connect key ideas in secondary school mathematics. At the same time we need to clarify in our own minds what will subsequently have to be built (after the age of 16) on the foundations that we are laying, and how that should affect the goals for lower secondary mathematics.

While many of the details that underpin such an extended professional map are determined by the nature of mathematics and by the way children learn mathematics, there are no God-given tablets of stone on which such things are written in canonical form. Rather each country has to formulate its own sketch-map – so that the profession establishes a common language and agreed landmarks, which can serve as evolving reference points for analysis, debate, criticism and improvement (whether at the local level – as in Chinese-style 'lesson study' within a single school, or at the global level – as in wholesale curriculum review).

To illustrate what we mean by such an extended 'professional map' of secondary mathematics, we step back for a moment and outline some of the key links in the transition from primary to secondary level.

Geometry becomes a fully-fledged part of (formal) elementary mathematics only in late primary or early secondary school, when

(a) the numerical groundwork has been sufficiently well laid to allow a serious treatment of *measures* (length; perimeter and area; surface area and volume; angle);
(b) dexterity has developed to a point where *mathematical constructions* (using ruler, protractor, and compasses) can be carried out in a spirit that allows pupils to appreciate the idea of *exactness in principle*;
(c) an appreciation of logic, and a willingness to analyse two-dimensional figures, leaves pupils in a position to engage in the *local deductions* related to simple angle-chasing, or ruler-and-compass constructions.

However, for such work to be effective, extensive preparatory work of a pre-mathematical kind is needed – where models are made; geometrical language is used; measurements are made and used to create copies of given objects; two-dimensional plans or pictures are used to analyse or to record information about three-dimensional objects; and so on. To assess the importance of this preliminary experience, and to shape it in a way that ultimately has the desired effect, it is essential to know *what it leads on to*. (The same is true of all 'preparatory experiences', since they will never be tested on centrally controlled assessments, so may be – wrongly – deemed to be dispensable.)

Measures arise whenever a concept has a calculational aspect in the form of 'numbers with units attached'; they pervade mathematics in primary and lower secondary school. (The relevant "units" may sometimes be invisible – as when counting collections of objects of a given kind, where the *units* may be sweets, or apples, or cars, or girls.)

The didactics of teaching *number* is therefore inextricably interwoven with the didactics of measures; yet professional insight into the didactics of measures often gets stuck at the level of petty pedantry ('always include the units with the answer, or you might lose a mark').

Initially it may seem artificial to insist on the separation of numbers arising in some context from their associated units. But by the time one reaches lower secondary school it becomes almost impossible to resist this separation and still to carry out calculations systematically.

Units generally arise as a result of an apparently mathematical problem being in some way embedded in the 'real world'. Any application, or use, of mathematics to solve such a 'real world' problem obliges us

◉   to move *from* this 'real world'

- *into* the mathematical world,

where calculations can be carried out with **pure numbers**, before

- moving *back* to the original context

where we can sort out the appropriate units and take the results of our calculations in the *purely mathematical world* and re-interpret them in the language and context of the original problem.

Like all such frameworks, this one can probably not be implemented *ab initio* except by arbitrary *fiat*. But it is essential to consider the advantages of making such a systematic distinction at some stage (between the 'real world' and the 'mathematical world'), and to decide whether such a distinction would help many more pupils organise their work and their *thinking*, and so allow them to produce mathematical solutions to 'real world' problems more reliably.

Algebra emerges from the shadows of work on measures (in the context of geometry and number), via the idea of a *formula*: for the area of a rectangle; or for the area of a triangle; or for the circumference of a circle. In the absence of a formal symbolic language in which to express such relationships, there is a temptation to fudge the whole idea by treating formulae as a kind of private linguistic shorthand. Unfortunately, this appears to encourage misleading notions that stay with students and that handicap them in later life – all of which suggests that we have not thought sufficiently deeply about how symbols (and hence formulae) are best introduced. Consider the following example:

> *Tom and Dick take 2 hours to do a job. Dick and Harry take 3 hours to complete the same job. Harry and Tom take 4 hours to complete the job. How long would all three take working together?*

The problem has been used extensively with teachers and with pupils, with frightening results. In a typical class of honours mathematics undergraduates, the number obtaining the correct answer is typically zero. Much more important is the fact that 75% of students go wrong for the crassest possible reason – namely that they

> translate the problem into symbols as though 'algebra' were simply a 'linguistic shorthand' for colloquial speech, writing $T + D = 2$, etc.

Remember, these students are among the most successful products of school mathematics. Six or more years of school algebra have somehow managed to embed the totally misguided idea that the letter 'T' can be used to stand for 'Tom'! This may be partly due to the fashion for encouraging 'informal algebra', such as one used to find in coursework mark schemes, where marks were awarded for a conjectured formula 'expressed in words'. Such informality may appear to provide a 'half-way house' between numbers and symbols; but if it leads our best students into such errors, it may be time to stand back and think again. Algebraic symbols need to be introduced and used in a very precise way. In elementary school algebra letters stand for numbers, never for 'objects'.

Number plays the central role, and so contributes in a more intricate way to an 'extended professional map' of mathematics at primary and lower secondary level. We have already seen indications of the links with geometry and with measures. We concentrate here on some of the main 'development lines' within the purely mathematical world of number and algebra – and even then we do little more than scratch the surface. The themes outlined here are summarised in Figure 2 on page 27.

Figure 2

Number

(from number to algebra: counting, the number line, hand calculation, tables, mental work, applications, factorisation, negatives, fractions, algebraic structure, powers and roots, index laws, ...)

Number in geometry	Number in life measures	Base 10 representation Place value	Natural numbers	Integers Algebraic structure	Rationals +
			Prime numbers		Fractions
			Factors		Unit fractions: 1/n
		Calculations	Multiples		
					Comparing
Length			Hcf/lcm		Equivalence
Angle		Written algorithms			
Perimeter				Negative integers	Arithmetic of fractions
Area		Decimals	Prime factorisation		
Volume					
Enlargement		Approximate calculation	Sequences	Arithmetic of negatives	
	Averages				Surd arithmetic
Pythagoras		Decimal fractions (tenths, hundredths, etc.)		Powers (roots)	
Formulae			Big numbers		Irrationals
	%	Fractions and decimals		Ratio and proportion	
	Rates				
	Prices	Other bases		Laws of arithmetic	
	Unit method			(Distributive law; inverses; index laws)	
	Rule of three	Recurring decimals			

W O R D

P R O B L E M S

I N V E R S E

P R O B L E M S

At primary level there are good reasons to concentrate first on the integers 0-5, where the distinction between 'numbers' and 'digits' does not arise, and where one can establish a firm foundation when combining numbers without having to confront the subtleties of 'trading' (which arise when combined quantities exceed 10).

One can then extend this foundation to the integers 0-9, and establish the basic 'trading' principle ('carrying a ten') which underlies the *base 10* notation for numbers, together with the distinction between 'numbers' and 'digits'. From here on the language and notation of 'counting' forces one to engage with 10s and 100s, collecting like terms (units and tens), and 'trading' to ensure that all digits lie between 0 and 9.

Counting leads naturally to 'measuring the size of *combined* collections', and to 'measuring the size of a collection from which a sub-collection has been removed', which may later be linked to the mental activity of movement along a number line (i.e. addition and subtraction).

From here it is but a short step to 'move by twos', or by threes, and to 'measure the size of 3 *lots* of 4 *sweets*', or to 'share 12 sweets among 3 people' (i.e. multiplication and division). Here an asymmetry inevitably arises in the constituent numbers, since they quantify different units, such as 'lots' and 'sweets'.

This leads naturally to work intended to achieve a robust mastery of addition facts and multiplication tables, and to regular and extensive mental arithmetic designed to establish that 'mental universe of number' on which all subsequent mathematics depends; this should encourage flexibility in looking for ways round 'brute force calculation' using the inner (algebraic!) structure of arithmetic (so that tasks like $5 \times 13 + 7 \times 5 = \square$ are experienced as if the '5's were a kind of temporary 'unit', of which precisely '13 + 7 = 20' are required).

Establishing the full labour-saving power of this 'algebraic' structure cannot be done through mental work alone: in order for the underlying arithmetico-algebraic rules (which cannot yet be stated in algebraic form) to sink in to the pupil's arithmetical psyche, extensive practice with *written* sums that incorporate these algebraic rules (like $13 \times 5 + 5 \times 7 = \square$) is needed.

At the same time written algorithms need to be mastered – ultimately in *standard form* (for reasons outlined in Section 2.2.18).

Once multiplication tables have been mastered, the inverse operation of 'factorising' can be developed – and can then be used to solve word problems of a suitable kind; the most important ideas here are those of 'common factors' and the 'highest common factor' (or *hcf*) of two integers – ideas which are rarely given the attention they require at primary level. Prime numbers arise here as the 'atomic particles' of the factorisation process, but their further exploration may be best left until the early secondary years.

In combination with work on measures, fractions arise as '(sub-unit) parts of a (unit) whole'; this leads naturally to the idea of analysing a given unit, or whole, using different sub-units, and so finding different ways of representing 'the same' fraction in 'equivalent' forms – an idea which lies at the heart of fraction arithmetic.

The inverse operation of (efficient) 'simplification' – namely, reducing a given fractional expression to its simplest terms – presupposes and reinforces a robust fluency in finding the *hcf* of two integers.

Fractions constitute a watershed in elementary mathematics: those who master the art of simplifying numerical fractions are likely to find algebra relatively straightforward; those who do not achieve automaticity (Section 2.2.10) in the simplification of fractions are likely to be permanently saddled with a fragile understanding of fractions (and ratios and percentages and all problems that depend upon them), and never achieve full mastery of algebraic thinking.

We should never underestimate the amount of work involved in establishing a robust mastery of the arithmetic of fractions. The key – whether teaching addition/subtraction or multiplication/division – is to root all calculation in the twin notions of 'equivalent fractions' and 'choosing a common unit' (which are particular instances of what is involved in 'change of units' when working with measures).

The advent of the calculator has not led to an improved understanding of decimals, or to a better sense of when their use is (and is not) appropriate. It may not be generally appreciated that *within mathematics itself* (as opposed to the simplest applications) *decimals are almost always a distraction*; fractions and surds are usually more appropriate and easier to manipulate in a mathematical spirit. However, decimals are important when number is linked to measures, so familiarity with decimals and their use is essential. Genuine familiarity with decimals (as so often in mathematics) is linked to the hands-on experience of learning to *calculate* reliably with them. This is one of the two main reasons why complete mastery of the classical *standard written algorithms* for integer arithmetic is essential. Unless the integer algorithms are mastered in a completely robust manner, there is no chance of extending them to handle decimals; and without a transparent way of calculating with decimals, these natural objects remain permanently 'alien'. (Recent substitutes for the classical algorithms are demonstrably ineffective as soon as the numbers become slightly more complicated, and so offer most pupils no chance of success when working with decimals – see Section 2.2.18.)

Meantime, 'zero' needs to be accommodated within the mathematical pantheon as a concept in its own right, with huge simplifying powers.

The place of *negative* integers (as opposed to the *subtraction* of *positive* integers) in the primary school mathematics curriculum remains confused. The basic language and notation may well arise naturally at a fairly early stage. But it may be best to concentrate on a deeper mastery of positive integers at primary level, while quietly preparing the ground for the full-blooded arithmetic of (positive and negative) integers in Year 7 or so.

The belief (in England) that the early introduction of negative numbers (or fractions, or probability), and their repeated treatment over a number of years, will somehow allow more pupils to accept their benefits and to master their use, is not justified by experience. *We need to reconsider the basis of this faith in the efficacy of the 'drip-feed' approach*, which not only fails to help more pupils master the higher notions being 'drip-fed', but compromises the teacher's focus on the basic routines relating to ordinary integers, fractions and decimals at a stage when very little progress can be made with the higher notions, thus leaving many pupils with an impoverished grasp of these basic concepts on which the higher notions depend. Hence we might do well to consider the approach adopted in many European countries and in the Far East, where they tend to concentrate on

- preparing the ground well, and
- *timing the introduction of each new topic in a way that allows serious progress to be made relatively quickly* (including the forging of strong connections with known methods).

Books *Alpha*, *Beta*, and *Gamma* illustrate explicitly how these mathematical themes of *number, measures, algebra* and *geometry* develop at age 11-15; they also indicate *implicitly* how these continue to evolve at higher levels.

2.2.3 Language, precision and logic

Pupils' understanding of mathematics is mediated through their understanding of 'English'. The consequences of this obvious remark are often overlooked, but are perhaps sufficiently subtle to warrant some elaboration. We do not attempt to offer a balanced analysis: certain 'facts' that appear to be important are presented, and the reader is invited to reflect on what is written, and to add the necessary nuances.

The use of English traditionally takes two quite distinct forms: a colloquial, street-corner 'vernacular', and a more disciplined version which forms the basis of all forms of formal communication.

The *vernacular*, or colloquial English, is generally reliable only between friends, where the subject matter is unproblematic, where understanding is likely to be rooted in un-stated common assumptions, and where there is no need to develop extended chains of logical reasoning. No formal instruction is needed for children to master the vernacular, which is learned in social settings – in the nursery, on the street corner, and through social interactions with one's peers. It *is the language of unanalysed feelings*: it does not need to be taught.

In contrast, *formal English* is **the language of thought**, and is based on precision in its local structure (grammar and style), and in its global architecture. Interpreted narrowly, formal English provides the pedant, the lawyer and the bureaucrat with the tools of their respective trades; interpreted broadly, it liberates the mind to allow the poet and the mathematician to weave tapestries of their own devising, which enrich lives way beyond the immediate street corner. The struggle to conform to the demands of formal English forces us to clarify our thinking, challenges our assumptions, opens our minds and provides us with our main means of intellectual growth. It also allows us to glean from others knowledge which transcends our own personal experience: Galileo's greatness stems not only from the originality of his scientific thinking, but from the way he communicated this in lucid and eminently readable form to his contemporaries. Formal language provides the basis for all intellectual progress, and in helping pupils master formal language one needs to cultivate the arts of

- 'dictation' (reliable copying with accurate spelling and punctuation to conserve the intended meaning);
- 'comprehension' (reading a given short text and extracting the underlying meaning); and
- 'précis' (the art of summarising, or 'précis-ion').

Mathematics is more precise than English, and refers to a more restricted domain of human experience. But mathematical ideas are not absorbed from the air around us; they have to be taught and learned through the medium of a *formal* language such as English, which, when used for this purpose, must be used *with considerable care*. In particular, formal English has to be taught in a way that underlines this need to use terms and statements with precision. It is not only mathematical *ideas* that have to be mediated through English in this way; the *logic* on which mathematics depends is also rooted in the correct use of formal English.

Where formal English has not been learned (perhaps because it is no longer taught, or is taught inadequately), mathematics stands little chance. Where pupils do not know that every piece of text has to be read with care, and where they do not accept the responsibility to 'apprehend and comprehend' it systematically – from *top left* to *bottom right* – the expectation that they should 'solve mathematical problems' is likely to remain an empty fiction. Many of our current difficulties arise because we (and others) have dodged the fact that all education depends upon the effective teaching of *formal* English. We try to get by using informal language – which may appear to work for a while, but is ultimately inadequate. Until this awkward nettle is grasped, and the necessary changes in expectation are in place, mathematics teachers may have no choice but to step in and 'do it themselves'; otherwise success in mathematics may be increasingly restricted to those whose parents ensure that their children master the old-fashioned art of using formal English correctly.

2.2.4 One-step routines versus two-step and multi-step tasks

Much was promised as a result of the introduction in the late 1980s of **Ma1**: *Using and applying mathematics* as an integral part of the English national curriculum. For example, we were told that, whilst students might 'know' less, they should be much better 'problem solvers'. Yet the 1995 LMS report *Tackling the mathematics problem* included the serious complaint – supported by TIMSS results (1995, 1999, 2003) – that:

> '4B Compared with students in the early 1980s, there is a marked decline in students' analytical powers when faced with simple two-step or multi-step problems.'

Achieving mastery of one-step routines is an important part of school mathematics teaching. But one-step routines give a false impression of the character of mathematics and do not prepare students for the kinds of application they will need to master if their mathematics is to be of any use in later life.

Mathematics proper *at every level* begins only when pupils

- are routinely required to *coordinate* the simple one-step routines which they have nominally mastered into *longer chains of calculation and reasoning* in order to solve multi-step *exercises* (like *The two cyclists* problem: see Section 1.5), and

- are also expected to select and combine familiar one-step routines to tackle less routine, and apparently unfamiliar *problems* (such as arise in the '24 game': see Section 2.2.5).

2.2.5 Direct and inverse operations

A challenge such as '$15 \times 9 = \ldots$' invites us to carry out a *direct* operation. The procedure is deterministic, and if implemented correctly, will routinely generate the required output.

Compare this with the following task.

> **24-game:** *'Given any four numbers (such as 6, 9, 5, 2), use them once each, together with the four rules (and brackets), to make 24'*

Here one is given the answer and the permitted ingredients (inputs and rules), and has to search among all possible combinations to find a way of obtaining the required 'target number' 24. The task requires the same kind of elementary arithmetic as '$15 \times 9 = \ldots$' for its successful completion: the ingredients remain the positive integers and the 'four rules' of elementary arithmetic. But the strategy needed to find a solution is no longer deterministic, and success is no longer guaranteed. This is an *inverse* problem.

A slightly different insight into the character of inverse operations and their place in school mathematics arises from a systematic attempt to 'make 24' for each set of four numbers in these two lists:

List A: 1,2,3,4; 1,2,3,5; 1,2,3,6; 1,2,3,7; 1,2,3,8; 1,2,3,9; 1,2,3,10;
   1,2,3,11; 1,2,3,12; 1,2,3,13; 1,2,3,14; 1,2,3,15; 1,2,3,16; 1,2,3,17;
   1,2,3,18; 1,2,3,19; 1,2,3,20; 1,2,3,21; 1,2,3,22; 1,2,3,23; 1,2,3,24
List B: 3,3,2,2; 3,3,3,3; 3,3,4,4; 3,3,5,5; 3,3,6,6; 3,3,7,7; 3,3,8,8; 3,3,9,9

The reader is encouraged to tackle these elementary tasks before reading on, in order to provide a reference point for understanding the distinction between *direct* and *inverse* processes in mathematics. They may also help to underline the facts:

- that *inverse problems* are intrinsically 'harder' – for the teacher to teach and for the pupil to master – than merely implementing 'direct' processes;

- that an *inverse* problem ('*Find a way to make 24 using 6, 9, 5 and 2*') is only tractable if one has already achieved a robust mastery of the relevant *direct* processes (mental addition, subtraction, multiplication and division of small numbers).

Recognition of these two facts may make it easier to consider the more controversial suggestions:

- that **the main thrust of mathematics is to tackle inverse problems**;

- that a sufficiently robust mastery of direct processes is achieved far less often than we imagine; and

- that as a result of this weakness, and of political pressures to guarantee increasing success, **we have in recent years systematically neglected inverse problems.**

Like any classification, the distinction between 'direct' and 'inverse' processes needs to be used with care. At one level, *subtraction* is the inverse of *addition*. But in the context of the 24-game both operations constitute part of the 'direct' processes for which the 24-game problem represents an 'inverse' problem.

With this proviso it now seems to be generally accepted:

- that this distinction between 'direct' and 'inverse' operations is helpful

- that inverse problems are especially important when planning extension work for the top 25% or so, and

- that the following list highlights the distinction between direct and inverse processes in a way that most teachers recognise, and find enlightening and useful.

<u>Direct</u>	<u>Inverse</u>
Counting	'What's six less than …?'
Addition	Subtraction
Multiplication	Division
Powers	Extracting roots
Multiplying out brackets	Factorising
Plotting graphs	Sketching and recognising
Construction	Proof
Differentiation	Integration
Calculating	Problem solving

The words *direct* and *inverse* used here have been chosen for a good reason. The notion of 'inverse problems' is well developed in higher mathematics, and what is being illustrated here is a low level instance of this more general phenomenon.

2.2.6 Simplification and 'local' meaning

For the language of elementary mathematics to become familiar, and to be available to pupils as a tool, its objects and expressions need to acquire *meaning*. Such meaning can never be attached to uncomprehended sequences of symbols, or to arbitrary arrangements of lines and curves. We make sense of the world around us by applying two fundamental strategies.

(i) **First we learn to identify a small number of *basic objects*.**

These 'basic objects' are in part chosen so that they can be clearly recognised and easily analysed: that is, they are chosen partly for psychological and pedagogical reasons. But there are two important mathematical reasons for their choice: basic objects should arise 'naturally' in some sense, and should also have the property that *a significant universe of more complicated configurations and expressions* are easily understood as being built out of these basic objects. For example:

- *positive integers* and their arithmetic arise naturally, and then become integral parts of our understanding of fractions and the arithmetic of fractions, and of decimals and the arithmetic of decimals;

- *triangles* are the simplest two-dimensional figures, and the geometry of triangles (angle-sum, area, Pythagoras' theorem, trigonometry, etc.) plays a central role in analysing more complicated polygons in two dimensions and in calculating lengths and angles in three dimensions;

- an understanding of the calculus of *elementary functions* (polynomials, trig functions, exponentials and their inverses) allows one to analyse the behaviour of a whole universe of functions which are built up from these basic ingredients.

In each case, the basic objects need to be understood first, after which more complicated mathematical structures can be analysed in terms of the 'basic objects' from which they are constructed.

(ii) Having encountered these basic objects, we then get to know them thoroughly, and learn to recognise them in all sorts of different settings – in particular, by routinely *simplifying* whenever a basic object (such as $\frac{1}{2}$, or 370, or $x + 1$) crops up in a possibly unfamiliar guise $\left(\text{such as } \frac{18}{36}, \text{ or } 975 + 371 - 976, \text{ or } \frac{(x^2 + 1 + 2x)}{x + 1}\right)$.

In mathematics the habit of *simplification* is the most basic way in which we construct *meaning*. Only if expressions and configurations are actively and systematically simplified at key junctures can we make sense of mathematical objects and expressions, or 'see' the inner structure within a calculation, an expression, a figure, or an answer. And the weaker a pupil is, the more elusive meaning is likely to be without this habit of simplification.

Routine simplification makes *meaning* possible. The absence of the habit of *simplification* indicates the absence of (or a complete indifference to) *meaning*.

2.2.7 Connections and 'global' meaning

As explained above, there is thus a strong link between the way we establish low-level meaning in mathematics and the habit of simplification. We refer to this aspect of meaning as 'local meaning', because its origins are 'localised', with any resulting insight into the nature of specific objects or expressions arising from *the objects themselves and the way they are presented*. Simplification allows us to tell at a glance whether an object is familiar or unfamiliar, and how it relates to other known entities of the same kind.

However, every learner also needs to make sense of what mathematical objects 'are' in terms of the way different ideas 'fit together': we refer to this as establishing *global meaning*.

The most important everyday examples of 'global meaning', or of 'ideas being seen to fit together', arise when one topic or idea is shown to extend, to be closely related to, or to tell us something new about, an apparently quite different topic or idea which we thought we had already understood.

Mathematics is hard; its subject matter is inescapably abstract; its inherent logic is unforgiving. A calculation is either right or wrong. New material often confronts both learner and teacher with unavoidable difficulties, and can all too easily appear arbitrary, disconnected, or even alien – until, that is, *its links with things that are already familiar become clear*.

The initial discomfort is often unavoidable; but it can be short-lived, provided the pupil comes to understand the web of *connections* that embed the new topic into the larger tapestry of elementary mathematics. The struggle with each new topic is then resolved by seeing how it fits naturally into a larger, and more familiar framework, making the new idea not only more natural, but also more memorable.

The most common such connections are *structural*, as

◉ when one realises that *simplifying fractions* is just an exercise in finding the highest common factor of two integers; or

◉ when one comes to see that fractions, percentages, and ratio and proportion problems are all aspects of a single idea; or

◉ when the arithmetic of negative numbers reveals *subtraction* to be the same as *adding a negative*; or

◉ when the arithmetical structure of long multiplication (multiplying out brackets)

$$249 \times 17 = 249 \times (10 + 7)$$
$$= 249 \times 10 + 249 \times 7$$

is seen to echo many other *familiar mental strategies*, such as

$$15 \times 9 = (10 + 5) \times 9$$
$$= 90 + 45;$$

```
    2 4 9
  ×   1 7
  -------
  2 4 9 0
  1 7 4 3
  .........
```

or

◉ when one discovers that

  ◉ the opening gambit 'Let *x* be the unknown quantity', together with

  ◉ a willingness to write simple symbolic expressions
  provide a unified approach to hundreds of problems at a stroke.

But there are also occasional mildly surprising connections, or unexpected correspondences, such as

◉ when one links the '$\frac{1}{2}$' in the formula for the area of a triangle to the fact that a rectangle can be cut into two identical right-angled triangles with the same 'dimensions' (or later with the '$\frac{1}{2}$' which arises in the indefinite integral of the linear function ax); or

- when one realises that the formula for the area of a trapezium incorporates the formula for the area of a triangle; or

- when one realises *why* the number of chords created in a circle by n marked points on the circumference is just the binomial coefficient 'n choose 2'; or

- *why* the number of crossing points created by chords joining n points on the circumference of a circle has to be the binomial coefficient 'n choose 4'.

However, one of the main reasons all pupils study mathematics is its astonishing applicability. Thus, whilst *internal* connections are important in helping pupils to make sense of the mathematical universe, regular detailed examples from other subjects, and persistent efforts to establish connections between mathematics and the *external world*, help to give mathematics a different kind of meaning. The kind of applications that can be treated in detail in the classroom are relatively elementary; so we also need to be willing to use a broad brush to indicate the importance of mathematics in understanding, and in allowing us to predict, or to control, certain aspects of the real world which cannot be analysed in detail at school level.

There is also considerable scope for exploring links between mathematics and historical events. For example: (i) Herodotus' striking description of the way Xerxes counted the size of his army by requiring his men to successively fill a 'pen' which was known to hold 10 000 men (see Section 2.2.12); or (ii) Archimedes' ideas for using machines in the defence of Syracuse; or (iii) the differences between the Ptolemaic and the Copernican systems; or (iv) the crucial role of geometry in the science of navigation; or (v) code-breaking in the second World War.

Unfortunately, though such *connections* are an essential ingredient in human understanding, they are unlikely to appear on centrally controlled assessments (for reasons outlined above in Section 2.2.1). This may explain why programmes of study and textbooks have in recent years tended to suppress such connections (both between parts of mathematics, and between elementary mathematics and certain features of the world at large that can be better understood with the help of elementary mathematics). Yet it is precisely these connections that make the subject attractive and accessible.

2.2.8 Memory: What you don't 'know' (and so can't access instantly), you can't use!

In recent years those who specify what a typical pupil should be expected to learn and to remember have downplayed the importance of *memorisation*. (The role of *speed* in achieving, and in assessing, genuine mastery has been subjected to similar neglect: cf Section 2.2.10.)

The official position has vacillated. In the late 1980s and early 1990s *children were increasingly no longer expected to learn their tables*. One reason was that we were consistently told that primary pupils should be expected to use a calculator from the early primary years. (This remains a statutory requirement, but one that is now quietly overlooked.)

The message was rarely stated as clearly as in the italicised words in the previous paragraph, but it was transmitted loudly, and was received clearly. For some reason educationists disapproved of the idea that children should be expected to learn their tables (or almost anything else for that matter). But even the most progressive educationists found it hard to object if a child *happened to learn his or her tables 'by accident'.* The practice of actually *teaching* children to learn their tables was frowned upon as outmoded, but was never entirely eradicated. The results were clear for all to see: for example, most children could no longer perform simple calculations unaided; they routinely failed to simplify fractions; and they increasingly failed to develop a 'feeling for number'. Unfortunately, calculator use to some extent camouflaged (and continues to camouflage) the profound consequences for pupils' lack of understanding.

Despite this new orthodoxy of the 1980s and the early 1990s, in private homes and in those parts of the educational system which felt able to ignore central diktat, parents and teachers refused to abandon what seemed so obvious – namely that 'learning one's tables' conferred a marked 'selective advantage' on children. Some made sure that this unfashionable milestone was achieved in the privacy of their own homes, or at the hands of private tutors or prep schools. While many mathematics teachers in ordinary schools understandably hesitated to insist that the pupils in their own classrooms should continue to learn their tables, one had the impression that they still made sure that their own offspring practised at home! Moreover, a good number of traditional primary teachers quietly ignored the official strategy which, on the basis of their everyday experience seemed bound to disadvantage those in their charge; so they quietly closed their classroom doors and continued to insist that their pupils should learn their tables, and that they were subjected to regular mental quizzes. Thus the tradition survived in *samizdat* form.

In late 1995 the results of TIMSS, combined with complaints from employers and from higher education, forced politicians to question the then prevailing educational consensus. This led to the *Numeracy Pilot*, and later the *Numeracy Strategy*, where the 'tables were truly turned': calculators were quietly sidelined, and learning one's tables again became *de rigeur*.

But the victory was only partial, and the change remained superficial.

In 1981 we had failed to learn from the explicit embarrassment, openly declared in the Cockcroft report (1982), that, although official policy had turned England into a lucrative market for Japanese calculators, those who visited Japanese schools were astonished that 'in such a technologically advanced country they never saw a single calculator being used in schools'. By 1995 we appeared more willing to concede that we might have got something wrong.

However, precisely as we repented of our error at primary level, the official curriculum agency embraced the same error at secondary level by advocating the adoption of electronic substitutes for algebraic and geometric understanding *before* the necessary preliminary conceptual foundations have been established. This official encouragement for the premature use of computer algebra systems and geometry packages seems likely to repeat the errors of the 1980s in the teaching of arithmetic. If this impression turns out to be accurate, and if the policy continues, we can anticipate that the basic arts of exact calculation in algebra and in euclidean geometry will suffer in much the same way as basic arithmetic suffered in the late 1980s and 1990s.

We clearly need an open debate about the underlying issue:

> **What role does memory play in mastering elementary mathematics?**

Such a debate would quickly be seen to be part of the larger questions:

> What role does memory play in seeking to master any subject?
>
> And what role does memory play in shaping who we are, or how we see ourselves?

George Steiner and others have written eloquently about the way memory contributes to, and allows each of us to hold on to, what we are – especially when those around us seek to 'airbrush away' the coordinates which assert where we come from, and what we 'are'. His observations may yet prove to be more significant in a consumerist age than in the Holocaust and the Gulag that inspired his original thoughts on the subject.

Memory (or its absence) is like eating (or starving), and like breathing (or suffocating). Memorising things cannot be what life is about; but where it is neglected, nothing else is possible. In other words, it is essential – but as a means to a higher end rather than an end in itself.

The indications of our failure towards the current generation are all around us. Free access to calculators – designed to cover up our own failure as teachers; formula books in exams – which we hope will conceal our failure to insist that 'What you don't know you can't use'; the unstoppable drift towards 'rule-based' teaching, where pupils no longer even look for 'reasons' and imagine that marks can be magic-ed by appeals to garbled, uncomprehended rules; our confusion – at the very highest levels – about the place of standard written algorithms and the reasons why they are important; our failure to recognise the centrality of *connections*, *reasons* and *proof* as the glue which holds all of mathematics together.

As generations of students have shown us, a formula book is of little value to someone who has never been required to learn the basic facts. Many of us can probably picture some exasperated colleague exclaiming 'But did you not realise that it was there in the formula book?'.

Students' failure to use the formula book intelligently should come as no surprise to those of us who sometimes reach for a dictionary when faced with a cryptic crossword, only to lay it down unopened: for one often simply does not know what words to 'look up'. What matters when tackling a crossword is instant recall of a repertoire of possible words, which can be quickly scanned in one's head: in other words, to operate effectively **one needs to memorise far more than is needed to answer any given question!**

Similarly,

◎ when confronted by a multi-step problem, one needs everything to be robustly internalised, so that one can scan quickly through possible intermediate steps to see which is the most promising;

◎ given a typical 'inverse' problem (such as arises routinely in the *24-game*) one has to survey the whole range of options, and assess their efficacy using calculations instantly acessible to memory, to decide which works.

The amount one should ideally know by heart is more extensive than is often believed – especially when first learning a subject. **Practice and the process of "memorisation" are an integral part of the subtle process of working towards understanding.** Serious jazz musicians, actors, and other apparently spontaneous performers practise far more than most people realise – *especially if they want to avoid their performances becoming stereotyped!* Yet they must never imagine that everything can be reduced to rote, and must leave room for freshness (and risk). In the same way we should never give the impression that rote learning can be used as a substitute for flexibility.

Memory provides us with a sketch map of each domain. We do not need to remember everything; but we **need to remember enough to find our way**

around quickly and easily. It is the teacher's job to know what are the central landmarks, and how they can be used to allow ordinary pupils with a limited range of elementary mathematical techniques to solve a vast range of problems.

Children who have been required to submit relevant material to memory in this flexible spirit approach unfamiliar problems with a confidence that is worlds away from the half-hearted (and doomed) attempts of those who have been deceived into imagining that there is no need to learn things by heart.

Facts liberate; rules bind.

2.2.9 Mental compression and compression-rich mathematics

Human beings can only hold a limited amount of information at the front of their minds – ready for instant use. As we learn more and more mathematics we need strategies for *compressing* what we know in more efficient ways.

When we first come to grips with individual fractions, we interpret each fraction as a compound notion. We first get to know simple *unit fractions* – such as $\frac{1}{2}$, $\frac{1}{4}$, and $\frac{1}{3}$: that is, 'fraction' means 'part of *a whole*'. Then, to make sense of $\frac{3}{4}$, we imagine $\frac{1}{4}$ and take '3 lots of $\frac{1}{4}$'. In time we must learn to compress these steps and accept '$\frac{3}{4}$' as a single entity. Only then are we ready for the surprise that when we try to make sense of sharing '3 wholes between 4 people', the answer is (very conveniently) $\frac{3}{4}$: that is, $3 \div 4 = \frac{3}{4}$. From that point on, the previously separate ideas of 'fraction', of sharing, and of division become compressed into a single, multi-faceted composite notion.

When we first need to evaluate 3×12 we may struggle with ungainly repeated addition; but in time we compress this perception into multiplication without explicit reference to repeated addition (using the distributive law to grasp this as '$3 \times 10 + 3 \times 2 = 30 + 6 = 36$', and later as the instant response '36'.

On one level problems such as *The two cyclists* have to be painstakingly unpacked step by step; but effective instruction means that the separate steps are soon compressed into a single mental schema. On higher levels the compression which takes place is even more striking:

- the identity '$\cos^2\theta + \sin^2\theta = 1$' is just a restatement of Pythagoras' theorem;

- given the circle theorems, the 'double angle formula' for $\sin 2\theta$ $(= 2\sin\theta\cos\theta)$ is just a restatement of our old friend 'half base times height' for the area of a triangle; and

- the addition formulae for $\cos(A + B)$ and $\sin(A + B)$ begin life as magical 'poems' – learned by rote and recited under one's breath each time they are used, with little or no insight beyond the scansion of the recited poem; but they are later seen to be simple consequences of the basic index law $e^{iA} \cdot e^{iB} = e^{i(A + B)}$, and the magical poem is either safely sidelined, or becomes part of some higher synthesis.

Mental compression is important for mathematical thinking because of the way mathematics is structured. In addition to promoting mental agility in moving between concepts, it strengthens the links between the cognitive structures being built in the mind of the learner.

This feature of elementary mathematics – that internal connections replace the need for more and more memorising of unrelated rules, and allow us to operate more efficiently and more meaningfully – is so important that it needs to be built into both the choice of curriculum material and the way it is taught. Thus we should deliberately emphasise those 'compression rich' topics – such as integer arithmetic (without a calculator), fractions and proportion, algebra, ruler and compass constructions and elementary euclidean geometry, etc. – which are not only mathematically 'important', but embody this feature of mathematics most effectively.

This and the previous section highlight the twin pillars on which elementary mathematics rests:

◎ *knowing by heart* (and understanding) *the basic steps,*

and

◎ *understanding that, since these simple steps can be combined to solve less familiar problems, there is at first no need to remember more than this.*

Curiously, recent trends have managed to neglect both pillars at the same time! Not only has the need to 'know by heart' the basic steps been downplayed, but the subtle art of linking these basic steps to solve multi-step problems has been generally neglected (because it cannot be assessed in tests that are obliged to achieve year-on-year improvement). Moreover the internal connections within school mathematics, which reduce the need for *additional* memorisation, have been quietly sidelined (because they cannot be centrally assessed) – with a resulting explosion in the number of unjustified 'rules' to be learned blindly (often displayed in 'boxes' within the text)!

2.2.10 Fluency and automaticity

Pupils need to attain fluency in handling a wide range of basic arithmetical, algebraic, trigonometric and geometrical facts and procedures.

A new topic or technique is at first inevitably unfamiliar and unnatural. But these initial difficulties diminish with time, partly as a result of practice, and partly as one comes to see the new procedure as a natural extension of processes that are already familiar. To encourage and to cement this change from 'unfamiliar' to 'familiar', it is essential to expect (and to test for) increased speed, fluency and flexibility, so that each new procedure can eventually be exercised *automatically, quickly,* and *accurately* – thereby freeing up mental space for serious thinking. What the brain does not know inside out repeatedly clogs the pathways of the mind to such an extent that *it can no longer focus on those matters that require genuine thought*.

As *The two cyclists* problem illustrates, whenever one is faced with an exercise or problem that is more complicated than one is used to, if the constituent steps cannot yet be implemented automatically and reliably, one or more of the basic steps, or the 'executive control' of the overall strategy of which these basic steps are atomic parts, is likely to malfunction. As many of the TIMSS items show, there are large tracts of basic school mathematics – including many fundamental topics – where English schools at present rarely achieve the necessary robust fluency.

2.2.11 The importance of being 'open-middled'

Recommendation 4.5 of the Smith Report *Making mathematics count* (2004) explicitly addressed the need for 'an extension curriculum and assessment framework'. It included a rough list of material that deserved to be included in such a curriculum, ending with the words: '*more open-ended problem solving*' (fortunately without the usual hyphen between 'problem' and 'solving').

In the last 15 years the expression 'open-ended' (with hyphen!) has been used in an increasingly uncritical way – if for superficially laudable reasons.

Those who are responsible for mathematics education are often aware that too much teaching is restricted to unimaginative drilling in one-step *direct* routines (even though they may not have thought of it quite like that). The expression 'open-ended' is then often used to refer to any task which requires the pupil to do more than implement some standard one-step routine.

Yet the label is **wrong** – even for many of the activities that it is used to describe.

While there are exceptions, it is generally true to say that good problems in school mathematics are almost never open-**ended**! A problem in which the *end* is 'open' is a recipe for chaos, and conveys a false image of mathematics. Good school mathematics problems – like good mathematics problems in general – usually have a clear answer: that is, they are **closed**-ended.

And while it may be closer to reality to consider problems which have an 'open' *beginning*, to use such problems too often in the classroom would make unreasonable demands on the pupils (and on the teacher!).

What we should be trying to encourage in the first instance is neither the property of being 'open-ended', nor that of being 'open-beginninged', but rather that of being

open-middled.

The best kind of problem material generally has a *clear statement*, and a *clear conclusion* – which may be given as part of the problem, or may be left implicit as part of what is to be found.

What remains 'open' is the route which leads from the statement to the conclusion!

Whether the route to be found is unique, or whether there are several different possible solutions is less important than the fact that the ultimately successful route is *initially opaque*, or 'covered-up', and so has to be actively dis-covered. It is the process which is needed in order to discover the solution to such a problem that largely determines its educational value.

Thus, problems that are referred to as 'open-ended' should often more properly, and more instructively, be referred to as **open-middled**!

2.2.12 Exactness and approximation

Integers and integer arithmetic are 'discrete' – and hence *exact*. Yet sooner or later work with large numbers, or with the decimal system, confronts us with the need to *approximate* and to *estimate*. The mathematical and pedagogical basis of approximation and estimation seem to be rather poorly understood.

Estimation and approximation are rooted in the basic notion of 'change of units', whose rules need to be clearly understood. In real life, measures (whether counting discrete objects, or measuring distances) are rarely exact, but are more honestly interpreted as indicating that the stated measure lies 'somewhere between' two limits. These limits may be explicitly given – for example, as a 'tolerance', or in the form of declared 'significant figures', or in the form '$\pm \varepsilon$'. The implied limits of accuracy may also remain implicit – as when we assume that the last non-zero digit in a given continuous quantity indicates the degree of 'rounding'.

Faced with a multiplication such as 3594×273, we may treat the given factors as 'approximate measures', which can be re-interpreted in tens, or in hundreds. Thus we may interpret the 3594 as 'slightly more than $33\frac{1}{3}$ hundreds' and the 273 as 'slightly less than 3 hundreds', whence the required answer is 'approximately 100 hundred hundreds', or 1 million. In a similar spirit, the size of a roughly rectangular park may be estimated by mentally picturing 'the number of football pitch *widths*' that would appear to fit one way and 'the number of football pitch *lengths*' that would fit the other way. A more striking example occurs in Herodotus, *The histories*, Book 7:

> 'As nobody has left a record, I cannot state the precise numbers provided by each separate nation [towards the army that Xerxes was leading against the Persians], but the grand total, excluding the naval contingent, turned out to be 1 700 000. The counting was done by first packing ten thousand men as close together as they could stand and drawing a circle round them on the ground; they were then dismissed, and a fence about navel-high, was constructed round the circle, finally the other troops were marched into the area thus enclosed and dismissed in their turn, until the whole army had been counted.'

The *mathematical* character of 'approximation' is compromised whenever estimation is implemented in an uncontrolled fashion – often as little more than (un)inspired *guesswork*. In contrast, mathematical approximation demands that we operate in a way that allows us to *simplify* while *retaining control over the approximate answer obtained*. In particular, when replacing an exact calculation by an estimate, one often needs to know the answer to such questions as:

- Is my estimate larger or smaller than the exact answer?
- How large is the possible error?

Moreover, the appropriate strategy when approximating may well depend in subtle ways on what kind of question we are being asked, and what the answer turns out to be. For example: when faced with such questions as

> 'Could a million £1 coins fit in an old-fashioned telephone kiosk?', or
> 'Do human beings live for as long as a million hours?',

one must somehow *underestimate* the number (of coins that fit in a telephone kiosk, or of hours in a human life) and still come up with more than a million if the answer is to be 'Yes', but must *overestimate* the number (and come up with a number less than a million) if the answer is to be 'No'. Hence the appropriate strategy depends on the answer – which one does not yet know!

For pupils to master the art of 'approximating' arithmetical calculations in integers, they first need to master the art of *exact calculation*. Only then can they use their knowledge of exactness as a 'fulcrum' for thinking precisely about more elusive *approximation*. And when they later come to analyse the errors introduced by such approximations, they will discover that this is done via the *exact calculations* of elementary algebra! Thus, even when seeking to transcend the inherent 'exactness' of *integer arithmetic* by developing the art of approximation, there is no escape from the maxim:

> *Mathematics is the science of exact calculation.*

Respect for, and the ability to handle, *exactness* correctly is the essence of elementary mathematics. Despite their youth, primary pupils are often well-aware of this fact. In contrast, our over-familiarity with calculator output can blind us to the subtleties involved in approximation, and lure us into thinking that we no longer need to respect the above fundamental constraint. Many secondary pupils (and their examiners) have become unthinkingly cavalier in this regard.

In the absence of a sufficiently rich experience of multiplication, it is often hard to see how pupils are expected to 'approximate' without resorting to guesswork, or to some imposed 'rule'. Their mental experience of exact calculation may suffice for small numbers, where they may have a very real sense that '38 × 7 is slightly less than 40 × 7' – and may even know exactly how much less. But it is a substantial step from this to conclude that ordinary pupils can make sense of the instruction 'approximate first' when faced with 3594 × 273. One could bully them by insisting that it is 'obviously more than 3000 × 200', and they might even agree – but it would be unclear what they were thinking. Their resulting assent would be reminiscent of the very young child who, having failed to answer his father's question 'What is 4 times 30?', is impatiently asked the apparently unrelated question 'What's 4 times 3?'. The child may know the answer to the latter question, yet – in the absence of a robust feeling for place value and for the mechanics of multiplication – see no apparent connection between this familiar fact and the original question.

The advantages – and the difficulties – of respecting 'exactness' become clear when students are confronted with fractions. It takes effort to learn to treat individual fractions, such as $\frac{3}{4}$ and $\frac{2}{3}$, as entities in their own right rather than as 'incomplete calculations' begging to be 'evaluated'. Yet it is only by learning to accept them as genuine entities can one handle such calculations as

$$8 \times \frac{3}{4} = 2 \times \left(4 \times \frac{3}{4}\right) = 2 \times 3 = 6, \text{ and}$$

$$6 \times \frac{2}{3} = 2 \times \left(3 \times \frac{2}{3}\right) = 2 \times 2 = 4$$

using integer arithmetic – without mindlessly multiplying everything out, or resorting to inscrutably messy (and usually inaccurate) decimals. Only then can simple linear and quadratic equations, and more general polynomials with rational coefficients, be handled appropriately, which is essential if fluency in elementary algebra is to be accessible to more students.

A similar phenomenon arises in learning to accept, and to work with, surds, and later with trigonometry.

This notion of **exactness** is an inescapable part of the essence of school mathematics. But insistence on respecting exactness also helps to convey – possibly subliminally – the fact that all of mathematics depends on *precision*, in the sense that

- technical terms need to be used correctly,
- statements and equations need to be transformed according to precise rules, and
- methods have to be *comprehended*, and algorithms have to be remembered and implemented completely accurately if their results are to be trusted.

In recent years these simple principles have been noticeably (and increasingly) absent among students with the very best A level mathematics grades. One apparent cause is the indiscriminate *way* in which students are encouraged to use calculators. Where a decimal answer is required, a calculator may be indispensable; but its use is usually best postponed *until the very last line of a calculation*, so that the derivation up to that point can remain *mathematically exact*.

2.2.13 Algorithms

Modern applications of mathematics are derived in much the same way mathematics has always been derived; but they often exploit the possibility of computer *implementation*. That is, they involve one or more *algorithms*. An *algorithm* is a general procedure, which begins with an arbitrary input (of some fixed type), which is then transformed, via a sequence of elementary steps, into a standard output.

Algorithms are quintessentially mathematical. Thus it is desirable that all youngsters emerging from school mathematics should have some direct experience of proven algorithms – starting with the most elementary and proceeding to examples which convey the spirit of 'algorithmics', namely that a sequence of simple steps can deliver far more than one has a right to expect.

The simplest prototype of all modern algorithms is perhaps the Euclidean algorithm for finding the *highest common factor* of two given integers. But while the algorithm itself is accessible to pupils in Year 10, its astonishing effectiveness (especially for pairs of large integers) is likely to be appreciated only some time after pupils have mastered more primitive methods for finding *hcfs*; and its inner logic can scarcely be appreciated without a degree of algebraic sophistication.

Another elementary algorithm is that which underlies Euclid's proof that 'the prime numbers are more than any assigned multitude'. Here an initial prime p_1 is used as 'seed' to generate an arbitrarily long sequence of distinct prime numbers

$$p_1, p_2, p_3, p_4, p_5, \ldots\ldots\ldots$$

But again, though the procedure is elementary, its overall architecture combines arithmetical, logical and algebraic sophistication!

These and other considerations force one to reassess the merits of the *standard written algorithms* of elementary integer arithmetic (see 2.2.18). They have the advantage that they deal with material that is entirely familiar. These basic algorithms are rooted in, and reinforce, aspects of elementary arithmetic that are available to Everyman, including

◎ place value and our *base 10* numeral system, and

◎ the addition facts and the multiplication tables for the digits 0-9.

They also open the door to a wide variety of excellent problem material (from simple 'missing digit' puzzles, to questions about 'Beginnings and ends' – see Section E8 in Book *Alpha*). But most importantly, they provide natural access to the arithmetic of decimals for ordinary pupils.

Thus there are good reasons to see these traditional procedures as having a renewed justification in a truly 'modern' curriculum. Naturally, we need to do more than simply reinstate them in their traditional form and declare the job to be 'done'. Their prototypical algorithmic character should be used as a starting point for a re-interpretation of other aspects of secondary mathematics to see how this algorithmic facet of modern mathematics might be best represented. (For example, one obvious candidate is to develop work on prime numbers and prime factorisation – replacing the 'tree diagram' method for factorising integers by a genuinely algorithmic procedure; one might also implement simple primality tests and sieve methods in algorithmic form. Another candidate is to explore convergence of simple iterations, especially where these reinforce important ideas within the existing curriculum: see Section T2 in Book *Gamma*.)

2.2.14 First steps to using and applying mathematics: Word problems

It is twenty years since the introduction of a national curriculum with its significant component dedicated to 'using and applying mathematics'. Sadly, the inclusion of this component has never been properly thought through (as one sees from *The two cyclists*, the emergency introduction of the *Numeracy Strategy*, the abolition of coursework, and the desperate invention by politicians and civil servants of *functional mathematics*).

Using and applying elementary mathematics is a delicate art – as anyone who has ever struggled to make sense of an income tax return can probably confirm. So school mathematics might be well advised to avoid being excessively ambitious on this score. This short subsection aims to do no more than to suggest that we may have neglected the simplest available 'stepping stones' that help to link classroom mathematics to full-blooded applications: namely *word problems*.

The expression *word problem* refers to a task whose mathematical character has to be extracted from a *relatively short* verbal statement.

We accept the outward form of the claim (taken from the Standards Site: 'Solving word problems') that 'Word problems are a traditional part of mathematics lessons'. However, the examples given there suggest an almost flippant disregard for what word problems are and why they are important. And we strongly dispute the claim made there that 'nearly all textbooks (in England) contain exercises of them'; for insofar as textbooks do contain such problems, they fail to make sufficient or systematic use of them.

Word problems have two main functions.

The first is purely mathematical, in that they provide a simple way of adding a layer of mild disguise to what would otherwise be a mere exercise, so transforming it into an educationally richer *problem*, which gives the teacher a better indication of how robustly and flexibly the underlying techniques have been understood and mastered. The simpler problems used in the national *Challenges* provide good illustrations of this first function, and the results reveal each year how ill-prepared pupils in ordinary schools are for the experience! A much richer source of word problems, and the role they should be expected to play, is to be found in the standard texts and workbooks used in Flemish Belgium, in Eastern Europe, in Singapore and in the Far East.

The second function (partly related to the first) is the way word problems can be used to help ordinary pupils achieve an insight into the interaction between elementary mathematics and its application to problems arising in the world around us. Word problems are not 'real world' problems; they are artificial attempts to capture certain aspects of 'using and applying' within three or four short sentences. *The two cyclists* may serve as a very elementary example. Word problems require pupils to read, to select information from a simple formulation, to choose an appropriate calculation, and to interpret the result of that calculation. While word problems are certainly not full-blooded applications, their regular use can serve as a systematic way of routinely linking the abstract world of school mathematics with the outside world. They constitute an invaluable stepping-stone on the path from abstract classroom arithmetic, algebra and geometry to the confident use of simple methods to solve given problems, and should be a routine part of school mathematics for all pupils.

We need to develop a clear pedagogical understanding of what word problems have to offer, and of the extent to which they are currently being trivialised or neglected. We then need to engage in a careful didactical analysis of the use of word problems in school mathematics at all levels.

2.2.15 The myth of 'problem-solving'

As we have already seen, those in England who teach mathematics, or who administer our national curriculum and its assessment, often overestimate how much of the curriculum should be devoted to one-step routines. But at the same time they are aware that the detailed curriculum document, with its fragmented and isolated one-step routines (statutorily condemned to be assessed in a fragmented way!) cannot possibly tell 'the whole story' of elementary mathematics.

However, having shirked the necessary didactical analysis which might yield a clearer picture of 'the rest of elementary mathematics', they have little option but to resort to crude portmanteau labels (such as 'problem-solving') in order to humanise an otherwise bare curriculum. Thus the hyphenated term 'problem-solving' has become a kind of shorthand for 'everything that is worth doing, but which is passed over in silence by the fragmented national curriculum'. So whenever something is not a recognisable curriculum topic, but is nevertheless perceived as being worthwhile, the only obvious way of allowing it to be included is to classify it under an officially acceptable, but professionally unhelpful, heading such as 'problem-solving'.

For example, many teachers who are challenged for the first time to reflect upon the distinction between *direct* and *inverse* processes – as illustrated, for example, by the 24-game (see Section 2.2.5) – recognise the phenomenon being described, but lack a suitable language with which to organise their thinking about the fundamental importance of, and the differences between, these contrasting processes. As a result, there is a danger that activities (like the 24-game), which cry out to be used to exercise a *specific* 'inverse' process, are simply classified under the general heading of 'problem-solving', and their significance is thereby misconstrued.

Much has been written on the subject of 'problem-solving'; but most users of the word never subject the idea to detailed scrutiny. Could it be that the hyphenated word 'problem-solving' (as currently used) has no clear meaning? Or that its use generates more confusion than it resolves? Or that the value of the expression lies mainly in the fact that it reflects a vague awareness that *something important has been omitted* in the remaining curriculum detail?

Despite its apparent lack of any clearly defined meaning, and despite the fact that its official introduction into the curriculum has patently failed to deliver what was promised on its behalf (as evidenced by complaint **4B** in the 1995 London Mathematical Society report *Tackling the mathematics problem* – see 1.3 above), this upstart has risen to the point where it is now assumed to be what is often called a 'generic skill'. Worse, it has increasingly supplanted that down-to-earth staple of all good mathematics teaching – namely, the central need for all students to engage in the *regular detailed work of struggling to solve* **particular problems of a particular kind**.

The situation has been made worse by 'curriculum generalists', by Human Resources types from business, and by politicians, who all seize on the fashionable expression 'problem-solving' as something whose absence is bemoaned by senior managers from time to time. These people understand little about the mathematics that is needed in the workplace, or about the necessary foundations that need to be laid in school; yet they imagine that there is some magic 'transferable skill' called *problem-solving*, which cuts across disciplines, and which might somehow replace the *hard graft* needed to master the art of solving *particular* problems in *particular* settings.

There is little evidence that any such transferable skill exists. The ability to 'identify and deploy known strategies, and to find and exploit promising stepping-stones' depends on *familiarity with specific subject matter*, and much information is lost if we try to encapsulate these activities under a single heading as if they were merely instances of some universal 'generic skill'.

2.2.16 Exercises and problems; short and extended tasks

As intimated in the previous subsection, official guidance regularly misconstrues the subtlety and the simplicity of 'the art of problem solving' in mathematics. Problem solving is neither a 'generic skill' that transcends specific subject matter, nor a portmanteau word that can usefully describe everything that is not 'functional mathematics'.

The extent of our misconceptions is visible on the simplest levels. We are told (Standards Site: 'Solving word problems', Section 2) that

> *'Children should have regular opportunities in the daily mathematics lesson to use and apply their mathematics. The problems you ask them to solve need to vary in type and extent, and include:*
>
> ◎ *short problems, taking from a few seconds to a minute or two to solve*
>
> ◎ *medium length problems, taking up half a lesson or more*
>
> ◎ *extended problems, such as an investigation, which might be spread over several lessons.'*

The implied belief in the virtues of 'extended investigation' is totally misplaced. **Most successful mathematics teachers base their teaching largely on problems that are either short, or very short!** The quality of the teaching has nothing to do with the 'extent' of the tasks used, and everything to do with their *character*. (The tasks used in most mathematics lessons are inadequate not because they are short, but rather because they lack content, and are too often designed simply to give pupils a sense of cheap success.)

An extended task risks running out of control: different pupils are likely to pursue different avenues and the teacher is left unable to orchestrate the desired outcomes. As a result, after tackling an extended task pupils often have no clear sense of what they were meant to have learned.

In contrast a series of carefully chosen short tasks *that force pupils to think* may look less impressive, but can allow the teacher to retain a measure of control, and the pupils to discern the intended inner lessons.

The most important distinction in mathematics teaching should be, not between short and extended tasks, but between an *exercise* and a *problem*.

An **exercise** is a task, or a collection of tasks, that provides routine practice in some technique, or combination of techniques. The techniques will have been explicitly taught, and the meaning of each task will be clear. All that is required of pupils is that they implement the procedure as taught to produce an answer. Each collection of such exercises should be designed to 'exercise' the given skill in order to establish the relevant technique in a suitably robust form; in particular it should highlight and help eliminate standard misconceptions and errors.

Exercises are not meant to be exciting, or especially stimulating. But without a regular diet of suitable exercises – ranging from the simple to the suitably complex – pupils are likely to lack the repertoire of basic technique which they need in order to make sense of mildly more challenging tasks. So it is *exercises* that constitute the 'bread and potatoes' of the mathematics curriculum.

However, bread and potatoes do not by themselves constitute a healthy diet. Pupils need activities of a more challenging kind to help whet their mathematical appetites, and to cultivate a willingness to tackle and to solve simple but unfamiliar problems. A **problem** is any task which we do not immediately recognise as being of a familiar type, and for which we know no standard solution method. Hence, when faced with a problem we may at first have no idea how to begin.

The first point to recognise is that a task does not have to be very unfamiliar before it becomes a *problem* rather than an exercise! In the absence of an explicit and realistic problem solving culture, it is often enough simply to set an exercise whose solution method has not been mentioned for a week or so, or which has been worded in a way that fails to announce its connection with recent work.

Too many exercises get stuck at the level of *one piece jigsaws*, so conveying the message that mathematics consists exclusively of such mindless activities. International comparisons suggest that this tendency may lie at the heart of the 'English disease'; so every set of exercises should include one or two tasks that force pupils to think flexibly, and to string simple steps together in a reliable way, and so to discover the astonishing increase in power that results. Pupils need to learn from their everyday experience that the whole purpose of achieving fluency in routine 'bread and potatoes' exercises is to be able to marshal these skills to handle slightly more demanding multi-step exercises and more interesting, if mildly unsettling problems.

2.2.17 Flexibility in marshalling simple techniques: problem solving 'Japanese'-style

As we have seen, the essence of elementary mathematics lies in the way simple techniques can be combined to solve problems that would otherwise be completely out of reach. Hence all pupils need *extensive first-hand experience that renders this fact so obvious as to be taken for granted*.

One-step routines remain dangerously fragile unless they can be routinely, reliably and correctly implemented within the larger context of the solution of simple multi-step problems. Thus all pupils need a regular diet of suitably chosen two-step and multi-step challenges.

On the simplest level this diet should include two-step and multi-step **exercises**: that is, questions like *The two cyclists* (Section 1.5), which require little more than the ability to read, to extract information, and to carry out the relevant simple routines in the correct sequence to obtain the required answer. These skills may seem so simple as to be scarcely worthy of remark. However, the evidence relating to *The two cyclists* shows that many of our mathematically 'most successful' students emerge from the present school system without having been expected to coordinate simple routines in a reliable way. This must be largely due to lack of practice at all stages of their school careers.

Achieving a robust mastery of basic routines is important; but most mathematics cannot be reduced to 'exercises' – that is, to predictable routines in standard settings. Pupils need to develop a 'suppleness of thought', which will allow them to operate *flexibly*, and to use their native intelligence to decide – *on the basis of the mathematical evidence* – how to proceed when confronted with simple **problems** of a less deterministic character than *The two cyclists*. One simple, and under-used, class of such problems are often referred to as 'angle-chasing' (see Book *Alpha*, Section T9; or Book *Beta*, Section T17).

Such 'problems' are often simple to state, yet constitute a very different kind of challenge from mere exercises. Their multi-step character means that there is likely to be a significant chasm between the stated problem and the required solution. In addition, the problem may be so worded as to appear unfamiliar, and hence may provide no immediately obvious clue about where, or how, to begin. It is not easy to give crisp examples out of context, but the following simplified specimens may suffice to convey the central idea:

- $181 - 182 + 183 - 184 + 185 - 186 + 187 - 188 + 189 = \ldots$.

- Simplify $\frac{142\,857}{999\,999}$.

- Find 30% of 40% of 50.

- What is the angle between the two hands of a clock at 1:30? Find another time when the angle between the two hands of a clock has the same size.

- Factorise $x^4 + x^2 + 1$.

- Use angle chasing and congruence to find an angle in a given geometric configuration.

Even where it *seems* clear how to begin (as in the first example), it may be better to stand back and think for a moment! In the other examples, the inexperienced solver is likely to have no immediate idea 'where to begin', and may notice no obvious 'clue' about what ideas to draw upon. Pupils need to learn, and teachers need to teach, in a way that encourages them to welcome regular challenges that make them **think**, and to realise that 'being temporarily stumped' marks the *beginning* of the solving process, rather than a reason to quit, or to demand outside help!

Problem solving 'Japanese'-style

While it is part of the teacher's role to try to avoid *unnecessary* difficulties, it is also important for pupils to learn *to be uncomfortable*, to experience *frustration* (and failure), and to realise that *this is an integral part of the learning process*. We all – teachers and pupils alike – have to learn to be unsettled and to take considered risks in simple settings. But such words remain 'pie-in-the-sky' unless pupils learn from regular classroom experience that new, and apparently difficult, kinds of problems **can** be solved using the methods they already know: this is the essence of what we call *'problem solving Japanese-style'*.

This 'Japanese-style' approach to school mathematics would appear to be extremely rare in England; but it is – or used to be – standard practice in Japan, in Russia, and in some other European countries.

Mathematics teaching in all countries is often based on an approach where each new topic is introduced through one or more 'worked examples', which are supposed to provide pupils with a 'model' for them to follow when they come to tackle similar problems for themselves. However, the principles underlying the choice of 'worked examples' varies markedly from country to country.

In England (and in many English-speaking countries) conventional wisdom assumes that the initial 'worked examples' should be chosen to be *as simple as possible*. **The 'Japanese-style' is to do the exact opposite!** The reasons behind such differences tell us much

- about the goals of school mathematics in different countries,

- about their perceptions of the nature of elementary mathematics and of children's potential,

- about the way classrooms are managed, and

- about how different countries work to achieve the best for their pupils.

The first thing to stress is that **the 'Japanese' approach is adopted precisely because teachers are concerned about *all* pupils, not just about the favoured few.** Japan is now facing, for the first time, many of the social problems which we know all too well; and they are not finding it easy to adjust. However, the traditional effectiveness of school mathematics teaching in Japan has been rooted in part in a common curriculum designed for, and delivered to, **all** pupils, with no selective schools and no official 'streaming'. (The reality is more complicated, in that almost all pupils and parents used to accept responsibility for contributing to their own learning, so attendance at *juku* – after school tutoring – was accepted from an early age. Also entrance to the better universities is highly competitive, so the more ambitious high schools and high school students find other ways of preparing to meet the demands of university entrance tests.)

The second thing to stress is that Japanese educational goals and values are not like the English 'comprehensive' system, where we oblige pupils to attend the same type of school and at the same time *continue to accept widespread pupil failure as if it were God-given*. Traditional Japanese school mathematics teaching would appear to have been successful precisely because it concentrated on the task of **optimising the performance of the weakest students**. Indeed, there was little or no formal provision for the 'well above average' students – except insofar as teachers and curriculum planners realised that an approach which is carefully designed to lay appropriate foundations *for all pupils* to allow them to build the higher mathematical structures they may later need, but which also strives to make things clear to weaker students, can hardly fail to make things clear to more able students.

A typical 'Japanese-style' lesson begins with a deliberately *hard* problem, which none of the pupils would at first know how to solve. The problem is carefully chosen, and developed, by the teacher

- because it can be made interesting to the children;
- because there is an accessible (but not immediately obvious) natural strategy which the teacher is fairly sure the children will propose;
- because the necessary ideas and mathematical techniques to implement this strategy are all available from *recently learned* material; and
- because the resulting communal solution will bring out the *key principles* which underlie the general method being introduced.

The teacher then involves the whole class in *extracting* not just 'any old solution', but a specific, carefully planned approach, which incorporates the desired *general solution method*: that is, the teacher purposefully and unashamedly orchestrates the ideas that emerge, so that

- the class succeeds in solving the problem *in the desired standard way*, and
- explicit attention is drawn to the key features of the method used.

Naturally some ideas are sidelined *en route*, but only when their limitations have been explored and understood.

> **An example** Sometimes the initial problem may be deliberately ill-posed, and so may require extensive clarification before one can attempt an approximate solution. For example, a teacher of Year 9 or 10 might show a picture of the local town lake, and say: '*Suppose the lake needs to be treated by*

> *adding a chemical 'agent' (or an organism) at a given concentration. How can officials decide how much "agent" to order?'*

The first move is for the teacher to help the class to recognise that the words 'at a given concentration' mean that the main mathematical task is to find a way of estimating the volume of the lake.

The next move may be to extract the idea that the profile of a typical lake basin means that using cuboids is probably too crude an approximation; so that the best available method may be to find a way of approximating the vertical cross-section of the lake in a way that will allow use of the only general volume formula they know, namely that for the volume of a (probably triangular) *prism*.

The teacher may then produce, or direct pupils to a predetermined source to find, cross-sectional maps of the lake taken at various points. The lake can then be systematically approximated by a sequence of triangular prisms, its approximate volume calculated, and the original question answered.

Despite the effort already expended, the teacher will rarely be satisfied with 'solving' the stated problem, but rather looks for ways of extending or adapting the solution method to extract more than was originally required.

(What if we wanted the answer in litres instead of cubic metres? What if the required concentration were dependent on the level of fish stocks in the lake: how would we estimate the average number, or weight, of fish per cubic metre? Etc.)

Much more is being absorbed in this example than merely the intended 'mathematical method'. However, the teacher avoids being sidetracked into thinking that 'anything goes', but makes sure that the intended method is explicitly formulated and fully understood. The principles underpinning the general method of solution are extracted and listed prominently on the board, and pupils are then required to use the same principles to solve problems – which are often at first *considerably easier* than the communal introductory problem which has just been solved. At the end of the session, the principles that pupils have been using may be emphasised once again.

The approach is strikingly different from the common English approach in which the teacher's exposition routinely begins with misleadingly simple examples, chosen in the belief that there is some 'spontaneous gain' in pupils' understanding if the first couple of exercises can be completed by most pupils using nothing but 'mindless mimicry'.

Curiously we persist in this approach even when our experience repeatedly confirms what should be obvious: namely that the resulting understanding is often frighteningly superficial. Of course, one way to hide from this conclusion is to ensure that *complete sets* of exercises (in the textbook, or on a worksheet) *remain at the level of misleadingly simple examples* – as when additions are restricted to two summands, or when a succession of linear equations to be 'solved' are all given in the form '$ax + b = c$'. The superficiality of such apparent "progress" is shown up as soon as pupils are confronted by exercises for which these simple examples have systematically failed to prepare them. In such a setting, mathematical progress is limited to those who manage to identify the general principles for themselves despite the smokescreen of misleading simplicity created by the initial worked examples!

The 'English' approach is designed to *minimise the **initial** difficulties* experienced when the class and teacher are working together, in the belief that more pupils will then 'succeed' *on the first couple of exercises*; but this approach guarantees that *most pupils fail to extract the general principles* that might allow them to tackle harder problems of the kind the method was originally designed to solve. Moreover, in trivialising the initial 'worked examples', the procedure being taught often fails to engage pupils' attention at the level that is required if they are to perceive the more difficult underlying principles. The approach also positively encourages pupils to *home in on their own imagined 'rules'* – which may appear to work for misleadingly simple problems, but which are often false in general.

> **An example:** Students from English schools and colleges, who enter some of our best universities to study nothing but mathematics for three or four years imagine that the way to solve simultaneous equations is to use *substitution*. In fact the key principle that should be conveyed at school level is that of *eliminating a variable*. Deeper probing suggests that this misconception is often the result of having been trained *using misleadingly simple examples* (where it is easy to extract y in terms of x and then to substitute). With more general examples, either this first step cannot be carried out effectively, or – if y can in fact be isolated – their algebraic skills are incapable of handling the resulting symbolic mess. Even if their algebra were good enough to make the approach work in simple cases, **it is a lousy method** that is unlikely to work for equations which are not linear. And the method becomes disastrously inefficient for larger systems of equations.

Our current habit of using misleadingly simple initial worked examples not only guarantees low levels of fluency; it also increases (in a very roundabout way) the pressure on those who set assessment questions not to expect candidates to solve problems 'in general form' – thereby reinforcing the impression that the current approach is successful. It isn't.

The 'Japanese' approach puts more responsibility on the teacher. But if used wisely, it has a marked effect on the whole atmosphere and sense of purpose of the mathematics classroom, and clearly increases the percentage of pupils who achieve the kind of mastery which is needed.

2.2.18 The place of standard written algorithms

This subsection is concerned with standard written methods for arithmetic. In general, successful mathematics teaching of any given topic has to attend to three things.

- One must start from a position which pupils recognise and can make sense of.

- One should end by **achieving mastery of the topic** in a form **that provides a basis for subsequent work**.

- One should proceed from the start to the end *via a bridge* which brings out the inner structure of the material in a form that can be understood by those who have not yet achieved final mastery, and which is chosen to optimise the likelihood of most pupils making this transition to mastery.

Much effort has been devoted in recent years to choosing user-friendly starting positions. But we have neglected the question of how to ensure that more pupils make the transition from these naive beginnings to any mathematically useful endpoint.

On the subject of 'standard written methods' the original *Framework* takes a none-too-promising stance. On page 11 of the Introduction we read: '*Standard written methods [...] are of no use to someone who applies them inaccurately.*' It might have been more honest to point out that *no method* is of much use if it is applied inaccurately!

The confusion is immediately made worse by the statement: *'For each operation, at least one standard written method should be taught to most pupils.'* It appears that we are not supposed to notice that the word 'standard' is incompatible with the words *'at least one'*. If we need a 'standard' written method, then we owe it to teachers to say which method is to be adopted as 'standard'. This attempt at limp-wristed compromise suggests we have missed the whole point of curriculum design in mathematics. So it may be necessary to state the obvious.

> **Digression:** A curriculum may be conceived as a collection of 'curriculum patches' – each being in some sense self-contained; except that each patch has to build on certain prerequisites, and has to establish the prerequisites (in spirit as well as in detail) on which other patches will subsequently have to build. The whole art of curriculum design is:
>
> ◉ to specify the collection of patches in a way that respects both the subject (mathematics) and the 'subjects' (the pupils and teachers);
>
> ◉ to devise and to implement each individual patch with suitable care;
>
> ◉ to order the patches in a way that makes mathematical and developmental sense; and
>
> ◉ to ensure that, where two patches 'overlap', or are interdependent, the language, concepts and methods of the earlier patch lay the necessary foundations, and prepare the relevant modes of thought, to support the subsequent development.
>
> This whole scheme breaks down if a teacher in Year 5 has no idea what the teacher in Year 8 is going to need; or if the teacher in Year 8 has no idea which 'written method' (if any) was felt to constitute a reasonable endpoint of the work in Year 6.

The evident official confusion about the importance of 'standard written algorithms' has led teachers to conclude that the expression 'standard written algorithms' has no clear meaning, can therefore never be effectively tested, and so must be optional! In this climate it is scarcely surprising that many of those who persist in trying to teach the traditional 'standard written algorithms' devote too little time and effort to the task for it to become robustly reliable.

The result is a complete mess. Most pupils are exposed to 'a range of methods', but never master any single effective method. The written methods they resort to when pressed are too unwieldy ever to be effective. For example, most able 14 year olds have no available effective procedure when confronted with a simple multiplication, such as 9009×37. They try to devise a procedure (based on the grid method, or repeated addition); but it is painfully slow and totally unreliable. So they never experience the quiet satisfaction of generating the slightly surprising answer! The 'grid' method is simply too unwieldy for able pupils to use reliably with integers having more than two digits, and has no chance of extending to the multiplication of decimals. And in the absence of an effective standard method for multiplication, long division has become completely unthinkable in most schools.

In mathematics, there are often good reasons why preliminary work should remain oral and informal; but lasting progress ultimately depends on establishing and mastering standard methods in written form. Teachers have worked hard to lay improved "mental" foundations on which a 'feeling for number' could be based, but have failed to realise the crucial need to cap off this preparatory work by ensuring that it culminates in mastery of standard written procedures.

Whether or not one introduces addition and subtraction by means of some physical interface, the ultimate goal has to be

- to establish an algorithm of complete generality;
- which exploits and reinforces the *base 10* structure of our numeral system;
- which depends on the simplest possible atomic steps and so is accessible to all pupils;
- whose implementation has, if possible, other positive pay-offs; and
- which is completely general – in that it can be extended in the obviously needed ways (for example, to decimals, and later to polynomials).

In almost every respect, the standard written algorithms for addition and subtraction knock spots off the alternatives. The structure of the underlying procedures are as simple as they could be – being based on iteration of the single requirement to combine two single digits 0-9. Their implementation depends on, and provides lots of practice that strengthens the basic addition facts for numbers 0-9. They cultivate discipline and accuracy, and they transform problems that are patently non-trivial in a way that offers the instantly available reward of success to all pupils. For more able pupils they also open up a tantalising universe of inverse problems (such as 'word sums', and missing digit puzzles – see Sections T13, T25, C8, C16 in Book *Alpha* and Sections T3, C36 in Book *Beta*), which allow one to further develop and strengthen pupils' grasp of the *base 10* numeral system.

The arguments in favour of long multiplication and division are analogous, but stronger. The basic step of long multiplication requires one to know one's tables (and reinforces this knowledge through use). The only other ingredient is that the algorithm depends on exploiting the *base 10* structure of the multiplier via the distributive law (though little time need be spent labouring this fact, any more than one labours the fact that the addition algorithm depends on decomposing both addends into their separate powers of 10 before using the commutative and associative laws of addition!). Yet, given these simple ingredients, and the discipline to lay out and to carry through the procedure systematically, the pay-off is astonishing, with answers to otherwise totally inaccessible problems being generated almost automatically, and one's feeling for the number system being strengthened in the process.

The world of inverse problems that is opened up by long multiplication is more impressive than for addition. But its main advantages lie elsewhere. The procedure we use to work out 14×14 and 1414×1414 makes it possible to work out the answer to such calculations as 1.4×1.4 and 1.414×1.414, and so to begin to get a feeling for what multiplication of decimals means *from the inside*. Long multiplication provides the key to understanding the much more interesting algorithm for the inverse operation – long division – and opens up the possibility of understanding the wonderful world of 'the decimal equivalents of fractions'.

Calculation may not be the ultimate purpose of mathematics. But it is often the only easily available means whereby ordinary mortals can begin to achieve genuine insight. Naturally, this requires teachers (and curriculum designers) who understand that,

- while one should never undervalue the satisfaction to be gained from grinding out answers, or the long-term benefits of developing the required reliability,

- an equal, and for many a stronger, justification for the work lies in ensuring that it is tackled in a way that *allows any calculational activity to give rise ultimately to insight*.

2.2.19 The place of standard layout

There is a similar failure in other aspects of school mathematics to appreciate the benefits of 'standard layout'.

Standard layout provides pupils with a potentially liberating framework, within which they are freed to concentrate on those aspects of a problem that demand more serious thought. As with standard spelling, punctuation and grammar in 'formal English', standard layout provides a framework

- which is partly self-correcting, and so helps the pupil to avoid and to identify errors; and

- through which pupils' final results can be more effectively and reliably communicated to others.

A classroom is not a military barracks; but there are similarities. Military training prepares raw recruits so that they can ultimately do a decent job 'under fire'. Mathematics teaching may be more relaxed, but should still be structured with a view to ensuring that as many pupils as possible master the key procedures of elementary mathematics in a way that will allow them to be reliably implemented 'under fire'. Insofar as procedures need to be completed quickly and reliably (so leaving thinking space for pupils to concentrate on more demanding and more interesting aspects of the work), or insofar as errors are likely to be made, standard layout allows more pupils to succeed and to concentrate on central ideas.

When undergraduates are invited to tackle *The two cyclists* they have no standard way of thinking about or laying out their solution. The exercise is so easy that most (70-75%) of them appear to 'succeed'; but they pay a heavy price – which becomes visible immediately after this hard-won success. For they have exhausted their powers of concentration and begin to make all sorts of 'silly mistakes' on the immediately following problems!

Simple examples of 'standard layout' include the following:

- Symbols or names used in a calculation should be declared at the outset (for example, 'Let x denote the number of apples', or 'Let x *pence* be the price of a single apple').

- The mathematical statements (such as equations), which constitute the successive steps of a mathematical calculation or solution, should be *aligned vertically*, with one statement per line.

- The correct logical connective between successive lines of such a calculation is the 'therefore' symbol $\therefore$ (and definitely not the logically subtle, and in this context totally incorrect, symbol '$\Rightarrow$').

- Mental effort should be required so that everything is expressed using standard notation and correct terminology.

- Where the justification for any given statement is less than obvious, reasons should be given (if a brief reason suffices, it may be indicated in brackets at the end of the line).

The benefits of standard layout become increasingly important throughout the secondary years.

2.2.20 Topic A in context B

Textbooks, and Programmes of Study, should be designed to introduce topics in a natural *sequence*. Thus when a topic is introduced and 'exercised', it is natural that the associated exercises should relate to the subject matter of the relevant 'patch' in the sequence.

However, the reason for learning the material is to be able to use it *outside* the context of the chapter in which it was introduced! It is therefore crucial that we convey – in our teaching, in the kind of exercises we set every day, and in the way school mathematics is assessed – the clear message that school mathematics is **not** just about answering predictable questions in predictably narrow contexts, but that elementary mathematics derives its power from the way simple methods from one part of mathematics can be used to solve problems in an apparently different area.

One feature of 'topic A in context B' is that each example is in some sense 'particular': if one could give 'generic' descriptions of types of examples, textbooks would long since have introduced chapters on such themes!

An elementary (but not necessarily easy) *particular* problem such as
   Do human beings live for as long as a million hours?
requires one to make connections:

- first to think of 'changing units' (from hours to days to years),
$$1\,000\,000 \text{ hours} = \frac{1\,000\,000}{24} \text{ days}$$
$$= \frac{1\,000\,000}{(24 \times 365)} \text{ years}$$

- then to think about approximation (*If the answer is 'Yes', then I want to overestimate the length of a human life. But if the answer is 'No', then I need to underestimate*),

and finally

- to implement the relevant arithmetic – preferably in a 'proto-algebraic' form
$$\frac{1\,000\,000}{24 \times 365} > \frac{1\,000\,000}{25 \times 400} = \frac{1\,000\,000}{10\,000} = 100 \text{ years.}$$

The following list of examples fails to capture the richness of this theme, but is included simply to ensure that this important aspect of school mathematics (and especially of any extension programme) is not overlooked.

- Counting problems involving 'posts and gaps' (*How many two digit integers – that is, from 10 up to 99 – are there?*), or problems requiring one to calculate average speeds (*I average 2 mph on the uphill walk to Granny's – only to find she is out. I then walk straight home averaging 4 mph. What is my average speed for the whole journey?*) regularly fool able students, because they ignore the context and treat them as problems in pure arithmetic.

- The arithmetic of fractions arises naturally within problems involving rates, percentages and measures.

- Percentage *increases* sound like 'addition', but are best interpreted *multiplicatively*.

- Surds and their simplification arise naturally in finding distances using Pythagoras' theorem.

- The algorithm for division arises naturally in proving that every rational number gives rise to a recurring decimal.

- Linear equations arise in showing that every recurring decimal corresponds to a rational number.

- Problems in statics often depend on interpreting the associated geometrical configuration.

- Elementary algebra arises so ubiquitously that it seems unfair to identify any particular instance; but algebra is too often left meaningless – being linked neither to arithmetic (substituting particular values is rarely used as a way of demonstrating that an error has been made), nor to detailed work with *formulae* in which the symbols have a concrete meaning which can be used as a guide in calculation.

2.2.21 Reasoning, proof and calculation

The *original* English National Curriculum constituted a failed attempt to re-interpret school mathematics as if it were an 'inductive' discipline. This attempt had its roots in a healthy distaste for premature formalism. However, instead of helping all pupils to lay a foundation in experience *which could then be formalised at a suitable stage*, the original structure produced a whole generation of students who had no notion of the distinction between 'induction' and 'deduction'. English school mathematics presents its material as a largely inductive form of knowledge, which is starkly at odds with the unique deductive character of the subject.

The 1995 LMS report *Tackling the mathematics problem* included (page 8) the complaint:

> **4C** Most students entering higher education no longer understand that mathematics is a precise discipline in which exact, reliable calculation, logical exposition and proof play essential roles; yet it is these features which make mathematics important.

The changes of the coming years present us with an opportunity to rethink what 'proof' should mean in school mathematics, and how an understanding of proof can be developed.

We suggest that a (proto-)*proof* consists:

- of any sequence of statements, each of which is clearly formulated and clearly laid out, and is either self-evident from standard known facts or from the structure of the argument presented, or is clearly justified in terms of previous steps, or known results;

- with the first statement being known to be true (or being a clearly identified hypothesis which will be disproved), and the last statement being that which was wanted.

This broader-than-usual conception of proof is aimed at curriculum developers, and is not intended (at least not initially) for pupils. It applies to, but extends far beyond, those areas traditionally associated with 'proof', such as euclidean geometry. Indeed it has been deliberately worded so as to apply to any mathematical argument or calculation involving at least two steps. As preliminary examples we offer:

> **Example 1:** *Evaluate 13 + 26 + 37 + 44 as efficiently as possible.*
> **Solution:** $13 + 26 + 37 + 44 = (13 + 37) + (26 + 44)$
> $= 50 + 70$
> $= 120$

> **Example 2:** *I buy 7 apples and get 16p change from £1. What does each apple cost?*
> This kind of problem is best introduced in Years 5 – 7 as a mental

word problem, before algebra is available. But once the algebraic approach of setting up and solving equations is introduced in Year 8 or Year 9, it is worth revisiting such familiar numerical problems to embed them in the new algebraic methodology. Pupils will already have numerical strategies for 'finding the answer'; so the goal then becomes that of establishing the line-by-line format for laying out solutions – emphasising the initial hypothesis, and the way each line is derived from the line before.

Solution: Suppose each apple costs x pence.
$$\therefore 7x + 16 = 100$$
$$\therefore 7x = 84$$
$$\therefore x = 12.$$

Example 3:   *Multiply out $(a - b + c)(a + b - c)$ as efficiently as possible.*
Solution: $(a - b + c)(a + b - c) = [a - (b - c)][a + (b - c)]$
$$\therefore (a - b + c)(a + b - c) = a^2 - (b - c)^2$$
$$\therefore (a - b + c)(a + b - c) = a^2 - b^2 - c^2 + 2bc.$$

In the context of 'learning to prove', these examples need to be embedded in a classroom setting where the 'standard template' (or some alternative) which underpins each example has already been made available as a natural frame of reference. In particular, each standard format needs to be developed, practised and internalised by writing out solutions to lots of simple exercises and problems, before it can be used to extend the range of problems which can be solved successfully by all students.

Such problems could of course be tackled and solved by individual pupils using 'their own reasonings'. One may even hope that most such approaches would arrive at the right answer. But some would inevitably be flawed, and many would lack clarity. Requiring students to present their solutions in the agreed line-by-line format of a standard protocol would help to make the inner logical structure of their solution explicit.

The proposed approach is scarcely sophisticated. Yet honesty compels one to concede how much work would be needed to implement such an approach on a wide scale. Proof is *a way of organising calculations within a given framework* – whether with numbers, with symbols, with geometrical entities, or with logical propositions – which allows solutions to be, in some sense, 'self-checking' in that errors can be identified relatively easily. There is no escape from the fact that this presupposes two things:

◉ First, a social discipline which allows the teacher to insist on a measure of conformity in adopting and using mundane frames of reference and deductive principles, which are common rather than idiosyncratic, and which are perceived not as shackles, but rather as the soil within which creativity can flourish.

◉ Second, a three-fold appreciation on the part of the pupil
  – that mathematics is *exact*;
  – that if one looks at things in the right way, one can expect answers to be comprehensible (and frequently simpler than expected); and
  – that proof, or exact calculation, offers the only reliable way of harvesting this simplicity.

To echo what we wrote earlier, the fundamental problem – at least with English 18-year-olds entering university to study numerate disciplines – would seem to be *not* that students have some incidental difficulty in adhering to and implementing such common procedures, but rather that they have *no clear conception of the deductive character of calculation,* and so do not see the need to work within a standard framework which might allow them to take responsibility for, and to evaluate the correctness of, their own solutions. However, if we are to teach mathematics at school level, such difficulties need to be understood and faced.

Example 1 and Example 3 above illustrate the pedagogical advantages of using 'contrived calculations' to counteract the incomprehension referred to in the previous paragraph. Problems involving 'real data' often encourage pupils to 'hack through' every calculation from the beginning, without ever internalising the routine expectation that what at first sight appears complex is often simpler than it looks, and can be analysed and comprehended by the human mind. If one wishes to encourage structured thinking, with solutions laid out in a standard way to make the internal logic clear, then the numbers need to be chosen to reward and to cultivate the kind of *irrational optimism* without which the beginner sees no reason to look beneath the surface to identify the hidden structure in a problem. In the absence of this instinct for sense-making, students resort too easily to unstructured, and hence error-prone, calculation, or to apparently random moves. Effective mathematics education actively cultivates 'irrational optimism' in students, so that they learn to look for – and expect to find – helpful structure just below the surface.

None of our three Examples is what is normally understood by a 'proof'. Yet each provides pupils with a clear yardstick which can help them refine their own (subjective) 'reasonings' into a mathematical proof.

- In the first example – as with most calculations at this level – the goal is to reduce the calculation to a short sequence of indisputable steps, which effectively remove all doubt, even if the deductive character of each step remains implicit.

- The second example adopts a standard approach and layout which makes the underlying logical structure explicit: each line represents a new step, and the connections between successive steps are established via the use of the 'therefore' symbol $\therefore$.

- The third example is an algebraic variation of the first – avoiding the error-prone strategy of multiplying out all nine terms before 'cancelling and collecting up', seeking instead to reduce all calculation to the two well-known identities for $(a + b)(a - b)$ and for $(a + b)^2$.

There is another important aspect of Example 1 (at age 6-7), of Example 2 (at age 12-13) and of Example 3 (at age 15-16). Pupils' own calculations at each level are often inefficient, even when successful. If they are ever to appreciate the decisive, objective character of the underlying steps, it is important to have a standard format which allows one to summarise those calculations which can be presented simply in short objective *written* form – so that the advantages of re-grouping in Example 1, of the standard approach to Example 2, and of recognising the difference of two squares in Example 3 can be clearly grasped, and the indisputability of the answer recognised.

These examples should be seen as simple instances within an extended sequence, which systematically exploits children's early appreciation of 'objective' reasoning (reinforced, as Piaget showed, by experience of the world and by the use of language) to help them develop over time a clear idea of what is meant by deductive proof, and its marked difference from subjective reasoning.

Early examples from the realm of calculation – whether with numbers or with symbols – are sufficiently simple that the sequence of steps can usually be chosen so that each line follows naturally from the previous line, with no need to appeal to interim conclusions or external results. The justification for each step is then clear *from the ordering of the steps*. Thus, while each step should be explained verbally when presenting such a proof, there is no need to require that it be written out explicitly. Moreover, with arithmetical calculations, or with 'linear' problems, each step is reversible; while there may be good psychological reasons to insist that the answer be checked, it would be pedantic to see this as part of the proof structure at this level.

However, the advent of problems involving squares or square roots leads to steps which are definitely not reversible. There is then no escaping from the need to confront (in some form) the fact that deduction yields a list of *candidate* answers, rather than guaranteed answers. At this point – if not before – it becomes clear that each step in a proof sequence may need to appeal to more than just the immediately preceding step, and that where this is needed, the justification (for example, when eliminating certain candidate values) has to be made *explicit*.

Non-example 4: $\pi = 3$.

Solution: Let $x = \dfrac{(\pi + 3)}{2}$

$\therefore \quad 2x = \pi + 3$

$\therefore \quad 2x(\pi - 3) = (\pi + 3)(\pi - 3)$

$\therefore \quad 2\pi x - 6x = \pi^2 - 9$

$\therefore \quad 9 - 6x = \pi^2 - 2\pi x$

$\therefore \quad 9 - 6x + x^2 = \pi^2 - 2\pi x + x^2$

$\therefore \quad (3 - x)^2 = (\pi - x)^2$

$\therefore \quad 3 - x = \pi - x$

$\therefore \quad \pi = 3.$ **QED!**

More sophisticated proofs routinely involve steps which can only be justified by explicit reference to clearly identified *external results* (that is, results which have been established elsewhere). This is especially true of euclidean geometry, where in each given problem one looks for ways of exploiting one of a relatively small number of standard external results (the angle sum of a triangle; basic criteria for two angles to be equal – vertically opposite, alternating, etc.; isosceles triangles; the SAS and SSS congruence criteria; Pythagoras' theorem; similarity; formulae for the area of a triangle; the sine and cosine rule; angles in the same segment; etc.). Euclidean geometry may provide the richest accessible example, but the need to identify and apply some standard external result is typical of mathematics and characterises the solution of many beautiful elementary problems.

Implementing such an approach starting in upper primary school, and in a manner that avoids degeneration as one moves on to secondary level, will not be easy. But the present situation in which ideas of proof are never addressed, is unacceptable. And pressures to re-interpret mathematics-for-all in terms of 'numeracy' and 'functional mathematics' may yet make things worse! So it is essential for committed educators and mathematicians to work together to devise, to implement and to refine strategies which reflect both the discipline of mathematics and the way ordinary students learn.

2.2.22 Priorities

In recent years additional material has been repeatedly squeezed into the school mathematics curriculum without analysing sufficiently clearly *why* it deserves to be included, or which other topics deserve to be squeezed out in order to make room.

For example, the *applicability* of mathematics should be an integral part of the way the subject is taught at school level. But as previous subsections indicate, we have failed to take this requirement seriously. In particular, while the art of counting, ratio and percentages deserve to be taken seriously, the inclusion of 'data-handling' as a separate curriculum theme has proved to be little more than a pretentious distraction (which, incidentally, may have had the effect of turning many undergraduates *away from* the study of statistics).

We now have a curriculum that is too broad, and that is being neither effectively taught nor adequately assessed. As with 'data-handling' we have repeatedly introduced new material *for the whole cohort* without first analysing for which students (if any) the new material is more important at a given age than previously standard topics. This mistake may be about to be repeated with the imposition of a commitment to teach and to assess low level 'functional skills' and 'financial capability' (whatever these may mean). The main consequence has been that truly important material has been squeezed to the point where student learning – even on the part of very able students – is now painfully superficial. For example, in the last 15 years, more time has been devoted to discussing 'probability', but at the same time students' ability to handle fractions intelligently has collapsed.

We are not suggesting that new material, or changes of emphasis, are always inappropriate; rather that, any such proposed change *should automatically invoke a debate about* **priorities**.

If we manage to embrace the logic of distinctive 14-19 pathways for different groups of students, then priorities for those following different pathways may differ beyond the point where curricula for different groups begin to diverge. But **up to that point** *it is important to achieve a carefully considered common foundation for as many students as possible*. We must therefore face up to the facts that

◉ in mathematical terms some topics (such as integer arithmetic, measures, fractions, algebra, and euclidean and coordinate geometry) are *more central and more important* than others, and

◉ in educational terms some topics need to be taught at a relatively early age – both because they are more easily assimilated at that age, and because of the subsequent mathematical learning which they open up to those (and only those) who have mastered them.

At present we lack a historical consensus about the crucial notions of *importance* and *timing* in elementary mathematics. We need to engage in open debate between experienced professionals to establish a consensus as to *what* topics, attitudes and experiences constitute the central pillars on which school mathematics at upper primary and lower secondary school should be based, and *why* these topics are central.

Part 2
The Works

3 Comments on and answers to the problems: book-by-book and section-by-section

Comments on the listing of sections in each book by topic

The comments on each book begin with a *rough listing of sections by topic*. We restrict attention to *Taster* and *Core* sections making no attempt to classify *Extension* sections.

However, elementary mathematics derives its power by combining

- fluency in basic techniques
- the imagination to select and combine techniques *from different areas*
- the willingness to apply these techniques *flexibly* to solve problems.

One consequence is that good extension material cannot be pigeon-holed by forcing each and every task to address one specific statement in some fragmented curriculum or scheme of work. Even where it looks as though the subject matter in a particular section could be neatly pigeon-holed, it is important to remember that the underlying theme of the section is more likely to be the need to approach that particular subject matter imaginatively, and with a willingness to think flexibly. The attempt to reduce elementary mathematics to a sequence of fragmented curriculum statements contradicts everything that has given mathematics its central role in human culture and that has made it a universal language for the modern world. The grouping of sections should therefore be interpreted as offering a very rough guide to the progression within each curriculum area. In books *Beta* and *Gamma*, sections increasingly cut across curriculum headings; hence many sections have to be listed under more than one heading.

We begin with a short description of the headings used.

Number and ('pre-')algebra

Any mathematical activity (a) which is primarily numerical, without context or units, or (b) which is numerical but which emphasises algebraic structure.

Algebra

Any calculational activity which exploits the *structure* of generalised arithmetic – including the use of symbols in place of numbers.

Geometry

Any tasks (a) which use drawing, or coordinates or length/angle/area/volume in a geometric spirit, or (b) which contribute to the deductive structure of Euclidean geometry.

Using and applying mathematics (including measures)

Direct Exercises involving ideas (a) which may be mathematical but which are especially important for applications (such as 'ratio'), or (b) which include a significant element which is concerned with applications rather than mathematics (perhaps involving measures, units, percentages, money, time, etc.), or (c) which take the form of 'word problems'.

Oblique Tasks which may be relatively unfamiliar, but which require flexibility in using simple ideas in the spirit of 'using and applying' mathematics.

3A Alpha

Rough listing of sections by topic

Note The order of sections within each list is not the 'dependence order'. Early *Taster* sections tend to be more accessible than later sections and early *Core* sections tend to be more accessible than later sections. But *early Core sections can usually be tackled well before late Taster sections.*

Number and 'pre-algebra'

T1	Slick sums	T23	Buy one, get one free B
T2	Tens, hundreds and thousands	C1	Mental multiplication
T4	Intelligent grouping	C3	Multiplication: Integers B
T6	Buy one, get one free A	C5	Tables with remainders
T7	Finding hidden factors	C9	Division: Integers
T8	Multiplication: Integers A	C11	HCFs and LCMs A
T10	Cunning calculation A	C13	Multiplication: Decimals B
T12	Turning the tables	C14	Flexible fractions
T16	Cunning calculation B	C15	Which is larger?
T19	Order! Order!	C24	HCFs and LCMs B
T20	Multiplication: Decimals A	C25	Fractions and decimals

Geometry

T5	Perimeters	C7	Drawing conclusions B
T9	Angles	C17	Triangles
T11	Drawing conclusions A	C19	Areas
C4	Analogue angles		

Using and applying mathematics (including measures)

  Direct

T14	Percentages	C18	Weighing the baby
T21	Measures: Change of units	C21	Ratio problems
T22	Where did the money go? A	C22	Measures and decimal arithmetic
T24	Calculation with measures A	C23	Where did the money go? B
T26	Word problems A	C26	Calculation with measures B
C12	Word problems B		

  Oblique

T3	Counting the ways A	C6	Counting the ways B
T13	Misplaced digits	C8	Missing digits B
T15	Skittles A	C10	Tiling A
T17	Posts and gaps	C16	Missing digits C
T18	Think straight	C20	Tiling B
T25	Missing digits A	C27	Skittles B
C2	What's my number? A		

Comments and answers

Mathematics is about *methods* rather than just answers. So the answers given here are often written in structured form to indicate how it is intended that pupils should derive these answers.

◉ Where a reader can see at a glance *from the given form* what the numerical answer is, the answer is sometimes omitted.

α: T1 Slick sums   NC

Problem **0** may be written on the board, or projected onto a screen. In either case, it may make sense to show only part **a** in the first instance.

Invite answers and ask for an explanation of quick methods. Bring out the need to look ahead and to spot pairs of units digits (or more generally paired groups of terminal digits) that combine nicely. Make spot checks to ensure later problems are tackled in the intended spirit.

Answers

0	a 100 + 48	b 213 + 1	c 654 − 1

1 96 + 0
2 96 + 100
3 64 + 2
4 67 − 37
5 81 + 2
6 79 + 3 or 83 − 1
7 160 − 59
8 90 + 39
9 50 + 49
10 243 − 1
11 250 − 50

12	a 150 − 150	b 302 − 300	c 181 + 4

α: T2 Tens, hundreds and thousands   NC

Efficient use of the *base 10* numeral system depends on recognising pairs of factors that combine to make 10, or 100, or 1000, etc. This is often weak, for example, when estimating 4 × 23, pupils often choose to create a single '0' by switching to 4 × 20 and fail to notice the two '0's on the end of 4 × 25.

Answers

0	a 15 × 20 = 3 × (5 × 20)	c 375 × 8 = 3 × (125 × 8)
	b 12 × 75 = (3 × 3) × (4 × 25)	

1 16 × 25 = 4 × (4 × 25)
2 25 × 40 = 10 × (25 × 4)
3 65 × 20 = 13 × (5 × 20)
4 12 × 25 = 3 × (4 × 25)
5 15 × 12 = (3 × 6) × (5 × 2)
6 75 × 8 = (3 × 2) × (25 × 4)
7 15 × 16 = (3 × 8) × (5 × 2)
8 35 × 40 = (7 × 2) × (5 × 20)
9 75 × 16 = (3 × 4) × (25 × 4)
10 35 × 14 = (7 × 7) × (5 × 2)
11 12 × 75 = (3 × 3) × (4 × 25)
12 175 × 16 = (7 × 4) × (25 × 4)
13 75 × 36 = (3 × 9) × (25 × 4)
14 125 × 16 = 2 × (125 × 8)
15 375 × 8 = 3 × (125 × 8)
16 225 × 40 = 9 × (25 × 40)

17	a 75 × 28 = (3 × 7) × (25 × 4)	c 625 × 32 = 2 × (625 × 16)
	b 375 × 48 = (3 × 6) × (125 × 8)	d 875 × 56 = (7 × 7) × (125 × 8)

α: T3 Counting the ways A

At first write up (or project) Problem 0a only. Give pupils time to work on the problem individually or in pairs. (**Note** We are interested in the number of nuts eaten by the three monkeys – not in which monkey eats which nuts. Hence 3 + 5 + 7 is the same as 5 + 3 + 7, etc.)

When solutions are invited, make it clear that you expect *structure and reasons*, not just answers. Initially responses may well be incoherent, so expect to have to prompt, or to ask suitable probing questions. If pupils do not clearly use the restriction to *odd* numbers, you might quietly write on the board:

    (1,) 3, 5, 7, 9, 11, 13, 15, ...

and ask 'How many nuts does each monkey eat?', then work to elicit 'An *odd* number *greater than* 1.' If this, or the fact that the odd numbers have to be different, does not emerge, you might hint by writing

    1 + 5 + 9 ??
    3 + 3 + 9 ??

Answers

0	a 3 + 5 + 7 only	b 3 + 3 + 9 or 3 + 5 + 7

1 Total number of legs = 3 × 5 = (number of Bipods) × 2 + (number of Tripods) × 3
    ∴ Number of Bipods must be a multiple of 3.
    ∴ i **3** Bipods and **3** Tripods
    or ii **6** Bipods and **1** Tripod
        (or **0** Bipods and **5** Tripods).

2 Average number of eggs per bird = 15 ÷ 3 = 5
    ∴ Smallest clutch < 5 (since all are different)
    i If smallest = 3, we get 15 = **3 + 5 + 7**
    ii If smallest = 1, we get 15 = **1 + 3 + 11**, or **1 + 5 + 9**

3 a Total number of legs = 23 = (number of Tripods) × 3 + (number of Bipods) × 2
    ∴ Number of Tripods must be odd (and ≥ 2)
    i If number of Tripods = **3**, we get 23 = 3 × 3 + 7 × 2
    ii If number of Tripods = **5**, we get 23 = 5 × 3 + 4 × 2
        (Number of Tripods ≠ 7, or else number of Bipods < 2)
  b **1** Tripod, **10** Bipods; **7** Tripods, **1** Bipod

4 Average score ≤ 18 ÷ 3
    ∴ Minimum score < 18 ÷ 3 (since 'my three scores are all different')
  a Minimum score = **2 or 4**
  b 3 solutions:
    i If minimum score = 2, we get 18 = **2 + 4 + 12** or **2 + 6 + 10**
    ii If minimum score = 4, we get 18 = **4 + 6 + 8**

5	7 = 3 + 4		(8 = 2 × 4, 9 = 3 × 3 – forbidden 'at least one of each')
	10 = 1 × 4 + 2 × 3	11 = 2 × 4 + 1 × 3	(12 = 3 × 4 = 4 × 3 – forbidden)
	13 = 1 × 4 + 3 × 3	14 = 2 × 4 + 2 × 3	
	15 = 3 × 4 + 1 × 3	16 = 1 × 4 + 4 × 3	
	17 = 2 × 4 + 3 × 3	18 = 3 × 4 + 2 × 3	
	∴ **19** = 4 × 4 + 1 × 3 = 1 × 4 + 5 × 3 is the required smallest score.		

α: T4 Intelligent grouping   NC

In reviewing Problem **0** make sure that the answers are obtained *from the structure* of the sum without calculating each term separately. Make spot checks to ensure later problems are tackled in the intended spirit.

Answers

0 a $(14 \times 7) - (2 \times 14) = (7 - 2) \times 14$	b $(7 \times 8) + (6 \times 4) = (7 + 3) \times 8$

1 $(13 \times 8) - (3 \times 8) = (13 - 3) \times 8$
2 $(14 \times 7) - (4 \times 7) = (14 - 4) \times 7$
3 $(13 \times 7) + (7 \times 7) = (13 + 7) \times 7$
4 $(13 \times 8) + (7 \times 8) = (13 + 7) \times 8$
5 $(23 \times 6) - (3 \times 6) = (23 - 3) \times 6$

6 $(13 \times 6) + (7 \times 6) = (13 + 7) \times 6$
7 $(6 \times 27) + (6 \times 3) = 6 \times (27 + 3)$
8 $(4 \times 17) + (6 \times 17) = (4 + 6) \times 17$
9 $(7 \times 19) + (19 \times 3) = (7 + 3) \times 19$

10 a $(17 \times 12) + (13 \times 12) = (17 + 13) \times 12$	e $(12 \times 14) + (6 \times 32) = 12 \times (14 + 16)$
b $(14 \times 15) + (15 \times 16) = (14 + 16) \times 15$	f $(22 \times 26) + (6 \times 13) = (44 + 6) \times 13$
c $(83 \times 7) + (17 \times 7) = (83 + 17) \times 7$	g $(23 \times 51) + (31 \times 17) = (69 + 31) \times 17$
d $(6 \times 67) + (33 \times 6) = (67 + 33) \times 6$	

α: T5 Perimeters   NC

The goal of this section is for pupils to learn to *extract* additional information from what is given (rather than being given everything on a plate).

Answers

0 a $\frac{1}{2} \times (35.3 - 10.9) = 12.2$ cm	b Perimeter $= 2 \times (15 + 7) = 44$, area $= 78$

1 $30 + 40 + 45 = 115$ m
2 a 72 mm   b 7.2 cm   c 0.072 m
3 $\frac{1}{4} \times 10.52 = 2.63$ m
4 $2 \times (42 + 27) = 138$ m
5 $2 \times (18 + 11) = 58$

6 $2 \times (5 \times 4) = 40$ cm
7 $2 \times (15 + 12) = 54$ cm
8 $2 \times (12 + 15) = 54$ cm
9 a $2 \times (8 + 6) = 28$ cm
   b $4 \times 8 + 2 \times 6 = 44$ cm

10 $2 \times (17 + 17) = 68$ cm

α: T6 Buy one get one free A   NC

This section (and Section T23) may reveal weaknesses in pupils' understanding of arithmetic and place value. However even where the necessary insights prove to be in good shape, these simple problems remain a worthwhile exercise. Use spot-checks to make sure the intended method is being used, and being used effectively. (The acid test is whether pupils can work *quickly* and *accurately*. *Speed* suggests that they are trying to use the intended method, but without *accuracy* something is likely to be missing.)

Answers

0 a $33.5 + 6.5 = 40$	c $33.5 - 3.5 = 30$	e $3.35 - 1 = 2.35$
b $33.5 - 3.5 = 30$	d 33.5	f $0.263 + 0.37 = 0.3$

1 1573
2 $1573 + 1$
3 $1309 - 2$
4 $1573 - 1$
5 $1573 - 73 = 1500$

6 $1573 + 30 = 1603$
7 $1573 - 3 = 1570$
8 1573
9 157.3
10 0.264

11 $130.9 - 0.9 = 130$
12 $0.1573 + 0.0027 = 0.16$
13 $2000 + 264 = 2264$
14 $400 + 1309 = 1709$
15 15.73

3A Alpha

| 16 a 264 | b 264 − 24 = 240 | c 264 + 36 = 300 |
| 17 7878 | a 78.78 + 0.22 = 79 | b 94.94 + 6.06 = 101 | c 0.9494 + 0.0006 = **0.95** |

α: T7 Finding hidden factors NC

In reviewing Problem 0 make sure that the answers are obtained *from the structure* of the sum without calculating each term separately. Make spot checks to ensure later problems are tackled in the same spirit.

Answers

| 0 a 2 × 147 | b 7 × 1000 | c 100 × 69 |

1 2 × 24	6 3 × 80	11 2 × 42
2 3 × 16	7 4 × 21	12 6 × 40
3 4 × 12	8 4 × 60	13 15 × 75
4 2 × 120	9 3 × 28	14 10 × 90
5 6 × 14	10 5 × 48	

| 15 a 2100 | b 2700 | c 3000 |
| 16 30 boxes | | |

α: T8 Multiplication: Integers A NC

This section assumes that a suitable amount of preliminary work with short and long multiplication has already been done during Year 6 and Year 7. Problem 0 is therefore designed to 'blow away the cobwebs'. Problems 1-7 then highlight two important, but neglected, numerical facts: $111 = 3 \times 37$ and $1001 = 7 \times 11 \times 13$. The overall goal should be for as many pupils as possible to complete Problems 1-7 quickly and accurately, and then to tackle and solve Problem 9.

Answers

| 0 24 013 |

1 148 × 3 = **444**	5 91 × 11 = **1001**
2 143 × 7 = **1001**	6 429 × 21 = **9009**
3 303 × 22 = **6666**	7 3003 × 37 = **111 111**
4 77 × 13 = **1001**	

| 8 533 × 231 = **123 123** | |
| 9 a 373 × 83 = **30 959** | b 47 × 89 = **4183** |

α: T9 Angles

Angle-chasing is an excellent, if modest, test of flexibility, and can be highly satisfying. Problem 0 should be used to generate *insight* and *methods* not just answers. In particular, explicit reasons should be given (for example, 'base angles of an isosceles triangle are equal', or 'vertically opposite angles are equal' should be clearly stated where these are the appropriate reasons).

Answers

0	a $x = 45°$	b $y = 45°$	c $z = 90°$

1	40°	5	100°	9	$x = 45°, y = 35°, z = 15°$
2	115°	6	45°	10	$x = 30°, y = 75°, z = 150°$
3	35°	7	40°		
4	80°	8	35°		

α: T10 Cunning calculation A NC

Answers

0	a $5324 + 100 = \mathbf{5424}$	b $30 + 1.1 = \mathbf{31.1}$

1	$5632 + 500 = \mathbf{6132}$	7	$42.4 - 13.5 = \mathbf{28.9}$	13	$900 \times 9 = \mathbf{8100}$
2	$60\,416 + 900 = \mathbf{61\,316}$	8	**108.8**	14	$300 \times 13 = \mathbf{3900}$
3	$12\,367 - 700 = \mathbf{11\,667}$	9	$238.8 - 20 = \mathbf{218.8}$	15	$700 \times 18 = \mathbf{12\,600}$
4	$300 + 2688 = \mathbf{2988}$	10	$70 - 4.3 = \mathbf{65.7}$	16	**54 000**
5	$500 + 3542 = \mathbf{4042}$	11	$175.7 - 10 = \mathbf{165.7}$	17	$10\,000 \times 9 = \mathbf{90\,000}$
6	$9654 - 3500 = \mathbf{6154}$	12	$500 \times 11 = \mathbf{5500}$		

α: T11 Drawing conclusions A

Activities requiring hand-eye-brain coordination lead to understanding *provided the brain remains active*. In coordinating responses to Problem **0** it is important to cultivate correct use of geometric language and geometrical reasoning.

Answers

0	a	i $\angle OAB = \angle OBA$ (since $OA = OB$ so $\triangle OAB$ is isosceles)
		ii should be equal
	b	iv $\angle ACB = 180° - \angle ABC - \angle BAC = 60°$
		v $AC = AB$ (since $\angle ABC = \angle ACB = 60°$, so $\triangle ACB$ is isosceles)

1 a *ABCD* is a rhombus   b *ABCD* is a rectangle.
2 a $AB = AC$ (radii of circle C)   c By parts **a** and **b**, $\triangle ABC$ is equilateral.
    b $BA = BC$ (radii of circle C') $\therefore \angle ABC = \angle BCA = \angle CAB = 60°$
3 f *ABCD* should be a square

α: T12 Turning the tables NC

Answers

0	a $48 \div 6 = 8$	b $72 \div 18 = 4$

1	$15 \div 5 = 3$	5	$36 \div 9 = 4$	9	$63 \div 9 = 7$
2	$24 \div 4 = 6$	6	$77 \div 7 = 11$	10	$42 \div 7 = 6$
3	$28 \div 7 = 4$	7	$72 \div 8 = 9$	11	$91 \div 13 = 7$
4	$54 \div 9 = 6$	8	$56 \div 7 = 8$	12	$68 \div 17 = 4$

3A Alpha

α: T13 Misplaced digits   NC

Be prepared for a surprising *lack* of flexibility at first. But don't give up: things will improve. Those who progress more quickly should be routinely challenged with 'Are you sure that yours is the only possible solution?'

Answers

| 0 | a | $19 \times 3 = 57$ | b | $62 + 43 = 105$ or $63 + 42 = 105$ |

1	a	$11 \times 7 = 77$			d	$14 \times 3 = 42$
	b	$12 \times 4 = 48$ or $21 \times 4 = 84$			e	$23 \times 4 = 92$
	c	$14 \times 7 = 98$			f	$17 \times 4 = 68$
2	a	$88 + 43 = 131$ or $83 + 48 = 131$			c	$88 + 22 = 110$ or $82 + 28 = 110$
	b	$99 + 19 = 118$			d	$79 + 24 = 103$ or $74 + 29 = 103$
3	a	$5432 + 8715 = 14\,147$			b	$105\,737 - 81\,046 = 24\,691$
4	a	$25 \times 3 = 75$

4	b	i $23 \times 5 = 115$, or $45 \times 7 = 315$	ii $343 \times 7 = 2401$	iii $589 \times 4 = 2356$
	c	$1314 \div 73 = 18$	d i $986 \div 34 = 29$	ii $529 \div 23 = 23$
5	a	$22 \times 38 = 836$	b $27 \times 35 = 945$

α: T14 Percentages   NC

This section is the first of several designed to underline the advantages of recognising percentages as *multiplicative operators*.

Answers

| 0 | a | 25% of 360 = $\frac{1}{4}$ of 360 = 90 | c | 65% of 40 = $\frac{13}{20} \times 40 = 26$ |
| | b | 20% of 85 = $\frac{1}{5}$ of 85 = 17 |

1 $\frac{3}{4}$ of 40 = 30

2 $\frac{4}{10}$ of 75 = 30

3 $\frac{11}{20}$ of 60 = 33

4 $\frac{9}{20}$ of 40 = 18

5 $\frac{6}{10}$ of 55 = 33

6 $\frac{4}{10}$ of 45 = 18

7 $\frac{11}{20}$ of 60 = 33

8 $\frac{5}{4}$ of 24 = 30

9 $\frac{6}{25}$ of 125 = 30

10 $\frac{4}{10}$ of $\frac{1}{2}$ of 60 = 12

11 $\frac{1}{2}$ of $\frac{4}{10}$ of 60 = 12

12 $\frac{6}{10}$ of $\frac{1}{2}$ of 40 = 12

13 $\frac{1}{2}$ of $\frac{4}{10}$ of 30 = 6

14 $\frac{3}{10}$ of $\frac{4}{10}$ of 50 = 6

15 $\frac{3}{10}$ of $\frac{4}{10}$ of 150 = 18

16 $\frac{1}{5}$ of $\frac{3}{10}$ of $33\frac{1}{3} = 2$

17 $\frac{2}{10}$ of $\frac{3}{10}$ of $\frac{4}{10}$ of 250 = 6

18 Overall a **£5 loss**. (Cat: cost £75, a £15 loss. Dog: cost £50, a £10 gain.)

α: T15 Skittles A

On one level this section may be viewed as low-level revision of simple integer arithmetic in a context. Learning to read, and to interpret a context, are important. But there is some very pretty mathematics lurking just below the surface (Problems **1c, 2c, 4, 5**).

Answers

| 0 a **4, 4** | b **6, 5** (3, 4, 5, 6, 7) |

1 a i 1 way   ii **1** (10)   b i 1 way   ii **1** (0)
2 a i 4 ways   ii **4** (1, 2, 3, 4)   b i 4 ways   ii **4** (6, 7, 8, 9)
3 a 6 ways   b **5** (3, 4, 5, 6, 7)
4 Number of ways: **1, 4, 6, 4, 1**   Number of total scores: **1, 4, 5, 4, 1**

5 Number of ways: **1, 5, 10, 10, 5, 1**   Number of total scores: **1, 5, 7, 7, 5, 1**

α: T16 Cunning calculation *B*   NC

These problems may appear simple and repetitive. However, the ability to exploit arithmetical (and later algebraic) *structure* to simplify calculations has to be learned, and is central to later progress. Those who find the problems easy should be challenged to use their understanding to work *accurately* and *fast*.

Answers

| 0 a (1234 ÷ 6) × 12 = 1234 × 2 = **2468**   c ((123 ÷ 4) × 56) ÷ 7 = **246** |
| b (25 ÷ 6) × 78 = 25 × 13 = **325** |

1 a (12 × 5) ÷ 5 = **12**   6 a (12 ÷ 16) × 8 = 12 ÷ 2 = **6**
  b (13 × 10) ÷ 5 = 13 × 2 = **26**   b (13 ÷ 16) × 8 = 13 ÷ 2 = **6.5**
  c (14 × 5) ÷ 10 = 14 ÷ 2 = **7**   c (14 ÷ 16) × 8 = 14 ÷ 2 = **7**
  d (1234 × 5) ÷ 10 = **617**   d (1234 ÷ 16) × 8 = 1234 ÷ 2 = **617**
2 a (15 ÷ 5) × 5 = **15**   7 a (4 × 12) ÷ 4 = **12**
  b (20 ÷ 5) × 10 = 20 × 2 = **40**   b (5 × 12) ÷ 5 = **12**
  c (23 ÷ 10) × 5 = 23 ÷ 2 = **11.5**   c (6 × 12) ÷ 6 = **12**
  d (123 ÷ 15) × 5 = 123 ÷ 3 = **41**   d (7 × 12) ÷ 14 = 12 ÷ 2 = **6**
3 a (12 × 17) ÷ 17 = **12**   e (8 × 12) ÷ 24 = 8 ÷ 2 = **4**
  b (13 × 34) ÷ 17 = 13 × 2 = **26**   f (9 × 12) ÷ 36 = 9 ÷ 3 = **3**
  c (123 × 17) ÷ 51 = 123 ÷ 3 = **41** 8 a (12 ÷ 2) × 4 = **24**
  d (1234 × 17) ÷ 34 = 1234 ÷ 2 = **617** b (13 ÷ 3) × 6 = **26**
4 a (12 ÷ 16) × 16 = **12**   c (14 ÷ 4) × 8 = **28**
  b (13 ÷ 16) × 32 = 13 × 2 = **26**   d (1234 ÷ 6) × 12 = **2468**
  c (123 ÷ 16) × 16 = **123**   9 a (12 × 5) ÷ 5 = **12**
  d (123 ÷ 48) × 16 = 123 ÷ 3 = **41**   b (12 × 7) ÷ 14 = **6**
5 a (12 × 18) ÷ 6 = 12 × 3 = **36**   c (12 × 9) ÷ 27 = **4**
  b (13 × 34) ÷ 17 = 13 × 2 = **26**   d (1234 × 11) ÷ 22 = **617**
  c (14 × 17) ÷ 34 = 14 ÷ 2 = **7**
  d (1234 × 34) ÷ 68 = 1234 ÷ 2 = **617**

| 10 a (91 ÷ 26) × 14 = 7 × 7 = **49**   b (234 × 37) ÷ 222 = 234 ÷ 6 = **39** |

α: T17 Posts and gaps

This is a pervasive, but neglected theme. Answers are frequently 'one more' or 'one less' than pupils think. So pupils need to learn to think carefully

3A Alpha

each time and make sure that the method being used is appropriate and correct.

Answers

> 0 There are 999 integers 1–999. 99 of these are <100.
> ∴ 999 − 99 = **900** three-digit integers.

1 From 19 to 89 = 89 − 18 = **71** seconds.
2 Halfway between 179 and 837 = 179 + $\frac{1}{2}$(837 − 179) = **508**
3 a 12 − 1 = **11**
  b 12 × 12 − 1 = **143** (each tear increases the number of pieces by 1).
4 36 ÷ 3 = **12 panels**; 36 ÷ 3 + 1 = **13 posts**
5 Gap = 12 cm ÷ (4 − 1) = **4 cm**; ∴ 1st to 9th = 4 cm × (9 − 1) = **32 cm**
6 3953 − 3747 = **206 tickets sold**
7 Gap = 600 m ÷ (3 − 1) = 300 m; ∴ 1st to 10th = 300 m × (10 − 1) = **2.7 km**
8 10 + 1 edges; ∴ 2 × (10 + 1) = **22 drawing pins**

> 9 365 = 52 × 7 + 1, 366 = 52 × 7 + 2
> ∴ a 2009: 'Saturday − 1' = **Friday**
>   b 2011: 'Saturday + 1' = **Sunday**
>   c 2008: 'Saturday − 1 − 1' = **Thursday**
>   d 2012 (leap) 'Saturday + 1 + 2' = **Tuesday**
> 10 Eats through Volume 2 and Volume 3 only;   ∴ **8 cm**

α: T18 Think straight

The willingness to think carefully that is required in this section is needed throughout school mathematics. But it needs to be actively cultivated!

Answers

> 0 **C** is the only one (*all* cats have whiskers; ∴ *some* cats have whiskers)

1 Harold is 125 cm + 8 cm = 133 cm; ∴ Jim is 133 cm − 12 cm = **121 cm**
2 Bilbo has 8*k* + 4 cherry stones, Frodo has 8*m* + 6 cherry stones; ∴ **Tailor**
3 Olly, Mo, Kay, Ned, Pat, Jo
4 Ethel
5 (18 + 15 + 20) kg = **53 kg**
6 **No.** (Den is taller than Ben and Ann taller than Con; no information to compare Ann and Den)
7 A, B, C follow logically; D, E do not. (Each solution is in green **d**; ∴ each solution is untidy **b**; ∴ each solution is erroneous **e**; ∴ each solution scored 0 **c**; ∴ Mo scored 0)

> 8 **10 ways**. (W, T, S in order – slowest first, so 4 'gaps'.
>   ∴ 10 ways to fit in U and V – with U slower than V)
> 9 **None** of A–D can be deduced
> 10 Zaheer (Bacup), Wes (Derby), Vic (Cromer), Yvette (Esher), Xi (Ashton) or the reverse.

3A Alpha

ALPHA

α: T19 Order! Order!   NC

These problems are meant to be easy. But they may reveal areas where more basic exercises are needed.

Answers

> 0 a $\frac{3}{15} = \frac{1}{5} = 0.2 < 0.315$ b $0.16 < 0.1\dot{6} = \frac{1}{6} = \frac{3}{18} < 0.318$

1 $0.36 < 0.5 = \frac{1}{2} = \frac{3}{6} < \frac{6}{9} < 0.69$

2 $0.14 < 0.25 = \frac{3}{12} = \frac{1}{4} < 0.312$

3 $0.2128 < 0.34 < 0.75 = \frac{3}{4} = \frac{21}{28}$

4 $0.12 < 0.5 = \frac{1}{2} = \frac{5}{10} < 0.510$

5 $\frac{27}{50} = 0.54 < 1.25 = \frac{5}{4}$

6 $0.375 = \frac{3}{8} < 0.38 = \frac{19}{50}$

7 $0.04 = \frac{1}{25} < 0.125 = \frac{1}{8}$

8 $\frac{49}{50} = 0.98 < 1.125 = \frac{9}{8}$

9 $\frac{3}{75} = \frac{1}{25} = 0.04 < 0.375 = \frac{3}{8}$

> 10 $\frac{3}{25} = 0.12 < 0.325 = \frac{13}{40}$ 12 $0.27 < (0.28 <) \frac{2}{7} = \frac{6}{21} < 0.621$
>
> 11 $\frac{47}{50} = 0.94 < 2.25 = \frac{9}{4} = \frac{27}{12}$

α: T20 Multiplication: Decimals A   NC

The step from integer arithmetic to decimal arithmetic is fundamental to calculation with measures, and (given appropriate preparation) should be relatively straightforward. But it requires time and effort. For some pupils this section will be routine revision; for others it may reveal the need for more detailed groundwork.

Answers

> 0 a 2 m @ £9 per metre = £(2 × 9) = **£18**
>   b 17.3 m @ £9 per metre = £(17.3 × 9) = **£155.70**

1 30	7 64.4	13 186.2
2 17.5	8 38	14 365.4
3 14.4	9 105	15 616.4
4 28	10 42.5	16 570
5 34.2	11 62.4	17 243.86
6 50.4	12 133	18 319.74

> 19 2557.86   20 21 464.74

α: T21 Measures: Change of units   NC

This section was devised in response to clear evidence that able pupils entering Year 7 cannot switch between standard units as they need to.

Answers

> 0 a 16 km = 16 000 m; 16 km 37 m = 16 037 m = 1 603 700 cm;
>   ∴ 16 km 37 m 8 cm = **1 603 708** cm
>   b 16 km 37 m 8 cm = 16 km 37.08 m = **16.03708** km

3A Alpha

1. 3 kg = $\frac{3}{1000}$ tonne; $\frac{3}{10}$ litre = 30 cl; 0.003 kg = 3 g; 0.3 m = $\frac{3}{10000}$ km; 30 ml = $\frac{3}{100}$ litre; 0.03 tonne = 30 kg; 30 mm = 0.03 m

2. $2\frac{1}{3}$ hours = (2 × 60 + 20) minutes

3. 750 g = $37\frac{1}{2}$% of 2 kg

4.
   a 4.5 m > 45 cm
   b 91 kg > 910 g
   c 1230 cm > 1.23 m
   d 20 min > 1000 s
   e £16.20 > 162 p
   f 1.2 tonnes > 120 kg

5. 14 (14 × 60 cm = 8 m 40 cm)

6.
   a 2 m 12 cm = **212** cm
   b 2 h 20 min = **140** min
   c 28 kg 30 g = **28 030** g
   d 3 m 33 cm = **3.33** m
   e 4 h 15 min = **4.25** h
   f 7 m 7 mm = **7.007** m
   g 44 999 p = £**449.99**
   h 3 m 4 mm = **3.004** m
   i 9 km 81 m = **9.081** km
   j 796 cl = **7.96** litres
   k 27 cm 4 mm = **0.274** m
   l 7 cm = **0.07** m
   m 2 m 2 cm = **2.02** m
   n 23 kg 17 g = **23.017** kg
   o 23 m 76 cm = **0.02376** km

7.
   a 'eleven thousand, eleven hundred and eleven' = **12 111**
   b 'ninety-nine thousand, ninety-nine hundred and ninety-nine' = **108 999**

α: T22 Where did the money go? A   NC

Problem 0b illustrates the intended goal: to *think about* given information in order to remove the need for guesswork or for extensive trial-and-error.

Answers

0.
   a £17.55 ÷ 5 = **£3.51**
   b 48 is a multiple of 6; ∴ number of Swizzles must be a multiple of 6
      ∴ **0** Swizzles, **8** Stickies, or **6** Swizzles, **3** Stickies

1. **37 p** change   2. Rose £**36**, Jo £**24**
3. Number of angel fish must be a multiple of 5.
   ∴ **0** angel fish and **5** goldfish, or **5** angel fish and **2** goldfish.
4. £**200**   5. £**1.20**
6. £**2**   7. a John: £**50**   b Ben: £**80**
8. a **93 p** (= 4 × 20 p + 5 p + 4 × 2 p)   b £**1.43** (= 50 p + 4 × 20 p + 5 p + 4 × 2 p)

9. **1** goldfish and **13** angel fish, or **8** goldfish and **4** angel fish

10. i Let L, M, S denote the number of 'large', 'medium' and 'small' eggs bought.
       Then (L, M, S) = (6, 0, 0), or (3, 5, 5), or (0, 10, 10) if $M = S$;
                       = (5, 0, 5), or (4, 3, 4) or (3, 6, 3), or (2, 9, 2), or (12, 1, 12), or
                         (15, 0, 15) if $L = S$;
                       = (0, 0, 30), or (1, 1, 23), or (2, 2, 16), or (3, 3, 9), or (4, 4, 2) if $L = M$.
    ii **14** solutions

α: T23 Buy one, get one free B   NC

Work for *speed* and *accuracy* – especially in positioning the decimal point correctly. Use spot-checks to ensure the intended method is being used.

Answers

```
0  Given  12 × 3 = 36
   a  36 ÷ 12 = 3                    e  3600 ÷ 30 = 120
   b  12 × 30 = 36 × 10 = 360        f  1.2 × 3 = 36 ÷ 10 = 3.6
   c  360 ÷ 3 = 12 × 10 = 120        g  360 ÷ 12 = 30
   d  120 × 30 = 3600                h  1.2 × 30 = 12 × 3 = 36
```

1 1088 × 3 = **3264**

2 a 1088 × 30 = 3264 × 10 = **32 640**
    b 10 880 × 3 = 3264 × 10 = **32 640**
    c 108.8 × 3 = 3264 ÷ 10 = **326.40**
    d 3264 ÷ 3 = **1088**
    e 32 640 ÷ 3 = 1088 × 10 = **10 880**
    f 1088 × 300 = 3264 × 100 = **326 400**
    g 3.264 ÷ 1.088 = **3**
    h 3264 ÷ 30 = 1088 ÷ 10 = **108.8**
    i 1088 × 0.3 = 3264 ÷ 10 = **326.4**
    j 0.1088 × 3 = **0.3264**
    k 32.64 ÷ 0.3 = **108.8**
    l 1.088 × 0.3 = **0.3264**
    m 0.3264 ÷ 0.03 = **10.88**

```
3  a  823 × 15 = 12 345;  ∴ 0.12345 ÷ 0.015 = 8.23
   b  1286 × 96 = 123 456;  ∴ 0.0123456 ÷ 12.86 = 0.00096
```

α: T24 Calculation with measures A   NC

The goal of this section is to cultivate clear thinking and simple, common-sense methods. Only when the structure underlying simple ratio problems is understood does it make sense to develop general methods (see Book *Beta*).

Answers

```
0  a  1 hour = 60 minutes = 120 × 30 seconds
       ∴ Snail crawls 120 × 30 cm = 36 m in 1 hour
   b  1 day = 24 × 1 hour; ∴ Snail crawls 24 × 36 m = 864 m in 1 day
   c  1000 = 864 + 136, and 136 ≈ 4 × 36
       ∴ Slightly less than 1 day 4 hours to crawl 1 km
```

1 a 1 minute = 60 seconds; ∴ Travels 60 × 20 m = **1.2 km** in one minute
    b 1 hour = 60 minutes; ∴ Travels 60 × 1.2 km = 72 km in 1 hour: speed = **72 km/h**
    c Travels 1 km in $\frac{1}{72}$ hour; $\frac{1}{12}$ hour = 5 minutes = 300 seconds; ∴ 1 km in **50 seconds**

2 18 litres = 36 × 50 cl; ∴ **36** glasses can be filled

3 a Travels 4 × 25 m = **100 m** in 4 seconds
    b ∴ 10 × 4 = **40 seconds** to cover 1 km
    c Travels $1\frac{1}{2}$ km in 1 minute; ∴ Speed = **90 km/h**

4 **14** lengths (14 × 60 = 8 m 40 cm)

5 **6.5 km/h**

6 a **72 km/h** (6 km in 5 minutes; ∴ 12 × 6 = 72 km in 1 hour)
    b **50 seconds** (as in **1c**)

```
7  a  1 hour = 12 × 5 minutes; ∴ 12 × 2.4 km = 28.8 km in 1 hour
   b  2.4 km in 300 seconds; ∴ 1 km in 125 seconds (or 2 minutes 5 seconds)
8  a  1 kg makes 10 rolls; ∴ 2.4 kg makes 24 rolls      b  2.5 kg
```

α: T25 Missing digits A   NC

These problems – and their harder variants in Sections C8 and C16 – provide an excellent check on whether place value has been understood and whether the arithmetical algorithms have been robustly mastered.

Answers

> **0** Start in the units column. 67 + 86 = 153

1 83 + 14 = 97	**3** 33 + 78 = 111	**5** 938 + 62 = 1000	**7** 481 − 468 = 13
2 17 + 76 = 93	**4** 12 + 89 = 101	**6** 314 − 128 = 186	

> **8** Lots of solutions: e.g. 243 − 156 = 87, 351 − 264 = 87, 513 − 426 = 87, 513 − 486 = 27

α: T26 Word problems A   NC

Word problems are an essential stepping-stone on the path from arithmetic, algebra and geometry to the confident use of simple methods to solve given problems. They require a combination of reading, selecting given information, choosing an appropriate calculation, and interpreting the result of that calculation.

Answers

> **0** **127** (= 123 + 4 = 131 − 4 = 129 − 2)

1 1.64 m

2 **6** rabbits, **8** geese

3 5 bars between 7 people $\left(= \frac{5}{7} \text{ each}: \frac{2}{3} < \frac{5}{7}\right)$

4 **£18** (£756 − 4 × £180 = £36 = 2 × £18)

5 **22** miles

6 Total of all three = $\frac{1}{2}$ (17 + 15 + 20) stone = 26 stone; ∴ Bashful, **11 stone** (= 26 − 15), Dopey, **6 stone** (= 26 − 20), Sleepy, **9 stone** (= 26 − 17)

7 300 ml $\left(\frac{2}{3} - \frac{1}{2} = \frac{1}{6} \text{ glass} = 50 \text{ ml}\right)$

8 **18 coins** (turn over 3 tails), or **6 coins** (turn over 1 head and 2 tails)

9 34

10 a 260 g   b 560 g

11 65 years (= 30 + 5 × 7)

12 400 tarts

> **13** 89 = 45 + 45 − 1
> ∴ 45 × 45 = **2025 tiles**
>
> **14** **30 coins** (turn over 5 tails), or **18 coins** (turn over 1 head and 4 tails), or **6 coins** (turn over 2 heads and 3 tails)

α: C1 Mental multiplication   NC

This section (like many others) aims to develop specific *methods*, not just answers. The whole purpose may be missed if pupils are allowed to use methods other than those being rehearsed to obtain the answers.

Answers

> 0 $15 \times 75 \times 40 = 15 \times (3 \times 25) \times 40 =$ **45 000**

1. $25 \times 12 = (25 \times 4) \times 3 =$ **300**
2. $19 \times 13 = (20 - 1) \times 13 = 260 - 13 =$ **247**
3. $18 \times 15 = (9 \times 2) \times (5 \times 3) =$ **270**
4. $22 \times 15 = 11 \times (2 \times 5) \times 3 =$ **330**
5. $28 \times 75 = 7 \times (4 \times 25) \times 3 =$ **2100**
6. $19 \times 15 = (20 - 1) \times 15 = 300 - 15 =$ **285**
7. $99 \times 83 = (100 - 1) \times 83 = 8300 - 83 =$ **8217**
8. $35 \times 26 = 7 \times (5 \times 2) \times 13 =$ **910**
9. $22 \times 49 = 11 \times 98 = 11 \times (100 - 2) =$ **1078**
10. $35 \times 202 = 7 \times (5 \times 2) \times 101 =$ **7070**
11. $222 \times 15 = 111 \times (2 \times 5) \times 3 =$ **3330**

> 12 $125 \times 35 \times 52 \times 40 = 125 \times (7 \times 5) \times (13 \times 4) \times (5 \times 8)$
> $= (7 \times 13) \times 100\,000 =$ **9 100 000**

α: C2 What's my number? A   NC

These problems require pupils to scan all integers in a given range quickly and systematically, while keeping two or more ideas in their heads – thereby cultivating a greater flexibility in working with integers up to 100.

Answers

> 0   a 14   b Your number is 11 or 17 (20 is not included)

1. $8 \times 3 =$ **24**
2. 12 $(= 4 \times (1 + 2))$
3. $\left(\frac{1}{8}\text{ of the number is 9; } \therefore \frac{1}{2}\text{ is}\right)$ **36**
4. 21
5. 17
6. 28
7. It is 19, or 28, or 37, or 46, or 55, or 64, or 73, or 82, or 91
8. 44
9. 97

> 10   8 apples, 3 people
> 11   a 7 (12, 18, 20, 21, 24, 27, 30)   d 5 (72, 80, 81, 84, 90)
>   b 6 (36, 40, 42, 45, 48, 50)   e 0
>   c 4 (54, 60, 63, 70)

α: C3 Multiplication: Integers B   NC

Learning to implement a simple algorithm quickly and reliably is a significant part of elementary mathematics. Long multiplication is especially important because of the way it exploits algebraic structure (e.g. the distributive law) and the numeral system (place value, etc.) to reduce all problems of a particular type to *knowing one's tables*. The goal should be for as many pupils as possible to complete Problems **1-8** accurately and then to grapple with Problem **9**.

Answers

> 0 $649 \times 47 =$ **30 503**

3A Alpha

1	91 × 11 = **1001**	4	97 × 56 = **5432**	7	5439 × 143 = **777 777**
2	77 × 13 = **1001**	5	953 × 57 = **54 321**	8	15 873 × 49 = **777 777**
3	823 × 15 = **12 345**	6	9009 × 37 = **333 333**		

9 a 749 × 63 = **47 187**   b 87 × 85 = **7395**, or 97 × 85 = **8245**

α: C4 Analogue angles   NC

These neglected problems embody the essence of elementary mathematics in a familiar concrete setting. The need to think about *both* the minute hand and the hour hand at the same time means that even the simplest examples are non-routine, and the *inverse* challenge of 'finding a time with a specified angle between the two hands' (Problems **0b, 5b, 6b, 7b, 8b, 9b**) can be particularly delicate.

Answers

0 a 15° (the minute hand points at 6 and the hour hand is halfway to 7)
   b 5:30

1 a 360°   b 3 × 360° = 1080°   c $\frac{1}{2}$ × 360° = 180°
2 a 360° ÷ 12 = 30°   b 3 × 30° = 90°   c $\frac{1}{2}$ × 30° = 15°
3 a $\frac{1}{4}$ × 360° = 90°   c $\frac{5}{6}$ × 360° = 300°
   b $\frac{1}{3}$ × 360° = 120°   d $\frac{7}{12}$ × 360° = 210°
4 a $\frac{1}{4}$ × 30° = 7½°   c $\frac{5}{6}$ × 30° = 25°
   b $\frac{1}{3}$ × 30° = 10°   d $\frac{7}{12}$ × 30° = 17½°
5 a 90°   b 9 pm
6 a 2 × 30° = 60°   b 10 pm
7 a 4 × 30° = 120°   b 8 pm
8 5 × 360° = 1800°

9   a 120° − 15° = 105°   b 9:30 pm
10 a 90° − 15° = 75°   b 8:30 pm
11 a 10°   b 7:40 pm
12 a 120° + 7½° = 127½°   b 4:45 pm

α: C5 Tables with remainders   NC

The solutions to some of these problems require one to be flexible about the meaning of 'remainders', so that statements such as '5 ÷ 2 = 1 remainder 3' are viewed as formally correct (since 5 = 1 × 2 + 3).

Answers

0 a 21 ÷ 4 = 5 remainder 1   b 43 ÷ 7 = 6 remainder 1.

1 16 ÷ 5 = 3 remainder 1   5 79 ÷ 6 = 12 remainder 7   9   68 ÷ 7 = 9 remainder 5
2 58 ÷ 6 = 9 remainder 4   6 63 ÷ 8 = 7 remainder 7   10 53 ÷ 4 = 12 remainder 5
3 45 ÷ 6 = 7 remainder 3   7 38 ÷ 8 = 4 remainder 6   11 59 ÷ 13 = 4 remainder 7
4 56 ÷ 9 = 6 remainder 2   8 43 ÷ 7 = 6 remainder 1

12 a 3 solutions: 15 ÷ 1, 55 ÷ 6, 95 ÷ 11 all = 8 remainder 7 (in some sense)
    b 3 solutions: 13 ÷ 1, 53 ÷ 6, 93 ÷ 11 all = 8 remainder 5 (in some sense)

α: C6 Counting the ways *B*

This section encourages simple strategies to produce systematic listing of all possibilities in a simple context.

Answers

> 0 a Average = $\frac{17}{3}$ nuts ∴ **smallest number ≤ 5**
>
>   b i **1** solution: smallest = 3; ∴ **3 + 5 + 9**
>
>   ii **8** solutions: smallest = 1 or 3 or 5; ∴ 1 + 1 + 15, or 1 + 3 + 13, or 1 + 5 + 11, or 1 + 7 + 9; or 3 + 3 + 11, or 3 + 5 + 9, or 3 + 7 + 7; or 5 + 5 + 7

1 **3** solutions: 1 + 3 + 5 + 13, or 1 + 3 + 7 + 11, or 1 + 5 + 7 + 9

2 23 is odd ∴ number of Tripods must be odd (and > 1)
  ∴ **3** Tripods, **7** Bipods; or **5** Tripods, **4** Bipods

3 **5** solutions: 1 + 3 + 15, or 1 + 5 + 13, or 1 + 7 + 11, or 3 + 5 + 11, or 3 + 7 + 9

4 **5** solutions: 3 + 5 + 17, or 3 + 7 + 15, or 3 + 9 + 13, or 5 + 7 + 13, or 5 + 9 + 11

> 5 47 = 8 × 5 + 1 × 7 = 1 × 5 + 6 × 7. (If $N = 5a + 7b = 5c + 7d$, then $5(a - c) = 7(d - b)$, so $d - b$ is a multiple of 5; ∴ $d \geq 6$ and $c \geq 1$, $N \geq 1 \times 5 + 6 \times 7 = 47$)

α: C7 Drawing conclusions *B*

Remember that the aim of this section is

a for pupils to carry out the construction, and

b to *think about, to discuss, and to justify the underlying mathematics*, with a view to achieving an initial understanding of what we mean by *exact in principle*.

It is difficult to provide *brief* structured solutions to geometry problems. What pupils write will depend on their previous experience. But the ultimate goal is to write *formal proofs*, so the solutions are provided as a guide, leaving the teacher to decide whether pupils' answers are acceptable.

Answers

> 0 a OA = OB = OF (radii of the same circle C)
>
>   b AO = AB = AF (radii of the same circle C_1)
>
>   c ∴ △OAB and △OAF are *equilateral*
>
>   d ∴ ∠ABO = ∠BOA = ∠OAB = 60° (angles in an equilateral triangle)

1 a i BA = BC (radii of same circle C_2)   ii △OBC is equilateral
  b i CB = CD (radii of same circle C_3)   ii △OCD is equilateral
  c i DC = DE (radii of same circle C_4)   ii △ODE is equilateral
  d ED = DE = DC = CD = CB = BC = BA = AO = EO; ∴ C_5 passes through O.
     OE = OF (radii of circle C); ∴ △OEF is isosceles, so ∠OEF = ∠OFE.
     But ∠FOA = ∠AOB = ∠BOC = ∠COD = ∠DOE = 60°; ∴ ∠EOF = 60°
     ∴ △OEF is equilateral, so EF = EO, and circle C_5 passes through F.
     ABCDEF is a regular hexagon (i BA = BC (radii of C_2); CB = CD (radii of C_3); etc.
     and ii ∠FAB = ∠FAO + ∠OAB = 60° + 60° = 120°; similarly ∠ABC = 120°, etc.)

> 2 e ABCDE should be a regular pentagon.
>   AB = AE (radii of first circle); BA = BC (radii of second circle)
>   EA = ED (radii of third circle); CB = CD (radii of fourth circle)
>   ∴ AB = BC = CD = DE = EA
>   It is not so easy to prove that the five angles are congruent. Here is how to start:
>   ∠BAE = ∠ABC = 108° (by construction). △EAB and △ABC are congruent (SAS).
>   ∠EAC = ∠EAB − ∠CAB = ∠ABC − ∠EBA = ∠CBE, so △EAC and △CBE are congruent (SAS).

3A Alpha

> 3 c $OA = OB$ ($\angle OAB = \angle OBA = 54°$ by construction; so $\triangle OAB$ is isosceles)
> d i $OA = OE$ (radii of circle, centre O)
>   ii $\therefore \triangle OAE$ is isosceles; $\therefore \angle OEA = \angle OAE = 54°$. $\therefore \angle AOE = 72°$
>   iii $\therefore \triangle OEA$ and $\triangle OAB$ are congruent (SAS), so $EA = AB$
>   iv Similarly, $\triangle OBC$ is congruent to $\triangle OAB$; $\therefore AB = BC$
> e i $\triangle OCD$ is congruent to $\triangle OBC$ by SSS ($CD = CB$ are radii of the same circle, $OC = OB$ and $OD = OC$ since all are radii of the circle C)
>   ii $\angle DOE = 72°$, $DE = EA$ and $EA = AB$

α: C8 Missing digits B NC

These puzzles strengthen insight into place value and the way our *base 10* numeral system works. It may not be easy to make the process of analysing these problems *conscious* and *explicit*. So use these excellent exercises in using simple logic to actively encourage *reasoning* and to discourage guesswork.

Answers

> 0 $69 + 95 + 79 = 243$

> 1 $24 + 94 + 84 = 202$ 3 $647 + 968 + 396 = 2011$
> 2 $92 + 14 + 93 = 199$ 4 $217 + 915 + 949 = 2081$

> 5 a $531 - 396 = 135$ b $824 - 749 = 75$ c $3658 - 2779 = 879$
> 6 4 solutions: $621 - 543$; $612 - 534$; $243 - 165$; $234 - 156$

α: C9 Division: Integers NC

These short divisions should be used to make the standard layout *automatic*.

Answers

> 0 a $654 = 3 \times 218$ c $1001 = 11 \times 91$
>   b $123 = 3 \times 41$ d $924 = 3 \times 308$

> 1 $5432 = 4 \times 1358$ 5 $5432 = 7 \times 776$ 9 $5432 = 8 \times 679$
> 2 $12345 = 3 \times 4115$ 6 $123123 = 11 \times 11193$ 10 $2002 = 13 \times 154$
> 3 $54321 = 3 \times 18107$ 7 $11193 = 7 \times 1599$ 11 $3003 = 21 \times 143$
> 4 $12345 = 5 \times 2469$ 8 $1599 = 13 \times 123$

> 12 $333333 = 37 \times 9009$ 14 a $7 \times 15 = 105$ 15 $4 \times 13 = 52$
> 13 $777777 = 49 \times 15873$ b $8 \times 29 = 232$

α: C10 Tiling A

The practical aspect of this section should make it suitable for large numbers of pupils. However, intervention may be needed to move many pupils on from doodling, to *noticing*, and to *checking* and *proving* what they find. In particular, examples are needed to justify the answers to Problems **3d** and **4d**, and either a proof or a construction is needed for Problems **3c** and **5**.

Answers

> 0 a 2 tiles for a 2 by 2 square
>   b i 8 '1 by 1' squares   ii 4 tiles

> 1 a Easiest way: tile each row with two 2 by 1 tiles   b As part **a**
> 2 5 (the 4 corners and the centre square)

3 a 1   b 12 tiles

> c Tile a 4 by 4 sub-square as in **1a**, then tile the border leaving 1 square uncovered.
> d 13 (any square with the same 'colour' as a corner in the usual black/white colouring).

4 a 1   b 24

> c Imitate **3c**   d 25

5 a *n* even for a complete tiling. (When *n* is odd, the area is an odd number of unit squares, so a tiling with 2 by 1 tiles is impossible. When *n* is even, cut the *n* by *n* square into 2 by 2 sub-squares; then tile each 2 by 2 sub-square)

> b For a 7 by 7 square, cut a 5 by 5 square from one corner, leaving a border of width 2. Tile the 5 by 5 square leaving one empty square; then tile the border completely. For a 9 by 9 square, cut a 7 by 7 square from one corner; and continue as before, etc.

α: C11 Highest common factors and least common multiples A   NC

These problems are supposed to be tackled using only what pupils know about integers. A general method should wait until later.

Answers

> 0 $hcf(30, 500) = 10$, $lcm(30, 500) = $ **1500**

1 $hcf(5, 10) = 5$, $lcm(5, 10) = $ **10**   5 $hcf(9, 12) = 3$, $lcm(9, 12) = $ **36**
2 $hcf(6, 12) = 6$, $lcm(6, 12) = $ **12**   6 $hcf(15, 20) = 5$, $lcm(15, 20) = $ **60**
3 $hcf(20, 5) = 5$, $lcm(20, 5) = $ **20**   7 $hcf(16, 24) = 8$, $lcm(16, 24) = $ **48**
4 $hcf(15, 12) = 3$, $lcm(15, 12) = $ **60**   8 $hcf(20, 30) = 10$, $lcm(20, 30) = $ **60**

> 9 $hcf(108, 162) = $ **54**, $lcm(108, 162) = $ **324**

10 a 105   b 12 × 12, 15

α: C12 Word problems B   NC

A regular diet of word problems contributes to the process whereby pupils learn to identify and use basic techniques to solve simple problems.

Answers

> 0 a 5   b 8

1 12   3 16 years 1 month   5 1.2 litres
2 9   4 500   6 48 years old

> 7 4 m   9 12 years
> 8 288 apples 10 Equal numbers (average number of legs = 1 ∴ normal ducks and sitting ducks cancel out)

α: C13 Multiplication: Decimals B   NC

The goal here is to think primitively in terms of 'multiplying by 10 (or 100)', and 'dividing by 10 (or 100)'. If pupils already know some rule about how to position the decimal point, the connection with what is expected here should be established afterwards.

3A Alpha

Answers

0	0.037×0.3	$= 0.0111$

1	3.7×3	$= 11.1$	8	1.3×0.77	$= 1.001$	15	9.53×0.057	$= 0.54321$
2	3.7×0.03	$= 0.111$	9	82.3×1.5	$= 123.45$	16	90.09×3.7	$= 333.333$
3	0.037×0.3	$= 0.0111$	10	0.823×0.015	$= 0.012345$	17	0.9009×3.7	$= 3.33333$
4	1.1×1.1	$= 1.21$	11	0.97×5.6	$= 5.432$	18	5.439×14.3	$= 77.7777$
5	0.11×1.1	$= 0.121$	12	9.7×0.056	$= 0.5432$	19	0.5439×1.43	$= 0.777777$
6	9.1×1.1	$= 10.01$	13	0.0097×0.56	$= 0.005432$	20	0.049×158.73	$= 7.77777$
7	0.91×0.011	$= 0.01001$	14	0.0953×5.7	$= 0.54321$			

α: C14 Flexible fractions   NC

This simple – but slightly unusual – collection is intended to cultivate flexible thinking with fractions.

Answers

0	a $\frac{18}{24} = \frac{12}{16} = \frac{24}{32}$	b $\frac{36}{54} = \frac{24}{36} = \frac{54}{81}$

1 $\frac{5}{6} = \frac{15}{18} = \frac{25}{30}$ 4 $\frac{10}{8} = \frac{15}{12} = \frac{25}{20}$ 7 $\frac{12}{28} = \frac{36}{84} = \frac{15}{35}$

2 $\frac{12}{15} = \frac{36}{45} = \frac{16}{20}$ 5 $\frac{20}{15} = \frac{24}{18} = \frac{16}{12}$ 8 $\frac{10}{16} = \frac{15}{24} = \frac{25}{40}$

3 $\frac{8}{12} = \frac{12}{18} = \frac{18}{27}$ 6 $\frac{6}{10} = \frac{9}{15} = \frac{15}{25}$ 9 $\frac{15}{21} = \frac{10}{14} = \frac{35}{49}$

10	12 solutions: $\frac{2n}{12} = \frac{7n}{42} = \frac{15}{m}$, where $m \times n = 90, n = 1, 2, 3, 5, 6, 9, 10, 15, 18, 30, 45, 90$

α: C15 Which is larger?   NC

These problems are meant to be tackled with bare hands. The exercise is worthwhile whatever the outcome, but it may reveal areas where additional work is needed.

Answers

0	a $0.8 < 0.81 = 0.9 \times 0.9$	b $\frac{5}{9} = 0.\dot{5} < 0.59$	c $27 \times 29 = 28^2 - 1 < 28^2$

1 $1.1 \times 1.1 = 1.21 < 2.2$

2 $1000 = 25 \times 40 < 25 \times 50$

3 $\frac{8}{9} = 0.8888\ldots$ for ever < 0.89

4 $1.3 \times 1.3 = 1.69 < 1.7$

5 $80 < 90 = \left(\frac{9}{4}\right) \times 40$

6 $39 \times 41 = 40^2 - 1 < 40^2 = 1600$

7 $30 = \sqrt{900} < \sqrt{1000}$

8 $12 = 90 \div 7.5 < 100 \div 7.5$

9 $70 = \frac{630}{9} < \frac{640}{9}$

10 $1.2 < 1.21 = 1.1 \times 1.1$

11 $\left(\frac{25}{12}\right) \times 84 < \left(\frac{25}{12}\right) \times 96 = 200$

12 $2.7 \times 2.9 = (2.8)^2 - 0.01 < 2.8 \times 2.8$

13 $49 < 50 = \sqrt{2500}$

14 $\frac{(360 + 8)}{4} = 92 = 10(10 - 0.8)$

15 $29 \times 31 = 30^2 - 1 < 900$

α: C16 Missing digits C   NC

These puzzles strengthen insight into place value and the way our *base 10* numeral system works. It may not be easy to make the process of analysing these problems *conscious* and *explicit*. So use these excellent exercises in using simple logic to actively encourage *reasoning* and to discourage guesswork.

Answers

| 0 | 27 × 7 = 189 |

1. 86 × 4 = 344
2. 76 × 3 = 228, or 16 × 8 = 128, or 66 × 8 = 528
3. 139 × 6 = 834
4. 147 × 8 = 1176, or 247 × 8 = 1976
5. 8 × 54 = 432
6. 7 × 73 = 511, or 7 × 83 = 581

| 7 | 7 × 6518 = 45 626 | 8 | 3 × 859 = 2577 |

α: C17 Triangles

Elementary geometry analyses figures in terms of *triangles*. This exploratory section constitutes a gentle concrete beginning. The reasons pupils give to explain what emerges will vary, but they should be rooted in what is *given* explicitly in a construction (Problems **0, 1, 2, 3**) or what is known – such as

(a) that radii of a given circle are equal

(b) that the dot-lattice used in Problems **4-10** is a *square* lattice.

Answers

| 0 | a | AB = CD (△MAB and △MCD are congruent – by SAS) |
| | b | ∠ABM = ∠CDM (same reason) c ∠BAM = ∠DCM (same reason) |

1. ∠OAB = ∠OBA (OA = OB; ∴ △OAB is isosceles)
2. a CD = 2AB   b ∠ABM = ∠CDM   c ∠BAM = ∠DCM
3. d AM : BM = CM : DM   e AM : CM = BM : DM = AB : CD
4. a ∠ABC = 45° (△ABC is an isosceles right-angled triangle)
   b ∠ACB = 45° (same reason)
5. a ∠BAC = 90° (because AB = AC so △ABC is isosceles with ∠ABC = 45° - by Problem 3)
   b ∠ABC = 45°   c ∠ACB = 45°
   d ABDC is a rhombus with a right angle at A, so is a **square**.
6. a From B move down one step and 2 steps to the right.
   b From C move 2 steps up and 1 step to the right; then ABCD is a square.
7. a ∠ABC = ∠ACB (AB = AC so △ABC is isosceles)   b ABDC is a **rhombus**
8. a ∠BAC = 90° (△ABC is an isosceles triangle with ∠ABC = 45°)
   b ∠ABC = 45°   c ∠ACB = 45°   d ABDC is a **square**
9. a From B move 2 steps down and 3 steps to the right.
   b From C move 2 steps to the right and 3 steps up

α: C18 Weighing the baby

The symmetry implicit in these problems invites a particularly elegant kind of solution. The solutions expressed here are *in print*, and so are *algebraic*; pupils may well think and enunciate the same approach without using algebra.

Answers

0	a	Let the box be a cm by b cm by c cm.
		Then 40 = 2a + 2b, 60 = 2b + 2c, 60 = 2c + 2a
		∴ 2a + 2b + 2c = $\frac{1}{2}$(40 + 60 + 60) = 80,
		so 2c = 80 − 40, 2b = 80 − 60 2a = 80 − 60
		∴ Volume = 20 × 10 × 10 cm³ = **2000 cm³**

3A Alpha

> b Let the box be a cm by b cm by c cm. Then $40 = 2a + 2b$, $60 = 2b + 2c$, $80 = 2c + 2a$
> $\therefore 2a + 2b + 2c = \frac{1}{2}(40 + 60 + 80) = 90$,
> so $2c = 90 - 40$, $2b = 90 - 60$ $2a = 90 - 80$
> $\therefore$ Volume $= 25 \times 15 \times 5 \text{ cm}^3 =$ **1875 cm³**
> *[The fact that **b** has larger girth than **a** but smaller volume may seem counterintuitive!]*
>
> c Volume $= 17\frac{1}{2} \times 12\frac{1}{2} \times 7\frac{1}{2} \text{ cm}^3 =$ **1640.625 cm³**

1 a 13 kg

   b x weighs $(13 - 8)$ kg = **5 kg**, y weighs $(13 - 11)$ kg = **2 kg**,
      z weighs $(13 - 7)$ kg = **6 kg**

2 a 142 kg

   b Nurse: $(142 - 78)$ kg = **64 kg**; me: $(142 - 69)$ kg = **73 kg**
      baby: $(142 - 137)$ kg = **5 kg**

3 a Let the cuboid be a cm by b cm by c cm.
      Then $40 = 2a + 2b$, $60 = 2b + 2c$, $80 = 2c + 2a$
      $\therefore 2a = 90 - 60$, $2b = 90 - 80$, $2c = 90 - 40$, so $a =$ **15**, $b =$ **5**, $c =$ **25**
      (as in Problem 0)

   b $a = 17\frac{1}{2}$, $b = 12\frac{1}{2}$, $c = 7\frac{1}{2}$

> c $a = 22\frac{1}{2}$, $b = 12\frac{1}{2}$, $c = 2\frac{1}{2}$

4 a Curry, ice cream and tea: **£5.25**   b Curry: **£3.25**, ice cream: **£1.25**, tea: **£0.75**

5 **2** spheres   7 a **8** people (+ 1 table + 8 stools)

6 **100** silver coins (65 nickls and 35 dims)   b **10** people (+ 1 table + 10 stools + 1 joint)

> 8 Let the cuboid be a cm by b cm by c cm $\therefore 6 = 2a + 2b$, $8 = 2b + 2c$, $10 = 2c + 2a$
> $\therefore 2a + 2b + 2c = 12$, $a = \frac{1}{2}[(2a + 2b + 2c) - (2b + 2c)] = 2$, $b = 1$, $c = 3$.
> $\therefore$ Surface area $= 2(ab + bc + ca) \text{ cm}^2 =$ **22 cm²**, volume $= abc \text{ cm}^3 =$ **6 cm³**
>
> 9 Let the cuboid be a cm by b cm by c cm.
>
>   a $ab = 20$, $bc = 24$, $ca = 30$ $\therefore (abc)^2 = 20 \times 24 \times 30 \ (= 4 \times 5 \times 6)^2$
> $\therefore$ volume $= abc \text{ cm}^3 = 4 \times 5 \times 6 \text{ cm}^3 =$ **120 cm³**
> $a = \frac{abc}{bc} = 5$, $b = \frac{abc}{ca} = 4$, $c = \frac{abc}{ab} = 6$, so **edge lengths 5 cm, 4 cm, 6 cm**
>
>   b $ab = 36$, $bc = 60$, $ca = 135$ $\therefore (abc)^2 = 36 \times 60 \times 135 = (6 \times 10 \times 9)^2$
> $\therefore$ volume $= abc \text{ cm}^3 = 6 \times 10 \times 9 \text{ cm}^3 =$ **540 cm³**
> $a = \frac{abc}{bc} = 9$, $b = \frac{abc}{ca} = 4$, $c = \frac{abc}{ab} = 15$, so **edge lengths 9 cm, 4 cm, 15 cm**
>
> 10 Let the cuboid be a cm by b cm by c cm $\therefore ab + bc + ca = 200$
>
>   a $a = 4$, $b = 8$ $\therefore c = 14$: height = **14 cm**
>
>   b $a = 4$, $b = 14$ $\therefore c = 8$: height = **8 cm**
>
>   c $a = 8$, $b = 12$ $\therefore c = 5.2$: height = **5.2 cm**

α: C19 Areas

Everything in this section can be explained in terms of the familiar formulae for the area of a rectangle and of a triangle.

Answers

> 0 a Draw the diagonal AC. ($\triangle ABC$ and $\triangle CDA$ are congruent, so equal in area)
>
>   b Join A to M – the mid-point of DC
>
>   c Join A to K – the point two-thirds of the way from D to C

1 a $\frac{5}{8}$ cm   b $\frac{5}{8}$ cm

2 a $12\,cm^2$ b $8\,cm^2$; $4\,cm^2$

3 ($3 \times 5 + 12 \times 12 =$) **159 square units**

4 a Join *A* to the mid-point *M* of *BC*   b Join *A* to the mid-point *K* of *CM*

   c Join *A* to the point one-third of the way from *B* to *C*

5 a Join *M* to *C*   b Join *M* to the mid-point *N* of *BC*

---
   c Join *M* to the point two-thirds of the way from *B* to *C* (Why?)
---

6 a Join *M* to the mid-point *N* of *BC*   b Join *M* to *B* (or to *C*)

---
   c Join *M* to the point *P* one-sixth of the way from *B* to *C* (Why?)

α: C20 Tiling *B*

As with Section **C10** the practical aspect of this section leaves scope for large numbers of pupils. But work may be needed to convey the need to justify, or to criticise and improve, mere experimental observations.

Answers

---
0 a 3 tiles

   b i 1   ii 5 tiles   iii Use 4 tiles to cover a 4 by 3 rectangle,
                                         then tile the 4 by 1 border leaving 1 empty square
---

1 a Use 2 tiles to tile each row   b Use 3 tiles to tile each row

2 **4** (the empty square must be in a corner; this requires proof)

3 a 1   b 8 tiles

---
   c Place two horizontal tiles in the top left corner and the bottom right corner, then
      two vertical tiles in the top right corner and the bottom left corner – leaving the
      centre empty.

   d **1** (the empty square must be at the centre; this requires proof)
---

4 a 1   b 16

---
   c Place four horizontal tiles in the top left corner and the bottom right corner, then
      four vertical tiles in the top right corner and the bottom left corner – leaving the
      centre empty

   d **1 + 4 + 4** (the empty square must be either at the centre, or in a corner, or in the
      centre of an edge; this requires proof)
---

5 a If *n* is not a multiple of 3, then the area of an *n* by *n* square is not a multiple of 3, so
      a complete tiling is impossible. If *n* is a multiple of 3, cut the *n* by *n* square into
      3 by 3 sub-squares, and tile each sub-square in turn.

   b Write *n* in the form $3k + r$, where $r = 4$ or $r = 5$. Then cut the *n* by *n* square into
      a $3k$ by $3k$ square, two $3k$ by *r* rectangles, and an *r* by *r* square. Finally tile the
      $3k$ by $3k$ square as in **a**; tile the $3k$ by *r* rectangle by using *k* tiles in each long
      row or column; then tile the *r* by *r* square as in problem **0biii** or **3c**.

α: C21 Ratio problems   NC

Ratio lies at the heart of elementary mathematics. These problems are designed to be accessible on a naive level – without teaching specific methods. However, they may reveal the need for discussion of how *quantities* behave.

3A Alpha

Answers

| 0 | a | $2\,cm^2$ | | b | $100\,km^2$ |

1 68 boxes

2 135 litres

3 18 minutes

4 120 km

5 Who knows?

6 a 24 $\left(\frac{3}{2} = 2 \times \frac{3}{4}\right)$ b 20 $\left(\frac{4}{3} = \frac{5}{3} \times \frac{4}{5}\right)$

7 9 days

8 8 cm

9 42, 18 (7 parts to 3 parts, with difference (4 parts) = 24 ∴ 1 part = 6)

10 a 1 : 2   b 5 : 12

11 $\frac{3}{5}$

12 New : old = 108 : 125; ∴ An old second is longer than a new second

13 6 : 7

14 3.2112 kg

α: C22 Measures and decimal arithmetic   NC

Arithmetic is applicable to problems involving simple measures precisely because those measures are defined so as to behave *linearly*.

Answers

0 a $1.2 \times £10 = £12$
   b i $1.2 \times £9.90 = £11.88$ iii $1.2 \times £9.80 = £11.76$
      ii $1.2 \times £10.10 = £12.12$ iv $1.2 \times £10.20 = £12.24$
   c $1.35 \times £9.60 = £12.96$

1 a $5 \times £1.30 = £6.50$ b $5 \times £1.35 = £6.75$ c $9.6 \times £1.35 = £12.96$

2 a $5 \times £2 = £10$ b i $5.2 \times £2 = £10.40$ ii $5.2 \times £1.90 = £9.88$
   c $5.4 \times £2.35 = £12.69$

3 a $7 \times 5p = 35p$ b i $7.5 \times 5p = 37.5p$ ii $7.5 \times 4.7p = 35.25p$

4 a i 1.5×30 miles = **45 miles**   ii 48.6 miles   b i 35 miles   ii 35.5 miles
   c i 22.5 miles   ii 24.3 miles

5 a $12 \times £25 = £300$ b $4.2 \times 2.8 \times £37.5 = £441$ (plain carpet!)   6 £3.78

α: C23 Where did the money go? B   NC

Answers

0 **0** Swizzles and **12** Stickies, or **4** Swizzles and **3** Stickies (the number of Swizzles must be multiple of 4)

1 28 p   2 a £2.64 (66 p each)   b £2.13 (71 p each)

3 a 12 @ 10p, 4 @ 20p;   b 25 @ 10p, 5 @ 20p   c 10 @ 10p   d 40 @ 10p

4 40 Chinos = $\left(40 \times \frac{25}{30}\right)$ Afros = $\left[\left(40 \times \frac{25}{30}\right) \times \frac{15}{20}\right]$ Euros = 25 Euros

5 **12 solutions.**
   Let L, M, S denote the number of 'large', 'medium' and 'small' eggs bought.
   Then $L + M + S = 100$ and $50L + 10M + 5S = 1000$
   ∴ $45L + 5M = 500$, i.e. $9L + M = 100$
   ∴ $(L, M, S) = (0, 00, 0)$, or $(1, 91, 8)$, or $(2, 82, 16)$, or $(3, 73, 24)$, or $(4, 64, 32)$,
         or $(5, 55, 40)$, or $(6, 46, 48)$, or $(7, 37, 56)$, or $(8, 28, 64)$, or $(9, 19, 72)$,
         or $(10, 10, 80)$, or $(11, 1, 88)$

6 £48 $\left(= \frac{4}{25} \times £300\right)$ 7 **8** goldfish and **4** angel fish, or **1** goldfish and **13** angel fish

8 **4** chocolate bars and **22** fruit bars, or **13** chocolate bars and **9** fruit bars

α: C24 Highest common factors and least common multiples B NC

These problems are considerably more demanding than *HCFs and LCMs A*, so Problem **0** must be used to bring out aspects of HCFs and LCMs that make the required naive search easier. However, the intention is still to postpone explicit instruction of a standard method (e.g. based on prime factorisation). Before teaching such an algorithm, pupils need to know in their bones

a that a *large* HCF means the LCM will be a relatively *small* multiple

b that to be a multiple of *both* numbers, the LCM must equal the product of the HCF and its two complements in the factorisation of each number.

One consequence of **b** that may emerge in the discussion is the fact that
$hcf(m, n) \times lcm(m, n) = m \times n$

Answers

0	a hcf(66, 99) = 33	lcm(66, 99) = 3 × 66 = 2 × 99 = **198**
	b hcf(135, 189) = 27	lcm(135, 189) = 7 × 135 = 5 × 189 = **945**

1	hcf(48, 60) = 12	lcm(48, 60) = 5 × 48 = 4 × 60 = **240**
2	hcf(48, 112) = 16	lcm(48, 112) = 7 × 48 = 3 × 112 = **336**
3	hcf(60, 108) = 12	lcm(60, 108) = 9 × 60 = 5 × 108 = **540**
4	hcf(66, 264) = 66	lcm(66, 264) = 4 × 66 = 1 × 264 = **264**
5	hcf(63, 105) = 21	lcm(63, 105) = 5 × 63 = 3 × 105 = **315**
6	hcf(135, 450) = 45	lcm(135, 450) = 10 × 135 = 3 × 450 = **1350**
7	hcf(144, 252) = 36	lcm(144, 252) = 7 × 144 = 4 × 252 = **1008**
8	hcf(252, 324) = 36	lcm(252, 324) = 9 × 252 = 7 × 324 = **2268**
9	hcf(168, 252) = 84	lcm(168, 252) = 3 × 168 = 2 × 252 = **504**
10	hcf(126, 294) = 42	lcm(126, 294) = 7 × 126 = 3 × 294 = **882**

α: C25 Fractions and decimals NC

Answers

0 a $0.75 = \frac{3}{4} \left(= \frac{3 \times 25}{4 \times 25} = \frac{75}{100}\right)$ c $\frac{1}{8} \left(= \frac{1 \times 125}{8 \times 125} = \frac{125}{1000} = 0.125\right)$

   b $0.28 \left(\frac{7}{25} = \frac{7 \times 4}{25 \times 4} = \frac{28}{100}\right)$ d $0.075 \left(\frac{3}{40} = \frac{3 \times 25}{40 \times 25} = \frac{75}{1000}, \text{ or } \frac{3}{40} = \frac{3}{4} \div 10\right)$

1 a $\frac{13}{5} = 2 + \frac{3}{5}$ c $6.805 = 6 + \frac{8}{10} + \frac{5}{1000}$

   b $4\frac{1}{2} = 9 \times \frac{1}{2}$ d $6 \times \frac{4}{5} = \frac{4}{5} + \left(5 \times \frac{4}{5}\right) = 4\frac{4}{5}$

2 a $0.2 = \frac{1}{5}$ c $0.5 = \frac{1}{2}$ e $0.8 = \frac{4}{5}$

   b $0.4 = \frac{2}{5}$ d $0.6 = \frac{3}{5}$ f $2.4 = \frac{12}{5}$

3 a $0.04 = \frac{1}{25}$ c $0.36 = \frac{9}{25}$ e $0.74 = \frac{37}{50}$

   b $0.375 = \frac{3}{8}$ d $0.625 = \frac{5}{8}$ f $0.875 = \frac{7}{8}$

4 a $1.25 = \frac{5}{4}$ c $2.35 = \frac{47}{20}$ e $5.125 = \frac{41}{8}$

   b $3.6 = \frac{18}{5}$ d $0.008 = \frac{1}{125}$ f $3.75 = \frac{15}{4}$

3A Alpha

5 a $\frac{1}{5} = 0.2$ d $\frac{3}{5} = 0.6$ g $\frac{24}{5} = 4.8$

   b $\frac{2}{5} = 0.4$ e $\frac{6}{5} = 1.2$

   c $\frac{4}{5} = 0.8$ f $\frac{12}{5} = 2.4$

6 a $\frac{1}{20} = 0.05$ d $\frac{11}{20} = 0.55$ g $\frac{5}{20} = 0.25$

   b $\frac{3}{20} = 0.15$ e $\frac{21}{20} = 1.05$ h $\frac{8}{20} = 0.4$

   c $\frac{7}{20} = 0.35$ f $\frac{4}{20} = 0.2$ i $\frac{2}{20} = 0.1$

7 a $\frac{1}{25} = 0.04$ d $\frac{4}{25} = 0.16$ g $\frac{44}{25} = 1.76$

   b $\frac{2}{25} = 0.08$ e $\frac{5}{25} = 0.2$ h $\frac{1}{40} = 0.025$

   c $\frac{3}{25} = 0.12$ f $\frac{11}{25} = 0.44$ i $\frac{7}{40} = 0.175$

α: C26 Calculation with measures B   NC

This section continues to lay the foundations for later work with ratio. The problems have been chosen so that simple methods and arithmetic without a calculator suffice. Pupils should be encouraged to discuss the methods they use and to *think* carefully whether they are appropriate.

Answers

> 0 a **40 m 80 cm** (1 hour = 3600 seconds)   c Just over $24\frac{1}{2}$ hours
>   b **979.2 m** (= 24 × 40.8 m)

1 a 30 km/h   b 2 minutes

2 a 1.8 km   b 108 km/h   c $\frac{5}{9}$ minute = $33\frac{1}{3}$ seconds

3 14 lengths (= 910 ÷ 65)

4 a 200 m   b 25 seconds   c 144 km/h

5 60 glasses   6 a £12.80   b £8.96

7 a $\frac{1}{3}$ km   b 20 km/h   8 a 31.2 km/h   b $8\frac{2}{3}$ m/s

>   c $\frac{25}{13}$ minutes $\left(= 5 \div 2.6\right)$
>
> 9 a 2.8 kg $\left(= \frac{1}{5} \times 14\,\text{kg}\right)$ c $12\frac{1}{2}$ $\left(= 175 \times \frac{1}{14}\right)$
>
>   b 60 $\left(= 175 \times \frac{4.8}{14}\right)$ d 80 g
>
> 10 a 36 seconds = **0.01 hours**, 40 cm 8 mm = **0.408 m**
>   b Distance (in metres) ÷ time (in hours) = speed (in metres per hour)

α: C27 Skittles B   NC

As with *Skittles* A the context is simple, but there are some subtle ideas here.

Answers

> 0 a **5** ways, **5** totals
>   b **10** ways (miss 12, 13, 14, 15, 23, 24, 25, 34, 35, 45)
>   **7** totals: minimum 6, maximum 12 — and everything in between
>   (but this must be checked)

3A Alpha

1. **a** i 1 way   ii 1 total
   b i 1 way   ii 1 total
   c The number of ways to hit five skittles must equal the number of ways to miss five!

2. **a** i 5 ways   ii 5 totals
   b i 5 ways   ii 5 totals
   c The number of ways to hit four skittles must equal the number of ways to miss four!

3. **a** i 10 ways
   ii 7 totals (everything between 3 and 9 – but this needs to be checked, or enumerate
   1 + 2, 1 + 3, 1 + 4, 1 + 5, 2 + 3, 2 + 4, 2 + 5, 3 + 4, 3 + 5, 4 + 5)
   b i 10 ways
   ii 7 totals (everything between 6 and 12 – but this needs to be checked, or enumerate
   15 − (1 + 2), 15 − (1 + 3), etc.)
   c The number of ways to hit three skittles must equal the number of ways to miss three!

4.

Number of skittles knocked down	0	1	2	3	4	5
Number of different ways to do this	1	5	10	10	5	1
Number of different total scores	1	5	7	7	5	1

5. **a** 0
   b 1, 5
   c 3 (= 1 + 2), 9 (= 4 + 5);
   2 + 1, 3 + 1, 4 + 1, 5 + 1 produce 3 to 6, and 5 + 2, 5 + 3, 5 + 4 produce 7–9.

6. **a** 10 (as in Problem 3)
   b Max = **23** (= 5 + 7 + 11), min = **10** (= 2 + 3 + 5)
   Only **10** different totals (not 14: can't score 11, 13, 17, 22)

3A Alpha

α: E1 How many solutions?   NC

Answers

0   a 8 (80 − 42, 81 − 43, up to 87 − 49)
    b 1 (80 − 49)
1   10 (20 − 10 up to 29 − 19)
2   10 (30 − 20 up to 39 − 29)
3   9 (41 − 30 up to 49 − 38)
4   9 (40 − 31 up to 48 − 39)
5   1 (59 − 40)
6   0
7   0
8   1 (80 − 69)
9   9 (80 − 61 up to 88 − 69)
10 10 (80 − 60 up to 89 − 69)
11 9 (81 − 60 up to 89 − 68)

   c 9 (71 − 40, 72 − 41, up to 79 − 48)

12 1 (89 − 60)
13 0
14 2 (88 − 40, 89 − 41)
15 2 (80 − 48, 81 − 49)
16 0
17 0
18 8 (22 − 11 up to 92 − 81)
19 1 (32 − 22)
20 1 (72 − 29)
21 5 (53 − 17 up to 93 − 57)
22 6 (47 − 11 up to 97 − 61)

α: E2 More angles   NC

These problems are relatively straightforward.

Answers

1   110°
2   90°, 45°, 45°
3   $157\tfrac{1}{2}°$
4   66°
5   66°
6   a 1:40   b 10:20
7   90°, 45°, 45°
8   80°
9   120°
10 30°
11 75°
12 180°
13 a 50°
    b $\left(90 - \tfrac{y}{2}\right)°$

α: E3 Arithmetic to ponder   NC

Answers

1   432 432 ÷ 1001 = **432**

2   12 345 679 × 9 = **111 111 111**

3   111 111 111 + 22 222 222 + 3 333 333 + 444 444 + 55 555 + 6666 + 777 + 88 + 9 = '136(10)(15)(21)(28)(36)(45)' = **137 174 205**

4   a 1 + 3 + 5 + 7 + 9 = **25**   c 1 + 3 + 5 + 7 + 9 + 11 + 13 = **49**
    b 1 + 3 + 5 + 7 + 9 + 11 = **36**

5   a 2 × **666** (twice 'the number of the B. East')

    b The digit 1 appears in the first column with each of the 6 arrangements of 2, 3, 4 in the other three columns (see part a). Similarly each digit appears 6 times in each column.
    ∴ each column adds to 6 × (1 + 2 + 3 + 4)
    ∴ sum = six times *ten thousand, ten hundred and tenty-ten*

6   1 (1 + 2 × 3 − 4 × 5 = − 13, 1 × 2 + 3 × 4 + 5 = 23, **1 + 2 × 3 × 4 = 25**,
    1 + 2 ÷ 3 + 4 × 5 = $21\tfrac{2}{3}$, 2 + 3 × 4 + 5 = 19)

7   1 + 2 = **3**, 4 + 5 + 6 = **7 + 8**,
    9 + 10 + 11 + 12 = **13 + 14 + 15**,
    16 + 17 + 18 + 19 + 20 = **21 + 22 + 23 + 24**

8   a $\tfrac{1}{2} \times \tfrac{2}{3} \times \tfrac{3}{4} \times \tfrac{4}{5} = \tfrac{1}{5}$ b $\tfrac{1}{2} \times (1 - \tfrac{1}{3}) \times (1 - \tfrac{1}{4}) \times (1 - \tfrac{1}{5}) = \tfrac{1}{5}$

9   a $\tfrac{1}{1 \times 2} + \tfrac{1}{2 \times 3} + \tfrac{1}{3 \times 4} = 1 - \tfrac{1}{4}$ b $\tfrac{1}{1 \times 2} + \tfrac{1}{2 \times 3} + \tfrac{1}{3 \times 4} + \tfrac{1}{4 \times 5} = 1 - \tfrac{1}{5}$

10 A *microcentury* = 52.56 minutes (just under an hour: 24 × 365 ≈ 10 000 hours per year)

11 $3^2 + 4^2 = 5^2$; $3^3 + 4^3 + 5^3 = 6^3$

12 a i $\dfrac{1}{(11-2)} = \dfrac{1}{9}$ iv $\dfrac{1234}{(11111-5)} = \dfrac{1}{9}$ vii $\dfrac{1\,234\,567}{(11\,111\,111-8)} = \dfrac{1}{9}$

   ii $\dfrac{12}{(111-3)} = \dfrac{1}{9}$ v $\dfrac{12345}{(111\,111-6)} = \dfrac{1}{9}$

   iii $\dfrac{123}{(1111-4)} = \dfrac{1}{9}$ vi $\dfrac{123\,456}{(1\,111\,111-7)} = \dfrac{1}{9}$

   b $\dfrac{12\,345\,678}{(111\,111\,111-9)} = \dfrac{1}{9}$, $\dfrac{123\,456\,789}{(1\,111\,111\,111-10)} = \dfrac{1}{9}$, $\dfrac{1\,234\,567\,900}{(11\,111\,111\,111-11)} = \dfrac{1}{9}$

13 $2 \times 3 - 1 \times 4 = 2$, $3 \times 4 - 2 \times 5 = 2$, $4 \times 5 - 3 \times 6 = 2$, $5 \times 6 - 4 \times 7 = 2$

14 $3 \times 4 - 1 \times 5 = 7$, $4 \times 5 - 2 \times 6 = 8$, $5 \times 6 - 3 \times 7 = 9$, $6 \times 7 - 4 \times 8 = 10$

15 $6 \times 7 = 42$, $66 \times 67 = 4422$, $666 \times 667 = 444\,222$

16 a 1089   b 9801 (digits in reverse order)   c $33^2 = 1089$, $99^2 = 9801$

α: E4 More integer problems   NC

The problems in this section vary in difficulty and sophistication. Their purpose is to convey the message that the simplest possible raw material (positive integers) still gives rise to plenty of genuinely serious problems.

Answers

1 a $3 + 5 + 11 = 19$ b $5 + 7 + 11 = 23$

2 101 (one hundred and one)   4 45

3 $31 + 41 + 61 + 71 + 101 = 305$ 5 $29 + 43 + 71 + 113 = 256$

6 a 1, 24, 120,   b 1, 48, 528, or 2, 23 98, or 4, 21, 60, or 5, 20 44; or …

7 $9 + 10 + 11 = 30$

8 a 11, 23, 83, or 17, 29, 89, or 23, 59, 83   b 11, 47, 71

9 a 217 (7 integers ∴ largest $= 329 - (1 + 2 + 3 + 4 + 5 + 97)$)

   b 1078 (list: 1, 2, 3, 4, 5, …, 46, 97, N, ∴ $N = 48 \times 47 - (1 + 2 + 3 + \ldots + 46 + 97)$)

10 288 (digit sum divisible by 9 and even)

11 a $2^2, 3^2, 2$ b $2 \times 3, 2^3, 2 \times 5; 5$ ($2 \times 7, 3 \times 5$)

    c $2^4, 3^4$ d 12, 18, 20   e $2^6, 3^6$

12 a i 28

    b i 38 (1, 2, 3, 4, 5, 7, 8, 9, 10, 11, 13, 14, 15, 16, 17, 19, 21, 22, 23, 25, 26, 27, 29, 31, 32, 33, 34, 35, 37, 38, 39, 41, 43, 44, 45, 46, 47, 49)

       ii 9 (12, 18, 20, 24, 30, 36, 40, 42, 48)

α: E5 Fair shares   NC

The solutions indicate the *portions*, for example, $4 \times \left(\dfrac{1}{3} + \dfrac{1}{6}\right)$ indicates that each of 4 people receives $\dfrac{1}{3}$ cake and $\dfrac{1}{6}$ cake – making $\dfrac{1}{2}$ cake in all. The reader should check how the cakes should be cut to produce these portions.

Answers

1 a $4 \times \dfrac{1}{2}$ b $4 \times \left(\dfrac{1}{4} + \dfrac{1}{4}\right)$; $4 \times \left(\dfrac{1}{3} + \dfrac{1}{6}\right)$ c $4 \times \left(\dfrac{1}{6} + \dfrac{1}{6} + \dfrac{1}{6}\right)$; $4 \times \left(\dfrac{1}{4} + \dfrac{1}{8} + \dfrac{1}{8}\right)$

2 a No ($3 = 2 + 1$, so one cake would remain uncut)

   b $3 \times \left(\dfrac{1}{3} + \dfrac{1}{3}\right)$; $3 \times \left(\dfrac{1}{2} + \dfrac{1}{6}\right)$ c $3 \times \left(\dfrac{1}{3} + \dfrac{1}{6} + \dfrac{1}{6}\right)$; $3 \times \left(\dfrac{1}{2} + \dfrac{1}{12} + \dfrac{1}{12}\right)$

3 a No (5 is odd; ∴ one cake is cut into an odd number of pieces, the other into an even number, so portions cannot be equal)

   b $5 \times \left(\dfrac{1}{5} + \dfrac{1}{5}\right)$; $5 \times \left(\dfrac{1}{4} + \dfrac{3}{20}\right)$; $5 \times \left(\dfrac{3}{10} + \dfrac{1}{10}\right)$

   c $5 \times \left(\dfrac{1}{5} + \dfrac{1}{10} + \dfrac{1}{10}\right)$; $5 \times \left(\dfrac{1}{5} + \dfrac{3}{20} + \dfrac{1}{20}\right)$; $5 \times \left(\dfrac{1}{4} + \dfrac{1}{10} + \dfrac{1}{20}\right)$

3A Alpha

4 a $4 \times \left(\frac{1}{2} + \frac{1}{4}\right)$; **only one way** (some cake is cut into 2 pieces, so largest part $\geq \frac{1}{2}$; if largest part were $> \frac{1}{2}$, then one could only create *three* such pieces; $\therefore$ largest part $= \frac{1}{2}$)

  b $4 \times \left(\frac{1}{4} + \frac{1}{4} + \frac{1}{4}\right)$; $4 \times \left(\frac{1}{2} + \frac{1}{8} + \frac{1}{8}\right)$; $4 \times \left(\frac{1}{3} + \frac{1}{3} + \frac{1}{12}\right)$

5 $5 \times \left(\frac{1}{2} + \frac{1}{10}\right)$; $5 \times \left(\frac{2}{5} + \frac{1}{5}\right)$

> 6 $6 \times \left(\frac{1}{2} + \frac{1}{3}\right)$. **Only one way** (Let the two sizes be a and b with $a \geq b$.
> One of the 5 cakes must produce 2 'large' pieces; $\therefore a \leq \frac{1}{2}$.
> Also $a + b = \frac{5}{6}$; $\therefore a \geq \frac{5}{12}$. If $a = \frac{1}{2}$, then $b = \frac{1}{3}$.
> Suppose $a < \frac{1}{2}$. Then in the cake that produces 2 large pieces, the remainder must be a small piece $\therefore 1 - 2a = b$
> But $1 - 2a \leq 1 - 2 \times \frac{5}{12} = \frac{1}{6}$ $\therefore b \leq \frac{1}{6}$ so $a + b < \frac{2}{3}$.)

α: E6 How many?

Answers

1 **14** (15, 24, 33, 39, 42, 48, 51, 57, 60, 66, 75, 84, 93, 99)

2 **54** (= 4 × 18 − 18)

3 **6** (if all the 8 left-handers were girls)

4 **25** (these are precisely the multiples of 4)

5 a **5**   b **14**

6 **(41, 23)**; **4** ((41, 23), (2, 431), (3, 241), (3, 421))

7 **9** (18, 27, 36, 45, 54, 63, 72, 81, 90)

8 **11** ways

9 **9** (11, 13, 17, 31, 37, 71, 73, 79, 97)

10 **7** (52 + 53, 34 + 35 + 36, 19 + 20 + ... + 23, 15 + 16 + ... + 20; 12 + 13 + ... + 18; 6 + 7 + ... + 15; 1 + 2 + ... + 14)

11 **7** (121, 144, 169, 441, 484, 676, 961)

12 **75** (= 10 + 10 + 12 + 14 + 14 + 14 + 1)

> 13 **41**
>
> 14 **25**
>
> 15 **388** (= 9 × 9 '2-digit years' + 9 × 9 × 3 '3-digit years' + [9 × 7 + 1] '4-digit years' including 2000)

α: E7 What's my number?   NC

Answers

1 a **2** (35, 42)   b **2** (14, 63)   5 a **1** (59)   b **2** (59, 119)

2 a **2** (10, 31)   b **5** (10, 31, 52, 73, 94)   6 a **3** (12, 16, 32)   b **7** (12, 16, 32, 52, 56, 76, 92)

3 a **2** (11, 41)   b **3** (11, 41, 71)   7 a **3** (9, 18, 36)   b **4** (9, 18, 36, 72)

4 a **3** (9, 29, 49) b **5** (9, 29, 49, 69, 89) 8 a **2** (25, 49)   b **4** (25, 49, 50, 98)

α: E8 Beginnings and ends   NC

Answers

1 a i **5**   ii **5, 50, 500, ...**   b i **4**   ii **4, 40, 400, ...**

> c i **25**   ii **25, 250, 2500, ...**

2 a i 20   ii 20, 200, 2000, ...   b i 25   ii 25, 250, 2500, ...

   c i 125   ii 125, 1250, 12 500, ...

3 45   4 36 (or 12, or 24, or 48); 4   5 72   6 18

α: E9 Crossnumbers   NC

The logic required to find all solutions can be hard to express compactly in written form (which explains why proofs are suppressed here). Teachers are encouraged to interrogate pupils to ensure that they recognise how logic should be used to avoid guesswork.

Answers

1
¹2	²7	■
³1	2	⁴1
⁵6	7	6

3
¹5	²3	³2
⁴6	7	6
⁵7	6	■

5
¹1	²4	³4
⁴6	8	6
■	⁵4	8

2
■	¹5	²1
³2	1	6
⁴7	2	9

4
■	¹2	²1
³8	■	0
⁴4	2	0

α: E10 Arithmetic in different bases

Answers

1 a $111_{base\,10}$ b $99_{base\,10}$ c $333_{base\,10}$

2 a $111111_{base\,2}$ b $1010101_{base\,2}$ c $1111_{base\,7}$ d $1111_{base\,12}$

3 $54321_{base\,8}$ 4 $12345_{base\,8}$ 5 $7777_{base\,8}$ 6 $777777_{base\,8}$

7 a 8 ($= 2^3$), 4 ($= 2^2$), 2 ($= 2^1$), 1 ($= 2^0$)   b 1 bag, (16 = 2^4)

8 a 10 weights: 1 g, 2 g, 4 g, 8 g, 16 g, 32 g, 64 g, 128 g, 256 g, 512 g

   b 7 weights: 1 g, 3 g, 9 g, 27 g, 81 g, 243 g, 729 g (2 = 3 − 1, 4 = 3 + 1, 5 = 9 − (3 + 1), ...)

α: E11 Fractions, ratio and pre-algebra   NC

Answers

1 £4.60   4 24   7 49 rungs

2 75 gallons   5 3 bars between 5 $\left(\frac{3}{5} > \frac{4}{7}\right)$ 8 40 : 3

3 64, 65   6 270 girls   9 a 93 p   b 93 p

10 4 : 9

11 a 5 : 6   b 5 : 4   c 27 : 28

12 1 hop = 1 jump (= $\frac{14}{15}$ steps = $\frac{14}{15} \times \frac{9}{8}$ skips = $\frac{14}{15} \times \frac{9}{8} \times \frac{20}{21}$ hops)

13 50% (at first, moisture : solid = 4 : 1; after drying = 1 : 1)

14 Answer = original tens digit (N = 'ab' = $10a + b$; N − 'digit-sum' = $9a$)

α: E12 It's a knockout

Answers

0 63 matches

1 6 matches   2 8 matches   3 9 matches

3A Alpha

4	a	64 teams ∴ 28 byes and 36 matches	b	99 matches
5	a	5 conkers	b	50 conkers
6	a	5 breaks	b	5 breaks
7	a	11 breaks	b	11 breaks

8	a	$N - 1$ matches	b	$m \times n - 1$ breaks

α: E13 Speeds and rates   NC

Answers

1. 30 minutes (1 km in 5 minutes)
2. 6:45 am
3. 3:50 pm
4. $1\frac{1}{2}$ hours, $7\frac{1}{2}$ km from walker's start
5. 4 km
6. 48 mph
7. 200.3 m
8. Length 270 m, speed 64.8 km/h
9. 5 minutes

10	a	12 mph	b	Impossible	11	80 steps high

α: E14 Rectangles and cuboids, squares and cubes   NC

Answers

1. 3 (cut at 45° through the reflex angle)
2. 24 cm²
3. 4 by 4, or 3 by 6 ($ab = 2a + 2b$
   ∴ $(a - 2)(b - 2) = 4$ with a, b integers)
4. $\frac{25\pi}{4}$
5. a i 125 cm³   ii 512 cm³
   b 216 cm²
6. $\frac{1}{3}$
7. Buz, $51 \times 51 = 2601$
8. $\sqrt{296} = 2\sqrt{74}$
9. $\frac{5}{24}$
10. 135 cm²

11	192 cm²	12	a	0.5 cm	b	2.5 cm

α: E15 More missing digits   NC

Proofs should be routinely expected – so try to spend a little time probing.

Answers

1. a $52 + 66 = 118$ b $6557 + 1581 = 8138$
2. $2572 \times 4 = 10\,288$
3. a $5369 \div 59 = 91$ c $996 \div 12 = 83$
   b $1428 \div 68 = 21$ d $948 \div 12 = 79$
4. All unique a $100\,056 \div 33 = 3032$ c $11\,401 \div 13 = 877$
                b $6821 \div 19 = 359$ d $13\,095 \div 45 = 291$

α: E16 Painting polyhedra   NC

Answers

1. 4 ways (1 way for each of 0 red, 1 red, 2 red, and 3 red vertices)
2. 6 ways (1 way for 0 red, 1 red, 3 red, and 4 red vertices; 2 ways for 2 red vertices)
3. 14 ways (1 way for 0 red, 1 red, 5 red, and 6 red vertices; 3 ways for 2 red and 4 red vertices; 4 ways for 3 red vertices)
4. 4 ways (painting edges of a triangle is just like painting vertices: so see Problem 1)
5. 5 ways (1 way for each of 0 red, 1 red, 2 red, 3 red, and 4 red faces)

6 **10** ways (1 way for each of 0 red, 1 red, 5 red, and 6 red faces; 2 ways for each of 2 red, 3 red, and 4 red faces)

7 **5** ways (painting vertices of a regular tetrahedron is just likes painting faces: see Problem 5)

8 **23** ways (1 way for each of 0 red, 1 red, 7 red, and 8 red vertices; 3 ways for each of 2 red, 3 red, 5 red, and 6 red vertices; 7 ways for 4 red vertices)

α: E17 Word sums

Answers

1 **8** solutions: 843 + 178 (and 873 + 148); 853 + 168 (and 863 + 158); 863 + 178 (etc.); 932 + 149 (etc.)

2 **13** solutions

3 **1** solution (138 × 138 = 19 044)

4 a **1** solution (5 × 401 = 2005)

   d **2** solutions (4 × 502 = 8 × 251 = 2008)

   b **0** solutions

   e **0** solutions

   c **0** solutions (e.g. 3 × 669 has "U" = "M")

   f **2** solutions (3 × 670 = 5 × 402 = 2010)

α: E18 Buckets and hoops

Answers

1 a **5**   b Yes   c **1 way**

2 a **10** (= 5 + 5)   b Yes

   c

Total score, S	0	1	2	3	4	5	6	7	8	9	10
Number of ways of achieving score S	1	1	2	2	3	3	3	2	2	1	1

3 It reads the same both forwards and backwards. (Given a list of 'all ways to score n', replace each individual bean bag score, s, by $5 - s$ to get a way of scoring $10 - n$.)

4 a **15**   b Yes

   c

Total score, S	0	1	2	3	4	5	6	7	8	9	10	11	12	13	14	15
Number of ways of achieving score S	1	1	2	3	4	5	6	6	6	6	5	4	3	2	1	1

   d It reads the same both forwards and backwards. (Given a list of 'all ways to score n', replace each individual bean bag score, s, by $5 - s$ to get a way of scoring $15 - n$.)

5 a **20**   b Yes

   c

Total score, S	0	1	2	3	4	5	6	7	8	9	10	11	12	13	14	15
Number of ways of achieving score S	1	1	2	3	5	6	8	9	11	11	12	11	11	9	8	…

   d It reads the same both forwards and backwards. (Given a list of 'all ways to score n', replace each individual bean bag score, s, by $5 - s$ to get a way of scoring $20 - n$.)

6 a 3 **b** 5 **c** 7 **d** 10 **e** 13

7 a i

Total score, S	0	1	2	3	4	5	6	7	8	9	10
No. of ordered score patterns	1	2	3	4	5	6	5	4	3	2	1

ii It reads the same both forwards and backwards. (Given a list of 'all ways to score n', replace each individual bean bag score, s, by $5 - s$ to get a way of scoring $10 - n$.)

b i

Total score S	0	1	2	3	4	5	6	7	8	9	10	11	12	13	14	15
No. of ordered score patterns	1	3	6	10	15	21	25	27	27	25	21	15	10	6	3	1

ii It reads the same both forwards and backwards. (Given a list of 'all ways to score n', replace each individual bean bag score, s, by $5 - s$ to get a way of scoring $15 - n$.)

α: E19 More tiling: Fun with *i*o*a**i

Answers

1 1 way   **2** 2 ways   **3** 3 ways   **4** 5 ways

5

n = 'length' of $2 \times n$ rectangle	0	1	2	3	4	5	...
R_n = number of ways of tiling $2 \times n$ rectangle with 2×1 tiles	1	1	2	3	5		

6 a Last tile is either vertical or horizontal; $\therefore R_4 = R_3 + R_2$

b $R_{20} = 10\,946$

7 b (8th term) $- 1$ **8 b** $2^6 - 1$

3B Beta

Rough listing of sections by topic

In Book *Alpha*, the structure of elementary mathematics which we could assume was available to all pupils and teachers remained rather slight, so it proved possible to group the sections by topic. As a result several sections designed to lay stronger foundations for number, algebra and geometry were classified under 'Using and applying mathematics'. Book *Beta* seeks to exploit the central pillars of elementary mathematics which become available from age 12 onwards. This means that extension items are much harder to classify under a single heading. The classification is still more-or-less possible, provided one accepts that some sections appear under more than one heading. Where this occurs, we have tried to identify which could be viewed as the main classification, and have entered *secondary* classifications *in italics*.

Note: The order of sections within each list is not a 'dependence order'.

Number and 'pre-algebra'

T1	Slick sums	C12	Percentage change
T4	Mental arithmetic	C13	Approximate calculation
T6	*Missing digits*	C16	Ordering fractions
T7	Intelligent grouping	C17	*Word problems B*
T9	*Sequences*	C19	Simplifying fractions B
T10	Powers	C20	Ratio
T14	*Word problems A*	C21	HCFs and LCMs B
T16	Simplifying fractions A	C22	Fractions, division and decimals
T19	Prime factorisation A		
T21	HCFs and LCMs A	C23	*Consecutive integers*
T22	Adding and subtracting fractions A	C24	*Fair shares*
		C28	Division: Integers
T23	TenTHs, hundredTHs, thousandTHs	C29	Prime factorisation C
		C30	Multiplying fractions
T24	Prime numbers	C31	Multiplication: Decimals and fractions
T25	*What's my number?*		
T27	Divisibility A	C32	In between
C1	Averages A: Use your loaf	C33	Division: Fractions and decimals
C3	Multiplication: Integers and decimals		
		C35	Negative numbers
C6	Totals	C37	Adding and subtracting fractions B
C8	Prime factorisation B		
C9	Fractions and decimals	C39	Divisibility B

Algebra

T7	*Intelligent grouping*	C25	Generalised arithmetic
T9	Sequences	C34	A formula for primes?
T18	Equations	C35	*Negative numbers*

Geometry

T2	Eyeing the dots	C4	Drawing conclusions C
T5	Analogue angles	C5	Ruler and compass constructions
T8	Enlargement A		
T11	Drawing conclusions A	C7	Drawing conclusions D
T15	Drawing conclusions B	C11	Calculating angles B
T17	Calculating angles A	C15	Drawing conclusions E
T20	Types of triangle	C18	Area of triangles and parallelograms
T26	Area and perimeter problems with rectangles		
		C26	Enlargement B
C2	Parallel lines and alternate angles	C27	Cuboids and volumes
		C38	Coordinates

Using and applying mathematics (including measures)

Direct

T5	Analogue angles	C13	*Approximate calculation*
T12	Change of units	C14	Calculating with measures
T14	Word problems A	C17	Word problems B
T15	*Drawing conclusions B*	C20	*Ratio*
C6	*Totals*		

Oblique

T3	Words sums A	C10	Knights and Knaves
T6	Missing digits	C23	Consecutive integers
T13	Counting the ways	C24	Fair shares
T25	What's my number?	C36	Word sums B
T28	Skittles		

Comments and answers

Mathematics is about *methods* rather than just answers. So the answers given here are often written in 'structured form' to indicate how it is intended that pupils should derive these answers.

◎ Where a reader can see at a glance *from the given form* what the numerical answer is, the answer is omitted.

◎ Where a numerical answer cannot be read off at a glance from the structured format we have often included the numerical answer as well.

β: T1 Slick sums   NC

Like most of the apparently *numerical* sections in books *Alpha* and *Beta* this opening section is designed to encourage *algebraic* thinking. *Extension mathematics* does not presume to teach basic algebra: rather it seeks to provide activities and exercises in numerical settings, which appear to be rather uncommon, yet which move pupils on

◎ from basic numerical calculation

◎ to an appreciation of algebraic structure and simplification.

To underline the intended approach, answers are given here mostly in factorised form (indicating that answers are not to be calculated term-by-term, but by grouping factors). This intended approach needs to emerge clearly from the experience of tackling and discussing Problem **0**. Teachers should make spot checks to ensure later problems are tackled in this spirit.

Answers

0 a 2	b 6 × 5	c 5 × 10	d 7	
1 5	3 9 × 11	5 7 × 11	7 40 × 4	9 7 × 5
2 5 × 10	4 9 × 10	6 24 × 2	8 9 × 7	10 13 × 7

11 a 3 × 23	b 3 × 49	c $\frac{3}{8}$	d $\frac{1}{8}$

β: T2 Eyeing the dots

There is unlikely to be much dispute about how to draw a line *parallel* to the given line *AB*: going from *A* to *B* involves moving '___ steps along' and '___ up', so it is natural to do the same starting from *X*.

Drawing the *perpendicular* to *AB* may well provoke more discussion! This is certainly not meant to be done either by eye or using a protractor – since neither is *exact* (though both approaches may be used to support the conclusion eventually reached).

Along and *up* are informal versions of 'in the (positive) *x*-direction' and 'in the (positive) *y*-direction'. The motion from *A* to *B* has already been naturally imagined in terms of these two components. When one turns through a right angle (say to the left),

the '*x* direction' changes to 'the (positive) ___ direction',
the '*y* direction' changes to 'the (negative) ___ direction',

so the motion 'along 2 and up 1' parallel to *AB* becomes 'up 2 and along − 1'.

Answers

0	b along 2, up 1	c down 2, right 1

1 b horizontal   c vertical
2 b vertical   c horizontal
3 a i down 3, right 2   ii left 3, down 2 (= XB)
   b i down 3, right 2   ii left 3, down 2
   c i down 3, right 2   ii left 3, down 2 (= ZA)

β: T3 Word sums A   NC

Each of these *word sums* has a good number of solutions (ranging from 7 to 72). To make sure that everyone knows the rules and appreciates how logic can help in the search for solutions, you might like to use Problem **0** to find *all* possible solutions.

Answers

0 For example: **246 + 246 = 492** (and 15 other solutions).
  [O must be even (from the units column); ∴ O = 2 or O = 4 (from the hundreds column)
  i   If O = 2, then E = 1 or E = 6.
     If O = 2 and E = 1, then T = 4 (**1** solution) or T = 5 (**3** solutions)
     If O = 2 and E = 6, then T = 4 (**3** solutions) or T = 5 (**1** solution)
  ii   If O = 4, then E = 2 or E = 7.
     If O = 4 and E = 2, then T = 8 (**1** solution) or T = 9 (**2** solutions)
     If O = 4 and E = 7, then T = 8 (**3** solutions) or T = 9 (**2** solutions)]

1 For example: 543 + 543 = 1086 (and 6 others)   3 For example: 258 + 3210 = 3468
2 For example: 5432 + 5432 = 10864   4 For example: 2910 + 2468 = 5378

5 a   T ≠ H, so carry 1 from hundreds column and H = T + 1
   ∴ H = 9 (in hundreds column), carry 1 from tens column, A = 0
   ∴ T = 8 (in thousands column), and I ≥ 5 (and I ≠ H = 9, I ≠ T = 8)
   ∴ I = 5 (**2** solutions), or 6 (**1** solution), or 7 (**3** solutions).
  b   THIS = 8956, or 8957, or 8967, or 8971, or 8973, or 8976

β: T4 Mental arithmetic   NC

As Problem **0** indicates, this is a mixed bag. But each problem should be solved as simply as possible – exploiting the built-in structure.

Answers

0 a   (21 × 25) ÷ 10 = **52.5**   c (22 + 13) × $\frac{3}{7}$ = **15**
  b   (21 ÷ 30) ÷ 10 = 7 ÷ 100 = **0.07**

1 −1	5 3.1	9 3	13 $\frac{5}{4}$
2 20 × 15 = **300**	6 12	10 $\frac{1}{3}$	14 37.2
3 $\frac{3}{8}$	7 13.2	11 1.69	15 44.1
4 17 × $\left(\frac{2}{5} + \frac{3}{5}\right)$ = 17	8 $\frac{9}{8}$	12 13.2	16 $\frac{11}{8}$ = **1.375**

β: T5 Analogue angles

Try to make sure that a clock is visible at the front of the room.

Use Problem **0c** to highlight the basic difficulty – namely, the need to allow for the movement of both the minute hand *and* the hour hand. This makes these problems excellent challenges. So invite responses from those who are normally confident, but who you know have written down the wrong answer! Allow others to contradict them, and so alert everyone to the existence of a problem. Everyone should get parts **a** and **b** right.

Answers

0	a 360°	b 30°	c 105°

1	a 360°	b 30°	2 a 240°	b 20°		
3	a 75°	b 110°	c 45°	d 10°	e 10°	f 20°
4	a 65°	b 145°	c 175°	d 95°	e $7\frac{1}{2}°$	f $37\frac{1}{2}°$
5	a 200 minutes ∴ 200 × 6°		b 200 minutes ∴ 200 × $\frac{1}{2}°$			

6 20°, 8:40	8 110°, 12:20	10 75°, 3:30	12 $172\frac{1}{2}°$, 2:45
7 45°, 7:30	9 130°, 8:20	11 $97\frac{1}{2}°$, 5:45	13 $37\frac{1}{2}°$, 7:45

14 125°, 5:50	15 $77\frac{1}{2}°$, 9:35

16 180°. The next time is 'just after 7:05'. More precisely, suppose the next 180° occurs at *m* minutes past 7. Then the minute hand has turned through $m \times 6°$ since passing 12 (= 0°), and the hour hand has turned $m \times \frac{1}{2}°$ beyond 7 (= 210°). ∴ $210 + \frac{1}{2}m - 6m = 180$, so $m = 5\frac{5}{11}$.

β: T6 Missing digits   NC

These puzzles strengthen insight into place value and the way our *base 10* numeral system works. It may not be easy to make the process of analysing these problems *conscious* and *explicit*. But these are excellent exercises in using simple logic, so actively encourage *reasoning* and discourage guesswork.

Answers

0 The hundreds digit in the answer must be 1. ∴ 95 + 8 = 103

1 The hundreds digit in the answer must be 1. ∴ 83 + 27 = 110

2 The multiplier = 4 or 9, so the carry to the tens column is odd. But the output, 8, is even. ∴ multiplier must be odd; ∴ 54 × 9 = 486

3 5 cannot go in the units column, ∴ answer = '5 *'. ∴ Units column contains at least one even digit – and hence two even digits. ∴ 13 × 4 = 52

4 Tens column must contain consecutive digits (3,4; or 4,5; or . . .).
∴ carry 1 from units column, so must be 46 + 7 = 53 (or 47 + 6 = 53)

5 Multiplier = 4 (from units column). And must produce a carry of 2 to the hundreds column; ∴ 57 × 4 = 228, or 67 × 4 = 268

6 Multiplier = 3 or 8 (from units column). And answer > 300, so multiplier = 8.
∴ 46 × 8 = 368

β: T7 Intelligent grouping   NC

Although this section works with *numbers* rather than with *symbols*, its spirit is thoroughly *algebraic*; treat it as an opportunity to develop the structured thinking that will be essential later to handle symbolic expressions.

Answers

0	a	i $20 \times (-7) = -140$	ii $8 \times (-7) = -56$			
	b	i $2 \times 7 = 14$	ii -70			
	c	i $14 \times (7-3) = 56$	ii $20 \times 7 = 140$	d 0		e 0

1	$20 \times (-7) = -140$	7	$10 \times 13 = 130$	13	0
2	$10 \times (-7) = -70$	8	$90 \times (-3) = -270$	14	$37 \times 20 = 740$
3	$20 \times (-3) = -60$	9	$50 \times (-3) = -150$	15	$18 \times 20 = 360$
4	$4 \times (-3) = -12$	10	$4 \times (-3) = -12$	16	$20 \times 18 = 360$
5	$4 \times 3 = 12$	11	$29 \times 10 = 290$	17	$34 \times 0 = 0$
6	$20 \times 3 = 60$	12	$9 \times 9 = 81$	18	$36 \times 0 = 0$

19	a $20 \times (-33) = -660$	b $10 \times (-42) = -420$	c $27 \times (-20) = -540$
20	$(100 \times 458) \div 8 = 25 \times 229 = 5725$		

β: T8 Enlargement A   NC

These tasks may appear light-hearted, but their intention is to exploit hand-eye-brain coordination to help internalise the consequences of *enlargement*.

Answers

0	a $XY = 5$ cm	b $X'Y' = 10$ cm

1 a $AC = 5$ cm   b $A'C' = 10$ cm   2 a $AZ = 5$ cm   b $A'Z' = 15$ cm

β: T9 Sequences

This section continues the delicate process of teasing apart the different aspects of sequences.

Answers

0	a	3, 5, 7, 9, 11, 13, 15, 17, 19, 21				
	b	i 4; add 1 to previous term	ii 10	iii n; n^{th} term = n		
	c	i 7 (or perhaps 8; or ...)	ii Unclear	iii Unclear		

1 a 16; $2 \times$ (previous term)   g 32; $2 \times$ (previous term)
   b 9; add 2 to previous term   h 16; add $n + 1$ to n^{th} term
   c 15; add $n + 1$ to n^{th} term   i 15; (previous term) + 3
   d 31; $2 \times$ (previous term) + 1 j 16; (previous term) + 3
   e 81; $3 \times$ (previous term)   k 14; (previous term) + 3
   f 10; (previous term) + 2   l 20; (previous term) + 4

2 a 2 (2, 1 + 1)   b 2 (2 + 1, 1 + 1 + 1)   c 3 (2 + 2, 2 + 1 + 1, 1 + 1 + 1 + 1)

d Amount made up	0p	1p	2p	3p	4p	5p	6p	7p	8p	9p	10p
Number of ways	1	1	2	2	3	3	4	4	5	5	6

e add 0, add 1, add 1, add 0, add 0, add 1, ...

f If $n = 2m$ is even, then can use 0, 1, 2, ..., m 2p's, so number of ways = $\frac{n}{2} + 1$

   If $n = 2m + 1$ is odd, then can use 0, 1, 2, ..., m 2p's, so number of ways = $\frac{n+1}{2}$

β: T10 Powers NC

Significant mathematics almost always involves *powers*. Powers are also central to calculation (logarithms, standard form) and to algebra (index laws).

Answers

0	a 5^2	b $2^3 - 1$	c $9^3 - 1^3 = 3^6 - 1$	d $9^2 = 3^4$
1	10^2	4 7^2	7 13^2	10 14^2	13 0
2	13^2	5 $4^2 - 1^2 = 2^4 - 1^2$	8 $6^3 + 1^3$	11 6^2	14 1
3	3^3	6 $12^2 + 1^2$	9 3^4	12 10^2	

15 $2^7 - 1^7$	17 6^4	19 2^5	21 $12^3 + 1^3$
16 $2^5 - 1$	18 $3^4 - 1$	20 2^7	22 6^3

β: T11 Drawing conclusions A: Isosceles triangles

Practical tasks can lead to understanding *provided the brain remains active*. When coordinating responses to Problem **0** try to cultivate correct use of geometric language and geometrical reasoning in order to prepare pupils for Problems **1-10**.

Answers

0 iv $\angle ABC = \angle ACB = \mathbf{63°}$ $\left(= \frac{1}{2}(180° - 54°)\right)$

1   a   70°, 70°   c   108°, 36°, 36°   e   72°, 54°, 54°
    b   55°, 70°   d   144°, 18°, 18°

2   a $DA = DP$, so $\triangle DAP$ is isosceles
       $\therefore \angle DAP = 75°$
       $\therefore \angle PAB = 15°, \angle APB = \mathbf{150°}$

    b $\triangle DAP$ is isosceles ($DA = DP$), $\angle ADP = 90° + 60°$
       $\therefore \angle DAP = 15°$
       $\therefore \angle PAB = \mathbf{75°}, \angle APB = \mathbf{30°}$

3   a $AM = \mathbf{5\ cm}$ (Seems to be an exact integer multiple of 1 cm.)
    b $BC = DC = \mathbf{13\ cm}$, $ABCD$ is a **rhombus** (C is the second point where the circles meet).

4   a   i $AB = AD$, so $\triangle ABD$ is isosceles
        $\therefore \angle ABD = \angle ADB = 70°$

      ii $BA = BC$, so $\triangle BAC$ is isosceles;
        $\therefore \angle BAC = \angle BCA$ (exact size unknown at this stage)
        Similarly $\triangle DAC$ is isosceles ($DA = DC$)
        $\therefore \angle DAC = \angle DCA$ (exact size unknown, but ...)
        $\therefore \angle BCD = \angle BCA + \angle DCA = \angle BAC + \angle DAC = \angle BAD = x°$

      iii $\triangle CBD$ is isosceles ($CB = CD$) and $\angle BCD = 40°$
        $\therefore \angle CBD = \angle CDB = \left(90 - \frac{x}{2}\right)°$
        $\therefore \angle ABC = \angle ABD + \angle CBD = 140°$, and $\angle ADC = \angle ADB + \angle CDB = 140°$

    b   i $AB = AD$, so $\triangle ABD$ is isosceles
        $\therefore \angle ABD = \angle ADB = \left(90 - \frac{x}{2}\right)°$

      ii $BA = BC$, so $\triangle BAC$ is isosceles
        $\therefore \angle BAC = \angle BCA$ (exact size unknown at this stage)
        Similarly $\triangle DAC$ is isosceles ($DA = DC$);
        $\therefore \angle DAC = \angle DCA$ (exact size unknown, but ...)
        $\therefore \angle BCD = \angle BCA + \angle DCA = \angle BAC + \angle DAC = \angle BAD = x°$

      iii $\triangle CBD$ is isosceles ($CB = CD$) and $\angle BCD = x°$
        $\therefore \angle CBD = \angle CDB = \left(90 - \frac{x}{2}\right)°$
        $\therefore \angle ABC = \angle ABD + \angle CBD = (180 - x)°$, and $\angle ADC = \angle ADB + \angle CDB = (180 - x)°$

3B Beta

5   AB = AD, so △ABD is isosceles
    ∴ ∠ABD = ∠ADB
    CB = CD, so △CBD is isosceles
    ∴ ∠CBD = ∠CDB
    ∴ ∠ABC = ∠ABD + ∠CBD = ∠ADB + ∠CDB = ∠CDA   QED

6 a OA = OX, so △OAX is isosceles
    ∴ ∠OXA = ∠OAX = 70°
    ∴ ∠AOX = **40°**, so ∠BOX = **140°**
    OX = OB, so △OXB is isosceles, and ∠BOX = 140°
    ∴ ∠OXB = ∠OBX = **20°**
    ∠AXB = ∠AXO + ∠OXB = 70° + 20° = **90°**

  b OA = OX, so △OAX is isosceles
    ∴ ∠OXA = ∠OAX = $x°$
    ∴ ∠AOX = **(180 − 2x)°**, so ∠BOX = **2x°**
    OX = OB, so △OXB is isosceles, and ∠BOX = 2x°
    ∴ ∠OXB = ∠OBX = (90 − x)°
    ∴ ∠AXB = ∠AXO + ∠OXB = x° + (90 − x)° = **90°**, so △AXB is a **right-angled** triangle.

7   OA = OB (radii of first circle), and AO = AB (radii of second circle)
    ∴ △OAB is equilateral.

  a ∴ ∠BAO = **60°**

  b ∠AOB = 60°
    ∴ ∠XOB = 120°. OX = OB, so △OXB is isosceles
    ∴ ∠OXB = ∠OBX = **30°**
    [Alternatively, use ∠ABX = 90° from Problem **6b**, and calculate in △ABX.]

8   AOC is a diameter ∴ ∠ABC = 90° and ∠ADC = 90° (from Problem **3b**)
    Similarly, BOD is a diameter
    ∴ ∠BCD = 90° and ∠BAD = 90° (from Problem **3b**)   QED

---

9 a **4**: every triangle involving three of the points A, B, C, D, E, O is congruent to one of △AOB, △AOC, △ABC, △ABD, and no two of these triangles are congruent (angles: 54°, 54°, 72°; 18°, 18°, 144°; 36°, 36°, 108°; 72°, 72°, 36°).
    ∴ Every triangle is isosceles.

  b △AOB: **5** copies; △AOC: **5** copies; △ABC: **5** copies; △ABD: **5** copies.

10 PQ = OQ, so △QPO is isosceles
    ∴ ∠OPQ = ∠POQ = ∠BOQ   (∗)
    ∠AOR = 180° − ∠POR   (angles on a straight line at O)
         = ∠OPR + ∠ORP   (angles in △ORP).
    OR = OQ, so △ORQ is isosceles
    ∴ ∠ORP = ∠OQR
    ∴ ∠AOR = ∠OPR + ∠OQR   (∗∗)
    Finally, ∠OQR = 180° − ∠OQP   (angles on a straight line at Q)
           = ∠POQ + ∠OPQ   (angles in △QOP)
           = 2 × ∠BOQ   (by equation (∗))
    ∴ (∗∗) ∠AOR = ∠OPR + ∠OQR = 3 × ∠BOQ   QED

β: T12 Change of units   NC

These problems provide a slightly light-hearted review of this fundamental theme, which arises in many applications of elementary mathematics to everyday problems.

Answers

0 a 1 cm = 10 mm, so 1 m = 100 × 10 = 10^3 mm
    ∴ 1 m² = **10^6** square millimetres

  b 1 cm³ of water weighs almost exactly 1 gram, 1 m = 100 cm
    ∴ 1 m³ = (10^6) cm³
    ∴ 1 m³ of water weighs 10^6 g = 10^3 kg = 1 tonne

1. **12** stone (= 12 × 14 lb = 168 lb; 1 kg ≈ 2.2 lb, so 75 kg ≈ 165 lb)
2. (12 × 300) ÷ 50 = **72** minutes
3. (120 × 85) ÷ 10 000 = **1.02** hectares
4. It's close! The answer would depend on the exchange rate. But at £0.70 per Euro, £2.45 ≈ €3.50 would buy just over $\frac{1}{2}$ litre (which is less than 1 pint = 0.568 litres).
5. **8** quonce (Let 1 quince weigh a grams, 1 quance weigh b grams, 1 quonce weigh c grams. Then $3a = 4b$ and $5b = 6c$; ∴ $15a = 20b = 24c$)
6. a **55** m, **32** m   b **2.5** cm

  c **44** tonnes (Volume in cm³ = (55 × 100) × (32 × 100) × 2.5 = 44 × 10⁶)
7. **55** years **3** months
8. **40** mpg (100 km = 62.137 miles; 1 gallon = 4.546 litres; 62.137 ÷ 8 < 8 < 40 ÷ 4.546)
9. **£9 000 000** (diameter of £1 coin = 2.25 cm (just over $\frac{7}{8}$ inch).
   125 miles ≈ 201 km = 201 × 10⁵ cm ∴ (201 × 10⁵) ÷ 2.25 ≈ 90 × 100 000)
10. a **1 000 000** seconds (10 days = 10 × 24 × 60 × 60 sec = 36 × 24 × 10³ sec < 40 × 25 × 10³ sec)
    b **100** weeks (100 weeks = 100 × 7 × 24 × 60 min = 1000 × 42 × 24 min > 1000 × 1000 min)
    c **1 000 000** hours (100 years = 100 × 365 × 24 hours < 100 × 400 × 25 hours)
11. a **1** day   b **2** hours   c ≈**1** month (30 days)   d $\frac{1}{2}$ week
    e **15** mph (1 furlong = $\frac{1}{8}$ mile; ∴ 7! miles per fortnight = [7! ÷ (14 × 24)] mph)
    f **6** weeks

β: T13 Counting the ways   NC

This section is an introduction to the application of the *product rule* for counting. Most of the problems are deliberately simple – being designed to make the underlying method seem obvious. However, just as multiplication vastly extends the range of applications of arithmetic, so the *product rule* for counting provides a technique that makes it possible for ordinary mortals to routinely solve many otherwise inaccessible counting problems.

Problem **8** illustrates the advantages of using the product rule to structure your thinking (as opposed to attempting any *listing* of possibilities, which becomes thoroughly unreliable when the number of possibilities being counted gets large). With a good class – or an older class – this problem may best be attempted collectively (in the spirit of a Problem 0).

Answers

0 a 2 × 3 = 6   b 3 × 5 = 15

1 a 2 × 3 = 6   b 2 × 3 = 6; 3 × 5 = 15
2 2 × 2 = 4   3 6 × 6 = 36   4 3 × 2 = 6
5 a 3 × 4 = 12

  b 121 = 11 × 11, and this is the only factorisation; ∴ 11 Starters and 11 Main Courses
  c 1001 = 7 × 11 × 13, and this is the only factorisation;
     ∴ Number of starters, main courses, sweets is 7, 11, 13 in some order.
6 6 (count *directed* paths from A to B: 4 choices for A, then 3 choices for B,
   ∴ 4 × 3 paths, but each ordinary path is counted *twice* – A to B and B to A)
7 a 25 (odd digits 1, 3, 5, 7, 9; ∴ 5 choices for tens digit, then 5 choices for units digit; ∴ 5 × 5)

> b **20** (even digits 0, 2, 4, 6, 8:
> ∴ 4 choices for tens digit (not 0), then 5 choices for units digit)
>
> c **45** (4 × 5 'even-odd' and 5 × 5 'odd-even')
>
> 8 a T = 1 (largest possible carry from tens column)
> I = 9 (with a carry from the units, so that I + O + 1 = 10 + O)
> M + N = 10 + P
>
> b M = 4 is the smallest possible value (see part **ci**)
>
> c M + N = 10 + P with P ≥ 4
>
> i When M = 2 there are no possible solutions (since P is non-zero, and N ≠ I)
> When M = 3, there are no possible solutions (since N = 8 would force P = T)
>
> ii When M = 4, N = 8 and P = 2 is the only possible solution for the units column – leaving 4 possibilities for O (3, 5, 6, 7)
> ∴ **4** solutions
>
> iii When M = 5, either N = 7, P = 2, or N = 8, P = 3
> Each of these **2** possibilities leaves **4** possible values for O
> ∴ **2 × 4** solutions
>
> iv When M = 6, either N = 7, P = 3, or N = 8, P = 4
> Each of these **2** possibilities leaves **4** possible values for O
> ∴ **2 × 4** solutions
>
> v When M = 7, we have N = 5, P = 2, or N = 6, P = 3, or N = 8, P = 5
> Each of these **3** possibilities leaves **4** possible values for O
> ∴ **3 × 4** solutions
>
> vi When M = 8, we have N = 4, P = 2, or N = 5, P = 3, or N = 6, P = 4, or N = 7, P = 5
> Each of these **4** possibilities leaves **4** possible values for O
> ∴ **4 × 4** solutions
>
> Hence 4 × (4 + 3 + 2 + 2 + 1) = **48** solutions altogether.

β: T14 Word problems A   NC

Regular exposure to word problems contributes to the process whereby pupils learn to identify and use basic techniques to solve simple problems.

Answers

> 0 a **Halfway – after 15 minutes** (son leaves 5 min later and arrives 5 min before the father)
>
> b **After 14 minutes** (14 minutes after son departs both have covered $\frac{1}{3}$ distance)

1 **26** (= 8 + 1 + 17)   4 **25 pupils** (14 girls)   6 **64 posts**

2 **$37\frac{1}{2}$ mph** $\left(5 \text{ miles in 8 min} = 7\frac{1}{2} \text{ miles in 12 min}\right)$

3 **14 years old**   5 **12 rabbits**   7 **55 p, 85 p**

> 8 **31 pages, 30 pages**   10 **175 boys**
> 9 **£48** (= £18 + £15 + £15)   11 **25 old monks, 75 novices**

β: T15 Drawing conclusions B: Asking why?

These tasks may seem to be purely practical, but they have been designed to produce outcomes that challenge pupils to distinguish between *numerical accidents* and *logical necessity*. Try to use the outcomes to encourage all pupils to look beyond the concrete task to what is going on underneath, and to think what can be *proved*. Pupils may vary in their readiness for a thorough proof, so use this as an opportunity to cultivate and to challenge that readiness.

Answers

> **0 a** Just under 13.5 cm **b** Exactly 15 cm
> Both interesting, but the exactness of **b** is more striking.

1 a Exactly 30 cm

  b Based on the same 3-4-5 right angled triangle: the triangle in Problem **0b** is a 3 times enlargement; that in Problem **1a** is a 6 times enlargement.

2 a Exactly 26 cm

  b The triangle here is a 2 times enlargement of a 5-12-13 right-angled triangle (compare Section **T11**, Problem **3**)

3 a Almost exactly 20 cm **b** Almost exactly 60° **c** Equilateral

4 a $BA = BC = BX = 20$ cm (radii of same circle)
     $DA = DC = DY = 20$ cm (radii of same circle)

  b $\angle ABC \approx 90°$; $\triangle BAC$ is isosceles
     $\therefore \angle BAC = \angle BCA \approx 45°$
     Similarly, $\angle ADC \approx 90°$ and $\angle DAC \approx 45°$
     $\therefore \angle DAB \approx 45° + 45°$

  c $ABCD$ is approximately a *square*.

5 b $AB = AF = AO = 10$ cm; $DC = DE = DO = 10$ cm

  c BC and EF also seem to equal 10 cm (for proof, see part **f**)

  d All exactly 60°

  e All exactly 60°

  f $ABCDEF$ is a **regular** hexagon.

> **Proof** $\triangle OAB$ is equilateral; similarly $\triangle ODC$ is equilateral.
> $\therefore \angle BOC = 60°$ and $OB = OA = OD = OC$
> $\therefore \triangle BOC$ is equilateral
> $\therefore BC = BO$, and $\angle ABC = \angle BCD = 120°$
> Similarly $FE = FO$ and $\angle AFE = \angle FED = 120°$ **QED**

6 a i All close to 20 cm **ii** All close to 90° **iii** $ACEG$ seems to be a *square*.

> **iv Claim** $ACEG$ is a square.
> **Proof** $\triangle AXE$ and $\triangle AYE$ are equilateral
> $\therefore \angle XAY = \angle XEY = 120°$
> $\triangle AXY$ and $\triangle EXY$ are congruent (by the SAS, or the SSS congruence criterion)
> $\therefore \angle AXY = \angle EXY = 30°$, so XY is perpendicular to AE – meeting at O.
> Now $\triangle AXO$ and $\triangle EXO$ are congruent so $AO = EO$.
> The circle with centre O through A passes through E.
> Let it meet XY at C and at G.
> $\therefore \triangle OAC, \triangle OCE, \triangle OEG, \triangle OGA$ are right-angled isosceles triangles
> $\therefore \angle GAC = \angle ACE = \angle CEG = \angle EGA = 45° + 45° = 90°$
> Also $\triangle AOC$ and $\triangle EOC$ are congruent (by the SAS congruence criterion)
> $\therefore AC = CE$. Similarly $CE = EG = GA$
> $\therefore ACEG$ is a square. **QED**

  b ii $ABCDEFGH$ seems to be a **regular** octagon.

> **iii** The proof is similar to Problem **6** part **a iv**, but a bit more involved.

β: T16 Simplifying fractions A NC

The need to simplify fractions is an important application of hard-won fluency with integer arithmetic. This section provides a slightly tongue-in-cheek set of basic exercises on this theme.

Answers

0 a $\frac{1}{823}$	b $\frac{3}{8}$		

1 a $\frac{1}{4}$	e $\frac{5}{14}$	i $\frac{1}{7}$	m $\frac{1}{7}$
b $\frac{2}{5}$	f $\frac{1}{4}$	j $\frac{1}{5}$	n $\frac{1}{8}$
c $\frac{1}{4}$	g $\frac{2}{11}$	k $\frac{1}{7}$	o $\frac{1}{9}$
d $\frac{1}{7}$	h $\frac{1}{3}$	l $\frac{4}{25}$	
2 a $\frac{1}{37}$	c $\frac{2}{29}$	e $\frac{1}{15}$	g $\frac{1}{26}$
b $\frac{2}{41}$	d $\frac{1}{26}$	f $\frac{2}{41}$	h $\frac{1}{28}$
3 a $\frac{5}{12}$	d $\frac{7}{24}$	g $\frac{1}{8}$	j $\frac{1}{15}$
b $\frac{5}{8}$	e $\frac{3}{8}$	h 1	k $\frac{1}{3}$
c $\frac{1}{2}$	f $\frac{1}{4}$	i $\frac{1}{7}$	l $\frac{3}{5}$

4 a $\frac{6}{17}$	c $\frac{1}{288}$	e $\frac{76}{13}$	g $\frac{23}{4526}$
b $\frac{41}{15}$	d $\frac{41}{152}$	f $\frac{29}{2181}$	h $\frac{26}{63}$

β: T17 Calculating angles A NC

Problem **0** is an excellent exercise in coordinating the *four basic facts* in the text. It may make sense for pupils to tackle Problem **0** in pairs at first – both to ensure that all pupils understand and engage with the details and to allow the teacher to assess how to coordinate the class discussion.

With some classes it might be interesting to tackle Problem **13** together at the end in order to bring out the intriguing differences between two apparently identical problems (namely that though *y* and *z* are determined, they cannot be calculated using the *four basic facts* currently available).

Answers

0 a $BA = BC$ (given); $\therefore \angle BCA = \angle BAC = 60°$
$\therefore \angle ABC = 60°$
$\therefore x = 180° - 100° - 60° = \mathbf{20°}$, $w = 180° - 100° - 40° = \mathbf{40°} = \angle ABD$, so $AB = AD$.
b △ABC is equilateral
c $\therefore AC = AB = AD$; $\therefore$ △ADC is isosceles
$\therefore z = \mathbf{70°}$, $y = \mathbf{30°}$

1 150°	3 20°	5 15°	7 95°	9 20°	11 51°
2 30°	4 10°	6 25°	8 80°	10 40°	12 40°

> 13 a i 100° ii Not using the four basic facts
>   b ii ∠BAC = 70°, ∠ABC = 40° ∴ the position of C is determined
>   ∠BAD = 110°, ∠ABD = 30° ∴ the position of D is determined
>   ∴ the angles ∠ACD and ∠BDC are determined (but cannot be calculated easily).
>   iii In fact, if AC and BD meet at X, then ∠BDC = y = 20° and ∠ACD = z = 80°, so △DXC is isosceles with height (measured from the apex D to XC) = $\frac{1}{2}$ × AB.

β: T18 Equations   NC

Some of the problems in this section can be solved more simply in other ways. However, the section is an *exercise in setting up and solving linear equations in a standard way*. By all means encourage those who can see how to do things differently, but explain that, in this context,

◉ each solution should start by declaring the chosen variable (line 1); for example, 'Let the cost of each pencil be x pence'
◉ letters should only be used for *pure numbers* (not for numbers-with-units, so discourage 'Let x be the cost of a pencil')
◉ each new step should begin on a new line, starting, where appropriate, with the symbol ∴.

Though *not* a symbol of formal logic, ∴ has a clear *informal* meaning (being read as 'therefore'), which declares that 'this line follows from what has gone before'. (In contrast, ⇒ has a technical meaning which makes it completely wrong, and mathematically misleading, to use it at the beginning of a line. The symbol is best avoided at this level.)

Answers

> 0 a **26 p** Let each pencil cost x pence.
>   ∴ 200 = 7x + 18
>   ∴ 7x = 182, so x = 26
>   b $\frac{4}{3}$ **gram** Let the box weigh b grams and each drawing pin weigh d grams.
>   ∴ b + 42d = 84 and 42d = b + 28
>   ∴ b + (b + 28) = 84
>   ∴ b = 28, so 42d = 56, d = $\frac{4}{3}$

1 £1.80	5 £5 loss	9 26 cm, 13 cm	13 6 years old
2 135 litres	6 48 years old	10 £8.24	14 14
3 a 260 g b 560 g	7 18 minutes	11 12 years old	15 5 kg
4 a £50 b £80	8 18, 42	12 72 oranges	

> 16 a k = 12   b k = 5   c k = 12
> 17 i Man: 6(t – 1) km, Woman: 16(t – 3) km
>   ii 6(t – 1) + 16(t – 3) = 45   ∴ t = $\frac{9}{2}$ (i.e. 4:30)
> 18 25 old monks, 75 novices

β: T19 Prime factorisation A   NC

Left to themselves most pupils will solve these problems by *listing factors*. However, the whole purpose of the section is to move them on to recognise the advantage of thinking in terms of

◉ the prime factorisation, and
  the *product rule* for counting (see Section T13)

3B Beta

The first two parts of Problem **0** should be used as a bridge, so that pupils

a write a list of factors of 6 and also come to
- understand the significance of the prime factorisation $6 = 2 \times 3$,
  because for the factor 1: take no 2s (or 2^0) and no 3s (or 3^0)
  for the factor 3: take no 2s (or 2^0) and one 3 (or 3^1)
  for the factor 2: take one 2 (or 2^1) and no 3s (or 3^0)
  for the factor 6: take one 2 (or 2^1) and one 3 (or 3^1)

b write a list of factors of 12 and also come to
- understand the significance of the prime factorisation $12 = 2^2 \times 3$,
  because for the factor 1: take no 2s (or 2^0) and no 3s (or 3^0)
  for the factor 3: take no 2s (or 2^0) and one 3 (or 3^1)
  for the factor 2: take one 2 (or 2^1) and no 3s (or 3^0)
  for the factor 6: take one 2 (or 2^1) and one 3 (or 3^1)
  for the factor 4: take two 2s (or 2^2) and no 3s (or 3^0)
  for the factor 12: take two 2s (or 2^2) and one 3 (or 3^1)

The solutions are written as though pupils are already familiar with $2^0 = 1$. However, this is to convey the underlying structure to the teacher; pupils may well apply the product rule procedure correctly to count factors whilst not yet thinking of 'no 2s' as '2^0'.

Answers

---

0 a i $6 = 2^1 \times 3^1$
  ii ∴ factors are: $1 = 2^0 \times 3^0$, $3 = 2^0 \times 3^1$; $2 = 2^1 \times 3^0$, $6 = 2^1 \times 3^1$
b i $12 = 2^2 \times 3^1$
  ii ∴ factors are: $1 = 2^0 \times 3^0$, $3 = 2^0 \times 3^1$; $2 = 2^1 \times 3^0$, $6 = 2^1 \times 3^1$;
  $4 = 2^2 \times 3^0$, $12 = 2^2 \times 3^1$
c i $36 = 2^2 \times 3^2$
  ii ∴ factors are: $2^0 \times 3^0, 2^0 \times 3^1, 2^0 \times 3^2$; $2^1 \times 3^0, 2^1 \times 3^1, 2^1 \times 3^2$;
  $2^2 \times 3^0, 2^2 \times 3^1, 2^2 \times 3^2$

---

1 $15 = 3^1 \times 5^1$
∴ **2 × 2** factors: $1 = 3^0 \times 5^0, 5 = 3^0 \times 5^1$; $3 = 3^1 \times 5^0, 15 = 3^1 \times 5^1$

2 $22 = 2^1 \times 11^1$
∴ **2 × 2** factors: $1 = 2^0 \times 11^0, 11 = 2^0 \times 11^1$; $2 = 2^1 \times 11^0, 22 = 2^1 \times 11^1$

3 $35 = 5^1 \times 7^1$
∴ **2 × 2** factors: $1 = 5^0 \times 7^0, 7 = 5^0 \times 7^1$; $5 = 5^1 \times 7^0, 35 = 5^1 \times 7^1$

4 $51 = 3^1 \times 17^1$
∴ **2 × 2** factors: $1 = 3^0 \times 17^0, 17 = 3^0 \times 17^1$; $3 = 3^1 \times 17^0, 51 = 3^1 \times 17^1$

5 $65 = 5^1 \times 13^1$
∴ **2 × 2** factors: $1 = 5^0 \times 13^0, 13 = 5^0 \times 13^1$; $5 = 5^1 \times 13^0, 65 = 5^1 \times 13^1$

6 $91 = 7^1 \times 13^1$
∴ **2 × 2** factors: $1 = 7^0 \times 13^0, 13 = 7^0 \times 13^1$; $7 = 7^1 \times 13^0, 91 = 7^1 \times 13^1$

7 $143 = 11^1 \times 13^1$
∴ **2 × 2** factors: $1 = 11^0 \times 13^0, 13 = 11^0 \times 13^1$; $11 = 11^1 \times 13^0, 143 = 11^1 \times 13^1$

8 $20 = 2^2 \times 5^1$
∴ **3 × 2** factors: $1 = 2^0 \times 5^0, 5 = 2^0 \times 5^1$; $2 = 2^1 \times 5^0, 10 = 2^1 \times 5^1$;
$4 = 2^2 \times 5^0, 20 = 2^2 \times 5^1$

9 $28 = 2^2 \times 7^1$
∴ **3 × 2** factors: $2^0 \times 7^0, 2^0 \times 7^1$; $2^1 \times 7^0, 2^1 \times 7^1$; $2^2 \times 7^0, 2^2 \times 7^1$

10 $45 = 3^2 \times 5^1$
∴ **3 × 2** factors: $3^0 \times 5^0, 3^0 \times 5^1$; $3^1 \times 5^0, 3^1 \times 5^1$; $3^2 \times 5^0, 3^2 \times 5^1$

11 $63 = 3^2 \times 7^1$
    ∴ **3 × 2** factors: $3^0 \times 7^0$, $3^0 \times 7^1$; $3^1 \times 7^0$, $3^1 \times 7^1$; $3^2 \times 7^0$, $3^2 \times 7^1$

12 $98 = 7^2 \times 2^1$
    ∴ **3 × 2** factors: $7^0 \times 2^0$, $7^0 \times 2^1$; $7^1 \times 2^0$, $7^1 \times 2^1$; $7^2 \times 2^0$, $7^1 \times 2^1$

13 $75 = 5^2 \times 3^1$
    ∴ **3 × 2** factors: $5^0 \times 3^0$, $5^0 \times 3^1$; $5^1 \times 3^0$, $5^1 \times 3^1$; $5^2 \times 3^0$, $5^2 \times 3^1$

14 $242 = 11^2 \times 2^1$
    ∴ **3 × 2** factors: $11^0 \times 2^0$, $11^0 \times 2^1$; $11^1 \times 2^0$, $11^1 \times 2^1$; $11^2 \times 2^0$, $11^2 \times 2^1$

15 $245 = 7^2 \times 5^1$
    ∴ **3 × 2** factors: $7^0 \times 5^0$, $7^0 \times 5^1$; $7^1 \times 5^0$, $7^1 \times 5^1$; $7^2 \times 5^0$, $7^2 \times 5^1$

16 $24 = 2^3 \times 3^1$
    ∴ **4 × 2** factors: $2^0 \times 3^0$, $2^0 \times 3^1$; $2^1 \times 3^0$, $2^1 \times 3^1$; $2^2 \times 3^0$, $2^2 \times 3^1$; $2^3 \times 3^0$, $2^3 \times 3^1$

17 $54 = 3^3 \times 2^1$
    ∴ **4 × 2** factors: $3^0 \times 2^0$, $3^0 \times 2^1$; $3^1 \times 2^0$, $3^1 \times 2^1$; $3^2 \times 2^0$, $3^2 \times 2^1$; $3^3 \times 2^0$, $3^3 \times 2^1$

18 $135 = 3^3 \times 5^1$
    ∴ **4 × 2** factors: $3^0 \times 5^0$, $3^0 \times 5^1$; $3^1 \times 5^0$, $3^1 \times 5^1$; $3^2 \times 5^0$, $3^2 \times 5^1$; $3^3 \times 5^0$, $3^3 \times 5^1$

19 $189 = 3^3 \times 7^1$
    ∴ **4 × 2** factors: $3^0 \times 7^0$, $3^0 \times 7^1$; $3^1 \times 7^0$, $3^1 \times 7^1$; $3^2 \times 7^0$, $3^2 \times 7^1$; $3^3 \times 7^0$, $3^3 \times 7^1$

20 $250 = 5^3 \times 2^1$
    ∴ **4 × 2** factors: $5^0 \times 2^0$, $5^0 \times 2^1$; $5^1 \times 2^0$, $5^1 \times 2^1$; $5^2 \times 2^0$, $5^2 \times 2^1$; $5^3 \times 2^0$, $5^3 \times 2^1$

21 a $64 = 8^2$; $64 = 4^3$ b $9^3 = 27^2 = 729$

β: T20 Types of triangle   NC

How much time is needed here will depend on pupils' previous experience. In Problem **0** those who are unsure *must* draw an accurate version of each triangle in order to generate the evidence for the intended conclusion in Problem **3** (namely, that the shortest side is opposite the smallest angle, and the longest side is opposite the largest angle).

Answers

0 Completing the table may be slow, but should be mostly straightforward. Triangles 5, 9 and 10 are slightly more subtle, in that the information given in the table about the longest and shortest sides has to be used to decide which two angles are equal.

Triangle	A	B	C			Longest side	Shortest side
5	60°	90°	30°	right-angled		b	c
9	32°	74°	74°		isosceles		a
10	32°	116°	32°		isosceles	b	

1 a Yes   c No   e Yes   g No   i Yes
   b Yes   d Yes   f Yes   h Yes

2 a i C   c i A
       ii c   ii a
   b i C   d i A
       ii c   ii a

3 a The shortest side is opposite the smallest angle.
   b The longest side is opposite the largest angle.

β: T21 Highest common factors and least common multiples NC

The corresponding sections in Book *Alpha* concentrated on *small* integers, because their goal was to ensure that the idea of *hcf* and *lcm* was understood without confusing the underlying *idea* with any prescribed *method*.

The integers occurring here are larger – so some method is needed. The method advocated in the text is:

◎ factorise the two integers a, b to find $hcf(a,b)$;
◎ if $a = m \times hcf(a,b)$, then $lcm(a,b) = m \times b$.

Problem **0** should be used to clarify why this simple method does indeed produce the *lcm*.

Answers

> **0 a** $hcf(66, 99) = 33$; $lcm(66, 99) = 2 \times 99$
> **b** $hcf(135, 189) = 27$; $lcm(135, 189) = 5 \times 189 = 945$

1 $hcf(36, 84) = 12$; $lcm(36, 84) = 3 \times 84$
2 $hcf(60, 156) = 12$; $lcm(60, 156) = 5 \times 156$
3 $hcf(45, 162) = 9$; $lcm(45, 162) = 5 \times 162$
4 $hcf(99, 264) = 33$; $lcm(99, 264) = 3 \times 264$
5 $hcf(105, 147) = 21$; $lcm(105, 147) = 5 \times 147$
6 $hcf(345, 405) = 15$; $lcm(345, 405) = 23 \times 405$
7 $hcf(252, 1728) = 36$; $lcm(252, 1728) = 7 \times 1728$
8 $hcf(648, 672) = 24$; $lcm(648, 672) = 27 \times 672$
9 $hcf(648, 675) = 27$; $lcm(648, 675) = 24 \times 675$
10 $hcf(665, 1190) = 35$; $lcm(665, 1190) = 19 \times 1190$
11 $hcf(253, 460) = 23$; $lcm(253, 460) = 11 \times 460$

> **12 a** 6×6 ($hcf(54, 78) = 6$); 9×13
> **b** 810 mm by 810 mm ($lcm(45, 162) = 810$); 18^2, 5^2
>
> **13 a** $\frac{1}{2}$ **e** $\frac{3}{4}$ **i** $\frac{4}{5}$ **m** $\frac{7}{5}$ **q** $\frac{27}{28}$
> **b** $\frac{1}{2}$ **f** $\frac{3}{4}$ **j** $\frac{13}{5}$ **n** $\frac{13}{8}$ **r** $\frac{19}{34}$
> **c** $\frac{1}{4}$ **g** $\frac{3}{2}$ **k** $\frac{5}{18}$ **o** $\frac{23}{27}$ **s** $\frac{11}{20}$
> **d** $\frac{4}{5}$ **h** $\frac{2}{3}$ **l** $\frac{3}{8}$ **p** $\frac{7}{48}$
>
> **14 a** $\frac{7}{60}$ **b** $\frac{5}{48}$ **c** $\frac{11}{270}$ **d** $\frac{1}{72}$ **e** $\frac{4}{245}$ **f** $\frac{2}{19 \times 17}$

β: T22 Adding and subtracting fractions A NC

The key to the arithmetic of fractions lies in integer arithmetic – and lots of practice. These exercises have been chosen to encourage the *expectation* that fractions will *simplify*, and to hint at some of the nice surprises that lie in store for those who regularly look for simplification.

Answers

> **0 a** $\frac{1}{2}$ **b** $\frac{1}{30}$

1 $\frac{1}{2} - \frac{1}{3} = 3 \times \left(\frac{1}{6}\right) - 2 \times \left(\frac{1}{6}\right) = \frac{1}{6}$

2 **a** $\frac{1}{2} + \frac{1}{6} = 3 \times \left(\frac{1}{6}\right) + 1 \times \left(\frac{1}{6}\right) = 4 \times \left(\frac{1}{6}\right) = \frac{2}{3}$ **b** $\frac{1}{3}$ **c** $\frac{1}{2}$ **d** $\frac{1}{12}$

3 **a** $\frac{1}{3} - \frac{1}{4} = 4 \times \left(\frac{1}{12}\right) - 3 \times \left(\frac{1}{12}\right) = \frac{1}{12}$ **b** $\frac{1}{20}$ **c** $\frac{1}{30}$ **d** $\frac{1}{42}$

4 a $\frac{2}{1} - \frac{2}{2} = \frac{1}{1}$ b $\frac{1}{3}$ c $\frac{1}{6}$ d $\frac{1}{10}$ e $\frac{1}{15}$

5 a $\frac{1}{6}$ c $\frac{1}{30}$ e $\frac{1}{84}$ g $\frac{1}{180}$ i $\frac{1}{330}$

   b $\frac{1}{15}$ d $\frac{2}{105}$ f $\frac{1}{126}$ h $\frac{2}{495}$

6 a $\frac{2}{3}$ b $\frac{1}{4}$ c $\frac{2}{15}$ d $\frac{1}{12}$

---

7 $\frac{9}{40}$

8 a $\frac{2}{3}$ b $\frac{3}{4}$ c $\frac{4}{5}$ d $\frac{5}{6}$

β: T23 TenTHs, hundredTHs and thousandTHs   NC

This simple section seeks to establish basic links between fractions and decimals, and a fluency in moving from one to the other in the simplest cases.

Answers

0 a i $\frac{1}{4} \times \frac{4}{100} = \frac{1}{100}$ $\frac{1}{5} \times \frac{5}{100} = \frac{1}{100}$

     ii $\frac{1}{2} \times \frac{2}{1000} = \frac{1}{1000}$ $\frac{1}{4} \times \frac{1}{250} = \frac{1}{1000}$ $\frac{1}{5} \times \frac{1}{200} = \frac{1}{1000}$

     iii $\frac{1}{20} \times \frac{1}{50} = \frac{1}{1000}$ $\frac{1}{25} \times \frac{1}{40} = \frac{1}{1000}$ $\frac{1}{8} \times \frac{1}{125} = \frac{1}{1000}$

   b i 0.01   ii 0.1   iii 0.01   iv 0.1

1 a $\frac{1}{5 \times 10} = 0.02$ b $\frac{1}{4 \times 5} = 0.05$ c $\frac{7}{1000} = 0.007$

2 a $2 \times \frac{1}{10} = 0.2$ e $\left(4 \times \frac{1}{10}\right) \times \frac{1}{40} = 0.01$ i 0.002   m 0.001

   b $4 \times 25 = 100$ f 0.03   j 0.003   n 0.01

   c $60 \times \frac{4}{100} = 2.4$ g 0.04   k 0.001

   d $3 \times 0.1 = 0.3$ h 0.03   l 0.1

---

3 a 0.03   b 0.003   c 0.001

β: T24 Prime numbers   NC

Prime numbers are interesting because integers can be factorised, or broken down, as products of smaller integers, and so as products of primes.

- 0 does not contribute in any way to this process and so is not a prime number.

- 1 does not contribute to the process of breaking down larger integers, and so does not count as a prime number.

Answers

0 i   A multiple of 4 would already be a multiple of 2 – and so would have been excluded.

   ii A multiple of 9 would already be a multiple of 3 – and so would have been excluded.

   iii Smallest possible factor ≥ 10.

1 i   A multiple of 4 would already be a multiple of 2 – and so would have been excluded.
   ii A multiple of 9 would already be a multiple of 3 – and so would have been excluded.
   iii Smallest possible factor ≥ 10.
       If $N = a \times b$ with $a, b \geq 10$, then $N \geq 10 \times 10 = 100$.

2 i   A multiple of 4 would already be a multiple of 2 – and so would have been excluded.
   ii A multiple of 9 would already be a multiple of 3 – and so would have been excluded.
   iii Smallest possible factor ≥ 11.
       If $N = a \times b$ with $a, b \geq 11$, then $N \geq 11 \times 11 = 121$.

3 e   A multiple of 4, 6 or 8 would already be a multiple of 2 – and so would have been excluded.
       A multiple of 9 would already be a multiple of 3 – and so would have been excluded.
       Smallest possible factor ≥ 10.
       If $N = a \times b$ with $a, b \geq 10$, then $N \geq 10 \times 10 = 100$.
   f   i   9   iii 21   v   36%   vii 28%
       ii 15   iv 25   vi 30%   viii 25%

4 g   Smallest possible factor ≥ 17.
       If $N = a \times b$ with $a, b \geq 17$, then $N \geq 17 \times 17 = 289$.
   h   i   30   iii 40   v   24%   vii $22\frac{6}{7}$%
       ii 35   iv 46   vi $23\frac{1}{3}$%   viii 23%

β: T25 What's my number? NC

These problems challenge pupils to find efficient ways to *scan* integers ≤ 100 systematically while checking two or more simple conditions.

Answers

| 0 | a Not exactly (14 or 74) | b Yes (44) |

1 28 or 91
2 a (20 or) 26   b 23 or 29
3 35 or 42
4 4 [or 5] ([20 or] 21, or 30, or 50, or 70)
5 52 or 87
6 21 or 56 or 98
7 61 or 85

8   86
9   2 (31 or 79)
10 39 or 93
11 1 person, 11 apples
12 192, 96, 64, 48
13 a 10, 11, 12, 13, 14
    b −2, −1, 0, 1, 2 is the only other solution
       2 (If $n − 2, n − 1, n, n + 1, n + 2$;
       then $(n − 2)^2 + (n − 1)^2 + n^2 = (n + 1)^2 + (n + 2)^2$, so $n^2 = 12n$.)

β: T26 Area and perimeter problems with rectangles   NC

These problems provide a simple test of whether the familiar facts about the area and perimeter of rectangles can be applied flexibly in slightly unusual settings. (Section C18 contains a systematic approach to areas of polygons.)

Answers

> 0 Shaded area = $\frac{3}{2}$; ∴ fraction = $\frac{3}{8}$

1 area = **76**, perimeter = 2 × (9 + 14) = **46**   5 $\frac{3}{8}$

2 50 cm²   6 $\frac{1}{6}$

3 area = 4 × (3 × 8) = **96**, perimeter = **62**   7 $\frac{1}{4}$

4 576 cm²

β: T27 Divisibility A: Does it go? How do you know?   NC

This section focuses on the easiest divisibility tests – by 10 and by 5, and by 2, 4, and 8. Pupils will think they know the tests for 10, 5 and 2 already: use the section to get them to think why these tests work, to construct proofs (using the fact that 10 – the *base* for our numeral system – is itself a multiple of 2 and of 5), and to extend these proofs to derive the less familiar tests for divisibility by 4 and by 8. Divisibility tests for 3, 6 and 9 are addressed in Section C41.)

Answers

> 0 a i 4   ii 8   iii 1   iv 5   v 6   vi 4   b See text

1 a i 4   ii 3   iii 1   iv 0   v 1   vi 4   b See text

2 a i 0   ii 0   iii 1   iv 1   v 0   vi 0

   b *N* is divisible by 2 *precisely when* the units digit of *N* is 0, 2, 4, 6, or 8.
   Proof Suppose the units digit of *N* is "*u*".
   Then *N* – *u* is a multiple of 10, and hence also a multiple of 2.
   ∴ *N* = (*N* – *u*) + *u* is a multiple of 2 precisely when *u* is a multiple of 2. **QED**

> 3 a i 2   ii 2   iii 1   iv 1   v 0   vi 2
>   b *N* is divisible by 4 *precisely when* the number formed by the tens and units digit of *N* is a multiple of 4.
>   *Proof* Suppose the tens digit of *N* is *t* and the units digit of *N* is *u*.
>   Let *tu* denote the number formed by the tens and units digits.
>   Then *N* – *tu* is a multiple of 100 (= 4 × 25), and hence also a multiple of 4.
>   ∴ *N* = (*N* – *tu*) + *tu* is a multiple of 4 precisely when *tu* is a multiple of 4. **QED**
>
> 4 a i 6   ii 2   iii 1   iv 1   v 0   vi 6
>   b *N* is divisible by 8 *precisely when* the number formed by the hundreds, tens and units digits of *N* is a multiple of 8.
>   *Proof* Suppose the hundreds digit of *N* is *h*, the tens digit of *N* is *t*, and the units digit of *N* is *u*.
>   Let *htu* denote the number formed by the hundreds, tens and units digits.
>   Then *N* – *htu* is a multiple of 1000 (= 8 × 125), and hence also a multiple of 8.
>   ∴ *N* = (*N* – *htu*) + *htu* is a multiple of 8 precisely when *htu* is a multiple of 8. **QED**

β: T28 Skittles   NC

On the simplest level, this section is an exercise in *being systematic* in a very simple context. However, there is some pretty mathematics lurking just beneath the surface. For example,

- The total number of outcomes (equal to the sum of all the entries in the second row of the table) is equal to 2^6 (because it counts the number of *subsets* of the set {1, 2, 3, 4, 5, 6} of skittles).

- The second row of the table in Problem **2a** has two surprising features:
  i it is *unimodal* – that is, the entries start small, increase slowly to a maximum, and then decrease
  ii it is *symmetrical* (or palindromic, in that it reads the same forwards and backwards).

The first of these features is likely to remain an experimental observation (though one that also occurs in many similar problems). The second is perfectly accessible; some pupils will find the proof aesthetically satisfying, while the rest need to be challenged that such observations demand proof.

Answers

> **0 a** i Largest: 6 + 5 + 4 + 3 + 2 + 1 = **21, 1** way;   ii smallest: **0, 1** way
> **b** **5** ways (use some systematic enumeration: for example, listing possibilities according to the largest skittle:
> 6 + 4, 6 + 3 + 1; 5 + 4 + 1, 5 + 3 + 2; 4 + 3 + 2 + 1)

1 a 1 way (1)
  b 1 way (2)
  c 2 ways (3; 2 + 1)
  d 2 ways (4; 3 + 1)
  e 3 ways (5; 4 + 1; 3 + 2)
  f 4 ways (6; 5 + 1; 4 + 2; 3 + 2 + 1)
  g 4 ways (6 + 1; 5 + 2; 4 + 3, 4 + 2 + 1)
  h 4 ways (6 + 2; 5 + 3, 5 + 2 + 1; 4 + 3 + 1)
  i 5 ways (6 + 3, 6 + 2 + 1; 5 + 4, 5 + 3 + 1; 4 + 3 + 2)
  j 5 ways (see Problem **0b**)
  k 5 ways (6 + 5, 6 + 4 + 1, 6 + 3 + 2; 5 + 4 + 2, 5 + 3 + 2 + 1; or, to score 11 *leave a total of 10 standing* – so use Problem **1j** and list, in reverse order *miss* 6 & 4; 6 & 3 & 1, 5 & 4 & 1, 5 & 3 & 2, 4 & 3 & 2 & 1)
  l 5 ways (leave a total of 9 standing)
  m 4 ways (leave a total of 8 standing)
  n 4 ways (leave a total of 7 standing)
  o 4 ways (leave a total of 6 standing)
  p 3 ways (leave a total of 5 standing)
  q 2 ways (leave a total of 4 standing)
  r 2 ways (leave a total of 3 standing)
  s 1 way (leave a total of 2 standing)
  t 1 way (leave a total of 1 standing)

2 a

Total score	0	1	2	3	4	5	6	7	8	9	10	11	12	13	14	15	16	17	18	19	20	21
Number of ways	1	1	1	2	2	3	4	4	4	5	5	5	5	4	4	3	2	2	1	1	1

> **b** The second row reads the same forwards and backwards (because to *knock down* a total of *n* you have to *leave untouched* a total of (21 – *n*), and the number of ways to *knock down* a given total is exactly the same as the number of ways to *leave untouched* that same total).
> **c** 2^6 (different outcomes correspond to choosing different combinations of skittles; counting all such combinations is like counting routes to the cheese in Section T13, Problem **0**:
>   skittle '1' is either included or excluded (2 possibilities)
>   then skittle '2' is either included or excluded (2 possibilities)
>   then skittle '3' is either included or excluded (2 possibilities), etc.
>   ∴ the total number of outcomes is 2 × 2 × 2 × 2 × 2 × 2   **QED**)

β: C1 Averages: Use your loaf

Use the class discussion of Problem 0 to bring out the simple idea that underlies these exercises. Stress (and check when pupils are tackling later exercises) that the goal is not just to produce answers, but to develop the ability to use-what-one-knows from the first part of each group of problems to find easy ways of solving later tasks in each group.

Answers

| 0 | a | 8,13 | i | 28 | ii | 88 | iii | 138 | iv | 13 888 |
| | b | 4 | i | 44 | ii | 44 | iii | 444 | iv | 4444 |

| 1 | 7 | a 17 | b 107 | c 117 | d 1707 | e 77 | f 707 | g 7777 | h 7777 |
| 2 | a 5 | | | | | | | | |

| b | i 35 | iii 985 | v 1005 | vii 5005 | ix 55 | xi 55 |
| | ii 50 | iv 500 | vi 2005 | viii 55 | x 55 | xii 65 |

| 3 | a | i 80 | ii 30 | iii 50 | iv 70 | v 55 | vi 99 |

	b	i 57	ii 56	iii 56	iv 52					
4	a 79	b 83	c 81	d 179	e 279	f 183	g 82	h 84	i 85	j 285
5	61	6 35		7 25 kg		8 50 more mice than spiders				

β: C2 Parallel lines and alternate angles

Problem 0 serves to introduce the section and paves the way for Problem 6. However, Problems 1 and 4 (and possibly Problem 7) deserve to be used as the basis for a closing plenary.

Answers

0 $x = 45°$ (Extend CB to meet m at Y.
   ∴ ∠ABY = 80°, so ∠AYB = 45° = x (alternate angles equal))

1 ∠XPQ = ∠RQP (alternate angles); ∠YPR = ∠QRP (alternate angles);
   ∠XPY = 180° (XPY straight line)

2 ∠QPR = 0°

3 △OAB is isosceles ∴ ∠OBA = $\frac{1}{2}(180° - 50°) = 65°$, and ∠BOC = ∠OBA (alternate angles).

   △OBC is isosceles ∴ ∠OCB = $\frac{1}{2}(180° - 65°) = 57\frac{1}{2}°$

4 **Claim** Angles in ABCD add to **360°**.
   Proof i 180° + 180° = 360°
   ii ∠A + ∠B + ∠C + ∠D = 360° + 180° − 180° = 360°   **QED**

5 **Proof** Extend the side AB to X. Then CB crosses the two lines AB and DC making alternate angles ∠XBC, ∠DCB ∴ ∠XBC = 180° − ∠ABC = 90° = ∠DCB ∴ AB∥DC.
   Similarly AD∥BC.
   Draw AC. Then ∠BAC = ∠DCA (since BA∥CD), and ∠BCA = ∠DAC (since BC∥AD)   **QED**

6 a 80°   b 65°   c 77°   d 360° − (x + y)   e y + z − x

7 a (△BAC is **isosceles**); (△DAC is **isosceles** with **DA = DC**)
   b ∠ABC = ∠ADC (angles at **opposite corners** of a rhombus are **equal** by part a)

8 Let ∠CBS = x. Then ∠RBC = 2x, so ∠ABC = 180° − 2x.
   ∴ ∠BCA = x (since △BCA is isosceles)
   ∴ ∠BCA = ∠CBS so AC∥BS (alternate angles equal)   **QED**

> 9 Let $\angle ADB = x$. Then $\angle ABD = 180° - 2x$ (△BAD is isosceles).
>   Also $\angle CDB = \angle ABD$ (AB||DC). △DBC is isosceles (given) ∴ $\angle CBD = x$
>   ∴ AD||BC (alternate angles equal).   QED
> 10 a Draw AC. Then $\angle BAC = \angle DCA$ (AB||DC) and $\angle DAC = \angle BCA$ (DA||CB).
>   ∴ $\angle A = \angle DAB = \angle DAC + \angle BAC = \angle BCA + \angle DCA = \angle BCD = \angle C$.
>   Similarly $\angle B = \angle D$.
>   b $\angle A + \angle B + \angle C + \angle D = 360°$ (by Problem 4), and $\angle A = \angle C$, $\angle B = \angle D$ (given).
>   ∴ $\angle A = 180° - \angle D$.
>   Extend BA to X, then $\angle XAD = 180° - \angle BAD = \angle D = \angle CDA$.
>   ∴ AB||DC (alternate angles equal). Similarly AD||BC.   QED
> 11 90° (△BXC is isosceles; $\angle XBC = 180° - \angle ABC = \angle BAD = 2x$ (say)
>   ∴ $\angle BXC = \frac{1}{2}(180° - 2x) = 90° - x$
>   △AYD is isosceles; $\angle YAD = 180° - \angle BAD = 180° - 2x$
>   ∴ $\angle AYD = x$ ∴ $\angle XOY = 180° - \angle AYD - \angle BXC = 90°$)
> 12 90° (The internal angles at A and at B are *corresponding angles* and so have sum 180°; so if the internal angle at A is 2x, then the internal angle at B is 180° − 2x.
>   ∴ $\angle XAB = x$, $\angle XBA = 90° - x$; ∴ $\angle AXB = 90°$)

β: C3 Multiplication (integers and decimals)

There is clear evidence that these tasks are widely neglected. Problems **1-10** are deliberately slightly tongue-in-cheek, but I hope the section is short enough that the joke will not obscure the underlying message. Problem **11** should provide a useful review.

Answers

> 0 a 111 111   b 10.01

1 111 111	5 9.99999	9 9.99999
2 1.11111	6 99.9999	10 7.77777
3 222 222	7 88.8888	
4 0.999999	8 33.3333	

> 11 a 726 × 89 (unique)
>   b 66 × 11 (unique)

β: C4 Drawing conclusions C: Side-Side-Side congruence

Pupils should ideally already have a clear sense that the lengths of the three sides of a triangle determine its shape. In this section this basic intuition is formalised in the form of the SSS congruence criterion.

Answers

> 0 b iv AB = 17.3 cm, BC = 20 cm, CA = 10 cm
>   v $\angle ABC = \angle A'B'C' = 90°$, $\angle BCA = \angle B'C'A' = 60°$, $\angle CAB = \angle C'A'B' = 30°$

1 a 90°   b 120°   c 60°

2 AC = AD (radii of same circle); BC = BD (radii of same circle); AB = AB (common).
  ∴ △ACB and △ADB are congruent (by the SSS congruence criterion)
  ∴ $\angle CAB = \angle DAB$ and $\angle CBA = \angle DBA$ QED

3 XB = XC (given), BM = CM (M is the mid-point of BC); XM = XM (common side).
  ∴ △XMB and △XMC are congruent (by SSS).
  ∴ $\angle XMB = \angle XMC = \frac{1}{2}$(straight angle BMC) = 90°   QED

4 See Problem 3.

5 a DA = BC (given), AC = CA (common side), CD = AB (given).
    ∴ △DAC and △BCA are congruent (by SSS). ∴ $\angle DCA = \angle BAC$ QED
  b i AC crosses DA and BC, making $\angle DCA$ and $\angle BAC$ equal alternate angles.
      ∴ DA||CB. Similarly AB||DC

6 Join AC. Then △ACB and △CAD are congruent (by SSS).
   ∴ ∠CAB = ∠ACD, so AB∥DC; and ∠CAD = ∠ACB, so AD∥BC.   QED

---

8 OA = OB (radii of same circle); AB = BC (given); OB = OC (radii of same circle).
   ∴ △OAB and △OBC are congruent (by SSS).
   Similarly △OBC, △OCD, △ODE, △OEA are congruent.
   ∴ ∠OAB = ∠OBC = ∠OCD = ∠ODE = ∠OEA, and ∠OBA = ∠OCB = ∠ODC = ∠OED = ∠OAE
   ∴ ∠EAB = ∠EAO + ∠OAB = ∠ABO + ∠OBC = ∠ABC, etc., so all five angles are equal.   QED

9 a △BAD and △BCD are congruent (by SSS).
      ∴ ∠ABD = ∠CBD, so BD bisects ∠ABC. Similarly BD bisects ∠ADC.   QED
   b Rub out BD, draw AC and mark the mid-point M of AC.
      Then △BMA and △BMC are congruent (by SSS).
      ∴ ∠ABM = ∠CBM, so BM bisects ∠ABC.
      ∴ M lies on BD (by part **a**), so BD bisects AC and is perpendicular to AC.   QED

β: C5 Ruler and compass constructions

Ruler and compass constructions form an accessible introduction to a simple deductive system. There are two basic constructions, and one conclusion.

- (**Ruler**) Given two points A, B, the line AB through these two points may be constructed.
- (**Compasses**) Given two points A, B, the circle with centre A and passing through B may be constructed.
- Whenever two lines, or a line and a circle, or two circles can be constructed, then the point(s) where these lines/circles meet can be constructed.

This section develops the basic constructions on which all others are based.

Answers

---

0 a AB = AD = AC (radii of same circle); CB = CD = CA (radii of same circle)
   b Join AC. Then △ABC and △ADC are equilateral.
      ∴ ∠CAB = 60° = ∠ACD; ∴ AB∥DC (alternate angles equal).
      Similarly ∠ACB = 60° = ∠CAD; ∴ CB∥DA   QED
   c ∠BAC = 60° = ∠DAC
   d △ABM and △CBM are congruent (by SSS). ∴ ∠ABM = ∠CBM.
      Now rub out AC and draw BD. △ABD and △CBD are congruent (by SSS).
      ∴ ∠ABD = ∠CBD, so BD bisects ∠ABC.
      ∴ M lies on BD so BD bisects AC.   QED
      [Note: AC also bisects BD. Let N be the mid-point of BD. Then △ANB and △AND are congruent (by SSS).
      ∴ ∠BAN = ∠DAN, so AN bisects ∠BAD – whence N lies on AC.]
   e ∠CAB = 60°, ∠ABD = ∠ABM = $\frac{1}{2}$∠ABC = 30°. ∴ ∠AMB = 90°

---

2 AB = AC (given); BM = CM (given); AM = AM (common side).
   ∴ △ABM and △ACM are congruent (by SSS).
   ∴ ∠BAM = ∠CAM so AM bisects ∠BAC, and
   ∠AMB = ∠AMC = $\frac{1}{2}$(straight angle) = 90°   QED

5 Draw the circle centre A through C and the circle centre C through A. Let these two circles meet at B and D. Then BD is the perpendicular bisector of AC (by Problem **0** and Problem **4**).

6 Draw a circle with centre M meeting the line *l* at A and at C. Now use Problem **5** to construct the perpendicular bisector of AC (which must pass through the mid-point M).

7 Draw a circle with centre B meeting *l* at A and at C. Construct the mid-point M of AC. Then △BCA is isosceles, and BM is the perpendicular from B to the line *l*.

9 b $AB = AD = CB$; $CB = CD$ ∴ $ABCD$ is a rhombus with a right angle at B.
∴ $\angle ADC = \angle ABC = 90°$ (opposite angles of a rhombus are equal – by **C4**,
Problem **5a** and $\angle BAD = \angle BCD = \frac{1}{2}(360° - \angle ADC - \angle ABC) = 90°$.
∴ $ABCD$ is a square. **QED**

d Let $ACEG$ be a square constructed just like $ABCD$ in part **b**. Let AE, CG meet at O.
Prove that $OA = OC = OE = OG$.
Draw the circle centre O through A, C, E, G.
Construct the perpendicular bisectors of AC, CE, EG, GA, and let these meet
the circle at B, D, F, H. Show $ABCDEFGH$ is regular.

10 a **35°** (Let $\angle BCD = 2x$. Show $\angle BAC = 2x - 70°$, so $\angle CAX = x - 35°$ and $\angle AXC = 35°$.)

b $\frac{1}{2}b°$ (Let $\angle BCD = 2x$. Show $\angle BAC = 2x - b°$, so $\angle CAX = x - \frac{1}{2}b°$ and $\angle AXC = \frac{1}{2}b°$.)

β: C6 Totals   NC

The easiest problems (**2, 4, 6**) concern linear diophantine equations, where the need to produce solutions in positive integers often means that there are fewer solutions than one might expect. The most interesting problems (**0, 1, 5, 7, 8, 9, 10**) involve symmetric functions of three or four unknowns, for example, 'Given the values of $a + b + c$, $ab + bc + ca$ and abc, find a, b and c'.

Answers

0 **6 cm by 9 cm by 12 cm**
(Let the cuboid by a cm by b cm by c cm, where $a \leq b \leq c$.
The total length of string measures each dimension four times,
so $4(a + b + c) = 108$, $a + b + c = 27$. ∴ $b = 9$ (average).
Volume $= (abc)$ cm³, so $ac = \frac{abc}{b} = \frac{648}{9} = 72$. ∴ $a = 6, c = 12$)

1 Combined weight $= \frac{1}{2}(76 + 87 + 98) = \mathbf{130\frac{1}{2}}$ kg

Louise $= 130\frac{1}{2} - 76 = \mathbf{54\frac{1}{2}}$ kg, Jane $= 130\frac{1}{2} - 87 = \mathbf{43\frac{1}{2}}$ kg

Katy $= 130\frac{1}{2} - 98 = \mathbf{32\frac{1}{2}}$ kg

2 a i **1, 2, 4, 7** (Once one finds $8 = 3 + 5$, $9 = 3 + 3 + 3$, $10 = 5 + 5$, all larger scores can be obtained by adding some multiple of 3.)

ii **All scores > 20** (all can be achieved by i; but maximum score with 4 darts $= 4 \times 5$); also $17 = 1 \times 5 + 4 \times 3$, and $19 = 2 \times 5 + 3 \times 3$ both need more than 4 darts.

b **32** $= 4 \times 5 + 4 \times 3$ and **34** $= 5 \times 5 + 3 \times 3$ both need more than 7 darts.

3 The only solution is shown on the right. Each house contains a different number of people so the total cannot be less than $1 + 2 + 3 + 4 + 5 + 6 + 7 + 8 = 36$, so each house contains ≤ 8 people.
The four side totals add to $4 \times 15 = 60 = 36 + 24$, so the four corners have sum 24.
List the six triples adding to 15 ($8 + 6 + 1, 8 + 5 + 2, 8 + 4 + 3; 7 + 6 + 2, 7 + 5 + 3; 6 + 5 + 3$). '1' is in just one triple, so cannot be in a corner
∴ $\boxed{8 : 1 : 6}$, and the other two corners have sum 10
∴ Neither 2 nor 5 can go in a corner. The rest follows.

8	1	6
4		2
3	5	7

4 a **13** Zids, **1** Zod; or **4** Zids, **6** Zods

b **17** Zids, **3** Zods; or **8** Zids, **8** Zods

5 Sleepy **33** stone, Bashful **22** stone, Dopey **11** stone, Lazy **10** stone.
(Let Bashful weight b stone, etc. Then $43 + 54 + 65 + 66 = 3(b + d + l + s)$,
so $b + d + l + s = 76$. Hence Sleepy weighs $(76 - 43)$ stone etc.)

6 a **19** ($74 = 17 \times 4 + 2 \times 3$): **17** chairs, **2** stools

b **24** ($74 = 2 \times 4 + 22 \times 3$): **2** chairs, **22** stools

7 Andy **6**, Ben **7**, Caz **11**, Den **12**
($3(a + b + c + d) = 30 + 29 + 25 + 24 = 108$, so $a + b + c + d = 36$
∴ Andy scores $36 - 30$ etc.)

8 a $3\frac{1}{2}, 2\frac{1}{2}, 1\frac{1}{2}$ b $4\frac{1}{2}, 3\frac{1}{2}, 2\frac{1}{2}$ c $4\frac{1}{4}, 3, 2\frac{1}{2}$

9 a Volume $(3 \times 5 \times 7)$ cm³; edges **7** cm, **5** cm, **3** cm (If a cm × b cm × c cm, then $15 \times 21 \times 35 = (abc)^2$)

   b Volume (5×15) cm³; edges 6 cm, 5 cm, $\frac{5}{2}$ cm

   c Volume (1) cm³; edges $\frac{15}{4}$ cm, $\frac{3}{5}$ cm, $\frac{4}{9}$ cm

10 **1 cm by 24 cm by 25 cm**
(Suppose a cm × b cm × c cm with $c \leq b \leq a$. Then $abc = 600$, $ab + bc + ca = 649$, $a + b + c = 50$. $c < 3$, or else the *largest* product of two dimensions $ab \leq 200$ so $ab + bc + ca$ cannot be 649.)

β: C7 Drawing conclusions *D*: Side-Angle-Side congruence

The SAS congruence criterion is one of the most basic building blocks of elementary Euclidean geometry. This and the basic property of parallel lines are what allow us to transfer information from one configuration to another. Ideally, the basic insight which underpins Problem **0** should already be known – in which case Problem **0** should be used to make this insight explicit and to prepare the way for the formal statement of the SAS congruence criterion and for its application to produce simple proofs of mildly non-obvious results.

Answers

0 e	i Equal	ii Equal	iii Equal

2   $CE = CB$ (radii of same circle); $\angle ACE = \angle DCE$ (vertically opposite angles);
    $CA = CD$ (radii of same circle).
    ∴ △ACE and △DCB are congruent (by SAS)
    ∴ $AE = DB$ **QED**

3   $PC = OC$ (radii of same circle); $\angle PCO = \angle OCY$ (same angle);
    $CX = CY$ (radii of same circle).
    ∴ △PCX and △OCY are congruent (by SAS)
    ∴ $\angle YOC = \angle XPC$ **QED**

4   $AM = BM$ (given); $\angle AMD = \angle BMD$ (vertically opposite angles);
    $MD = MC$ (given).
    ∴ △AMD and △BMC are congruent (by SAS)
    ∴ $AD = BC$ as required.
    Also $\angle YOC = \angle XPC$.
    ∴ $AD \parallel CB$ (alternate angles equal)   **QED**

5   △OAB is isosceles ∴ $\angle OAB = \angle OBA$. Also △YOA and △XOB are congruent (by SAS)
    ∴ $\angle OAY = \angle OBX$.
    ∴ $\angle YAB = \angle OAB - \angle OAY = \angle OBA - \angle OBX = \angle XBA$ **QED**

8   $30°$

9   Show $\angle CED = 35°$

10   △ABC is isosceles ($AB = AC$) ∴ $\angle ABC = \angle ACB$
     ∴ $\angle CBI = \frac{1}{2}\angle CBA = \frac{1}{2}\angle BCA = \angle BCI$
     ∴ △IBC is isosceles with $IB = IC$ **QED**

11   Join BD. Then △DBA and △BDC are congruent (by SAS) ∴ $AD = BC$
     Also $\angle ADB = \angle CDB$ ∴ $AD = BC$ (alternate angles equal).   **QED**

12 *This may prove highly elusive! The clue is to use ∠DAC + ∠ACB = 180° to create a straight angle at A, by constructing a copy of ∠ACB next to ∠DAC.*
Extend DA to B' such that AB' = CB.
Then △AB'C and △CBA are congruent (by SAS).
∴ CB' = AB = CD and ∠CB'A = ∠ABC = ∠B
∴ △CDB' is isosceles, so ∠CB'A = ∠CDA = ∠D.

β: C8 Prime factorisation B   NC

The context (rectangles and squares) is a way of encouraging pupils to think about factorisation of integers. It should be exploited to enhance the focus on *significant features of factorisation*. However the match between geometry and number theory is far from perfect; where the geometry gets in the way, try to emphasise the number theoretic classification.

Answers

0 3 (12 × 1, 6 × 2, 4 × 3)

1

Number of unit squares	Number of different rectangles	Number of squares
3	1	–
4	2	1
5	1	–
6	2	–
7	1	–
8	2	–
9	2	1
10	2	–
11	1	–
12	3	–
14	2	–
16	3	1
17	1	–
20	3	–
24	4	–
27	2	–
32	3	–
36	5	1
47	1	–
48	5	–
49	2	1
72	6	–
81	3	1
83	1	–
91	2	–
97	1	–

2 **a** 3, 5, 7, 11, 17, 47, 83, 97   **b** prime numbers

3 **a** 4, 6, 8, 9, 10, 14, 27, 49, 91

b A: **4, 9, 49** are squares of prime numbers (1 long thin rectangle and 1 square)
B: **8, 27** are the cubes of prime numbers (2 rectangles, 0 squares)
C: **6, 10, 14, 91** are the product of two distinct prime numbers (2 rectangles, 0 squares)

c A: 121, B: 125 = 5^3, C: 123 = 3 × 41

4 a 12, 16, 20, 32, 81

> b **12** (3 rectangles, 0 squares), **16** (3 rectangles, 1 square)
> Three groups: *A*: **16, 81** (4th powers of a prime number: 3 rectangles, 1 square)
> *B*: **32** (5th power of a prime number: 3 rectangles, 0 squares)
> *C*: **12, 20** (square of one prime times another: 3 rectangles, 0 squares)

β: C9 Fractions and decimals   NC

Fractions arise from sharing or dividing integers into parts. Decimals are strongly linked to our *base 10* numeral system and arise from measuring. The remarkable connection between these very different ways of representing numbers should be one of the jewels of school mathematics, but it presupposes an ease in moving from one to the other and back. This section constitutes a very simple beginning; the story continues to unfold in Sections **C22** and **C35** and more particularly in Book *Gamma*.

Answers

0 a i $\frac{4}{10} = \frac{2}{5}$ iii $\frac{125}{100} = \frac{5}{4}$ v $\frac{20\,032}{10\,000} = \frac{1252}{625}$

      ii $\frac{12}{100} = \frac{3}{25}$ iv $\frac{125}{1000} = \frac{1}{8}$ vi $\frac{625}{10\,000} = \frac{1}{16}$

   b i $\frac{1}{10}$ ii $\frac{15}{10}$ iii $\frac{2}{100}$ vii $\frac{25}{10\,000}$ viii $\frac{8}{1000}$

1 a i $\frac{75}{100}$ v $\frac{15}{100}$ vii $\frac{225}{100}$

      iii $\frac{625}{1000}$ vi $\frac{28}{100}$ ix $\frac{2}{1000}$

   b i $\frac{3}{10}$ v $\frac{125}{100} = \frac{5}{4}$ ix $\frac{1096}{1000} = \frac{137}{125}$

      ii $\frac{6}{10} = \frac{3}{5}$ vi $\frac{236}{100} = \frac{59}{25}$ x $\frac{16}{10\,000} = \frac{1}{625}$

      iii $\frac{24}{100} = \frac{6}{25}$ vii $\frac{1125}{1000} = \frac{9}{8}$ xi $\frac{2008}{1000} = \frac{251}{125}$

      iv $\frac{35}{100} = \frac{7}{20}$ viii $\frac{875}{1000} = \frac{7}{8}$ xii $\frac{13\,125}{10\,000} = \frac{21}{16}$

2 a $\frac{12}{5} = 2.4$ b $\frac{33}{10} = 3.3$ c $\frac{7}{4} = 1.75$ d $\frac{11}{8} = 1.375$

3 i $\frac{1}{2} = 0.5$ iv $\frac{4}{5} = 0.8$ ix $\frac{9}{10} = 0.9$ xv $\frac{3}{500} = 0.006$

   iii $\frac{3}{4} = 0.75$ vii $\frac{7}{8} = 0.875$ xiv $\frac{7}{4} = 1.75$ xvii $\frac{1}{200} = 0.005$

β: C10 Knights and Knaves

These problems are perfectly accessible provided one does not try to do too many at once. But they are far from easy. Don't expect all pupils to complete the same number of problems: it is better to complete two problems systematically and successfully than to rush ahead and get things wrong.

Because the material is likely to be unfamiliar, it may make sense for pupils to tackle Problem **0** in pairs – partly to allow the teacher to assess what needs to be brought out in the class discussion. Pupils need to learn to be systematic; but they also need to experience the confusion (and brain-ache) that results from *failing* to be systematic. So resist the temptation to provide a premature method.

3B Beta

Answers

> 0 a No
>
>   b **Yes** (If *C* is a Knight, then he would be telling the truth, so *B* is lying – and hence a Knave, but then *B*'s statement would be true! Hence **C is a Knave**, *C*'s statement is false, so *B*'s statement is correct and **B is a Knight**.)

1 **D Knave, E Knight** (If *E* is lying, then *E* is telling the truth! This is impossible; ∴ *E* is a Knight, so *D* must be a Knave.)

2 **F Knave, G Knave, H unclear** (If *F* was telling the truth, then *G* would be a Knight; but *G* contradicts *F*. ∴ *F* is a Knave.
If *G* was telling the truth, then *H* would be a Knight, but *H* contradicts *G* ∴ *G* is a Knave.
H may be either Knight or a Knave – we cannot tell.)

3 **J Knave, K Knight, L Knave** (*J* cannot be telling the truth – or he would be a Knight! ∴ *J* is a Knave, and at least one of the other two is a Knight.
If *K* were a Knave, *L* would be a Knight, and so *K*'s statement would be true - contradicting the fact that he is a Knave. ∴ *K* is a Knight and is telling the truth. ∴ *L* is a Knave.)

4 **M and N are both Knaves** (*M* cannot be telling the truth – or he would be a Knight; ∴ *M* is a Knave and is lying, so *N* is a Knave.)

> 5 a **Q is a Knave, R is a Knight** (Neither tribe can say 'I am a Knave', so *Q* is lying.)
>
>   b **T Knave, U Knight, S unknown** (*U* contradicts *T*, so *U* and *T* cannot both be Knights. If *T* were a Knight, then *U* would be a Knave; then *T*'s claim that *S* said 'There is just one Knight' would be true, so this is what *S* said, but then *S* would be a second Knight.)
>
> 6 1 Knight (*X*) and 4 Knaves
>
> 7 Tweedledum is a Knight, Tweedledee is a Knave
>
> 8 a γαβδε   b βεδαγ
>
> 9 a π is a **Knave**, θ is **Normal**, ρ is a **Knight**
>
>   b If σ speaks truly, then so does τ; so σ is Normal (and speaks truly).
>   If σ speaks falsely, then τ cannot be a Knight, but speaks truly – so τ is Normal.

β: C11 Calculating angles   NC

A significant (and important) part of this section is the expectation that pupils should interpret each problem themselves and *draw their own diagrams*.

Answers

> 0 $r = 41°$, $s = 48°$, $t = 91°$, $u = 57°$, $v = 32°$, $w = 29°$, $x = 62°$, $y = 47°$; z is elusive!

1 a 60°	b 270°	c 165°
2 a **2 × 360°** (= 12 × 60°)	b **9 × 360°** (=12 × 270°)	c $5\frac{1}{2}$ **× 360°** (= 12 × 165°)
3 106°, 74°	7 75°	
4 ∠BDA = 40°, ∠BDC = 77°	8 75°	
5 75°	9 114°	
6 ∠RTS = 61°, ∠TSR = 29°		

> 10 a $(180 - x - y)°$ b ∠ADB = $(x + y)°$, ∠ABC = $(180 - 2x - y)°$
>
> 11 $(x + y)°$ 12 $(2x - 180)°$

β: C12 Percentage change   NC

Be prepared to work quite hard in Problem 0. Insist on *multiplicative* methods and mental arithmetic, rather than allowing the language of increase and decrease to trigger addition and subtraction which leads to the need to calculate intermediate answers, consequent slowness, more frequent errors, and a lack of insight into problems like Problem **0c** and Problem **10**.

Answers

0	a	i	8	ii	6.4				
	b	i	32	ii	48	iii	38.4	iv	38.4
	c	i	£38.40	ii	£38.40				

1 a 32   b 38.4   c 38.4   d 48

2 95%   3 70%

4 a $\frac{120}{100}\left(=\frac{6}{5}\right)$ c $\frac{170}{100}\left(=\frac{17}{10}\right)$ e $\frac{200}{100}(=2)$

   b $\frac{117}{100}$ d $\frac{183}{100}$ f $\frac{239}{100}$

5 a $\frac{70}{100}\left(=\frac{7}{10}\right)$ c $\frac{50}{100}\left(=\frac{1}{2}\right)$ e $\frac{39}{100}$

   b $\frac{91}{100}$ d $\frac{63}{100}$ f $\frac{0}{100}(=0)$

6 a $\frac{108}{100} \times 300 = 324$ c $\frac{90}{100} \times 80 = 72$

   b $\frac{80}{100} \times 400 = 320$ d $\frac{130}{100} \times 60 = 78$

7 a $A:B = 113:100$ b $X:Y = 79:100$

8 a 107 : 100   b 7 : 107   c $\frac{100}{7}$

9 a $16\frac{2}{3}\%$ $\left(\frac{800}{4800} = \frac{x}{100}\right)$ b £135 $\left(\frac{x}{1125} = \frac{12}{100}\right)$

> 10 All give the same result $\left(\text{If the bill is } £B, \text{ each calculates } £\frac{90}{100} \times \frac{117.5}{100} \times \frac{112}{100} \times £B\right)$
>
> 11 a 20%   b 25%
>
> 12 a Just under **4 years**: $(1.2)^4 = 2.0736$
>
>   b Just under **4 years**: $(1.5)^4 = 5.065$
>
>   c Just under **8 years**: $(1.1)^2 = 1.21$ so use **a**; or $(1.1)^8 = 2.1435$
>
>   d Just under **15 years**: $(1.05)^{15} = 2.0789\ldots$ $((1.05)^2 = 1.1025$, so **c** gives <16 years)

β: C13 Approximate calculation: Addition and subtraction NC

Estimation is generally held to be 'a good thing'. But the mathematics and didactics of estimation and approximation are poorly understood.

Approximation depends on *exact calculation*: its methods are based on *tweaking* the procedures of exact calculation – which can only be done with understanding if those exact procedures have been clearly mastered. This section is concerned with the most basic aspect of this tweaking process: namely obtaining *upper* and *lower* bounds for the errors introduced.

Answers

> 0 a i **80 + 30** gives a *lower* bound; **90 + 40** gives an *upper* bound.
>   **85 + 35** may be closer, but it takes effort to see whether it is too small or too big.
>
>   ii **5600 + 3400** gives a *lower* bound; **5700 + 3500** gives an *upper* bound.
>
>   b i **80 – 40** gives a *lower* bound; **90 – 30** gives an *upper* bound.
>   **85 – 35** may be closer; but it takes effort to see whether it is too small or too big.
>
>   ii **5600 – 3500** gives a *lower* bound; **5700 – 3400** gives an *upper* bound.
>   Other methods make it hard to see whether the approximation is too big or too small.

3B Beta

1. **a** **i** 340 + 170 gives a *lower* bound; 350 + 180 gives an *upper* bound.
   ii 345 + 175 may be closer; but it takes effort to see whether it is too small or too big.
   b **i** 340 − 180 gives a *lower* bound; 350 − 170 gives an *upper* bound.
   ii 345 − 175 may be closer; but it takes effort to see whether it is too small or too big.

2. **a** **i** 3000 + 1700 gives a *lower* bound; 3100 + 1800 gives an *upper* bound.
   ii 4800 + 700 gives a *lower* bound; 4900 + 800 gives an *upper* bound.
   b **i** 3000 − 1800 gives a *lower* bound; 3100 − 1700 gives an *upper* bound.
   ii 4800 − 800 gives a *lower* bound; 4900 − 700 gives an *upper* bound.

3. **a** **i** 3055 + 1784: **4000 + 2000** gives an *upper* bound; **3000 + 1000** gives a *lower* bound.
   4860 + 721: **5000 + 1000** gives an *upper* bound; **4000 + 0** gives a *lower* bound.
   ii 3055 + 1784: **3100 + 1800** gives an *upper* bound; **3000 + 1700** gives a *lower* bound.
   4860 + 721: **4900 + 800** gives an *upper* bound; **4800 + 700** gives a *lower* bound.
   iii 3055 + 1784: **3060 + 1790** gives an *upper* bound; **3050 + 1780** gives a *lower* bound.
   4860 + 721: **4860 + 730** gives an *upper* bound; **4860 + 720** gives a *lower* bound.
   b **i** 20 (unless one of the numbers is an exact multiple of 10)
   ii 30 (unless one or more of the numbers is an exact multiple of 10)
   c **i** 200 (unless one of the numbers is an exact multiple of 100)
   ii 300 (unless one or more of the numbers is an exact multiple of 100)

4. If you make both numbers in 87 − 32 *larger*, you get 90 − 40 = 50 which is **less than 87 − 32**

5. **a** **i** 3055 − 1784: **4000 − 1000** gives an *upper* bound; **3000 − 2000** gives a *lower* bound.
   4860 − 721: **5000 − 0** gives an *upper* bound; **4000 − 1000** gives a *lower* bound.
   ii 3055 − 1784: **3100 − 1700** gives an *upper* bound; **3000 − 1800** gives a *lower* bound.
   4860 − 721: **4900 − 700** gives an *upper* bound; **4800 − 800** gives a *lower* bound.
   iii 3055 − 1784: **3060 − 1780** gives an *upper* bound; **3050 − 1790** gives a *lower* bound.
   4860 − 721: **4860 − 720** gives an *upper* bound; **4860 − 730** gives a *lower* bound.
   b 20 (unless one number is an exact multiple of 10)
   c 200 (unless one number is an exact multiple of 100)

6. **a** Upper: 8000 − 8000 + 8000 = **8000**; or 7900 − 8400 + 7300 = **6800**; or 7900 − 8430 + 7300 = **6770**
   Lower: 7000 − 9000 + 7000 = **5000**; or 7800 − 8500 + 7200 = **6500**; or 7890 − 8440 + 7290 = **6740**
   b Upper: 4000 − 7000 + 5000 = **2000**; or 3900 − 7200 + 4500 = **1200**; or 3870 − 7290 + 4440 = **1020**
   Lower: 3000 − 8000 + 4000 = **−1000**; or 3800 − 7300 + 4400 = **900**; or 3860 − 7300 + 4430 = **990**
   c Upper: 10000 − 3000 − 3000 = **4000**; or 9300 − 3700 − 3800 = **1800**; or 9240 − 3790 − 3860 = **1590**
   Lower: 9000 − 4000 − 4000 = **1000**; or 9200 − 3800 − 3900 = **1500**; or 9230 − 3800 − 3870 = **1560**

7. Must go for upper bound (assuming no wastage): 2 × 407.5 + 2 × 273.5 = **1362 m**

β: C14 Calculating with measures   NC

Calculating with measures is the most common everyday application of elementary mathematics. Hence it is important to provide a regular diet of challenging exercises that develop confidence in using more recently acquired arithmetical skills (fractions, compound measures, ratio, etc.).

Answers

> 0 a £18.48 $\left(= £14 \times 1.32 = £14 \times 1.3 + \left(£14 \times \frac{1}{50}\right)\right)$ b £18.41 to nearest penny

1 a £10.46 (= £2 × 5.23)   b £9.62
2 a 67 p (= 13.4 × 5)   b 63 p (= 13.4 × 4.7)
3 1.1 m
4 a 37.5 miles (= $\frac{5}{4}$ × 30 miles)   b 40.5 miles (= $\frac{5}{4}$ × 32.4 miles)   c 57.1 miles
5 a 16 800 litres (= 140 × 120 litres) b 32 310 litres (= 143.6 × 225 litres)
6 90 minutes
7 a £25 × (3 × 4) = £300   b £291.65
8 a £5.70 (= £2.20 + £0.14 × 25)   b 5.4 km

> 9 750 m

β: C15 Drawing conclusions E: Angle-Side-Angle   NC

Practical activities with a theoretical purpose are often neglected. Problem **0** is intended to cement the key physical insight which lies behind the ASA congruence criterion, and to provide teachers with an opportunity to extract the more general underlying principle.

Like all constructions based on measuring, Problem **0** requires you to be aware of, and to cultivate a sensitivity to, the distinction between 'the *exact* triangle *ABC*' determined by the given data, and the physical triangle you manage to construct yourself. (For example, Problem **0c** shows that the exact triangle *ABC* satisfies *AC* = *AB* = 10.5 cm – no matter what approximate measurement you yourself may arrive at.) Problem **0b** may appear straightforward, but it encapsulates what lies behind the congruence criteria, and so should not be treated too hastily.

Answers

> 0 c *AC* = 10.5 cm, *BC* ≈ 17 cm
>   d ∠*ACB* = 180° − 108° − 36° = 36° ∴ △*ABC* is isosceles, so *AC* = *AB* = 10.5 cm
>   e 5 (In a regular pentagon *VWXYZ* with sides of length *VW* = 10.5 cm, the five triangles *VWX*, *WXY*, *XYZ*, *YZV*, *ZVW* are all isosceles with apex angle 108° and legs of length 10.5 cm.)

1 (A) ∠*BAC* = ∠*DCA* (alternate angles, *AB*||*DC*)
   (S) *AC* = *CA*   (common side)
   (A) ∠*BCA* = ∠*DAC* (alternate angles *AD*||*BC*)
   ∴ △*ABC* and △*CDA* are congruent (by ASA) ∴ *AB* = *DC* and *BC* = *DA*
   Also ∠*ABC* = ∠*CDA* and ∠*BAD* = ∠*BAC* + ∠*CAD* = ∠*DCA* + ∠*ACD* = ∠*DCB*   QED

2 If ∠*ABD* = *x*, then ∠*CBD* = 90° − *x*; ∴ ∠*CDB* = *x* (angles in △*CBD*)
   ∴ *AB*||*DC* (alternate angles equal). Similarly *AD*||*BC*.   QED

3 Let *AC*, *BD* cross at *X*.
   Then (A) ∠*XAD* = ∠*XCB* (alternate angles, *AD*||*BC*)
        (S) *AD* = *CB*   (opposite sides of a parallelogram are equal by Problem 1)
        (A) ∠*ADX* = ∠*CBX* (alternate angles, *AD*||*BC*)
   ∴ △*XAD* and △*XCB* are congruent (by ASA), so *XA* = *XC* and *XD* = *XB*   QED

5 △ABC is isosceles. ∴ ∠ABC = ∠ACB. Hence
(A) ∠QBC = $\frac{1}{2}$∠ABC = $\frac{1}{2}$∠ACB = ∠PCB
(S) BC = CB (same side)
(A) ∠BCQ = ∠CBP (base angles of △ABC)
∴ △QBC and △PCB are congruent, so QC = PB. **QED**

6 ∠BXM = ∠CYM = 90°; ∴ BX∥YC (alternate angles equal). Hence
(A) ∠XBM = ∠YCM (= 90°)
(S) BM = CM (given: M is the mid-point of BC)
(A) ∠BMX = ∠CMY (vertically opposite angles)
∴ △XBM and △YCM are congruent (by ASA); ∴ BX = CY **QED**

β: C16 Ordering fractions   NC

These problems should be relatively straightforward; they may therefore highlight gaps and weaknesses more clearly than harder sections. In re-writing each pair of fractions with a common denominator, make explicit use of earlier work on *hcf*s and *lcm*s (T21).

Answers

0 a $\frac{5}{12}$ $\left(\frac{3}{8} = \frac{9}{24}; \frac{5}{12} = \frac{10}{24}\right)$ b $\frac{137}{57}$ $\left(\frac{137}{57} = \frac{5 \times 137}{5 \times 57}, \frac{228}{95} = \frac{3 \times 228}{3 \times 95}\right)$

1 $\frac{3}{4}$ $\left(\frac{3}{4} = \frac{9}{12}; \frac{2}{3} = \frac{8}{12}\right)$ 6 $\frac{11}{25}$ $\left(\frac{5}{12} = \frac{125}{300}; \frac{11}{25} = \frac{132}{300}\right)$ 11 $\frac{7}{12}$

2 $\frac{4}{7}$ $\left(\frac{1}{7} > \frac{1}{9}\right)$ 7 $\frac{5}{8}$ (= 0.625)   12 $\frac{13}{21}$

3 $\frac{2}{3}$ $\left(\frac{2}{3} = \frac{16}{24}; \frac{5}{8} = \frac{15}{24}\right)$ 8 $\frac{43}{50}$ (a mark of 86%)   13 $\frac{17}{12}$

4 $\frac{4}{7}$ $\left(\frac{4}{7} = \frac{36}{63}; \frac{5}{9} = \frac{35}{63}\right)$ 9 $\frac{5}{12}$

5 $\frac{4}{10}$ $\left(\frac{3}{8} = \frac{15}{40}; \frac{4}{10} = \frac{16}{40}\right)$ 10 $\frac{5}{8}$

14 $\left(\frac{8}{5}\right) \div \left(\frac{2}{8}\right)$ (= 6.4; $\left(\frac{5}{2}\right) \div \left(\frac{5}{8}\right)$ = 4)

15 It all depends how you measure.
If you assume the different denominators represent different amounts of work (so the first test was justifiably worth more than twice as much as the second), then it makes sense to add up the marks and work out the total as a percentage – ignoring the fact that Joanna missed the first test. Joe: $\frac{120}{130}$ (that is, 92.3%); Joanna: $\frac{73}{79}$ (that is, 92.4%).
If you assume that each test was in fact worth more or less the same, then it makes sense to work out each mark as a percentage and then to average the percentages: Joe: (90.2%, 95.8%, 96%, 90% with an average of) 93%; Joanna: (87.5%, 96%, 93.3%, average) 92.26%.

β: C17 Word problems B   NC

A regular diet of word problems helps to ensure that students can interpret written sentences and can use the simple mathematics they know; it also provides practice in thinking about unfamiliar elementary problems.

Answers

0 19-er (= (3 + 3 + 3 + 3 + 3) + 4)

| 1 | 24 000 km (= (30 000 × 4) ÷ 5) | 3 | 40 | 5 | 240 |
| 2 | 125 | | | 4 | 6:50 am |

> 6 150 girls 7 £96
>
> 8 864 (1 human pint = 12^3 'Lilliput pints')
>
> 9 1998 (Let Methuselah be y years old. Then Moses is $y - 666$ years old. When Moses is as old as Methuselah is now, Moses will be y years old! $\therefore y - 666 = 2 \times \frac{y}{3}$.)
>
> 10 15 years

β: C18 Area of triangles and parallelograms   NC

This section derives the familiar formulae for the area of triangles and parallelograms. Although both formulae should be known, the way in which they can be uniformly derived from the formula for the area of a rectangle is likely to be less familiar. That may be a place for a teacher-led plenary to summarise and review the important conclusions of the section.

Answers

> 0 They are *equal*. (The diagonal splits the rectangle into two congruent right-angled triangles (X and Y). It also splits the bottom left rectangle into two congruent triangles (A and B), and the top right rectangle into two congruent triangles (C and D). $\therefore X - A - C = Y - B - D$.)

1 a 148 m² (= 24 × 17 − 20 × 13)   b 190 m² (= 25 × 18 − 20 × 13)

2 390 cm² (= 46 × 378 − 41 × 32)   3 5.04 m² (= 4 × 5 − 4.4 × 3.4)

4 a 17 m²   b 32 m² (Shaded area = $2ab + b(2c + b) = b(2a + b + 2c)$)

5 Let the perpendicular from P to BC meet BC at X.
   $\therefore$ area(BXP) = $\frac{1}{2}$ area(BXPA), area(CXP) = $\frac{1}{2}$ area(CXPD),
   so area(BPC) = $\frac{1}{2}$ area(ABCD)

> 6 a △BMA and △BMC are congruent (by SAS):
>   (S) BM = BM = 1 (common side); (A) ∠BMA = ∠BMC = 90°; (S) MA = MC = 1.
>
>   b $\therefore$ BA = BC; △BMA, △BMC are isosceles triangles, ∠BAM = ∠BCM = **45°**, so ∠ABC = **90°**.
>
>   c Similarly BC = BX and ∠CBX = 90°.
> $\therefore$ (S) AB = CB
>   (A) ∠ABC = ∠CBX
>   (S) BC = BX,
>   so △ABC and △CBX are congruent (SAS), and are congruent to △XBY and △YBA.
> $\therefore$ area (ACXY) = 2^2 = 4 × area(△ABC), so area(△ABC) = 1.
>
>   d Taking AB as base, △ABC has height BC.
>   But BC = AB, so area(△ABC) = $\frac{1}{2}$(AB × BC).
> $\therefore$ 1 = $\frac{1}{2}$ AB², so AB = $\sqrt{2}$.
>
> 11 a Draw the line through P parallel to AB, meeting AD at Q.
>   Then area(ABP) = area(PQA).
> $\therefore$ area(ABPQ) : area(QPCD) = 4 : 3, so BP : PC = **4 : 3**.
>
>   b BP : PC = 6 : 4 = **3 : 2**.

β: C19 Simplifying fractions B   NC

This section exploits work on *hcfs* and *lcms* to show that many messy-looking fraction calculations are nicer than they seem.

Answers

0 a $\frac{1}{6} + \frac{1}{12} = \frac{1}{4}$ b $\frac{1}{6} - \frac{7}{48} = \frac{1}{48}$

1 a $\frac{1}{2}$ c $\frac{1}{6}$ e $\frac{1}{12}$ g $\frac{4}{5}$
  b $\frac{1}{4}$ d $\frac{1}{10}$ f $\frac{1}{4}$ h $\frac{5}{13}$

2 a $\frac{1}{4} - \frac{1}{4} = 0$ c $\frac{1}{6} + \frac{1}{12} = \frac{1}{4}$ e $\frac{1}{4} - \frac{1}{2} + \frac{1}{4} = 0$
  b $\frac{1}{4} + \frac{1}{12} = \frac{1}{3}$ d $\frac{4}{5} - \frac{1}{10} = \frac{7}{10}$

3 a $\frac{5}{18}$ c $\frac{5}{7}$ e $\frac{7}{48}$ g $\frac{19}{34}$
  b $\frac{3}{8}$ d $\frac{23}{27}$ f $\frac{27}{28}$ h $\frac{11}{20}$

4 a $\frac{3}{8} - \frac{1}{4} = \frac{1}{8}$ c $\frac{11}{20} - \frac{1}{10} = \frac{9}{20}$ e $\frac{27}{28} - \frac{5}{7} = \frac{1}{4}$
  b $\frac{5}{18} - \frac{1}{6} = \frac{1}{9}$ d $\frac{1}{6} - \frac{7}{48} = \frac{1}{48}$

5 a $\frac{4}{16} - \frac{3}{16} = \frac{1}{16}$ d $\frac{1}{12}$ g $\frac{3}{80}$ j $\frac{1}{45}$
  b $\frac{35}{42} = \frac{5}{6}$ e $\frac{1}{4}$ h $\frac{1}{240}$ k $\frac{1}{15}$
  c $\frac{1}{6}$ f $\frac{1}{4}$ i $\frac{2}{45}$

β: C20 Ratio   NC

Ratio and proportion are at the root of many applications of elementary mathematics; they are also important within mathematics itself. They are however poorly understood. This section (and sections in book *Gamma*) seek to plug this gap.

A *ratio* links two quantities with the same units; in this section ratios are represented schematically by line segments – initially horizontal, but later sometimes vertical. A *proportion* is an 'equality of ratios'; in this section, proportions are represented schematically by rectangular diagrams.

Answers

0 a i $\frac{5}{6}$ ii $\frac{14}{3} : \frac{28}{5} = 5 : 6$ c £14, £21; 14 : 21 = 2 : 3
  b i $\frac{3}{40}$ ii 60 : 800 = 3 : 40

1 a i $\frac{3}{10}$ ii $\frac{8}{9}$ iii $\frac{4}{9}$ iv $\frac{14}{33}$ v $\frac{14}{45}$
  b i $\frac{2}{5}$ ii $\frac{4}{25}$ iii $\frac{3}{25}$ iv $\frac{3}{2}$ v $\frac{7}{5}$
    vi $\frac{3}{5}$ vii $\frac{7}{27}$ viii $\frac{3}{14}$ ix $\frac{17}{7}$
  c i $\frac{6}{25}$ ii $\frac{13}{50}$ iii $\frac{9}{20}$ iv $\frac{30}{17}$ v $\frac{2}{45}$

2 a $\frac{32}{15} = 2\frac{2}{15}$ (cf **1aiii**)   b 60 p (cf **1biii**)   c 132 (cf **1cv**)

3 a £30   b $58\frac{2}{3}$ miles   c $19\frac{1}{4}$ hours   d $\frac{3}{5}$ kg = 600 g   e 14   f 540

4 a $33\frac{1}{3}$%; 1 : 3   b 40%; 2 : 5

5 a $\alpha = \frac{9}{8}$; $\beta = \frac{8}{9}$ c $\alpha = \frac{5}{7}$; $\beta = \frac{7}{5}$ e $\alpha = \frac{17}{30}$; $\beta = \frac{30}{17}$

   b $\alpha = \frac{33}{14}$; $\beta = \frac{14}{33}$ d $\alpha = \frac{7}{17}$; $\beta = \frac{17}{7}$ f $\alpha = \frac{5}{3}$; $\beta = \frac{3}{5}$

6 a i £24 : £36   ii £25 : £35   iii £48 : £12
   b i 18 kg : 30 kg   ii 8 kg : 40 kg   iii 27 kg : 21 kg
   c £3 : £1.20 : £5.40

7 13   8 £36 : £18 : £12

9 a 9   b $7\frac{1}{2}$ c −6 (−$13\frac{1}{2}$ is *less than* −9)   d 20 : 30

---

10 20, 30 or −20, −30 (numbers do not have to be positive, or integers)

11 *X*: **£200**; *Y*: **£250** (In 1 day *X* lays $\frac{1}{10}$ wall, *Y* lays $\frac{1}{8}$ wall: ratio 4 : 5)

12 Craftsman: **£308**; Trainee: **£132** (ratio of pay = 7 × 8 : 4 × 6 = 56 : 24)

---

13 a 60 p   b 30 p   17 a 120 km   b $\frac{x}{8} \times 48 = 6x$ km

14 a 8 mm   b 37.5 km   18 a 50 minutes   b $7\frac{1}{2}$ km

15 $\frac{4}{5}$ 19 £1.62

16 a £18   b £5.62 $\left(\frac{1}{2}\right)$ c £ $\left(\frac{9t}{2}\right)$ 20 a 42   b −34

21 a 27   b $6\frac{1}{2}$ c $\frac{32}{3}$ d $\frac{23}{7}$

22 160 (not 320: '60% *of the rest* are yellow')

β: C21 Highest common factors and least common multiples B   NC

Pupils need fluency with *hcfs* and *lcms* (for example, to support work with fractions). But they also need the experience of relating these numerical ideas to word problems. Some of the problems in this section may be surprisingly elusive.

Answers

0 a **12** pieces each **1.85 m × 1.85 m**
   b **819 cm × 819 cm** (= 13 × 63 cm by 9 × 91 cm); **13 × 9** tiles

1 9 × 7 patches, each 27 cm × 27 cm

2 118 (= 2 × (36 + 23)); 12 m

3 27 × 20

4 **8.19 m** (= 9 father's paces = 13 son's paces) before they put *a foot* down together; **16.38 m** (= 18 father's paces = 26 son's paces) before they put *the same foot* down together

5 11 (= *hcf*(176,231))

6 a **9 m**; **170** (= 2 × (41 + 44))   b **9 m**; **230** (= 2 × (71 + 44))

7 a *A*: 16, *B*: 15   b *A*: 7, *B*: 3

8 **7** hours, **11** minutes, **12** seconds (= *lcm*(77,84,98,112) seconds)

β: C22 Fractions, division and decimals   NC

As the text in this section indicates, Problem 0 is certainly not an isolated exercise in producing answers using rules for multiplication and division. Rather it is meant to be used to explore the first goal of this section – namely to strengthen the link between *fractions* and *division*. (The second goal of the section is to link fractions and division to *decimals*.) Thus

a $6 \times (5 \div 9) = ?$ is an invitation:
  - to interpret $5 \div 9$ as $\frac{5}{9} = 5 \times \frac{1}{9}$
  - to see that 6 lots of $5 \times \frac{1}{9}$ makes $30 \times \frac{1}{9}$, and

d $12 \div (9 \div 14) = ?$ is an invitation
  - to interpret $9 \div 14$ as $\frac{9}{14} = 9 \times \frac{1}{14}$
  - to think what $12 \div \frac{9}{14}$ means (namely 'that number which when multiplied by $\frac{9}{14}$ gives the answer 12': $\square \times \left(9 \times \frac{1}{14}\right) = 12$).

Allow time for pupils to make sense of this challenge, and to work their way towards the recognition that $4 \times \frac{14}{3} \left(= 12 \times \frac{14}{9}\right)$ works just fine!

Answers

0	a $\frac{10}{3}$	b $\frac{39}{2}$	c $\frac{3a}{5}$	d $\frac{56}{3}$
1	a $\frac{1}{2}$	b $\frac{1}{2}$	c $\frac{10}{3}$	d 10
2	a $\frac{1}{6}$	c $\frac{1}{4}$	e $\frac{1}{8}$	g $\frac{1}{9}$
	b $\frac{1}{8}$	d $\frac{3}{16}$	f $\frac{2}{9}$	h $\frac{1}{27}$
3	a $\frac{1}{2}$	b 2	c 8	
4	a 6	b 6	c 20	d 20
5	a $\frac{11}{10}=1.1$	b $\frac{3}{8}=0.375$	c $\frac{9}{4}=2.25$	d $\frac{57}{40}=1.425$
6	a i 16	ii $\frac{56}{3}=18\frac{2}{3}$	iii $\frac{10}{3}=3\frac{1}{3}$ miles	iv 16
	b i 16	ii £$\frac{56}{3}$ = £$18\frac{2}{3}$	iii $\frac{10}{3}=3\frac{1}{3}$ miles	iv 16

β: C23 Consecutive integers   NC

This section uses simple numerical work to generate conjecture *and proof*. In Problem 0a, the 'best' answer (11, 12, 13) is not the simplest (3, 4, 5). The questions should generate partial predictions, counter examples and refined conjectures. However, in Problem 0c you may have to cheat a little to elicit the (sensible, but incomplete) prediction

$$12k - 1,\ 12k,\ 12k + 1$$

before inviting someone to offer a counter example (3, 4, 5). The goal should be for as many pupils as possible to formulate correct conjectures and to proceed to provide proofs (Problems 3, 6, 9, 12).

Answers

0	a 11, 12, 13		b 3, 4, 5
	c i Easiest: $12k - 1, 12k, 12k + 1$		ii Probably not, see the triple in part **b**.

1 a 3, 4, 5 ; 7, 8, 9
   b 6, 7, 8; 13, 14, 15
   c 10, 11, 12; 21, 22, 23
2 a 2, 3, 4; 1, 2, 3
   b 5, 6, 7; 1, 2, 3
   c 8, 9, 10; 2, 3, 4

3 a $n - 1, n, n + 1$ for any n; sum = $3n$
   b $5k - 1, 5k, 5k + 1$ for any k; sum = $15k$
      No others: $5k, 5k + 1, 5k + 2$ have sum $15k + 3$; $5k + 1, 5k + 2, 5k + 3$ have sum $15k + 6$, etc.
   c $5k - 1, 5k, 5k + 1$ for any k; sum = $15k$
      No others: $5k, 5k + 1, 5k + 2$ have sum $15k + 3$; $5k + 1, 5k + 2, 5k + 3$ have sum $15k + 6$, etc.

4 a 2, 3, 4, 5, 6; 6, 7, 8, 9, 10
   b 5, 6, 7, 8, 9; 12, 13, 14, 15, 16
   c 9, 10, 11, 12, 13; 20, 21, 22, 23, 24
5 a 3, 4, 5, 6, 7; 1, 2, 3, 4, 5
   b 8, 9, 10, 11, 12; 2, 3, 4, 5, 6
   c 13, 14, 15, 16, 17; 1, 2, 3, 4, 5

6 a $3k - 2, 3k - 1, 3k, 3k + 1, 3k + 2$ for any k; sum = $15k$.
      Proof Sum of any five consecutive integers = $5 \times$ (middle term).
      ∴ Middle term must be multiple of 3 (and any such sequence works). **QED**
   b $n - 2, n - 1, n, n + 1, n + 2$ for any n; sum = $5n$.
   c $3k - 2, 3k - 1, 3k, 3k + 1, 3k + 2$ for any k; sum = $15k$.
      Proof Sum of any five consecutive integers = $5 \times$ (middle term).
      ∴ Middle term must be multiple of 3 (and any such sequence works). **QED**

7 a 2, 4, 6; 6, 8, 10
   b 12, 14, 16; 26, 28, 30
   c 20, 22, 24; 42, 44, 46
8 a 4, 6, 8; 2, 4, 6
   b 2, 4, 6; 4, 6, 8
   c 16, 18, 20; 4, 6, 8

9 a $2k - 2, 2k, 2k + 2$ for any k; sum = $6k$
      Proof Sum of any three consecutive even integers = $3 \times$ (middle integer), so is always a multiple of 3, so we only have to ensure that all three integers are even. **QED**
   b $10k - 2, 10k, 10k + 2$ for any k; sum = $30k$
      Proof Sum of any three consecutive even integers = $3 \times$ (middle integer), so to have sum a multiple of 5, middle integer must be a multiple of 5 – and must be even. **QED**
   c $10k - 2, 10k, 10k + 2$ for any k; sum = $30k$
      Proof Sum of any three consecutive even integers = $3 \times$ (middle integer), so to have sum a multiple of 15, we only need to ensure that the middle integer is a multiple of 5 – and is also even. **QED**

10 a 4, 6, 8, 10, 12; 0, 2, 4, 6, 8
    b 10, 12, 14, 16, 18; 24, 26, 28, 30, 32
    c 18, 20, 22, 24, 26; 40, 42, 44, 46, 48
11 a 6, 8, 10, 12, 14; 2, 4, 6, 8, 10
    b 6, 8, 10, 12, 14; 2, 4, 6, 8, 10
    c 2, 4, 6, 8, 10; 8, 10, 12, 14, 16

12 a $6k - 4, 6k - 2, 6k, 6k + 2, 6k + 4$ for any k; sum $= 30k$
Proof Sum of any five consecutive even integers $= 5 \times$ (middle integer).
∴ For sum to be a multiple of 3, middle integer must be a multiple of 3, and even. **QED**

b $2k - 4, 2k - 2, 2k, 2k + 2, 2k + 4$ for any k; sum $= 10k$
Proof Sum of any five consecutive even integers $= 5 \times$ (middle integer).
∴ We only have to ensure that all five integers are even. **QED**

c $6k - 4, 6k - 2, 6k, 6k + 2, 6k + 2$ for any k; sum $= 30k$
Proof Sum of any five consecutive even integers $= 5 \times$ (middle integer), so to have sum a multiple of 15, we only need to ensure that the middle integer is a multiple of 3 – and is also even. **QED**

β: C24 Fair shares   NC

This section combines the simple arithmetic of fractions with the need to visualise. This may prove surprisingly challenging – but thoroughly worthwhile.

Answers

0 a $4 \times \left(1 + \frac{1}{4}\right)$ – which is short for: leave 4 whole cakes uncut, and cut the fifth cake into 4 quarters; then give each of 4 people $1 + \frac{1}{4} = $ '1 whole cake and 1 quarter'.

b $2 \times \left(1 + \frac{1}{4}\right) + 2 \times \left(\frac{3}{4} + \frac{1}{4}\right)$ (which is short for: leave 2 whole cakes uncut, cut 2 cakes into $\frac{3}{4} + \frac{1}{4}$, and cut the fifth cake into 2 halves; then give 2 people $1 + \frac{1}{4}$ and 2 people $\frac{3}{4} + \frac{1}{2}$).

1 a i $2 \times \frac{2}{3} + 1 \times \left(\frac{1}{3} + \frac{1}{3}\right)$ (which is short for: cut each cake into $\frac{2}{3} + \frac{1}{3}$; then give 2 people $\frac{2}{3}$ and 1 person $\frac{1}{3} + \frac{1}{3}$).

  ii No (since one cake would remain completely uncut, and this piece would be too large)

b i $4 \times \frac{1}{2}$

  ii No (one cake would remain uncut)

c i $4 \times \frac{2}{5} + 1 \times \left(\frac{1}{5} + \frac{1}{5}\right)$ (cut each cake into $\frac{2}{5} + \frac{2}{5} + \frac{1}{5}$)

  ii No (one cake would be cut into at most 2 pieces, so some piece would be $\geq \frac{1}{2}$)

d i $6 \times \frac{1}{3}$

  ii No (one cake would be cut into at most 2 pieces, so some piece would be $\geq \frac{1}{2}$)

e i $6 \times \frac{2}{7} + 1 \times \left(\frac{1}{7} + \frac{1}{7}\right)$ (cut each cake into $\frac{2}{7} + \frac{2}{7} + \frac{2}{7} + \frac{1}{7}$)

  ii No (one cake would be cut into at most 3 pieces, so some piece would be $\geq \frac{1}{3}$)

f i $8 \times \frac{1}{4}$

  ii No (one cake would be cut into at most 3 pieces, so some piece would be $\geq \frac{1}{3}$)

2 a i $2 \times \left(1 + \frac{1}{2}\right)$

  ii No (all three cakes would remain uncut)

b i $3 \times \frac{3}{4} + 1 \times \left(\frac{1}{4} + \frac{1}{4} + \frac{1}{4}\right)$

  ii No (one cake would remain uncut)

3 a i 7 $\left(\text{If some cake remains uncut, then cannot give each person } \frac{3}{5} \text{ of a cake.}\right.$
Hence < 6 pieces is impossible.
Suppose 6 pieces is possible, and each cake is cut – so is cut into two pieces.
Then the larger piece of each cut cake is $\geq \frac{1}{2}$ and $\leq \frac{3}{5}$, so the smaller part is $\geq \frac{2}{5}$,
and two smaller pieces cannot combine to make up a 'fair share' of $\left.\frac{3}{5}.\right)$

   ii $3 \times \frac{3}{5} + 2 \times \left(\frac{2}{5} + \frac{1}{5}\right)$

 b i **6** pieces. (Need at least 1 piece each; $\therefore$ number of pieces ≥ 6.)
   ii $6 \times \frac{1}{2}$ is possible.

 c i **9** pieces $\left(\text{Need at least 1 piece each; } \therefore \text{ number of pieces} \geq 7. \text{ If number of}\right.$
pieces is < 9, then some cake is cut into at most 2 pieces, so the largest piece
is $\geq \frac{1}{2}$ so cannot be part of any fair share of $\left.\frac{3}{7}.\right)$

   ii $6 \times \frac{3}{7} + 1 \times \left(\frac{1}{7} + \frac{1}{7} + \frac{1}{7}\right)$

4 a **10** pieces $\left(\text{Need at least 1 piece each; } \therefore \text{ number of pieces} \geq 8.\right.$
Each piece $\leq \frac{3}{8}$. $\therefore$ Each cake is cut into at least 3 pieces. If no cake is cut into
4 pieces, then the smallest piece from each cake is $\geq 1 - \frac{3}{8} - \frac{3}{8} = \frac{1}{4}$ and so cannot
be combined to make a fair share of $\left.\frac{3}{8}.\right)$

 b $6 \times \frac{3}{8} + 2 \times \left(\frac{1}{4} + \frac{1}{8}\right)$

5 a $5 \times \frac{5}{6} + 1 \times \left(\frac{1}{6} + \frac{1}{6} + \frac{1}{6} + \frac{1}{6} + \frac{1}{6}\right)$ $\left(\text{cut } \frac{1}{6} \text{ from each cake}\right)$

 b $5 \times \frac{5}{7} + 2 \times \left(\frac{2}{7} + \frac{2}{7} + \frac{1}{7}\right)$ (cut $\frac{2}{7}$ from each cake, and cut one $\frac{2}{7}$ piece in half)

 c $4 \times \frac{5}{8} + 4 \times \left(\frac{3}{8} + \frac{1}{4}\right)$, or $5 \times \frac{5}{8} + 2 \times \left(\frac{3}{8} + \frac{2}{8}\right) + 1 \times \left(\frac{3}{8} + \frac{1}{8} + \frac{1}{8}\right)$

6 $6 \times \frac{6}{7} + 1 \times \left(\frac{1}{7} + \frac{1}{7} + \frac{1}{7} + \frac{1}{7} + \frac{1}{7} + \frac{1}{7}\right)$ $\left(\text{cut } \frac{1}{7} \text{ from each cake}\right)$

7 $12 \times \left(\frac{1}{2} + \frac{1}{12}\right)$ $\left(\text{or } 7 \times \frac{7}{12} + 7 \times \left(\frac{5}{12} + \frac{1}{6}\right) + 1 \times \left(\frac{5}{12} + \frac{1}{12} + \frac{1}{12}\right)\right)$

8 a

Number of people, p	1	2	3	4	5	6	7	8	9	10
Minimum number of pieces required, N	2	2	4	4	6	6	8	8	10	10

 b p (If $p = 2n$, cut each cake into n equal pieces of size $\frac{1}{n} = \frac{2}{p}$ and give one piece to
each person. If the number of pieces is < p, then one cake is cut into fewer than
n pieces, so the largest piece will be > $\frac{1}{n}$, and so is too big for a fair share.)

 c $p + 1$ (If $p = 2n - 1$, cut each cake into $n - 1$ pieces each of size $\frac{2}{p}$ and one piece
of size $\frac{1}{p}$. Then give 1 piece of size $\frac{2}{p}$ to $p - 1$ people, and 2 pieces of size $\frac{1}{p}$ to
one person. If the number of pieces is < $p + 1$, then one cake is cut into $\leq n - 1$
pieces, so the largest piece is too big for any fair share.)

β: C25 Generalised arithmetic   NC

This section is intended more as a general review to indicate themes that may need further attention. In particular, Problems **0**, **1** and **3** may reveal basic weaknesses and Problem **2** may reveal a curious blinkered-ness (failing to notice that the expressions to be evaluated have just been simplified). The

3B Beta

teacher is encouraged *not* to pre-empt such mistakes, but rather to use them as the basis for subsequent reflection.

Answers

> 0 a $12 \times (17 - 6) - 6 \times 22 = 12 \times 11 - 6 \times 22 = 0$
> b $2 \times 17 + 12 = 46$
> c $2a + 1$
> d $20 \times (20 - 1) + 1 \times (20 - 1) = 20 \times 20 - 1 = 399$
> e $a \times (a - 1) + 1 \times (a - 1) = a^2 - 1$

1 a y c 0 e $3 - 2y$ g $4y$
   b $-2a$ d $3 - 3d$ f 2 h 0
2 a 2 b 0 c 6 d 5
3 a $a + b + c$ e $x^2 + 5x + 6$ i 1 m x^2
   b $2a$ f $x^2 - 7x + 12$ j $-2a$
   c $a^2 + 2$ g $2x^2 - 5x - 3$ k $5xy - 5zy$
   d $1 - a^2$ h $x^2 + 6x + 9$ l 0
4 $V = xyz$; $A = 2(xy + yz + zx)$; $L = 4(x + y + z)$
5 a i $ax(y - ay)$ ii $(x - ax)ay$ iii a^2xy iv $(x - ax)(y - ay)$
   b *XWZC* and *VAYW*

> 6 a Volume = $4 \times 5 \times 6$ cm³ (Suppose cuboid is x cm × y cm × z cm; $10 \times 30 \times 48 = xy \times yz \times zx = (xyz)^2$)
> Edges: 4 cm, $\frac{5}{2}$ cm, 12 cm: $\left(x = \frac{xyz}{yz} = \frac{4 \times 5 \times 6}{30}, \text{etc.}\right)$
> b Volume = 75 cm³, edges: 6 cm, 5 cm, $\frac{5}{2}$ cm

β: C26 Enlargement B   NC

This section is clearly supposed to reinforce pupils' feeling for the way enlargements affect all lengths; but it is also intended as an opportunity for reflection. The quality of the proofs offered (and whether they are accepted or challenged), will depend on the teacher's judgement. However, since the enlargements are 2× and 3× enlargements, the enlarged figures can be easily decomposed into congruent copies of the initial figure, which means that the proofs in Problems **0**, **1** and **3** are more accessible than one might anticipate. In Problem **2** each length to be measured is the hypotenuse of a right-angled triangle whose 'legs' consist of so many steps (*along* and *down*) on the dot-lattice; hence each length to be measured in part **b** decomposes into parts, each being identical to the corresponding length in part **a**.

Answers

> 0 a 5 cm
> b 10 cm; divide rectangle *WXYZ* into four copies of *ABCD*; diagonal *WY* = 2 × *AC*

1 **15 cm**; divide rectangle *STUV* into 3 × 3 copies of rectangle *ABCD*; then diagonal *SU* = 3 × *AC*
2 a i *MD* $\frac{5}{2}$ cm = 2.5 cm   ii *AC* = $\sqrt{5}$ cm ≈ 2.24 cm   *AD* = $2\sqrt{2}$ cm ≈ 2.83 cm
   b i *M'D'*   = 5 cm   ii *A'C'* = $2\sqrt{5}$ cm ≈ 4.5 cm   *A'D'* = $4\sqrt{2}$ cm ≈ 5.66 cm
   c i *M"D"*   = 7.5 cm   ii *A"C"* = $3\sqrt{5}$ cm ≈ 6.7 cm   *A"D"* = $6\sqrt{2}$ cm ≈ 8.5 cm

3 a i Let the horizontal through A meet the vertical through B at X, and let the vertical through B meet the horizontal through C at Y.
Then $AX = BY = 2$, $\angle AXB = \angle BYC = 90°$, $XB = YC = 1$.
∴ $\triangle AXB$ and $\triangle BYC$ are congruent (by SAS).
∴ $AB = BC$ and $\angle ABC = 180° - \angle ABX - \angle CBY = 90°$ QED

iii $5\ cm^2$

b ii $20\ cm^2$ c ii $45\ cm^2$

4 a $BC \approx 17\ cm$ b $B'C' = 2 \times BC \approx 34\ cm$ c $B''C'' = 3 \times BC \approx 51\ cm$

5 a $BL = 2.4\ cm$ b $B'L' : BL = 2 : 1$, $B'L' = 4.8\ cm$

6 a i Equilateral ($PR = PQ$ (radii of the same circle), $RP = RQ$ (radii of same circle))

ii $\triangle PQS$ and $\triangle RQS$ are congruent (by SSS); $\triangle PQM$ and $\triangle RQM$ are congruent (by ASA); $QS : QM = 2 : 1$

b i $Q'M' : QM = 2 : 1$, $Q'S' : QS = 2 : 1$

ii $\triangle Q'N'L'$ is isosceles with $\angle N'Q'L' = 60°$; ∴ $\triangle Q'N'L'$ is equilateral.
Similarly $\triangle P'M'N'$ and $\triangle R'L'M'$ are equilateral.
If we use $N'L' = 10\ cm$ in place of PR, and then part **a** constructs $Q'M'$ in place of QS.
∴ $Q'M' : QM = QS : QM = 2 : 1$ (by **a ii**)   QED

β: C27 Cuboids and volumes   NC

This mixed collection cultivates flexibility in using the familiar formula for the volume of a cuboid.

Answers

0 $4 \times 40 \times 30\ cm^3$ = **4.8** litres

1 a $3 \times 4 \times 5$ = **60** cubes
  b surface area = $2 \times (6 \times 8 + 8 \times 10 + 10 \times 6)\ cm^2$ = **376** cm^3

2 $10 \times 16 \times 8\ cm^3$ = **1.28** litres   8 20 cm
3 42 cm   9 18 cubes
4 12 cm   10 $1\frac{1}{2}$ minutes
5 $40 \times 30 \times 6\ cm^3$ = **7200** cm^3 11 16 minutes
6 **10.29** litres (= $(25 \times 30 \times 15 - 8 \times 10 \times 12)\ cm^3$) 12 38 cm
7 $60 \times 35 \times 10\ cm^3$ = **21 000** cm^3

β: C28 Division: Integers   NC

Short and long division need to be part of the stock-in-trade of all pupils. The standard layout for long division may be less familiar than it should be - in which case Problem **0** will need to be supplemented to give extra practice.

Answers

0 a i $1001 = 7 \times $ **143**   ii $688 = 43 \times $ **16**   b $18\,323 = 73 \times $ **251**

1 $7007 = 11 \times $ **637**   3 $7015 = 23 \times $ **305**
2 $7007 = 13 \times $ **539**   4 $7004 = 34 \times $ **206**

5 a $648 = 12 \times $ **54**   b $252 = 12 \times $ **21**
  c **10** solutions (solutions come in pairs, as the divisor and the answer can be interchanged; ∴ 30×31, 30×32, 30×33, 31×32: **8** solutions; 30×30, 31×31 self-paired: **2** solutions)

6 a $15 \times 5 = 75$, $25 \times 3 = 75$, $35 \times 2 = 70$, $75 \times 1 = 75$
  b $90 \times 11 = 990$; 90×10, 91×10, 92×10 up to 99×10

| 7 | $4683 = 21 \times 223$ | 9 | $147844 = 46 \times 3214$ |
| 8 | $3703 = 23 \times 161$ | 10 | $70863 = 237 \times 299$ |

11 $5478 = 11 \times 498$, or $6678 = 14 \times 477$

β: C29 Prime factorisation C NC

Pupils need an effective procedure for factorising any given integer as a product of powers of primes. The factor tree method is unsatisfactory and error-prone. Having left pupils to their own devices up to now, this section introduces the standard procedure – which is proven and much more compact.

Answers

0 $72 = 2^3 \times 3^2$

1	$216 = 2^3 \times 3^3$	4	$147 = 3 \times 7^2$
2	$600 = 2^3 \times 3 \times 5^2$	5	$686 = 2 \times 7^3$
3	$720 = 2^4 \times 3^2 \times 5$	6	$162 = 2 \times 3^4$

| 7 | a 216, 600, 720, 162 | c 216, 600, 720 |
| | b 147, 686 | d 216, 720, 162 |

8	$160 = 2^5 \times 5$	11	$980 = 2^2 \times 5 \times 7^2$
9	$240 = 2^4 \times 3 \times 5$	12	$10800 = 2^4 \times 3^3 \times 5^2$
10	$270 = 2 \times 3^3 \times 5$	13	$6615 = 3^3 \times 5 \times 7^2$

14 C ($451\,066 = 2 \times 7 \times 11 \times 29 \times 101 = 7 \times 29 \times \left(\frac{1}{2} \times 404\right) \times \left(\frac{1}{2} \times 22\right)$ shows that C is possible; further reasoning is needed to rule out each of the other four options)

β: C30 Multiplying fractions NC

This section provides a routine review of cancellation for simple products of fractions.

Answers

0 a $\frac{1}{3}$ b $\frac{1}{4}$

| 1 | $\frac{2}{5}$ | 3 | $\frac{5}{16}$ | 5 | $\frac{21}{32}$ | 7 | $\frac{5}{16}$ | 9 | $\frac{1}{10}$ | 11 | $\frac{1}{70}$ |
| 2 | $\frac{1}{2}$ | 4 | $\frac{16}{35}$ | 6 | $\frac{7}{20}$ | 8 | $\frac{1}{4}$ | 10 | $\frac{1}{20}$ | | |

12 Volume = 1 cm^3; edges $\frac{15}{4}$ cm, $\frac{6}{25}$ cm, $\frac{10}{9}$ cm

β: C31 Multiplication: Decimals and fractions NC

This section is a more general exercise in multiplication of decimals (concentrating on where to put the decimal point), and of fractions (concentrating on changing mixed fractions to $\frac{\text{numerator}}{\text{denominator}}$ form and looking for unexpected cancellation).

Answers

0 a 16.38	b 4		
1 305.9	3 0.21836	5 0.001638	7 0.0988
2 21.836	4 0.0000988	6 0.003059	8 21.836

9 £221

| 10 112 | 11 7 | 12 $\frac{21}{4}$ | 13 $\frac{30}{77}$ | 14 $\frac{3}{70}$ | 15 $\frac{1}{33}$ |

16 £32

β: C32 In between   NC

As the parenthetical remarks in Problems **4**, **5** and **6** indicate, these simple numerical questions are routinely tackled without sufficient thought! Check that errors made in the first half of the section are corrected in the second half, rather than being reproduced unthinkingly.

Answers

0 a 3	b $\frac{3}{8}$						

1 a 2	b 3	c 4	4 a $\frac{2}{3}$	b $\frac{3}{8}$	c $\frac{4}{15}$	7 a $\frac{6}{35}$	b $\frac{11}{15}$
2 a 1	b $\frac{3}{2}$	c 2	5 a $\frac{4}{3}$	b $\frac{3}{4}$	c $\frac{8}{15}$	8 a $\frac{4}{15}$	b $\frac{8}{15}$
3 a $\frac{1}{2}$	b $\frac{3}{4}$	c 1	6 a $\frac{8}{3}$	b $\frac{3}{2}$	c $\frac{16}{15}$		
9 a 1	b 1	c 1	d −1	e −1	f −1		
10 a $-\frac{1}{15}$	b $-\frac{1}{8}$	c $-\frac{1}{3}$	d $\frac{1}{15}$	e $\frac{1}{8}$	f $\frac{1}{3}$		
11 a i $\frac{1}{3}$ hour	ii $\frac{1}{5}$ hour		iii $\frac{15}{4}$ mph		b $\frac{8}{3}$ mph		
12 a 2, 4	b 8, 1	c 8 (or −8), −1					

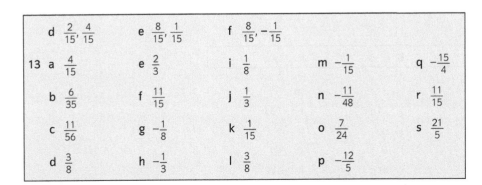

β: C33 Divison: Fractions and decimals   NC

Division of fractions is never as robust as one would like. Even if pupils 'know' how to divide fractions, it is worth using this short section to review how they think about the procedure in the spirit of the text in the section.

Answers

> 0 a i $\left(3 \times \frac{1}{4}\right) \div \left(5 \times \frac{1}{4}\right) = \frac{3}{5}$ ii $\left(9 \times \frac{1}{12}\right) \div \left(10 \times \frac{1}{12}\right) = \frac{9}{10}$
>   b 0.31

1 $\frac{3}{4}$ 2 2   3 $\frac{2}{3}$ 4 $\frac{3}{4}$ 5 $\frac{35}{8}$ 6 $\frac{10}{11}$

> 7 $\frac{1}{3} \div \frac{4}{5} = \frac{5}{12}$ cm

8 0.3   9 0.009   10 5150   11 87.148   12 0.314

> 13 19 short strips, remainder 0.053 m

β: C34 A formula for primes?   NC

The theme here has its own appeal, and is being exploited to provide a useful exercise in *making sense of quadratics* – using substitution to develop a feeling for how such expressions behave. It should also serve as a valuable antidote to mindless pattern-spotting.

Answers

> 0 a 3   b $n = 4$ (65)

1 $n = 4$ (21)   5 $n = 11$ (121)   9 $n = 2$ (33)
2 $n = 6$ (55)   6 $n = 16$ ($289 = 17^2$) 10 $n = 40$ (41^2)
3 $n = 6$ (91)   7 $n = 17$ (289)   11 $n = 41$ (41^2)
4 $n = 10$ ($121 = 11^2$) 8 $n = 1$ (33)   12 $n = 2$ (21) (next: $n = 7$ (361))

> 13 a $n = 11$ b $n = 17$ 14 b $n = 11$ (155)

β: C35 Negative numbers   NC

It is worth using this simple review as a challenge for pupils to work fast and accurately, aiming to get everything right (though they should be prepared to slow down a bit for Problems **3** and **5**).

Answers

> 0 a i –2   ii 15   b i –2a   ii 11y

1 a 1   e –5   i a m –5a
   b –3   f –10   j –3a   n –10a
   c 8   g 2   k 8a   o 2a
   d 0   h –8   l 0   p –8a
2 a 2   e 18   i 8x   m –18x
   b 2   f –4   j –2x   n –4x
   c –2   g –18   k 2x   o 4x
   d –8   h 4   l –8x   p 18x

3	a	6	e	−6	i	−4	m	−20
	b	−40	f	−42	j	10	n	−6
	c	−6	g	42	k	6	o	−10
	d	40	h	6	l	20	p	4

4	a	1	c	−1	e	5
	b	5	d	−5	f	−5

5	a	$\frac{5}{4}$	e	$-\frac{1}{12}$	i	$\frac{3}{10}$
	b	$\frac{1}{4}$	f	$-\frac{17}{12}$	j	$\frac{13}{10}$
	c	$-\frac{1}{4}$	g	$\frac{17}{12}$	k	0
	d	$-\frac{5}{4}$	h	$\frac{1}{12}$	l	$\frac{8}{5}$

β: C36 Word sums B   NC

These word sums provide an excellent way of strengthening insight into the structure underlying our *base 10* place value system. Although most of these word sums don't work, the challenge is to identify quickly and clearly *why* they don't work – and to keep alert just in case there is the occasional solution.

Answers

> 0 a **No** (Lots of reasons: for example, N = 0 in units column, so E = V in tens column)
>   b **No** (For example, E = 0 in units column, so N = V in tens column)

1 **No** (Y = 0 in units column, whence T = 0 = Y in tens column)
2 **No** (R = 0 in units column, ∴ no carry to tens column. Then U = 0 = R in tens column)
3 **No** (F = 9 in thousands column – with carry of 1, so E = 0, then O = N in units column)
4 Lots of solutions, for example, 1970 + 1264 = 3234
5 **No** (T = 8 or 9 – neither of which works)
6 **No** (Too many different letters)
7 **No** (No carry to hundred thousands column, so E = 0 in ten thousands column)
8 **No** (Carry to hundred thousands column, so L = 9, W = 0, and E + 1 = T; also E + N = Y + 10 in units column, so E + N + 1 = T + 10 in tens column whence N = 10)
9 **No** (S ≠ E, so L = 9, I = 0, S = 8 ∴ carry 1 to tens column so N = H.)
10 **No** (E = T + 1 in ten thousands column ∴ E + E = T + 10 in units column, so T = 8. ∴ V = H.)
11 **No** (Too many different letters)

β: C37 Adding and subtracting fractions B   NC

This short review provides more necessary practice – some simple (Problem 1) and some not quite so simple (Problems 2 and 3).

Answers

> 0 a $\frac{17}{12}$ b $\frac{1}{12}$

3B Beta

1 a 1   d $\frac{1}{2}$ g $\frac{6}{5}$ j $\frac{3}{2}$ m 1

   b $\frac{1}{2}$ e $\frac{1}{4}$ h $\frac{3}{2}$ k $\frac{4}{3}$ n $\frac{1}{3}$

   c $\frac{2}{3}$ f $\frac{2}{5}$ i $\frac{3}{2}$ l $\frac{3}{2}$

2 a $\frac{3}{6} + \frac{4}{6} = \frac{7}{6}$ d $\frac{21}{10}$ g $\frac{53}{60}$ j $\frac{9}{16}$ m $\frac{161}{44}$

   b $\frac{4}{12} + \frac{9}{12} = \frac{13}{12}$ e $\frac{13}{30}$ h $\frac{29}{24}$ k $\frac{49}{60}$ n $\frac{29}{210}$

   c $\frac{8}{20} + \frac{15}{20} = \frac{23}{20}$ f $\frac{19}{12}$ i $\frac{23}{40}$ l $\frac{11}{42}$

3 a $\frac{1}{3}$ e Leave as it is, or write as $\frac{3a + 2b}{6}$ i $\frac{ab}{12}$

   b $\frac{14}{5}$ f $\frac{a}{12}$ j $\frac{2}{a}$

   c 0   g $\frac{a^2}{12}$

   d $\frac{5a}{6}$ h $\frac{3a}{10}$

4 Rows: $\frac{5}{8} + \frac{5}{16} = \frac{15}{16}$; $\frac{3}{8} + \frac{1}{4} = \frac{5}{8}$; $1 + \frac{9}{16} = \frac{25}{16} = 1\frac{9}{16}$

β: C38 Coordinates   NC

These problems all relate to 'along and up', and *hcf*s. After the event, you may need to point out that pupils have overlooked the direct connection between each part of Problem **2** and the corresponding part of Problem **3**.

Answers

0 b A, O, S lie on the line $y = 0$;   B, D, G, J, O, R lie on the line $x = 0$;
   A, H, L lie on the line $y + 3x = 12$;   B, I, L lie on the line $5y - 3x = -30$;
   D, H, M lie on the line $3y + 10x = 39$;   E, G, S lie on the line $3y - 2x = 12$;
   E, H, O, P lie on the line $y = x$;   K, O, N lie on the line $4y + 3x = 0$.
   c $OA = OG = 4$; $OB = OS = 6$; $OD = OF = 13$; $OI = ON = 10$

2 a **3** (*hcf*(12, 20) = 4; ∴ segment joining (0, 0) to (12, 20) passes through 4 points with non-zero integer coordinates, including (12, 20); ∴ 3 = *hcf*(12, 20) − 1 such points. Gradient = $\frac{20}{12} = \frac{5}{3}$; ∴ first such point is (3, 5): the three points are **(3, 5)**, **(6, 10)**, **(9, 15)**)

   b **17** (= *hcf*(36, 90) − 1): (2, 5), (4, 10), (6, 15), ...

   c **23** (= *hcf*(48, 72) − 1): (2, 3), (4, 6), (6, 9), ...

   d **23** : (5, 7), (10, 14), (15, 21), ...

   e **7** (To find the minimal step – along and up – think about the parallel segment from O = (0, 0) to P' = (24, 40) based at the origin; then proceed as before: *hcf*(24, 40) = 8; ∴ (7 + 3, 3 + 5), (7 + 6, 3 + 10), (7 + 9, 3 + 15), ...)

   f **11**: (−11 + 5, 13 + 7), (−11 + 10, 13 + 14), (−11 + 15, 13 + 21), ...

   g **11**: (23 + 2, −15 + 3), (23 + 4, −15 + 6), (23 + 6, −15 + 9), ...

   h **35**: (−20 + 9, 11 + 5), (−20 + 18, 11 + 10), (−20 + 27, 11 + 15), ...

   i **26**: (57 + 9, 3 + 11), (57 + 18, 3 + 22), (57 + 27, 3 + 33), ...

   j **62**: (98 + 8, 81 + 13), (98 + 16, 81 + 26), (98 + 24, 81 + 39), ...

3 a $\frac{5}{3}$ c $\frac{3}{2}$ e $\frac{5}{3}$ g $\frac{3}{2}$ i $\frac{11}{9}$

	b $\frac{5}{2}$		d $\frac{7}{5}$		f $\frac{7}{5}$		h $\frac{5}{9}$	j $\frac{13}{8}$
5 a	(3, 0)		c $\left(\frac{1}{2}, 4\right)$		e $\left(\frac{1}{2}, -\frac{1}{2}\right)$		g $\left(-\frac{5}{2}, -5\right)$	
	b (0, 1)		d $\left(\frac{13}{2}, \frac{9}{2}\right)$		f (−2, 9)		h $\left(-\frac{3}{2}, 1\right)$	

β: C39 Divisibility B: Does it go? How do you know?   NC

This section moves on from *Divisibility A* to introduce, prove, and extend the tests for divisibility by 3 and by 9 (or rather for calculating the *remainder* when a given integer is divided by 3 or by 9). It is worth using a plenary review to revisit the proofs in Problem **1b** and Problem **5b**, and the condition for an integer to be divisible by 6 (see before Problem **3**).

Answers

0 a	i 0	ii 0	iii 2	iv 0	v 0	vi 0
b	i 15, 0	ii 18, 0	iii 11, 2	iv 15, 0	v 12, 0	vi 21, 0

c Given *N* written in *base 10*, with digit-sum *D*, the remainder on dividing *N* by 3 is equal to the remainder when the digit sum *D* is divided by 3.

1 a	i 1	ii 1	iii 1	iv 0	v 0	vi 0
2 a	0	b 0	c 0	d 0	e 0	f 1

3 e, f, i, j only

4 a It is not entirely obvious how to proceed; somehow the remainder on division by 2 (*odd* and *even*) and by 3 have to be matched up with the remainder *r* on division by 6:

	odd, r = 1	even, r = 2	odd, r = 0	even, r = 1	odd, r = 2	even, r = 1
remainder mod 6	1	2	3	4	5	0
i 4	iii 1	v 0	vii 3	ix 0	xi 3	
ii 4	iv 3	vi 0	viii 3	x 0	xii 1	
b i 0	ii 1	iii 2	iv 4	v 3	vi 5	

5 a	i 4	ii 4	iii 7	iv 3	v 3	vi 0

β: E1 More missing digits NC

Proofs should be routinely expected – so try to spend a little time probing. In this section most proofs depend on 'case analysis' (for example, in Problem **1**, the multiplier must be ≥ 7; for 7 the only possible answer in the 'two hundreds' is $29 \times 7 = 203$, 8 leads to 28×8, and 9 leads to 26×9; Problem 2 is messier). Such proofs are sometimes suppressed here to save space.

Answers

1 $28 \times 8 = 224$; $26 \times 9 = 234$ (multiplier ≥ 7)   3 $165 \times 3 = 495$ (multiplier ≤ 3)

2 $52 \times 6 = 312$; $62 \times 6 = 372$; $57 \times 6 = 342$ 4 $967 \times 9 = 8703$; $969 \times 7 = 6783$

5 **$54 \times 3 = 162$** (Units column must be 2×3, 3×2, 3×4, or 4×3; only the last can be made to work)

6 $261 \times 97 = 25\,317$ (unique)   7 No

β: E2 Divisibility problems NC

Problems **4** and **5** help to explain the puzzle in Problems **9** and **10**. Problem **6** provides the background to the test (Problem **7**) for divisibility by 11.

Answers

1 a 0 b 0 c 0 d 0 e 0 f 0 g 3 h 3 i 3 j 1 k 1 l 1

2 **b, c, d, e, h, i, j, l** only   3 **b, c, d, e, g, i, j, l** only

4 a i 7 ii 7 iii Same remainder 7, so differ by an exact multiple of 9 ($8 + 5 + 3 = 16$, so $853 = 9m + 7$; similarly $358 = 9n + 7$; $\therefore 853 - 358 = 9(m - n)$)

   b $853 - 358 = 9 \times 55$

5 a Same remainder 3, so differ by an exact multiple of 9 ($9 + 8 + 7 + 6 = 30$, so $9876 = 9m + 3$; similarly $6789 = 9n + 3$; $\therefore 9876 - 6789 = 9(m - n)$)

   b $9876 - 6789 = 9 \times 343$

6 a 11×0 b 11×1 c 11×9 d 11×91 e 11×909 f 11×9091

7 a $11 \times $ **8669** b $11 \times 943 + 3$

8 a i, iii, iv, v, vi, vii, viii, x, xi only   9 a 1089

10 a Adapt the answer to Problem **4** to show that '*abc*' – '*cba*' is exactly divisible by 9.

   b i For a three-digit integer '*abc*' (in *base 10*), the *remainder* on division by 11 is the same as the remainder when you divide the alternating digit-sum $c - b + a$ by 11.

     ii $\therefore$ '*abc*' and '*cba*' leave the same remainder on division by 11
$\therefore$ '*abc*' – '*cba*' is exactly divisible by 11 (as well as by 9), and hence by 9×11.
$\therefore$ '*def*' = 99, or 198, or 297, or 396, or 495, or 594, or 693, or 792, or 891 (or 990, though 990 cannot in fact occur)

     iii $099 + 990 = 1089$; $198 + 891 = 1089$; etc.

β: E3 More word problems

This set of word problems contains some awkward examples (Problems 2, 5, 8, 9, 10), but may still be suitable for use with a much larger group.

Answers

1 $75 \times 10\,\text{p}$ coins; $25 \times 50\,\text{p}$ coins   3 40, 56

2 Eve 96 kg, Abel 99 kg, Cain 103 kg, Adam 104 kg   4 12 km

5 a **24** miles ($= 83 + 42 - 101$)

   b Infinitely many? If all distances are positive integers, then **17**
($DF = 18$ miles; $D \neq E \neq F$; $\therefore DE = 1$, $BC = 53$ down to $BC = 37$, $DE = 17$)

6 a 93p	b £1.43	7 9 days

8 £0 to Alex; £7 to Bob	9 $71\tfrac{1}{8}$%	10 70 children

β: E4 More angles

These problems are relatively straightforward. If Problem **1** is used as a communal Problem **0**, the section might well serve a complete top set.

Answers

1 540° (= 3 × 180°)

2 a 70°   b 110°   c 109°   d 70°   e 30°   f 35°

3 45°   4 $67\tfrac{1}{2}$°

5 90°	6 50°
7 75° (Let circle centre *N*, through *M* meet *CD* at *X*, *AB* at *Y*; then *NX* = *NY* = *XY*.)	
8 120°	

β: E5 More ratios

This section extends the idea of ratio to provide a way of comparing *three* quantities with the same units.

Answers

1 a 5 between 11 $\left(\tfrac{4}{9} < \tfrac{5}{11}\right)$ b *n* between 2*n* + 1 $\left(2n^2 - n - 1 < 2n^2 - n; \therefore \tfrac{n-1}{2n-1} < \tfrac{n}{2n+1}\right)$

2 £1.35 : 60 p : 15 p

3 £60 : £40 : £8

4 8 cm, 12 cm, 16 cm

5 a 32 : 16 : 48 = 2 : 1 : 3   c 78 : 60 : 36 = **39** : **30** : 18

   b 36 : **72** : 40 = **18** : **36** : 20

6 35% $\left(\tfrac{7}{4+7+9}\right)$

7 200   8 6, 10   9 22.5 cm   10 *A* pays *B* **£7**; *C* pays *B* **£15**

11 75 $\left(£1.08 = 12 \times 9\,\text{p; so }£1.08 \text{ buys } 108 \times 12 \times \tfrac{50}{70} \times \tfrac{1}{48} \times \tfrac{28}{18} \times \tfrac{25}{10} \text{ pears}\right)$

β: E6 More HCFs and LCMs   NC

This section extends the idea of *hcf* and *lcm* to *triples* of integers.

Answers

1 hcf = 1, lcm = 30   5 hcf = 1, lcm = 715

2 hcf = 3, lcm = 210   6 hcf = 13, lcm = **10 010** = 2 × 5 × 7 × 11 × 13

3 hcf = 5, lcm = 210   7 hcf = 1, lcm = 2 × 3 × 5 × 7 × 11 × 13^2

4 hcf = 1, lcm = 1001   8 8.06 am ($2^3 \times 3^2 \times 5$ seconds later)

9 54 pieces (hcf = 2 × 7 ∴ 10 + 17 + 12 + 15 pieces)

10 4860 = $2^2 \times 3^5 \times 5$ buttons in each packet
(388 800 = $2^6 \times 3^5 \times 5^2$,
3 542 940 = $2^2 \times 3^{11} \times 5$, 1 244 160 = $2^{10} \times 3^5 \times 5$)

β: E7 Number squares

Problem **1** invites pupils to construct the 3 by 3 magic square and to prove that it is *unique*. Problems **2–6** build on this in an unusual way that requires a simple willingness to think in a mildly creative way. Problems **7–11** move in a slightly different direction – exploring *Latin squares* (or Sudoku-like squares).

3B Beta

Answers

1. The three *rows* (horizontal) contain the numbers 1, 2, 3, 4, 5, 6, 7, 8, 9 in some order. So if the *row-sum* = s, the sum of the three rows must be $3s = 1+2+3+4+5+6+7+8+9 = 45$, so $s = 15$. Moreover, the four lines through the centre square use up every square once and the centre square 4 times, so if the entry in the centre square is c, $4s = 45 + 3c$, so $c = 5$.

   The only triples with sum 15 that include 1 are $1 + 9 + 5$ and $1 + 8 + 6$ ∴ 1 cannot go in a corner. The rest follows.

6	1	8
7	5	3
2	9	4

2.
7	2	9
8	6	4
3	10	5

4.
12	2	16
14	10	6
4	18	8

6.
51	1	71
61	41	21
11	81	31

3.
11	1	15
13	9	5
3	17	7

5.
66	11	88
77	55	33
22	99	44

7. a
1	2	3
2	3	1
3	1	2

   b Suppose such an arrangement is possible, with a in the top left corner and b in the top right corner. The central square is on a diagonal with both a and b, so contains c where $a \neq c \neq b$. ∴ a, b, c are 1, 2, 3 in some order. But then cannot fill the bottom right corner.

8.
1	2	3	4
3	4	1	2
4	3	2	1
2	1	4	3

9.
3	2	4	1
1	4	2	3
2	3	1	4
4	1	3	2

10. 2 solutions (Top left could be 2 or 4; each produces a unique solution)

2	1	4	3
4	3	2	1
3	4	1	2
1	2	3	4

11. 2 solutions (Top left could be 3 or 4; each produces a unique solution)

2	1	4	3
3	4	1	2
1	2	3	4
4	3	2	1

β: E8 More prime factorisation   NC

These problems may appear to repeat ideas broached in earlier sections (linked to prime factorisation and using the product rule to count factors). These ideas are simple and powerful, but they are often not easily absorbed. If they have been understood, they may be cemented by completing this section fairly quickly; if not, then it is worth struggling with them further.

Answers

0 a $9 = 3 \times 3 = 3^2$; factors $3^0, 3^1, 3^2$
  b $10 = 2 \times 5$; factors $1 = 2^0 \times 5^0$, $5 = 2^0 \times 5^1$; $2 = 2^1 \times 5^0$, $10 = 2^1 \times 5^1$
  c $18 = 2 \times 3^2$; factors $1 = 2^0 \times 3^0$, $3 = 2^0 \times 3^1$, $9 = 2^0 \times 3^2$;
  $2 = 2^1 \times 3^0$, $6 = 2^1 \times 3^1$, $18 = 2^1 \times 3^2$

1 a $14 = 2 \times 7$; factors $1 = 2^0 \times 7^0$, $7 = 2^0 \times 7^1$; $2 = 2^1 \times 7^0$, $14 = 2^1 \times 7^1$
  b $21 = 3 \times 7$; factors $1 = 3^0 \times 7^0$, $7 = 3^0 \times 7^1$; $3 = 3^1 \times 7^0$, $21 = 3^1 \times 7^1$
  c $28 = 2^2 \times 7$; factors $1 = 2^0 \times 7^0$, $7 = 2^0 \times 7^1$; $2 = 2^1 \times 7^0$, $14 = 2^1 \times 7^1$;
  $4 = 2^2 \times 7^0$, $28 = 2^2 \times 7^1$
  d $50 = 2 \times 5^2$; (2×3 factors)
  e $27 = 3^3$; (4 factors)
  f $35 = 5 \times 7$; (2×2 factors)
  g $75 = 3 \times 5^2$; (2×3 factors)
  h $77 = 7 \times 11$; (2×2 factors)
  i $91 = 7 \times 13$; (2×2 factors)
  j $49 = 7^2$; (3 factors)
  k $98 = 2 \times 7^2$; (2×3 factors)
  l $25 = 5^2$; (3 factors)
  m $44 = 2^2 \times 11$; (3×2 factors)
  n $63 = 3^2 \times 7$; (3×2 factors)

2 a 6: $1 = 2^0 \times 3^0$, $2 = 2^1 \times 3^0$; $3 = 2^0 \times 3^1$, $6 = 2^1 \times 3^1$
  10: $1 = 2^0 \times 5^0$, $5 = 2^0 \times 5^1$; $2 = 2^1 \times 5^0$, $10 = 2^1 \times 5^1$
  14: $1 = 2^0 \times 7^0$, $5 = 2^0 \times 7^1$; $2 = 2^1 \times 7^0$, $14 = 2^1 \times 7^1$
  21: $1 = 3^0 \times 7^0$, $7 = 3^0 \times 7^1$; $3 = 3^1 \times 7^0$, $21 = 3^1 \times 7^1$
  35: $1 = 5^0 \times 7^0$, $7 = 5^0 \times 7^1$; $5 = 5^1 \times 7^0$, $35 = 5^1 \times 7^1$
  77: $1 = 7^0 \times 11^0$, $11 = 7^0 \times 11^1$; $7 = 7^1 \times 11^0$, $77 = 7^1 \times 11^1$
  91: $1 = 7^0 \times 13^0$, $13 = 7^0 \times 13^1$; $7 = 7^1 \times 13^0$, $91 = 7^1 \times 13^1$
  b All have factor diagrams that are simple rectangles: 2×2 vertices $\therefore 2 \times 2$ factors
  c 6, 10, 14, 15, 21, 22, 26, 33, 34, 35, 38, 39, 46

3 a 18: $1 = 3^0 \times 2^0$, $2 = 3^0 \times 2^1$; $3 = 3^1 \times 2^0$, $6 = 3^1 \times 2^1$; $9 = 3^2 \times 2^0$, $18 = 3^2 \times 2^1$
  28: $1 = 2^0 \times 7^0$, $7 = 2^0 \times 7^1$; $2 = 2^1 \times 7^0$, $14 = 2^1 \times 7^1$; $4 = 2^2 \times 7^0$, $28 = 2^2 \times 7^1$
  b 50: $1 = 5^0 \times 2^0$, $2 = 5^0 \times 2^1$; $5 = 5^1 \times 2^0$, $10 = 5^1 \times 2^1$; $25 = 5^2 \times 2^0$, $50 = 5^2 \times 2^1$
  98: $1 = 7^0 \times 2^0$, $2 = 7^0 \times 2^1$; $7 = 7^1 \times 2^0$, $14 = 7^1 \times 2^1$; $49 = 7^2 \times 2^0$, $98 = 7^2 \times 2^1$
  c All factor diagrams have two equal rectangles end to end; 2×3 vertices $\therefore 2 \times 3$ factors
  d $20 = 2^2 \times 5^1$
  e 12, 18, 20, 28, 44, 45, 50, 52, 63, 68, 75, 76, 92, 98, 99

4 a i 14, 21, 35, 77, 91   ii 28, 44, 50, 63, 75, 98   iii 25, 49   iv 27
  b i 2×2 factors   ii 3×2 factors   iii 3 factors   iv 4 factors

5 a i 6, 10, 14, 91   ii 4, 9, 49   iii 8, 27
  b i 12, 18, 20, **28, 44, 45, 50**   ii 16, 81   iii 32
  c i The above together with: 52, 63, 68, 75, 76, 92, 98, 99   ii 16, 81   iii 32

6 a $52 = 2^2 \times 13$ factors $1 = 2^0 \times 13^0$, $13 = 2^0 \times 13^1$; $2 = 2^1 \times 13^0$, $26 = 2^1 \times 13^1$;
  $4 = 2^2 \times 13^1$, $52 = 2^2 \times 13^1$
  b $99 = 3^2 \times 11$ factors $1 = 3^0 \times 11^0$, $11 = 3^0 \times 11^1$; $3 = 3^1 \times 11^0$, $33 = 3^1 \times 11^1$;
  $9 = 3^2 \times 11^0$, $99 = 3^2 \times 11^1$
  c $39 = 3 \times 13$
  d $125 = 5^3$
  e $54 = 2 \times 3^3$ (1st new family)
  f $24 = 2^3 \times 3$ (1st new family)
  g $9 = 3^2$
  h $40 = 2^3 \times 5$ (1st new family)
  i $121 = 11^2$
  j $143 = 11 \times 13$
  k $135 = 3^3 \times 5$ (1st new family)
  l $72 = 2^3 \times 3^2$ (2nd new family)
  m $30 = 2 \times 3 \times 5$ (3rd new family)
  n $144 = 2^4 \times 3^2$ (4th new family)
  o $108 = 2^2 \times 3^3$ (2nd new family)
  p $200 = 2^3 \times 5^2$ (2nd new family)
  q $42 = 2 \times 3 \times 7$ (3rd new family)
  r $32 = 2^5$ (5th new family)
  s $70 = 2 \times 5 \times 7$ (3rd new family)
  t $96 = 2^5 \times 3$ (6th new family)

7
a $16 = 2^4$ (new family; 5 factors)
b $46 = 2 \times 23$ (like 14; 2×2 factors)
c $169 = 13^2$ (like 49; 3 factors)
d $56 = 2^3 \times 7$ (new family; 4×2 factors)
e $48 = 2^4 \times 3$ (new family; 5×2 factors)
f $125 = 5^3$ (like 27; 4 factors)
g $32 = 2^5$ (new family, 6 factors)
h $81 = 3^4$ (like a16, 5 factors)
i $96 = 2^5 \times 3$ (new family; 6×2 factors)
j $72 = 2^3 \times 3^2$ (new family; 4×3 factors)
k $343 = 7^3$ (like 27; 4 factors)
l $200 = 2^3 \times 5^2$ (like j 72; 4×3 factors)
m $108 = 2^2 \times 3^3$ (like j 72; 4×2 factors)
n $250 = 2 \times 5^3$ (like d 56; 2×4 factors)
o $135 = 3^3 \times 5$ (like d 56; 4×2 factors)
p $500 = 2^2 \times 5^3$ (like j 72; 3×4 factors)
q $1000 = 2^3 \times 5^3$ (new family; 4×4 factors)
r $30 = 2 \times 3 \times 5$ (new family; $2 \times 2 \times 2$ factors)
s $144 = 2^4 \times 3^2$ (new family; 5×3 factors)
t $42 = 2 \times 3 \times 7$ (like r 30; $2 \times 2 \times 2$ factors)
u $70 = 2 \times 5 \times 7$ (like r 30; $2 \times 2 \times 2$ factors)

β: E9 Crossnumbers   NC

The logic required to find all solutions can be hard to express compactly in written form (which explains why proofs are only indicated here). Teachers are encouraged to interrogate pupils to ensure that they recognise how logic should be used to avoid guesswork.

Answers

1

¹7	²5
³8	1

2 1D must end in 1 or 9 ∴ 5A = 16.
1A and 1D are two squares of primes with the same hundreds digit
∴ 1D = 121, 1A = 169, etc.

¹1	²6	³9
⁴2	7	7
⁵1	6	

3 3D = 27 or 64. Work is needed to eliminate 27 and to show 64 leads to a unique solution.

	¹7	²2
³6	2	5
⁴4	9	6

4 1D is odd; 3A and √(3A) have the same first digit – which is therefore 1.
Since the tens digit of 3A must be odd, 3A = 196.
The rest follows.

	¹1	²3
³1	9	6
4		1

5

¹5	²2	
³7	1	⁴2
⁵6	7	6

6

¹3	²6	
³6	7	6
⁴1	6	

¹6	²4	
³7	8	4
⁴6	4	

β: E10 1089 and all that   NC

This section is included under *Extension* (rather than under *Taster* or *Core*) only because it strays from the official curriculum. However, it is best tackled by a complete class.

Answers
1. a 99

   c Only 99 ('*cd*' and '*dc*' are both divisible by 9 – by the solution to **E2** Problem 4
      ∴ '*cd*' + '*dc*' is divisible by 9.
      Moreover '*cd*' ≠ 99; ∴ $c + d = 9$; ∴ '*cd*' + '*dc*' = $(c + d) \times 11 = 9 \times 11$

3. a $88_{base\ 9}$

   c Only $88_{base\ 9}$ ('*cd*' and '*dc*' are both divisible by 8; ∴ '*cd*' + '*dc*' is divisible by 8,
      And '*cd*' ≠ 88 ∴ $c + d = 8$ ∴ '*cd*' + '*dc*' = $(c + d) \times 11_{base\ 9} = 8 \times 11_{base\ 9} = 88_{base\ 9}$)

4. a $77_{base\ 8}$

   c Only $77_{base\ 8}$ ('*cd*' and '*dc*' are both divisible by 7 ∴ '*cd*' + '*dc*' is divisible by 7,
      And '*cd*' ≠ 77 ∴ $c + d = 7$ ∴ '*cd*' + '*dc*' = $(c + d) \times 11_{base\ 8} = 7 \times 11_{base\ 8} = 77_{base\ 8}$)

5. a $1078_{base\ 9}$ b $8701_{base\ 9}$ (same digits reversed)   c $1078_{base\ 9}$
6. a $1067_{base\ 8}$ b $7601_{base\ 8}$ (same digits reversed)   c $1067_{base\ 8}$

β: E11 Integer problems   NC

The problems in this section vary in difficulty and sophistication. Their purpose is to convey the message that the simplest possible raw material (positive integers) still gives rise to plenty of genuinely serious problems.

Answers
1. a 5478 (or 8745)   b 3267 (or 7623)   c 8745 (digits of a reversed)
2. a 25 (multiples of 4)
   b 22 (the perfect squares $< \sqrt{500} \approx 22.36$: $1^2 = 1 \times 1$, $2^2 = 4 \times 1$, etc.)
3. a 200 000   b 6
4. a 24; 4   b 120; 0   c 720; 0   d 7!:1; 8!:1; 9!:1; 10!:2;
   e 15!:3 zeros; 20!:4 zeros; 25!:6 zeros
5. a $\frac{1}{2}$ (3 of the 6 possible scores are even, and all are equally likely)

   b $\frac{1}{2}$ (This is not so obvious! 6 of the 11 possible scores are even, but they are not all equally likely)

   c $\frac{15}{36} = \frac{5}{12}$ (5 of the 11 possible scores are prime, but they are not all equally likely)

6. 4×4 or 3×6 (Want $ab = 2(a + b)$; that is $4 = ab - 2a - 2b + 4 = (a - 2)(b - 2)$ with a, b integers)
7. i 20 @ 1p, 20 @ 4p, 0 @ 12p; or ii 28 @ 1p, 9 @ 4p, 3 @ 12p
8. a 3^{33} b 4^{4^4}
9. a 11 111 = 100 × 111 + 11, so $hcf(11\ 111,111) = hcf(111,11) = 1$)
   b 1 111 111 111 111 111 = $10^{10} \times 111\ 111 + 10^4 \times 111\ 111 + 1111$;
      ∴ $hcf(1\ 111\ 111\ 111\ 111\ 111,\ 111\ 111) = hcf(1111, 111\ 111) = hcf(1111, 11) = 11$
10. 45, 54   11 7; 121, 144, 169, 441, 484, 676, 961

> 12. a 5, 41, 263
>   b 16 (The only possible units digits for a multi-digit prime are 1 and 3, hence there must be *at least one* single digit prime.
>   First suppose there are *two* single digit primes: i 2, 3, or ii 2, 5, or iii 3, 5
>   If i, third prime must use digits 4,5,6 and end in 1 – only 4561, 4651, 5641, 6451 work.
>   ii Third prime must use digits 3,4,6 and end in 1 – only 3461 works; or third prime uses digits 1, 4, 6 and ends in 3 – only 6143 works.
>   iii Third prime must use digits 2,4,6 and end in 1 – only 4261, 4621, 6421 work.

> Next suppose there is *just one* single digit prime (which can't be 3): **i** 2, or **ii** 5
> **i** Other two primes must end in 1 and 3: ∴ 41, 563 or 41, 653; 53, 461 or 53, 641
> **ii** Other two primes must end in 1 and 3: ∴ 41, 263; 23, 461 or 23, 641)

13 $2^2 + 2^5 = 6^2$ Multiply all three terms by any even power of 2 to get another such triple.

14 A 3-gon and the 6-gon both use a multiple of 3 matches. ∴ $N = 3k$. A 4-gon and a 6-gon each use an even number of matches. ∴ $N = 3k$ is a multiple of 2, so $k = 2m$, $N = 6m$.
To make a 5-gon and a 6-gon, if each edge of the 5-gon has a matches and each edge of the 6-gon has b matches, then $6m = N = 5a + 6b$. ∴ a must be a (positive) multiple of 6
∴ $N \geq 30 + 6 = 36$. Now show the conditions are fulfilled for every multiple of 6 which is ≥ 36.

15 See answer to *Alpha* Section **E4**, Problem **12**.

β: E12 More word sums   NC

This collection presents a very varied level of challenge. For more serious pupils there is much to be said for working on several such problems one after the other (in order to get into the swing of things). However, teachers may also choose to use individual problems with a complete top set as one way of providing something that feels more relaxed, but which remains serious.

Answers
1 a This clearly won't work! (T ≠ 0, so the only way the thousands column could work is if T = 9 with a carry of 1 from the hundreds *and a carry of 1 to the ten-thousands*)
  b This doesn't appear to work either – but don't give up too easily! In fact it has a unique solution! (It is not too hard to get going: the two left-hand columns show that O = 9, I = 0, E = D + 1; then in the thousands column E + carry = 10, so E = 8 – since a carry of 3 is impossible; now focus on the tens column, where there must be a carry from the units, but it can't be just 1, since 3 × N + 1 cannot then end in 8)

2 a **4** solutions (5386 + 5386; 6385 + 6385; 7832 + 7832; 7943 + 7943)
  b **2** solutions (6546 + 6546; 8548 + 8548)
  c **25** solutions (for example, 354 + 354 + 354 = 1062)

3 a **1** solution (68 782 + 650 + 68 782)
  b **1** solution (850 + 850 + 29 786)
  c **2** solutions (82 524 + 19 722 + 106, and the same with N and O interchanged)

4 a 92 836 + 12 836   b 96 233 + 62 513   c 3457 + 98 636

5 a 2 + 97 455 + 6928
  b 14 992 ÷ 4; 56 778 ÷ 6; 67 004 ÷ 7
  c 31 770 ÷ 5; 18 990 ÷ 6; 19 002 ÷ 6; 35 112 ÷ 8

6 (See **T13**, Problem **8** for a different solution when all digits are non-zero.)
  a T = 1, I = 9 (with carry of 1 from units column), O ≠ 0
  b P = 0: **30** solutions
    i   M = 8, N = 2 (or vice versa), and 5 choices for O: 2 × 5 solutions
    ii M = 7, N = 3 (or vice versa), and 5 choices for O: 2 × 5 solutions
    iii M = 6, N = 4 (or vice versa), and 5 choices for O: 2 × 5 solutions
  c P = 1: **0** solutions (since P ≠ T = 1)
    P = 2: i M = 8, N = 4 (or vice versa); 4 choices for O (since O ≠ 0): 2 × 4 solutions
        ii M = 7, N = 5 (or vice versa), and 4 choices for O (since O ≠ 0): 2 × 4 solutions

> P = 3: **i** M = 8, N = 5 (or vice versa); 4 choices for O (since O ≠ 0):
> 2 × 4 solutions
> **ii** M = 7, N = 6 (or vice versa); 4 choices for O (since O ≠ 0):
> 2 × 4 solutions
> P = 4: M = 8, N = 6 (or vice versa); 4 choices for O (since O ≠ 0):
> 2 × 4 solutions
> P = 5: M = 8, N = 7 (or vice versa); 4 choices for O (since O ≠ 0):
> 2 × 4 solutions
> Total number of solutions = 30 + 16 + 8 + 8 + 8 = **78**

β: E13 100% proof   NC

Each problem in this final section links with previous work.
Teachers may prefer to extract individual problems to link with earlier sections (Problem 1 with **T22** and **C37**, Problems 2 and 3 with **C11** and **T20**).

Answers

1 a i 0   ii 0 (fluke)   c i 1   ii 1 (fluke)
   b i 1   ii $\frac{1}{2}$ d i $\frac{1}{6}$ ii $\frac{1}{5}$

> e We shall revisit this problem in book *Gamma*, Section **E4**, by which time pupils' algebra should be much stronger. Meantime they might like to try to prove that:
>
> i if $a, b, c, d > 0$, and $\frac{a}{b} = \frac{c}{d}$, then $\frac{a}{b} = \frac{c}{d} = \frac{a+c}{b+d}$
>
> ii if $a, b, c, d > 0$, and $\frac{a}{b} < \frac{c}{d}$, then $\frac{a}{b} < \frac{a+c}{b+d} < \frac{c}{d}$

2 a △*TYU* and △*WZV* are congruent right-angled triangles (by ASA), and slide together so that *TU* and *WV* coincide to form an equilateral triangle with side $TY = WZ = \frac{1}{3}YZ$, and with *TU* = *WV* as the perpendicular bisector of the base. Hence $YU = ZV = \frac{1}{6}YZ$.

   b i *TX*, *XW* and *UV* are the longest sides.

   ii ∠*T* = 150° (opposite side *WV*), ∠*U* = 90° (opposite side *XW*), ∠*V* = 90° (opposite *XT*), ∠*W* = 150° (opposite *TU*), ∠*X* = 60° (opposite *UV*);
   ∴ ∠*T* and ∠*W* are the largest angles

   iii *WV* is opposite ∠*T*, and *TU* is opposite ∠*W*.
   (The two *shortest* sides are opposite the two *largest* angles, and the three *smallest* angles ∠*X*, ∠*U*, ∠*V* are opposite the three *longest* sides.)

3C Gamma

Rough listing of sections by topic

'Extension' tasks often cut across curriculum topics – for example, using arithmetic in a geometric context, or reasoning in an arithmetical problem. In Book *Alpha*, the structure of elementary mathematics which could be assumed to be available to all pupils and teachers remained rather slight; so it proved possible to group sections which sought to explore interesting elementary themes 'by topic'.

In book *Beta* the attempt to group sections by topic became more awkward. However, partly because this series has striven to give algebraic ideas a firm numerical meaning (through problems involving measures, integers, ratios, fractions, surds and geometrical applications) before dressing them up in symbolic garb, the classification was still more-or-less possible.

Now that we have reached book *Gamma* it is no longer possible to pretend that individual sections can be classified in this simple-minded way. We have nevertheless tried to give a similar listing – subject to the proviso that many sections appear under more than one heading.

Note: The order of sections within each list is not a "dependence order".

Number and "pre-algebra"

T1	Algebraic arithmetic	C18	The unitary method
T2	$\sqrt{2}$, a curious sequence, and A4 paper	C19	Estimation C: Arithmetic meets geometry
T3	Substituting values in algebraic expressions	C21	Integer problems
T5	Simplifying *A*	C22	From fractions to decimals *A*
T9	Power play *A*	C23	Averages
T11	Number chains	C24	Index laws *B*
T12	Simplifying *C*: Cancelling	C25	Missing digits
T14	Index laws *A*	C26	Equations
T15	Surd arithmetic *A*	C28	Surd arithmetic *B*
T18	Power play *B*	C29	Adding and subtracting fractions
T20	From fractions to decimals and back	C31	Index laws *C*
T22	Calculating and comparing: a miscellany	C32	Approximate calculation
C1	Estimation *A*	C34	From fractions to decimals *B*
C2	How to tell when an integer is prime	C37	Sequences *C*
C4	Estimation *B*	C40	Estimation *D*: Big numbers
C5	How to decide the meaning of $(-1) \times (-1)$	C42	Sequences *D*: Guess my rule
C6	Number puzzles	C43	What's my number?
C11	Ratios	E1	Integers, digits and algebra
C12	Power play *C*	E2	From fractions to decimals *C*
C14	Word problems	E3	Consecutive integers

Algebra

T1	Algebraic arithmetic	T9	Power play *A*
T3	Substituting values in algebraic expressions	T12	Simplifying *C*: Cancelling
T4	Sequences *A*	T14	Index laws *A*
T5	Simplifying *A*	T15	Surd arithmetic *A*
T6	How to decide the meaning of 2^0	T16	Simplifying *D*
T7	Simplifying *B*	T18	Power play *B*

T19 Factorising quadratics
T22 Calculating and comparing: a miscellany
T23 Solving quadratic equations
C5 How to decide the meaning of (–1) × (–1)
C6 Number puzzles
C7 Linear equations and inequalities
C9 Negative numbers
C11 Ratios
C12 Power play C
C14 Word problems
C16 From formula to function
C18 The unitary method
C23 Averages
C24 Index laws B
C26 Equations

C27 Sequences B
C28 Surd arithmetic B
C29 Adding and subtracting fractions
C31 Index laws C
C36 Algebra review
C37 Sequences C
C38 Index laws D
C40 Estimation D: Big numbers
C42 Sequences D: Guess my rule
C43 What's my number?
E1 Integers, digits and algebra
E3 Consecutive integers
E4 How many?
E5 Primes in arithmetic progression
E6 More missing digits

Geometry
T2 √2, a curious sequence, and A4 paper
T8 Circles A: Arc lengths and areas of sectors
T10 Parallel lines
T12 Similar triangles A
T17 Pythagoras' theorem A
T21 Scale factors A: Length and area
T24 Loci
C3 Geometry problems A
C7 Linear equations and inequalities
C8 Circles B: Circumference and area

C10 Angles in regular polygons
C13 Similar triangles B
C15 Volume and surface area of right prisms
C19 Estimation C: arithmetic meets geometry
C20 Similar triangles C
C33 Similar triangles D
C35 Pythagoras' theorem
C37 Sequences C
C39 Geometry problems B
C41 Scale factors B

Using and applying mathematics (including measures)
   Direct
T2 √2, a curious sequence, and A4 paper
T22 Calculating and comparing: a miscellany
C1 Estimation A
C4 Estimation B
C11 Ratios
C14 Word problems

C18 The unitary method
C19 Estimation C: Arithmetic meets geometry
C23 Averages
C32 Approximate calculation
C40 Estimation D: Big numbers
E8 Identical portions

   Oblique
T6 How to decide the meaning of 2^0
T11 Number chains
C2 How to tell when an integer is prime
C5 How to decide the meaning of (–1) × (–1)
C6 Number puzzles
C17 Black hats and white hats
C25 Missing digits

C30 Algorithms and strategies
E3 Consecutive integers
E4 How many?
E5 Primes in arithmetic progression
E6 More missing digits
E7 Tiling

Comments and answers

Mathematics is about *methods* rather than just 'answers'. We have tried to give answers in 'structured form' to indicate how it is intended that pupils should derive these answers. Where a reader can see at a glance *from the given form* what the numerical answer is, the answer is often omitted. Where a numerical answer cannot be read off 'at a glance' from the structured format the numerical answer is often included as well.

Two related changes affect book *Gamma*. The problems in book *Gamma* are often harder, and require longer solutions than those in the earlier books; so it is not always possible to provide the ideal level of support in a *Teachers' Book*. However, teachers using book *Gamma* should already have extensive experience of the format and expectations of the earlier books, and so should be in a better position to judge for themselves what is required.

γ: T1 Algebraic arithmetic   NC

Like most of the apparently 'numerical' sections in this series this opening section is blatantly *algebraic*. *Extension mathematics* does not presume to teach basic algebra: rather it seeks to provide activities and exercises in numerical settings, which move pupils on from basic numerical calculation, and which cultivate an appreciation of algebraic structure and simplification. The intermediate answers given here underline the intended approach.

Answers

0	a	$48 \times (1 + 49) = 2400$	b	$0.48 \times (1 + 49) = 24$

1	$25 \times (25 - 1) = 600$	7	$48 \times (49 + 1) = 2400$
2	$19 \times (19 + 1) = 380$	8	$98 \times (99 + 1) = 9800$
3	$21 \times (21 - 1) = 420$	9	$48 \times (48 + 2) = 2400$
4	$51 \times (49 + 51) = 5100$	10	$49 \times 50 + 50 \times 51 = 5000$
5	$199 \times (199 + 1) = 39\,800$	11	$(n + 1)[(n - 1) + (n + 1)] = 2n(n + 1)$
6	$201 \times (201 - 1) = 40\,200$		

12	$25 \times (1 + 25) = 650$	15	51
13	$(n - 1)n + n(n + 1) = 2n^2$	16	$0.98 \times (1 + 99) = 98$
14	$(2n + 1)(2n + 2)$	17	$0.48 \times (49 + 1) + 1 = 25$

γ: T2 √2, a curious sequence, and A4 paper

The term-to-term recurrence which underlies Problems **0-4** is part of a much more extensive theme. However, it is enough here for pupils to be struck by how quickly the process converges towards $\sqrt{2}$. Problem **5** then highlights the way $\sqrt{2}$ arises inescapably in the series A0, A1, A2, A3, A4, A5, ... (The series is precisely specified by two requirements: that all sizes be similar, and that size A0 should have area 1 square metre – so has width $2^{-\frac{1}{4}}$ metres!)

Answers

0	i	$1, \frac{3}{2}, \frac{17}{12}, \frac{577}{408}$	ii	$1, 1.5, 1.416666\ldots, 1.414215687\ldots$

1 a $2.006944444\ldots$ b $2.000006007\ldots$

  c That the terms of the sequence are 'converging' very quickly towards $\sqrt{2}$

  d $1.414213562\ldots$; my calculator claims (wrongly) that its square is *exactly* 2

2 a i $2, \frac{3}{2}, \frac{17}{12}, \frac{577}{408}$ ii 2, 1.5, 1.416666..., 1.414215687...

  b Identical from the second term onwards

3 a 1.4, 1.414285714..., 1.414213564..., 1.414213563...

  b 1.96, 2.000204081..., 2.000000005..., 2.000000002...

4 The sequence remains constant, with every term equal to $\sqrt{2}$.
  Proof: 2nd term = $\left[\left(\sqrt{2} + \frac{2}{\sqrt{2}}\right) \div 2 = 2\sqrt{2} \div 2 = \sqrt{2}\right]$

5 a 'length' = 2y, 'width' = x   c $r' = \frac{2}{r} = r$; ∴ $r^2 = 2$; ∴ $r = \sqrt{2}$.

  b i $r = \frac{2x}{2y} = \frac{x}{y}$ ii $r' = \frac{2y}{x} = \frac{2}{r}$

γ: T3 Substituting values in algebraic expressions   NC

In Problem 0c you may need to stress the advantages of thinking about the *powers* in the expression to be evaluated.

Answers

0 a	0	b	8	c	$\frac{4}{3}$						

1 a	4	d	36	g	8	j	60	m	$\frac{8}{3}$	p	$\frac{2}{3}$
b	6	e	3	h	0	k	0	n	$\frac{10}{3}$	q	0
c	8	f	8	i	32	l	16	o	$\frac{8}{7}$		
2 a	8	d	16	g	$\frac{1}{48}$	j	$\frac{1}{8}$	m	9	p	3
b	12	e	$\frac{1}{40}$	h	$\frac{1}{20}$	k	$\frac{5}{6}$	n	8^2		
c	105	f	$\frac{1}{24}$	i	$\frac{1}{10}$	l	$\frac{1}{10}$	o	1		
3 a	19	d	11	g	6	j	85				
b	0	e	36	h	36	k	6				
c	7	f	14	i	18	l	96				

γ: T4 Sequences A: From a term-to-term rule to a closed formula

Pupils should emerge from this section able to implement a term-to-term rule quickly and reliably. They should also appreciate that translating a term-to-term rule into a closed formula is sometimes very easy (Problem 2), but can also be surprisingly elusive (Problem 4).

Answers

0 i	39 (perhaps)	ii 39, 47, 56, 66	iii Probably not

1 2, 4, 6, 8, 10

2 a nth term = 2n   b 10th term = 2 × 10 = 20, 20th term = 2 × 20 = 40   c 2 × 99

3 a i 4, 8, 16   ii 8, 16, 32   iii 6, 12, 24
  b i 7, 15, 31   ii 11, 23, 47   iii 7, 15, 31
  c i 13, 29, 61   ii 17, 37, 77   iii 9, 21, 45
  d i 25, 676, 458 329   ii 100, 10201, 104 080 804   iii 16, 289, 84100
  e i 5, 26, 677   ii 26, 677, 458330   iii 10, 101, 10202
  f i 5, 9, 44   ii 14, 69, 965   iii 7, 13, 90
  g i 121, 16900, 289 714 441   ii 784, 654 481, 4 293 7222 0225   iii 49, 2809, 816 8164
  h i 29, 866, 750 797   ii 13, 178, 31 853   iii 25, 641, 411 506

| 4 3aii 2^n | 3bi $2^n - 1$ | 3cii $5 \times 2^{n-1} - 3$ |

γ: T5 Simplifying A: Collecting repeated brackets NC

Use Problem 0 (and subsequent spot checks) to stress the advantages of the *algebraic* approach, where we identify some fraction which occurs in each term (often a 'unit fraction' – such as $\frac{1}{3}$ in Problem 0ai), treat each term as a *multiple* of this fraction, and collect up terms as though this fraction were a symbol (like 'x').

Answers

| 0 a i $18 \times \frac{1}{3} = 6$ | ii $2 \times \frac{1}{3} = \frac{2}{3}$ | b i $2(y - x)$ | ii $2x - y$ | iii $-y$ |

1 $20 \times \frac{1}{5} = 4$	10 $70 \times \frac{6}{7} = 60$	19 $20(x + y)$
2 $14 \times \frac{1}{7} = 2$	11 $55 \times \frac{7}{11} = 35$	20 $7(y - x)$
3 $12 \times \frac{1}{3} = 4$	12 $68 \times \frac{1}{17} = 4$	21 0
4 $26 \times \frac{1}{13} = 2$	13 $1 \times \frac{1}{4} = \frac{1}{4}$	22 $10(x + y + 4)$
5 $32 \times \frac{1}{8} = 4$	14 $39 \times \frac{1}{6} = \frac{13}{2}$	23 $8 \times \frac{1}{x} = \frac{8}{x}$
6 $52 \times \frac{2}{13} = 8$	15 $20(x + 1)$	24 $46 \times \frac{1}{a} = \frac{46}{a}$
7 $102 \times \frac{1}{17} = 6$	16 $11(x + 2y)$	25 $10 \times \frac{1}{a} = \frac{10}{a}$
8 $55 \times \frac{1}{11} = 5$	17 $50(2y - 3)$	26 $3 \times \frac{1}{a} = \frac{3}{a}$
9 $70 \times \frac{2}{7} = 20$	18 $x - 1$	

| 27 $\frac{27x}{x-1}$ | 29 -12 |
| 28 15 | 30 -12 |

γ: T6 How do we decide the meaning of 2^0? NC

The goal of this section is to convey that the definitions of 2^0, 2^{-1} and $2^{\frac{1}{2}}$ make perfect sense and are in fact forced upon us if the index law

$$2^m \times 2^n = 2^{m+n}$$

is to hold for all powers.

Where pupils have limited previous experience of fractional exponents, it may be necessary to extend the discussion in Problem 0 to address the meaning of such expressions as $2^{\frac{1}{3}}$, $2^{\frac{2}{3}}$, $2^{-\frac{1}{2}}$, $2^{\frac{1}{4}}$ and $2^{-\frac{1}{4}}$ (Problem 2e, f, i, j).

Answers

0 a i $2^2 = 4$, $2^1 = 2$, $2^0 = 1?$, $2^{-1} = \frac{1}{2}?$, $2^{-2} = \frac{1}{4}?$ iii $1, \frac{1}{2}, \frac{1}{4}$

 ii $2^2 = 4$, $2^0 = 1$, $2^{-2} = \frac{1}{4}$

b In ai: $\frac{2^2}{2^1} = 2^1$, $\frac{2^1}{2^0} = 2^1$, etc. In aii: $\frac{2^4}{2^2} = 2^2$, $\frac{2^2}{2^0} = 2^2$, $\frac{2^0}{2^{-2}} = 2^2$.

If $2^{\frac{1}{2}} = x$, then in the sequence $2^1 = 2$, $2^{\frac{1}{2}} = x$, $2^0 = 1$, $2^{-\frac{1}{2}}$, ...

we may expect $\frac{2}{x} = \frac{x}{1}$; that is $2^{\frac{1}{2}} = x = \sqrt{2}$.

1 a $2^0 = 1$ b $2^{-1} = \frac{1}{2}$ c $2^{\frac{1}{2}} = \sqrt{2}$

2 a 2   d $\frac{1}{\sqrt{2}}$ g 4   j $\sqrt{2}$
  b 4   e 2   h $\frac{1}{2}$
  c $\sqrt{2}$ f 4   i 2

3 a 8   c $2^1 - 2^0 = 1$ e $3^1 - 2^0 = 2$
  b $4^0 = 1$ d $3^1 - 2^1 = 1$ f $4^1 - 8^{\frac{2}{3}} = 0$

4 a $2\sqrt{2}?, 4?$ b $4\sqrt{2}?, 8?$ c $2^{\frac{3}{2}} + 2^2 = 2\sqrt{2} + 4?, 2^2 + 2^{\frac{5}{2}} = 4 + 4\sqrt{2}?$

5 a $\sqrt{2}$ units   b $\frac{1}{\sqrt{2}}$ units

6 a Volume = $2^{-1} \times 2^0 \times 2^1 = 1$ cubic units;
  surface area = $2 \times (2^{-1} \times 2^0 + 2^0 \times 2^1 + 2^1 \times 2^{-1}) = 7$ square units;
  total edge length = $4 \times (2^{-1} + 2^0 + 2^1) = 14$ units

  b Volume = $2^{-\frac{1}{2}} \times 2^0 \times 2^{\frac{1}{2}} = 1$ cubic units;
  surface area = $2 \times \left(2^{-\frac{1}{2}} \times 2^0 + 2^0 \times 2^{\frac{1}{2}} + 2^{\frac{1}{2}} \times 2^{-\frac{1}{2}}\right) = 2 + 3\sqrt{2}$ square units;
  total edge length = $4 \times \left(2^{-\frac{1}{2}} + 2^0 + 2^{\frac{1}{2}}\right) = 4 + 6\sqrt{2}$ units

  c Volume = $2^0 \times 2^{\frac{1}{2}} \times 2^1 = 2\sqrt{2}$ cubic units;
  surface area = $2 \times \left(2^0 \times 2^{\frac{1}{2}} + 2^{\frac{1}{2}} \times 2^1 + 2^1 \times 2^0\right) = 4 + 6\sqrt{2}$ square units;
  total edge length = $4 \times \left(2^0 + 2^{\frac{1}{2}} + 2^1\right) = 12 + 4\sqrt{2}$ units

7 a $2\sqrt{2} = 2.828427125\ldots$. All five other expressions give rise to the same approximate value

  b ii $2^{\frac{3}{2}} = 2^1 \times 2^{\frac{1}{2}} = 2\sqrt{2}$ v $3 - \left(2^{\frac{1}{2}} - 1\right)^2 = 3 - (\sqrt{2} - 1)^2 = 2\sqrt{2}$

  iii $\left(2^{\frac{1}{2}} + 1\right)^2 - 3 = (\sqrt{2} + 1)^2 - 3 = 2\sqrt{2}$ vi $\frac{2}{\sqrt{2}} + \sqrt{2} = \sqrt{2} + \sqrt{2} = 2\sqrt{2}$

  iv $8^{\frac{1}{2}} = \sqrt{8} = 2\sqrt{2}$

8 a All three expression should produce the same approximate value
  $\approx 2.414213562\ldots$

  b i $\frac{1}{2^{\frac{1}{2}} - 1} = \frac{1}{\sqrt{2} - 1} = \sqrt{2} + 1$ iii $7 + 5\sqrt{2} = (3 + 2\sqrt{2})(1 + \sqrt{2})$

  ii $3 + 2^{\frac{3}{2}} = 3 + 2\sqrt{2} = (1 + \sqrt{2})^2 = \left(1 + 2^{\frac{1}{2}}\right)^2$

γ: T7 Simplifying B: Collecting up like terms   NC

If this review seems likely to prove relatively straightforward, you might consider using it as a challenge to begin to develop *speed* and *accuracy*.

Answers

0 a x^2	b $-a$	c $u + 1$

1 $x + 24$	5 $5 + x$	9 $6y + 24$	13 $3a$
2 $5x$	6 $5a + 4b$	10 $-c + 2$	14 $26a - 10b - 3c$
3 $3a$	7 $5a - 7b$	11 $12x$	
4 0	8 -1	12 $-6a$	

15 a $4a$	b $a - b$

γ: T8 Circles A: Calculating arc lengths and areas of sectors

NC

The 'No Calculator' instruction is included partly to emphasise the injunction to give all answers 'in *exact* form (in terms of π)'.

Answers

> 0 a has circumference $2\pi r = 10\pi = \sqrt{100\pi^2}$
> b has circumference $20 = 2\pi r$, so $r = \frac{10}{\pi}$ and area $= \pi r^2 = \frac{100}{\pi}$
> c has circumference $2\pi r = 25\pi$

1. a 10π cm b 25π cm²
2. a circumference = 31.4 cm d circumference = 25.1 cm
   b circumference = 37.7 cm e circumference = 18.8 cm
   c circumference = 62.8 cm f circumference = 94.2 cm
3. a $(28 + 14\pi)$ cm b $(20 + 10\pi)$ cm
4. $(10 + \frac{5}{2}\pi)$ cm
5. a $6\pi + 4\pi = 10\pi$ cm
   b perimeter = 12π cm; area = $18\pi + 3 \times 2\pi = 24\pi$ cm²
6. a Perimeter = $(24 + 10\pi)$ cm; b area = $(120 + 25\pi)$ cm²
7. a area = 153 cm² c area = 113 cm² e area = 227 cm²
   b area = 95 cm² d area = 707 cm² f area = 201 cm²
8. $3 \times \left(\frac{1}{2\pi}12^2\right) + 2 \times 24^2 + 4 \times (24 \times 5) = (216\pi + 1632)$ cm²
9. $15\pi \div \frac{1}{2}\pi = 30$
10. a $2 : 3$
    b $4 : 9$
    c The region between the two circles is larger ($900\pi - 400\pi$ to 400π)
11. a $\frac{\pi}{4}$
    b $\frac{\pi}{4}$ (the figure includes exactly half of the circle and half of the square in **a**)
    c $\frac{\pi}{4}$ (the figure includes exactly half of the semicircle and half of the rectangle in **b**)
12. $(400 - 100\pi)$ cm²
13. a $\left(16 + \frac{49}{2}\pi\right)$ cm² b $(22 + 7\pi)$ cm
14. Perimeter = $(12 + 2\sqrt{85} + 7\pi)$ cm; area = $\left(84 + \frac{49}{2}\pi\right)$ cm²
15. $9\pi - \pi = 8\pi$ m²
16. $\left(\sqrt{3} - \frac{\pi}{2}\right)$ cm²
17. a $(6 + 9\pi)$ cm b $\left(36 - \frac{9}{2}\pi\right)$ cm²
18. a Perimeter = 3π cm; b area = 2π cm²
19. $(256 - 64\pi)$ cm²

γ: T9 Power play A

This slightly tongue-in-cheek set of exercises is designed to encourage the habit of 'thinking in powers'. (Interesting mathematics often involves powers; so answers are often more instructive if expressed multiplicatively using powers.)

Answers

> 0 a $2^2 \times 2^3 = 2^5$ c $2^3 \times 2^5 = 2^8$ e $2^5 \times 2^6 = 2^{11}$
> b $2^1 \times 2^4 = 2^5$ d $2^4 \times 2^3 = 2^7$

1 a $3^2 \times 3^3 = 3^5$ c 5^5 e 10^5
   b $4^5 = 2^{10}$ d 6^5

2 a 2^5 e $2^3 \times 3^5$ i $2^2 \times 5^3$ m $2^3 \times 3^2$
   b 3^4 f 3×2^3 j $2^3 \times 3^3$ n $3^3 \times 5^2$
   c $2^2 \times 3^3$ g $2^2 \times 3^3$ k $2^3 \times 3 \times 5^3$ o $2^7 \times 5^3$
   d 6×5^3 h $2 \times 3 \times 5^3$ l $2^2 \times 3^2$

3 a 2×10^2 c 6×10^2 e 3^4
   b 6×10^2 d 2^5

4 6^3 hours

5 a 6 days = 12^3 hours   c 42 weeks = $(42 \times 2 \times 60)^2$ seconds
   b 6 days = $(60 \times 12)^2$ seconds   d 20 days = $(8 \times 5 \times 3)^3$ seconds
6 a $9 = 1^3 + 2^3$
   b $16 = 2^3 + 2^3$. Multiply each of the three terms in $3^2 = 1^3 + 2^3$ by 2^6, or 2^{12}, or .....

γ: T10 Parallel lines   NC

You will need to stress that one of the goals of this section is that pupils should learn to extract information reliably from a written question and to *draw a suitable diagram*.

Answers

0 b △FMN   c ∠FGH = ∠FHG = ∠FMN = ∠FNM = 70°

1 X

2 a E, F, H, M, N, Z   b H, N, Z

3 a ∠BAC = ∠DCA; ∠ABD = ∠CDB; ∠ADB = ∠CBD; ∠DAC = ∠BCA
   b ∠BAC = ∠DCA = 25°; ∠ABD = ∠CDB = 35°;
      ∠AOB = ∠COD = 120°; ∠AOD = ∠COB = 60°
      (Note: ∠ADB = ∠CBD and ∠DAC = ∠BCA are both determined, but cannot be calculated using what you know at this stage.)

4 $\frac{1}{2}(180° - 112°) = 34°$

5 ∠ACB = 72°, ∠CAB = 75°, ∠ABC = 33°

6 ∠KCD = 45°, ∠ABC = 45°

7 ∠BDC = 65°, ∠BAD = 83°

8 ∠AXE = 79°

9 ∠DAC = ∠BCA = 30°; ∴ ∠AOD = 108° = ∠BOC.
   ∠BAD = 80°; ∴ ∠CAB = 50° = ∠ACD.

10 ∠AXY = ∠DZX = 140° (alternate angles); ∴ ∠YXZ = 60°

11 ∠MSK = 55° = ∠QMR = ∠MQK = ∠LMS; ∠QKS = 125° = ∠QMS = ∠RML

12 Let the bisector of ∠ABC meet AD (extended if necessary) at P.
    Then ∠APB = $\frac{1}{2} \times 108°$;
    ∴ ∠DAB = ∠PAB = 180° − 52° − 29° = 99°;
    ∴ ∠BCD = 360° − 58° − 104° − 99° = 99°

γ: T11 Number chains

Digit-sum sequences link naturally to the test for divisibility by 9. Starting with any integer N, the digit-sum sequence of N converges very quickly to a single

3C Gamma

digit. In contrast, factor-sum sequences behave in a much more interesting and unpredictable way.

Answers

> 0 a $56765 \to 5+6+7+6+5 = 29 \to 2+9 = 11 \to 1+1 = 2$
> b i $16 \to 1+2+4+8 = 15 \to 1+3+5 = 9 \to 1+3 = 4 \to 1+2 = 3 \to 1$
> ii $20 \to 1+2+4+5+10 = 22 \to 1+2+11 = 14 \to 1+2+7 = 10 \to 1+2+5 = 8 \to 1+2+4 = 7 \to 1$

1 a $N = 10a + b > a + b$
  c $N = 1000a + 100b + 10c + d > a + b + c + d$
  b $N = 100a + 10b + c > a + b + c$

2 a $10 \to 1$
  b $11 \to 2$
  c $12 \to 3$
  d $13 \to 4$
  e $17 \to 8$
  f $18 \to 9$
  g $19 \to 10 \to 1$
  h $27 \to 9$
  i $28 \to 10 \to 1$
  j $29 \to 11 \to 2$
  k $30 \to 3$
  l $89 \to 17 \to 8$
  m $90 \to 9$
  n $91 \to 10 \to 1$
  o $92 \to 11 \to 2$
  p $98 \to 17 \to 2$
  q $99 \to 18 \to 9$
  r $100 \to 1$
  s $101 \to 2$
  t $189 \to 18 \to 9$
  u $199 \to 19 \to 10 \to 1$

3 a $199 \to 19 \to 10 \to 1$
  b $1999 \to 28 \to 10 \to 1$
  c $2999 \to 29 \to 11 \to 2$
  d $3999 \to 30 \to 3$
  e $56789 \to 35 \to 8$
  f $45678 \to 30 \to 3$
  g $98789 \to 41 \to 5$
  h $87878 \to 38 \to 11 \to 2$

> 4 199 is the smallest integer with a 'four-term digit-sum sequence'.
> 19 999 999 999 999 999 999 999 (twenty two 9s) $\to$ 199, so has a 'five-term digit-sum sequence'. Any smaller integer has a smaller digit sum, so can't have a digit-sum with a 'four-term digit-sum sequence'. So this must be the smallest integer with a five-term digit-sum sequence.

5 $12 \to 1+2+3+4+6 = 16$; $18 \to 1+2+3+6+9 = 21$; $20 \to 1+2+4+5+10 = 22$; $24 \to 1+2+3+4+6+8+12 = 36$; $30 \to 1+2+3+5+6+10+15 = 42$; $36 \to 1+2+3+4+6+9+12+18 = 55$

6 i $6 \to 1+2+3 = 6 \to 1+2+3 = 6 \to \ldots$ ii $7 \to 1$ iii $8 \to 1+2+4 = 7 \to 1$

7 b $2^0 \times 7^0 = 1$, $2^0 \times 7^1 = 7$, $2^1 \times 7^0 = 2$, $2^1 \times 7^1 = 14$, $2^2 \times 7^0 = 4$, $2^2 \times 7^1 = 28$
[Note: $2^0 \times 7^0 + 2^0 \times 7^1 + 2^1 \times 7^0 + 2^1 \times 7^1 + 2^2 \times 7^0 + 2^2 \times 7^1 = (2^0 + 2^1 + 2^2) \times (7^0 + 7^1)$]
  c $28 \to 1+2+4+7+14 = 28$ d i $27 \to 1+3+9 = 13 \to 1$ ii $29 \to 1$

> 8 a i $495 = 3^2 \times 5 \times 11$ ii $2^4 \times 31$ iii 7×71
> c Good pupils who tackle the shaded problems should be left to work this out the hard way. But at some stage it is appropriate to let them in on a wonderful algebraic secret indicated in the 'Note' to Problem **7b** above. Given the prime factorisation of an integer – such as $495 = 3^2 \times 5 \times 11$ – simple algebra suggests a clever way of summing all its factors.
> If we multiply out $(1 + 3 + 3^2) \times (1 + 5) \times (1 + 11)$ then we get each factor exactly once *including* $3^2 \times 5 \times 11 = 495$;
> hence the factor-sum of 495 is equal to $13 \times 6 \times 12 - 495 = 441$.
> i $495 \to 441 \to 300 \to 568 \to 512 \to 511 \to 81 \to 40 \to 50 \to 43 \to 1$
> ii $496 \to 496 \to \ldots$ iii $497 \to 79 \to 1$
>
> 9 a $120 \to 240 = 2 \times 120$ b $672 \to 1344 = 2 \times 672$
> 10 a $220 \to 284$ b $284 \to 220$
> 11 $1184 \to 1210$ b $1210 \to 1184$
> 12 $2620 \to 2924$ b $2924 \to 2620$

γ: T12 Simplifying C: Cancelling NC

Mathematics depends on the art of simplification. This set of exercises provides a gentle introduction to multiplicative simplification.

Answers

> 0 a $49 \times 2 = 98$ b $\frac{3}{10}$ c $13a$

1	a	6	c	1	e	12×3	g	3×27	i	d	k	$3y$
	b	8×2	d	12	f	5×3	h	8×5	j	3	l	$8 \times 5b$
2	a	c	d	4	g	5	j	4	m	$\frac{n}{2q}$	p	$\frac{2r}{3t}$
	b	3	e	5	h	2×12	k	$\frac{x^3}{4}$	n	k^3	q	$2a^2$
	c	$\frac{3}{8}$	f	2	i	5×30	l	y^3	o	x	r	$\frac{9r}{4s}$
3	a	1	c	$\frac{5 \times 3}{2}$	e	2	g	$\frac{4a}{7b}$	i	$\frac{5c}{6a}$	k	$\frac{3r}{14t}$
	b	10	d	$\frac{2}{3}$	f	$\frac{13}{10}$	h	$\frac{4y^2}{7x^2}$	j	$\frac{4yz}{7x^2}$	l	$\frac{4b^4}{7a^4}$
4	a	$\frac{1}{3}$	c	$\frac{20}{13}$	e	1	g	abc
	b	6	d	$\frac{a}{c}$	f	$\frac{bdf}{ace}$	h	$\frac{1}{abc}$

> 5 −7
>
> 6 $\frac{x^2 + x}{x^3} = \frac{1}{x} + \frac{1}{x^2} = \frac{1}{x}\left(1 + \frac{1}{x}\right) = \frac{x^2 - 1}{x^3 - x^2} = \frac{1 + x}{x^2}$

γ: T13 Similar triangles A: The AAA and SSS similarity criteria

The *Midpoint theorem* (Problem 6) emerges from the world of congruent triangles; yet it provides a window into the world of *similarity*. Learning to identify and to use similar triangles is the single most powerful technique in elementary geometry.

Answers

> 0 b i $\angle AB'C' = \angle ABC$; $\angle AC'B' = \angle ACB$ ii $AC' = 2 \times AC$; $B'C' = 2 \times BC$

1 a For example, a 1×1 square and a 2×1 rectangle

   b For example, a 1×1 square and a 60° rhombus with sides of length 1

2 No. Corresponding angles are equal (all 90°); but corresponding sides are not in the same ratio (6×8 versus 4×6, and $6 : 4 \neq 8 : 6$)

3 **33.6 m** (height : 4 m = 21 m : 2.5 m)

4 Length = **91 m** (length : 130 m = 84 m : 120 m);
   distance from foot of mast = **35 m**

5 **22 cm** (height : 7 cm = 30.8 cm : 9.8 cm)

6 b $AN = ML$ and $MN = BL$ c $MN = LC$ and $ML = NC$

7 In $\triangle ABY$, M is the midpoint of AB and MD is parallel to BY;
   ∴ (∗) D is the midpoint of AY and $MD = \frac{1}{2}BY$ (by the *Midpoint theorem*).
   $MBXD$ is a parallelogram, so $MD = BX$; hence X is the midpoint of BY (by (∗)).

8 a Apply the *Midpoint theorem* to $\triangle AB'C'$.

9 a $MNOP$ appears to be a parallelogram.

> **b** Draw *AC*. Apply the *Midpoint theorem* to △*BAC* to show that *MN* is parallel to *AC*.
> Then apply the *Midpoint theorem* to △*DAC* to show that *PO* is parallel to *AC*.
> ∴ *OP*||*MN*.
> Draw *BD*. Apply the *Midpoint theorem* to △*ABD* to show that *MP* is parallel to *BD*.
> Then apply the *Midpoint theorem* to △*CBD* to show that *NO* is parallel to *BD*.
> ∴ *MP*||*NO*.
>
> **10** Applying the *Midpoint theorem* to △*BAC* shows that *MN*||*AC*.
> Applying the *Midpoint theorem* to △*DAC* shows that *PO*||*AC*.
> ∴ *MN*||*PO*.
> Similarly, in △*ABD*, *MP*||*BD* and in △*CBD*, *NO*||*BD*.
> ∴ *MP*||*NO*.
> Hence *MNOP* is a parallelogram.
> Two parallel line segments, such as *MN* and *PO*, necessarily lie in a plane.
>
> **11 a** ∠*PSM* = ∠*ARM* (alternate angles);
> *SM* = *RM*   (given);
> ∠*SMP* = ∠*RMA* (vertically opposite angles).
> ∴ △*PSM* and △*ARM* are congruent (by the ASA congruence criterion).
> ∴ *PS* = *AR*, but *PS* = *QR* (opposite sides of parallelogram).
> ∴ *AR* = *QR*, so *R* bisects *QA*.
>
> **b** Since △*PSM* and △*ARM* are congruent, *PM* = *MA*.
> As in part **a**, *S* bisects *PB*.
> So in △*PBA* we have *MS*||*AB* (by the *Midpoint theorem*),
> and *PQ*||*SR* (opposite sides of a parallelogram).

γ: T14 Index laws A   NC

These problems use the basic index law $a^m \times a^n = a^{m+n}$ to explore the world of powers, to achieve efficient cancellation (Problems 6, 7), and to take a brief look at the idea behind *logarithms* (Problems 0, 1, 2, 4).

Answers

> **0 a i** $64 = 2^6$ **ii** $4096 = 2^{12}$
> **b** ∴ $64 \times 64 = 2^6 \times 2^6 = 2^{12} = 4096$
> **c** $4096 \div 128 = 2^{12} \div 2^7 = 2^5 = 64 \div 2 = 32$

1 $2^1 = 2$; $2^2 = 4$; $2^3 = 8$; $2^4 = 16$; $2^5 = 32$;
$2^6 = 64$; $2^7 = 128$; $2^8 = 256$; $2^9 = 512$; $2^{10} = 1024$;
$2^{11} = 2048$; $2^{12} = 4096$; $2^{13} = 8192$; $2^{14} = 16\,384$; $2^{15} = 32\,768$;
$2^{16} = 65\,536$; $2^{17} = 131\,072$; $2^{18} = 262\,144$; $2^{19} = 524\,288$; $2^{20} = 1\,048\,576$

2 a 1024   **c** 8192   **e** 8   **g** 131 072   **i** 512
  b 2048   **d** 64   **f** 32 768 **h** 262 144

3 a 999   **b** −1002   **c** 499   **d** −1004

4 a $3^1 = 3$; $3^2 = 9$; $3^3 = 27$; $3^4 = 81$; $3^5 = 243$;
  $3^6 = 729$; $3^7 = 2187$; $3^8 = 6561$; $3^9 = 19\,683$; $3^{10} = 59\,049$
  b i $3^3 \times 3^4 = 3^7 = 2187$ **iii** $3^4 \times 3^5 = 3^9 = 19\,683$ **v** $3^9 \div 3^6 = 3^3 = 27$
     ii $3^2 \times 3^6 = 3^8 = 6561$ **iv** $3^6 \div 3^3 = 3^3 = 27$ **vi** $3^{10} \div 3^3 = 3^7 = 2187$

5 a 11^{-2} ($11^2 = 121 < 125 = 5^3$)   **c** 10^{-3} ($10^3 = 1000 < 1024 = 2^{10}$)
  b 3^{-5} ($3^5 = 243 < 256 = 2^8$)

> **6 a** 1   **c** 1   **e** 1   **g** 4   **i** 1
>   **b** 1   **d** 1   **f** 2   **h** 27   **j** 2
> **7 a** $\frac{2}{3}$ **b** 5   **c** $\frac{2^4}{5 \times 11}$ **d** $\frac{1}{5^5 \times 3^3 \times 2^4}$

γ: T15 Surd arithmetic A

Learning to calculate reliably with surds is (like working with fractions and later with algebra) part of 'the art of exact calculation'; it also serves as a natural preparation for algebra.

Answers

0	a i 4	ii 64	iii $\frac{5}{4}$	iv $\frac{3}{2}$
	b $2\sqrt{3}$	c 2	d 2	

1 a $2\sqrt{5}$ c 5   e 7   g 5
  b $5\sqrt{5}$ d 30   f 12   h 12

2 a i 4   ii $4\sqrt{2}$ iii 8
  b i $3\sqrt{3}$ ii 9   iii $9\sqrt{3}$
  c i x ii $x\sqrt{x}$ iii x^2

3 a $2\sqrt{2}$ d $2\sqrt{5}$ g $4\sqrt{2}$ j $3\sqrt{5}$
  b $2\sqrt{3}$ e $2\sqrt{6}$ h 6   k $4\sqrt{3}$
  c $3\sqrt{2}$ f $2\sqrt{7}$ i $2\sqrt{10}$ l $5\sqrt{2}$

4 i Second term $= \frac{1}{2} \times \left(\sqrt{2} + \frac{1}{\sqrt{2}}\right) = \frac{1}{2}(\sqrt{2} + \sqrt{2}) = \sqrt{2}$.
  ii Hence third and all subsequent terms $= \sqrt{2}$.

5 a $7\sqrt{3}$ b $6\sqrt{3}$ c 0   d 0

6 a i $\sqrt{6}$ iii $\sqrt{10}$ v $\sqrt{14}$ vii $3\sqrt{2}$
    ii $\sqrt{8} = 2\sqrt{2}$ iv $2\sqrt{3}$ vi 4   viii $2\sqrt{5}$
  b i $2\sqrt{3}$ ii $\sqrt{15}$ iii $3\sqrt{2}$ iv $\sqrt{21}$ v $2\sqrt{6}$ vi $3\sqrt{3}$

7 a 7   e 5   i $9\sqrt{2}$ m $3\sqrt{10}$ q $8\sqrt{6}$
  b $\sqrt{2}$ f $2\sqrt{6}$ j 4   n $\sqrt{6}$ r 5
  c $2\sqrt{3}$ g $5\sqrt{5}$ k 3   o $3\sqrt{8}$ s $\frac{\sqrt{5}}{2}$
  d $2\sqrt{10}$ h $4\sqrt{5}$ l $\sqrt{3}$ p 2

8 a $2\sqrt{3} + 3$ b $8\sqrt{3}$ c 0   d $\sqrt{5}$

9	a i 1	ii 2	c i $\sqrt{2}(1 + \sqrt{2})$	ii $\sqrt{3}(1 + \sqrt{3})$
	b i $\sqrt{2}$	ii $2\sqrt{3}$		

γ: T16 Simplifying D   NC

These simple exercises illustrate the range of tasks which pupils need to master when developing a fluency in *additive* algebra.

Answers

0	a $4a$	b $a - b$

1 a $47a$ c $-66c$ e $2ab$
  b $-26x$ d 0   f $-16z$

2 a x^2 c $-21a^3$ e $\frac{8}{5}b$
  b $-14a^2x$ d $2x$ f $\frac{1}{3}x^2$

3 a 0   c $4x + 4y + 4z$ e $6x$ g $13z$
  b $39x - 5y + 4z$ d $3ax - 3by + 3cz$ f $-20ab + 4ca$ h $a + b + c$

4 a $x^3 - 5x - 1$ c $x^2 + y^2 + xy$ e $a^3 + b^3 + c^3$ g $\frac{1}{4}a - \frac{2}{3}b$

   b abc d $xy + yz + zx$ f $15x^3 - 4x^2 + 3x - 1$ h $\frac{3}{8}x^2 - \frac{1}{2}y^2 - \frac{2}{5}xy$

5 a $2a + 5b + 2c$ c $8a^3 - 2a$ e $2x^2 + 7x - 3$

   b $2x^3 - 5x^2$ d $2x^3 - 2x^2$ f $3x^2 + 7x - 8$

γ: T17 Pythagoras' theorem A

The statement of Pythagoras' theorem leads you to ask whether there is some way to split the 'square on the hypotenuse BC' into two parts — one of which is equal to 'the square on the side AB' and the other equal to the 'square on the side AC'.

In Problem **0** try to bring out how natural the approach is. To split the square on BC we need a line to 'cut' along. A line is determined by either 'two points' (and there are no sensible natural candidates), or by 'one point and a direction'. The point A stands out as being the only possible 'special point'; and the only possible special direction which has a chance of working is the direction perpendicular to BC, and the line through A perpendicular to BC miraculously splits the square $BCTU$ exactly as required!

Answers

0 a A (right angle)

   c ii '$\triangle PBC$ and $\triangle PBA$ have the same base PB and same height BA'
          '$\triangle UBA$ and $\triangle UBM$ have the same base UB and same height BM'

1 $BC^2 = AC^2 + AB^2 = 9^2 + 12^2 = 3^2(3^2 + 4^2) = 15^2$; $\therefore BC = $ **15 cm**

2 a **7** $(AD^2 = BD^2 - 1^2 = 5^2 + 5^2 - 1^2 = 49)$

   b **1** $(BC^2 = BD^2 - 8^2 = 4^2 + 7^2 - 8^2 = 1)$

   c **9** $(AB^2 = BD^2 - 2^2 = 7^2 + 6^2 - 2^2 = 81)$

4 $AC = \sqrt{2}$

5 Height = $\sqrt{3}$ units $(AM^2 + BM^2 = AB^2; \therefore AM^2 = 2^2 - 1^2 = 3)$

   $\therefore$ Area $= \frac{1}{2} \times 2 \times \sqrt{3} = \sqrt{3}$ square units

6 $BC = 2\sqrt{3}$ units (If M is the midpoint of BC, then $\triangle BMC$ is congruent to $\triangle AMB$ in Problem **5**).

   $\therefore$ Area $= \frac{1}{2} \times 2\sqrt{3} \times 1 = \sqrt{3}$ ($\triangle ABC$ is obtained by taking $\triangle BMA$ and $\triangle CMA$ in Problem **5** and glueing BM to CM)

7 a ii $\triangle CXA$ has a right angle at X;
           $\therefore CX^2 + AX^2 = CA^2$; $\therefore CA > CX$.

      iii In the right angled triangle $\triangle CAP$, $CA^2 + PA^2 = PC^2$;
          in the right angled triangle $\triangle CBP$, $CB^2 + PB^2 = PC^2$.
          Also $CA^2 = CB^2 = r^2$. $\therefore PA^2 = PB^2$.

8 Join AC. $BA = BC$, so $\triangle ABC$ is isosceles with $\angle BAC = 60°$.
   $\therefore \triangle ABC$ is equilateral.
   $\therefore AC$ has length **2**.
   Join BD. $\triangle ABD$ is congruent to $\triangle ABC$ in Problem **6**.
   $\therefore BD$ has length $2\sqrt{3}$.
   $\therefore$ Area$(ABCD) = 2 \times$ area$(\triangle ABC) = 2\sqrt{3}$ (by Problem **5**).

9 If O is the midpoint of AD, then $\triangle ABO$, $\triangle BCO$ and $\triangle CDO$ are all equilateral.
   $\therefore AD = AM + MD = AB + CD = 4$.
   $\triangle ABC$ is congruent to $\triangle BAC$ in Problem **6**. $\therefore AC = 2\sqrt{3}$.
   $\therefore$ Area$(ABCDEF) = 6 \times$ area$(\triangle ABO) = 6\sqrt{3}$

γ: T18 Power play *B*

It is left to the teacher to emphasise the unstated message:

(a) given any positive integer $x > 1$, positive integer powers x^n of x can become arbitrarily *large*; and

(b) given any positive number $x < 1$, positive integer powers x^n of x can become arbitrarily *small*.

Answers

> 0 a £237 376   b £590 668

1 $2^{10} = 1024$; $\therefore 1000^2 < (2^{10})^2 = 2^{20}$

2 $(1.5)^2 = \left(\frac{3}{2}\right)^2 = \frac{9}{4} = 2.25 > 2$;
$\therefore 1\,000\,000 = 1000^2 < (2^{10})^2 = 2^{20} < ((1.5)^2)^{20} = (1.5)^{40}$
(This is just an easy estimate; in fact $(1.5)^{34} \approx 970\,740$, so $(1.5)^{35} > 1\,000\,000$.)

3 $(1.1)^5 = 1.61051 > 1.5$;
$\therefore 1\,000\,000 < (1.5)^{40} < ((1.1)^5)^{40} = (1.1)^{200}$
[This is just an easy estimate; it could be improved by replacing $(1.5)^{40}$ by $(1.5)^{35}$. In fact $(1.1)^{145} \approx 1\,004\,475$ is already slightly larger than $1\,000\,000$.]

4 $\left(\frac{1}{2}\right)^{10} = \frac{1}{1024} < \frac{1}{1000}$;
$\therefore \frac{1}{1\,000\,000} = \left(\frac{1}{1000}\right)^2 > \left(\left(\frac{1}{2}\right)^{10}\right)^2 = \left(\frac{1}{2}\right)^{20}$

5 $\frac{1}{1\,000\,000} = \left(\frac{1}{1000}\right)^2 > \left(\frac{1}{2}\right)^{20} > \left(\frac{4}{9}\right)^{20} > \left(\left(\frac{2}{3}\right)^2\right)^{20} = \left(\frac{2}{3}\right)^{40}$

6 $\frac{1}{1\,000\,000} = \left(\frac{1}{1000}\right)^2 > \left(\frac{2}{3}\right)^{40} > \left(\left(\frac{10}{11}\right)^5\right)^{40} > \left(\frac{10}{11}\right)^{200}$

> 7 Fewer than 80 cuts ($2^{10} > 10^3$; $\therefore 2^{80} > 10^{24}$)

γ: T19 Factorising quadratics   NC

Factorising quadratics is a good example of an 'inverse process', and provides an excellent opportunity to develop flexibility in a simple context. This set of exercises illustrates what pupils need to watch out for when factorising.

Answers

> 0 a $(x-2)(x-3)$ b $(x-6)(x+1)$

1 a $x(2x+3)$ c $3x(2x+3)$ e $2xy(3x+1)$ g $7x(1-3x)$
   b $x(x-5)$ d $3ab(1-3b)$ f $5uv(2-3uv)$ h $2a(2ab-5)$

2 a $(x+3)(x+5)$ d $(x+3)(x-5)$ g $(x-1)(x+15)$ j $(x+5)(x+5)$
   b $(x-3)(x-5)$ e $(x+1)(x+15)$ h $(x+1)(x-15)$ k $(x-5)(x-5)$
   c $(x-3)(x+5)$ f $(x-1)(x-15)$ i $(x-5)(x+5)$

3 a $(2x+1)(x+3)$ e $(2x+3)(x+1)$ i $(3x-10)(x-1)$ m $(3x-2)(x-5)$
   b $(2x-1)(x+3)$ f $(2x-3)(x-1)$ j $(3x+2)(x-5)$ n $(3x-5)(x-2)$
   c $(2x-1)(x-3)$ g $(2x-3)(x+1)$ k $(3x+2)(x+5)$ o $(3x-2)(x+5)$
   d $(2x+1)(x-3)$ h $(2x+3)(x-1)$ l $(3x+5)(x+2)$ p $(3x-10)(x+1)$

4 a $(3x+1)(2x+3)$ e $(6x+3)(x+1)$ i $(6x+1)(x-3)$ m $(6x-3)(x+1)$
   b $(3x+1)(2x-3)$ f $(6x-3)(x+1)$ j $(6x-1)(x+3)$ n $(6x+3)(x+1)$
   c $(3x-1)(2x+3)$ g $(6x-3)(x-1)$ k $(6x-1)(x-3)$
   d $(3x-1)(2x-3)$ h $(6x+1)(x+3)$ l $(6x+3)(x-1)$

3C Gamma

5 a	$(15x + 14)(x + 1)$	g	$(5x + 1)(3x - 14)$	m	$(5x + 7)(3x + 2)$
b	$(15x - 14)(x - 1)$	h	$(5x + 2)(3x - 7)$	n	$(5x + 1)(3x + 14)$
c	$(5x - 14)(3x + 1)$	i	$(5x - 1)(3x + 14)$	o	$(5x - 2)(3x - 7)$
d	$(15x + 7)(x + 2)$	j	$(5x + 7)(3x - 2)$	p	$(5x - 7)(3x - 2)$
e	$(15x + 7)(x - 2)$	k	$(5x - 1)(3x - 14)$	q	$(5x - 7)(3x + 2)$
f	$(15x - 7)(x + 2)$	l	$(5x + 2)(3x + 7)$		

γ: T20 From fractions to decimals – and back   NC

The link between fractions and decimals is mathematically important and provides welcome opportunities for satisfying calculation.

Answers

0 a 0.875   b $\frac{4}{9}$

1 a 0.5   c 0.2   e 0.1875
   b 0.25   d 0.625

2 a $1 + \frac{1}{2} = 1.5$ c $1 + \frac{1}{4} = 1.25$ e $1 + \frac{1}{5} = 1.2$ g $\frac{1}{2} + \frac{5}{80} = 0.5625$
   b $\frac{1}{2} + \frac{1}{4} = 0.75$ d $3 \times \frac{1}{5} = 0.6$ f $1 + \frac{7}{8} = 1.875$

3 a, c, d, g, i, o only

4 a 0.3636... for ever   b 0.567567... for ever

5 a 0.142857142857... for ever   b Remainder 1; after 6 steps

6 a 0.571428571428... for ever   b Remainder 4; after 6 steps

7 a 0.454545... for ever   b Remainder 5; after 2 steps

8 a 0.567567... for ever   b Remainder 21; after 3 steps

9 a 0.1666... for ever   b Remainder 4; after 2 steps

10 a $9x = 10x - x = 5; \therefore x = \frac{5}{9}$ d $999x = 1000x - x = 567; \therefore x = \frac{21}{37}$
   b $99x = 100x - x = 12; \therefore x = \frac{4}{33}$ e $999x = 1000x - x = 123; \therefore x = \frac{41}{333}$
   c $99x = 100x - x = 45; \therefore x = \frac{5}{11}$

γ: T21 Scale factors A: Length and area   NC

The goal here is for pupils to calculate without using similarity, but rather to use more primitive ways of calculating and so to appreciate how similarity is a natural extension of what they already know.

Answers

0 a A5
   b i   The two rectangles are **similar**
      ii A5 (= A4 folded in half, so) has length b and breadth $\frac{a}{2}$. $\therefore a : b = b : \frac{a}{2}$, so $\frac{a}{b} = \sqrt{2}$

1 a i $\sqrt{2}$ ii $\frac{1}{2}$
   b i $AB' = 2;\ AD' = 2$
      ii In $\triangle AB'C'$, B is the midpoint of AB' and C is the midpoint of AC' $\therefore BC \| B'C'$
          $\therefore \angle AB'C' = 90°$. Also $B'C' = 2 \times BC = 2$
      iii $AC' = 2\sqrt{2}$
      iv Area($\triangle AB'C'$) = 2 square units.

2 a $AB'C'D'$ is a parallelogram with $AB' = AD' = 2$ ∴ $AB'C'D'$ is a rhombus.
     Also $\angle B'AD' = 90°$, so $AB'C'D'$ is a square.
  b i $AC = 3\sqrt{2}$ ii $AB' = 6$; $AD' = 6$ iii $AC' = 6\sqrt{2}$
  c i 9 square units; 36 square units   ii $\frac{9}{4} = \left(\frac{3}{2}\right)^2$

3 a i $\sqrt{3}$ ii $\frac{3}{2}$ iii $\sqrt{\frac{3}{2}}$
  b i $AB' = 2\sqrt{2}$; $AD' = 2$
     ii $AC' = \sqrt{12} = 2\sqrt{3}$ ($AB'C'D'$ is a parallelogram with $\angle B'AD' = 90°$, and so is a rectangle)
     iii $C'D = 3$;
     iv $C'B = \sqrt{6}$; $\frac{\sqrt{6}}{\sqrt{\frac{3}{2}}} = 2$.
  c i In $\triangle AC'B'$, C is the midpoint of AC' and B is the midpoint of AB' ∴ $BC \| B'C'$.
     In $\triangle AC'D$, C is the midpoint of AC' and N is the midpoint of AD ∴ $CN \| C'D$.
     ii See bii.
     iii Area $(AB'C'D') = 4\sqrt{2}$; $\frac{4\sqrt{2}}{\sqrt{2}} = 2^2$.

4 a $\triangle AB'C'$ is isosceles ($AB' = AC'$) with apex angle $\angle B'AC' = 60°$.
     ∴ $\triangle AB'C'$ is equilateral. ∴ $\angle AB'C' = \angle ABC$; ∴ $B'C' \| BC$ (corresponding angles equal).
  b $AM \perp BC$ and $B'C' \| BC$; ∴ $AM \perp B'C'$.
     In $\triangle AMB'$, $\angle MAB' = 180° - 90° - 60° = 30°$. Similarly in $\triangle AMC'$, $\angle MAC' = 30°$;
     ∴ $\triangle MAB'$, $\triangle MAC'$ are congruent (by ASA). ∴ $MB' = MC'$
  c $AM = \frac{3\sqrt{3}}{2}$; $AM' = \sqrt{3}$
  d Area$(\triangle ABC) = \frac{1}{2} \times 3 \times \frac{3\sqrt{3}}{2} = \frac{4}{9}\sqrt{3}$; area$(AB'C') = \sqrt{3}$

5 a $AB \| FC$ ($\angle ABC + \angle FCB = 180°$); similarly $ED \| FC$, so $AB \| ED$; that is, opposite sides of a regular hexagon are parallel.
     In particular, $FE \| BC$. Hence $OBCF$ is a parallelogram.
  b i $OX = \sqrt{3}$; $AC = \sqrt{3}$ ($OACX$ is a parallelogram)
     ii $BF = AC = \sqrt{3}$
     iii $OC = \sqrt{7}$ (Let the perpendicular from C to AB produced meet AB produced at X.
          Then $CX = \frac{\sqrt{3}}{2}$, $OX = \frac{5}{2}$, and $CX^2 + OX^2 = OC^2$.)
     iv area$(OBCF) = OB \times CX = 2 \times \frac{\sqrt{3}}{2} = \sqrt{3}$ square units
  c i $BP = 2$; $BE = 2$; $PB' = EB = 2$; $OP = 2 \times OX = 2\sqrt{3}$.
     ii $OC' = 2\sqrt{7}$ (Let the perpendicular from C' to AB produced meet AB produced at X'. Then $C'X' = \sqrt{3}$, $OX' = 5$, and $C'X'^2 + OX'^2 = OC'^2$.)
     iii $C'B = OP = 2\sqrt{3}$
     iv Area$(OB'C'E) = 4\sqrt{3}$
  d In $\triangle OC'B$, C is the midpoint of OC' and A is the midpoint of OB; ∴ $CA \| C'B$.

6 a i Circumference$(\mathcal{C}) = 2\pi r$;
     ii $2r' = AB' = 3 \times AB = 6r$; ∴ circumference$(\mathcal{C}') = 6\pi r$
  b i Area$(\mathcal{C}) = \pi r^2$;   ii area$(\mathcal{C}') = 9\pi r^2$

γ: T22 Calculating and comparing: A miscellany NC

This mixed collection of word problems combines calculation and comparison.

Answers

| 0 a $\frac{11}{10}$ | b $\frac{11}{12}$ |

3C Gamma

1. 46 years old
2. 110 seconds
3. 79.2 km/h
4. Equal (because X lies on AC)
5. a $\frac{10\,001}{10\,002}$ c $\frac{1001}{2001}$ e $\frac{1001}{1002}$
   b $\frac{1002}{1001}$ d $\frac{20\,001}{10\,001}$ f $\frac{102}{101}$
6. 24 posts [gaps = 138 mm because hcf(690, 966) = 23 × 6 = 138]
7. £32.50
8. 30 km/h
9. Densest: olive oil; least dense: petrol
10. 60 steps

γ: T23 Solving quadratic equations   NC

Use Problem **0** to highlight the principle described in the text ('$ab = 0$ if and only if $a = 0$ or $b = 0$'); hence show why factorisation is effective, in that it reduces one quadratic equation to two simpler linear equations.

Answers

0. a $x = 0$ or $x = 5$ b $x = -1$ or $x = 6$ c $x = -\frac{8}{7}$ or $x = \frac{3}{2}$

1. a $x = -3$ or $x = 2$ c $x = -1$ or $x = 2$ e $x = 2$
   b $x = -3$ or $x = 1$ d $x = -4$ or $x = 1$ f $x = 3$

2. a $x = 1$ e $x = -3$ or $x = \frac{1}{2}$ i $x = \frac{14}{15}$ or $x = 1$
   b $x = -1$ f $x = -\frac{2}{3}$ or $x = 5$ j $x = -\frac{2}{3}$ or $x = \frac{7}{5}$
   c $x = -1$ or $x = 15$ g $x = -\frac{1}{6}$ or $x = 3$ k $x = -\frac{3}{2}$ or $x = \frac{1}{3}$
   d $x = \frac{1}{2}$ or $x = 3$ h $x = -1$ or $x = \frac{3}{2}$ l $x = \frac{2}{5}$ or $x = \frac{7}{3}$

3. a $x = -\frac{3}{2}$ or $x = 0$ f $x = 5$ k $x = -\frac{1}{2}$ or $x = 1$
   b $x = -5$ or $x = -3$ g $x = -3$ or $x = 5$ l $x = \frac{2}{3}$ or $x = 5$
   c $x = -5$ or $x = 3$ h $x = -3$ or $x = 1$ m $x = \frac{5}{3}$ or $x = 2$
   d $x = 1$ or $x = 15$ i $x = -3$ or $x = -\frac{1}{2}$ n $x = -1$ or $x = \frac{10}{3}$
   e $x = -5$ or $x = 5$ j $x = \frac{1}{2}$ or $x = 3$

4. a $x = \frac{1}{3}$ or $x = 2$ c $x = 1$ or $x = \frac{32}{3}$ e $x = \frac{2}{3}$ or $x = 13$
   b $x = -1$ or $x = 3$ d $x = 4$ or $x = \frac{11}{2}$ f $x = -\frac{1}{2}$ or $x = 3$

5. $x = -1$ or $x = 9$
6. 9 and 45
7. a $x = 3$ (-1 is impossible)   c $x = 9$ (-3 is impossible)
   b $x = 6$ (-2 is impossible)   d $x = 2$ ($-\frac{4}{3}$ is impossible)
8. 14 pieces

9. a $x = 5$ (-5 is impossible)   c $x = 5$ (-1 is impossible)
   b Both solutions are impossible
10. Two solutions: 7, 8; or $-\frac{8}{15}, \frac{7}{15}$ 11. 3 or -20
12. 7 hours   13. All values of $x > 1$.
14. $n = -3$ (The second condition also allows $n = 3$; but this does not satisfy the first condition.)

γ: T24 Loci   NC

Half the battle here is to get pupils to imagine the possible locus. The other half is cultivating accuracy. For example, the quarter circles in Problem **0** should start out vertically at X, enter Z horizontally, and emerge from Z with gradient 1 (at an angle of 45° to the horizontal).

Answers

> **0** A quarter circle centre W through X and Z; then a quarter circle centre U through Z and T; then a quarter circle centre S through T and R. The square then rotates about R, before repeating.

1 Locus of X : the perpendicular bisector of the segment AB.

2 Locus of X: a pair of lines, one either side of and both parallel to m, distance 5 cm from m.

3 $r = \sqrt{\frac{8000}{3\pi}} = 20\sqrt{\frac{20}{3\pi}} \approx 29.13$ **m** (which is – fortunately – less than each side of the field).

4 **a** Locus of X : the circle with centre O and radius 15 cm.

   b Locus of X : two concentric circles with centre O, one with radius 5 cm, the other with radius 15 cm.

5 Locus of X : the line parallel to m and n and halfway between them.

> 6 **a** $\frac{\pi\sqrt{5}}{2}$ ($AC \perp A'C$ ∴ quarter circle centre C)
>
>   **b** $\frac{5\pi}{4}$ square units
>
> 7 **a** Locus of centre: square of side 2 with same centre as the given square.
>
>   **b** 8 units   **c** $\frac{8}{2\pi} = \frac{4}{\pi}$ revolutions
>
> 8 **a** Locus of centre: square of side 6, with the same centre as the given square, *but with the corners replaced by quarter circles of radius 1* centred at the corners of the given square.
>
>   **b** $16 + 2\pi$
>
>   **c** $\frac{16}{2\pi} + 1 = \frac{8}{\pi} + 1$ revolutions
>
> 9 The locus of X: If m, n cross at O, then the locus consists of a pair of perpendicular lines through O, each being a bisector of two of the angles formed by m, n at the point O.
>
> 10 **a** The locus of X: the perpendicular bisector of the line segment joining the two centres (which is also the tangent to both circles at the point of contact).
>
>   **b** The locus of X: the perpendicular bisector of the line segment joining the two centres
>
>   **c** The locus of X: the perpendicular bisector of the line segment joining the two centres (which is also the line extending the common chord of the two circles).
>
>   **d** This cries out for some imaginative work using compasses and double polar coordinates. For example, in **a** mark two points A, B 12 cm apart.
> Draw circles of radius 5, 6, 7, 8, etc. with centre A, and circles with radius 7, 8, 9, 10, etc. with centre B.
> The two first circles in each sequence touch at the point O. The second circles in each sequence cut at points which are distance 1 from each of the two first circles. The third circles in each sequence cut at points which are distance 2 from the two first circles. In this way one constructs a 'dotted shadow' of one branch of a hyperbola with foci at A and at B $\bigl(|XB| - |XA| = 2\bigr)$.

γ: C1 Estimation A: Introductory problems   NC

A serious professional discussion of the didactics of teaching *estimation* is overdue. However, this section is deliberately *informal*: pupils are expected to use what they know about arithmetic to answer a varied collection of everyday problems, and to reflect (if possible together) on the likely accuracy of the methods used. Problem **0** is not meant to be hard; but it may be worth working to elicit and to discuss several different approaches.

Answers

> **0** ≈ 60 × 70 = **4200 cm²** (or 50 × 80 ≈ 4000 cm²)

1 ≈ 70 × 60 = **4200** beats per hour
2 $\frac{2}{3}$ of '30 rows' = 20 rows ∴ 20 × 45 = **900**
3 ≈ 12 000 ÷ 50 = **240** miles a week (or just over 1000 miles per month ∴ ≈ 250 miles a week)
4 128 ÷ 11 ≈ **12** litres (ignoring doors, windows, cupboards, etc.)
5 ≈ 26 × 20 = **520** (average row length = 20 seats)
6 77 × 38 × 150 grams ≈ 75 × 40 × 150 grams = 3 × 1000 × 150 grams = **450 kg**
7 4850 ÷ 22 ≈ **200** (*under*estimate)
8 2.2 km in 1.5 minutes ≈ (2.2 × 40) = **88 km/h**

> **9** 3 × 365 ≈ 1100 litres ∴ **1.1 tonnes**
> **10** Total length of path = 2 × (26 + 11) = 74 m;
> ∴ volume = 74 × 2 × 0.05 = 7.4 m³; cost ≈ **£ 300**
> **11** 12 345 678.9 ÷ 345 ≈ ??
>   i ≈ £ 12 000 000 ÷ 300 = £ 40 000 (but can't tell whether more or less)
>   ii ≈ £ 14 000 000 ÷ 350 = £ 40 000 (fairly clearly an *over*estimate)
>   iii ≈ £ 12 000 000 ÷ 400 = £ 30 000 (clearly an *under*estimate)

γ: C2 How can you tell when a given integer is prime?

Elementary mathematics begins with the step from addition to multiplication; and the procedure for testing whether an integer is prime is one of the simplest examples of the unexpected consequences of this step to multiplicative thinking, and the counterintuitive character of what emerges. The fact that 'if N is composite, then the smallest prime factor of N is $\leq \sqrt{N}$' comes as a surprise to almost all pupils who do not know (and accept) it already. This surprise arises partly because pupils hesitate to make the step from additive thinking to multiplicative thinking (additive thinking suggests that one needs to check for factors 'up to $\frac{1}{2}N$').

Problem **0** serves as a gentle introduction by looking for runs of *consecutive* composite numbers (8, 9, 10 or .....); but the meat of the section is contained in Problems **4** and **5**. With a suitable class teachers might like to round off the section by exploring 'prime deserts' (like 8, 9, 10, or 24, 25, 26, 27, 28) – in which all integers are composite. Provided you do not want the integers to be as small as possible, intervals of a specified length can be constructed using factorials (for example, between *n!* + 2 and *n!* + *n*).

Answers

> **0 a** 8 = 2 × 4; 9 = 3 × 3; 10 = 2 × 5   **b** 24, 25, 26, 27

1 c, f, g, i, j, k, l, m only

2 a 24, 25, 26, 27, 28
  b 90, 91, 92, 93, 94, 95
  c 90, 91, 92, 93, 94, 95, 96
3 a i No   ii No   iii No   iv No   v No
  c composite
4 a i No   ii No   iii No   iv No   v No
  c i 2, 3, 5, 7   ii Three (2, 3, 5 only)   iii $101 = 7 \times 14 + 3$; $\therefore$ 101 must be prime.
5 a i 2, 3, 5, 7, 11, 13, 17, 19, 23, 29, 31   ii $1001 = 2 \times 500 + 1$; $1001 = 3 \times 333 + 2$;
       $1001 = 5 \times 200 + 1$;
       $1001 = 7 \times 143 + 0$ so 1001 is composite.
  b $\therefore$ 1001 is composite
  c $1001 = 7 \times 11 \times 13$
6 b $111 = 3 \times 37$
  c $1111 = 11 \times 101$
  d $11\,111 = 41 \times 271$

7 3 (2, 11, 101)
8 Integers alternate odd-even-odd-....
  We know that $n \neq 2, 3$ (since then n is prime). $\therefore n \geq 4$.
  If n is even, $n + 10$ is also even, and hence composite.
  If n is odd, then $n - 1$ is even, and hence composite.
  [Note: You met this already in Problems **0**-**2**: the sequence in the answer to Problem **0b** extends to give an answer to Problem **2a**; and the sequence in Problem **2b** extends to give an answer to Problem **2b**.]

γ: C3 Geometry problems A   NC

These problems subject a variety of visual images to the discipline of calculation. Problem **0** is **not** intended as an exercise in applying the formula for the area of a trapezium! Rather it should be used to encourage different elementary strategies (e.g. split the quadrilateral into two triangles by drawing either diagonal; or draw a horizontal line to split the quadrilateral into a rectangle and a right angled triangle).

Answers

0 400 square units $(= 15 \times 20 + \frac{1}{2}(20 \times 10))$

1 48 units   2 318 square units $(= \frac{1}{2}(20 \times 15) + \frac{1}{2}(14 \times 24))$
3 $8a + 2b$ $(= 2 \times (4a + b))$
4 Perimeter = **29** units $(= 3 \times 5 + 2 \times 12$; this is independent of the given length '$\frac{5}{2}$').
  Area = $15\sqrt{3}$ square units $(= \frac{5}{2} \times 12\frac{\sqrt{3}}{2})$
5 Perimeter = **4** units; area = $\frac{23}{32}$ square units
6 Perimeter = **36** units (opposite sides of a parallelogram are equal; so perimeter unchanged)
7 Perimeter = $\sqrt{5} + \sqrt{10} + \sqrt{13}$; area = $\frac{7}{2}$ $(= 3^2 - \frac{1}{2}(2 \times 1) - \frac{1}{2}(1 \times 3) - \frac{1}{2}(2 \times 3))$

8 a $\frac{1}{4}$ (shaded area is equal to the central square, which is one-quarter of the large square)
  b $\frac{5}{16}$ $(= \frac{1}{4} + \frac{1}{4} \times \frac{1}{4}$ by using part a twice)
9 $\frac{1}{12}$
  ($\triangle XVY$ is $\frac{1}{4}$ of $WXYZ$. $\triangle XWT$ and $\triangle UYT$ are similar, and $XW = 2 \times UY$;
  $\therefore WT = 2 \times YT$.
  $\therefore VT = \frac{1}{3} \times VY$, so area($\triangle XVT$) = $\frac{1}{3} \times$ area($\triangle XVY$).)

γ: C4 Estimation B: Arithmetical methods

The goal of this section is to establish reasonable estimates for familiar surds and to extend these to provide estimates for less familiar surds. Though the problems have been carefully structured, effort may be needed to ensure that pupils 'read between the lines' and tackle things in the intended spirit.

Answers

> 0 a Side length $\sqrt{200}$ cm: slightly more than **14 cm** ($14^2 = 196$), and slightly less than 14.2 cm ($(14 + 0.2)^2 = 196 + 2 \times 2.8 + 0.04 = 201.64$).
>
>   b Side length **90 cm** exactly.

1 $2 \times 3 = 6$ a ≈ **600**   c ≈ **60 000**   e ≈ **300**
                      b ≈ **600**   d ≈ **6000**   f ≈ **20**

2 a $14^2 = 196$; ∴ $\sqrt{200} \approx 14$; $\sqrt{2} \approx$ **1.4**   c $22^2 = 484$; ∴ $\sqrt{500} \approx 22$; $\sqrt{5} \approx$ **2.2**
   b $17^2 = 289$; ∴ $\sqrt{300} \approx 17$; $\sqrt{3} \approx$ **1.7**

3 a $24^2 = 576$, $25^2 = $ **625**   b ∴ $\sqrt{6} \approx$ **2.45**

4 a $20^2 = 400$ ∴ $\sqrt{400} = $ **20**   f $\sqrt{50} = 5\sqrt{2} \approx$ **7**
   b i $(10\sqrt{2})^2 = 200$; ∴ $\sqrt{200} = 10\sqrt{2}$ g $\sqrt{72} = 6\sqrt{2} \approx$ **8.4**
      ii ≈ 14 ∴ $\sqrt{2} \approx$ **1.4**   h $\sqrt{96} = 4\sqrt{6} \approx 4 \times 2.45 =$ **9.8**
   c i $\sqrt{20} = 2\sqrt{5} \approx$ **4.5** (or 4.4)   i i $5^2 = 25 < 30 < 36 = 6^2$; ∴ $5 < \sqrt{30} < 6$
   d $\sqrt{12} = 2\sqrt{3} \approx$ **3.4**   ii $\sqrt{30} \approx$ **5.5**
   e $\sqrt{18} = 3\sqrt{2} \approx$ **4.2**

5 a $3.16^2 \approx 10$; $\sqrt{10} \approx$ **3.16**
   b i $\sqrt{40} = 2\sqrt{10} \approx$ **6.3**   v $\sqrt{640} = 8\sqrt{10} \approx$ **25.3**
      ii $\sqrt{90} = 3\sqrt{10} \approx$ **9.5**   vi $\sqrt{810} = 9\sqrt{10} \approx$ **28.5**
      iii $\sqrt{160} = 4\sqrt{10} \approx$ **12.6**   vii $\sqrt{1000} = 10\sqrt{10} \approx$ **31.6**
      iv $\sqrt{250} = 5\sqrt{10} \approx$ **15.8**

6 $7.1^2 = 49 + 1.4 + 0.01 =$ **50.41**; ∴ $7 < \sqrt{50} < 7.1$

7 a i $14.1^2 = 196 + 2.8 + 0.01 =$ **198.81**   c i $22.3^2 = 484 + 13.2 + 0.09 =$ **497.29**
      ii $14.2^2 = 196 + 5.6 + 0.04 =$ **201.64**   ii $22.4^2 = 484 + 17.6 + 0.16 =$ **501.76**
      iii ∴ $14.1 < \sqrt{200} < 14.2$, $1.41 < \sqrt{2} < 1.42$ iii ∴ $22.3 < \sqrt{500} < 22.4$, $2.23 < \sqrt{5} < 2.24$
   b i $17.3^2 = 289 + 10.4 + 0.09 =$ **299.49**
      ii $17.4^2 = 289 + 13.6 + 0.16 =$ **302.76**
      iii ∴ $17.3 < \sqrt{300} < 17.4$, $1.73 < \sqrt{3} < 1.74$

8 a $\sqrt{190} \approx$ **14**   c $\sqrt{500} \approx$ **22.4**   e $\sqrt{0.048} \approx$ **0.22**   g $\sqrt{1999} \approx$ **45**
   b $\sqrt{300} \approx$ **17.3**   d $\sqrt{0.2} \approx$ **0.45**   f $\sqrt{31.2} \approx$ **5.6**

> 9 a i $13^3 \approx$ **2210**   ii ∴ $\sqrt[3]{2.2} \approx$ **1.3**
>   b i $2^{10} =$ **1024**   ii ∴ $2^{21} \approx 2\,000\,000$; $2^7 =$ **128**   iv ∴ $\sqrt[3]{2} \approx$ **1.28**
>
> 10 **60** ($3.9 = 3 \times 1.3$, where $1.3 \approx \sqrt[3]{2.2}$ (underestimate) and $3 = \sqrt[3]{27}$; ∴ $3.91^3 \approx 2.2 \times 27 = 59.4$)
>
> 11 a $39^2 = 1521$, $11^3 = 1331$ e $118^2 = 13\,924$, $24^3 = 13\,824$
>   b $52^2 = 2704$, $14^3 = 2744$ f $125^2 = 15\,625$, $25^3 = 15\,625$
>   c $64^2 = 4096$, $16^3 = 4096$ g $134^2 = 17\,956$, $26^3 = 17\,576$
>   d $83^2 = 6889$, $19^3 = 6859$ h $157^2 = 24\,649$, $29^3 = 24\,389$

γ: C5 How do we decide the meaning of 'minus times minus'?

I assume that "$-1 \times -1 = +1$" is familiar *as a rule*. Hence this section is only intended to provide an opportunity for consolidation and reflection, to show that the rule is natural, and to confront one or two of its consequences (Problems 2-5).

Answers

> 0 a *Change* in weight from today to m months time = $(-2) \times m$ kg; that is, I shall have **lost** $2m$ kg
>
> b *Change* in weight m months ago relative to today = $(-2) \times (-m)$ kg = $2m$ kg; that is, I was $2m$ kg **heavier** then than I am now.

2 a 6   b 7

3 a $\frac{1}{4}$ b $\frac{1}{4}$ c $\frac{1}{4}$ d $\frac{1}{4}$

4 The step from the 4th to the 5th line is wrong: if $x^2 = y^2$, then one cannot conclude that $x = y$. (In this case, $1 - \frac{3}{2} < 0$ and $2 - \frac{3}{2} > 0$.)

5 $n = 0$, or $n = -2$. ($n^3 = (n + 2)^3 - 8$; $\therefore 6n^2 + 12n = 0$)

γ: C6 Number puzzles   NC

These problems are meant to provide an opportunity for reasoning and for algebraic thinking. Solutions to Problems **0** and **2** should (if possible) move beyond trial-and-error to identify general patterns. The logic behind Problems **8** and **9** may be less transparent; but Problems **1, 3, 5, 6, 7, 10** invite explicit algebraic analysis.

Answers

> 0 Impossible: $1 + 2 + 3 + 4 + 5 + 6 = 21$ is odd.

1 1 solution: **−9, 19, 26** ($17 + 45 - 10 = 2 \times$ (number at the top vertex))

2 a $1 + 4 = 2 + 3$ b **Impossible** ($1 + 2 + 3 + 4 + 5 = 15$ is odd)
  c $7 + 8 + 1 + 2 = 3 + 4 + 5 + 6$ d $10 + 11 + 12 + 1 + 2 + 3 = 4 + 5 + 6 + 7 + 8 + 9$

3 $\frac{33}{2}, \frac{53}{2}, \frac{71}{2}$ ($43 + 52 - 62 = 2 \times$ (number at the top vertex))

4 a **Yes**: $37 + 38 + \ldots + 12 = 13 + 14 + \ldots + 36$
  b **Yes**: $36 + 37 + \ldots + 11 = 12 + 13 + \ldots + 35$
  c **No**: $1 + 2 + \ldots + 46$ is odd.

5 1 solution. (Let bottom right number = x and let edge sum = s.
  The three edges have sum $3s$ (so is a multiple of 3);
  but this also equals $(1 + 2 + 3 + 4 + 5 + 6) + (6 + 5 + x) = 32 + x$. $\therefore x = 1$ or 4.
  If $x = 1$, then $s = 11$ and the bottom edge would be $5 + 5 + 1$. $\therefore x = 4$.)

6 2 solutions – up to reflection. (Let bottom left number = x, the bottom right number = y, and let the edge sum = s. The three edges have sum $3s$ (a multiple of 3); but this also equals $(1 + 2 + 3 + 4 + 5 + 6) + (6 + x + y) = 27 + x + y$.
  $\therefore$ i $x + y = 3$ ($s = 10$), or   ii $x + y = 6$ ($s = 11$), or   iii $x + y = 9$ ($s = 12$).
  i is impossible (x and y are 1 and 2 in some order, and the bottom edge would need a 7). Each of ii and iii works in just one way (up to reflection).

7 1 solution. (Let the top number = x, the bottom left number = y, the bottom right number = z, and let the edge sum = s. The three edges have sum $3s$ (a multiple of 3); but this also equals $(1 + 2 + 3 + 4 + 5 + 6) + (x + y + z) = 21 + (x + y + z)$. $\therefore x + y + z = 9$ (since $s = 10$), so the only options for x, y, z (in some order) are i 1, 2, 6, or ii 1, 3, 5, or iii 2, 3, 4.
  i impossible (one edge = $1 + 7 + 2$);   ii unique;   iii impossible (one edge = $3 + 3 + 4$).

3C Gamma

8 a 4, 21, 60   b 5, 20, 44

9 a 0, 1, 24, 25 (in order); or 1, 3, 46, 35   b 0, 1, 48, 16; or 3, 1, 48, 33

10 Apex = 48 $\left(=\dfrac{74 + 53 + 87 - \frac{1}{2}(65 + 44 + 31)}{3}\right)$

γ: C7 Linear equations and inequalities   NC

This simple section helps to link familiar algebraic manipulations with their natural geometric interpretations.

Answers

0   a $x > -\frac{3}{4}$ (all points to the right of $x = -\frac{3}{4}$)

    b $x > -3$ (all points to the right of $x = -3$)

    c $y < 2x + \frac{5}{2}$ (all points in the half-plane below and to the right of the line $y = 2x + \frac{5}{2}$)

1   $x > 4$ 2 $x > 6$

3   $x < 5$ and $x > -1$: that is, all points which satisfy *both*.
    ∴ All points between $x = -1$ and $x = 5$.

4   $x < 4$ and $x < 6$: that is, all points which satisfy *both*.
    ∴ All points to the left of $x = 4$.

5   $x < -1$ and $x > -\frac{3}{7}$: that is, all points which satisfy *both* – which is impossible, so no solutions.

6   a   This is correct.

    b $x < -\frac{3}{4}$ gives all solutions to the *second* inequality (not the first).

       $x > -\frac{3}{4}$ gives all solutions to the *first* inequality (not the second).

    c   Ditto

    d   Multiplying or dividing both sides by a negative constant *reverses* the inequality.

7   The line $y = 4x - 1$ crosses the y-axis at the point $(0, -1)$. All points in the half-plane below and to the right of this line are solutions of the inequality $y - 4x + 1 < 0$.

8   The line $y = 2x - \frac{5}{2}$ crosses the y-axis at the point $(0, -\frac{5}{2})$. All points in the half-plane below and to the right of this line are solutions of the inequality $2y - 4x + 5 < 0$.

9   The line $y = -x - \frac{5}{3}$ crosses the y-axis at the point $(0, -\frac{5}{3})$. All points in the half-plane below and to the left of this line are solutions of the inequality $4x - 2y + 8 < 3 - 5y + x$.

10   The line $y = 2x - \frac{5}{2}$ featured in Problem **8**, and the line $y = -x - \frac{5}{3}$ featured in Problem **9**. These two lines are not parallel and cross at the point $\left(\frac{5}{18}, -\frac{35}{18}\right)$.
All points in the lower wedge between these two lines are solutions of the given simultaneous inequalities.

γ: C8 Circles B: Proving the formulae for circumference and area   NC

The familiar formulae for the circumference and area of a circle depend on their analogues for regular polygons; hence the formulae for regular polygons need to be dealt with first. The extent to which the formulae for regular polygons are entirely analogous to those for a circle does not seem to be generally appreciated. Hence teachers may need to reflect on the problems in this section before using them with a class.

Answers

> 0 a $8r$ $(= 4 \times 2r)$ b $4r\sqrt{3}$ $\left(= 6 \times \frac{2r}{\sqrt{3}}\right)$
>
>   c $16r(\sqrt{2} - 1)$ ($= 8s$ where s is the length of a side; since $2r = s + 2\left(\frac{s}{\sqrt{2}}\right) = s(1 + \sqrt{2})$)
>
>   d 4 ; $\frac{6}{\sqrt{3}} = 2\sqrt{3}$; $8(\sqrt{2} - 1)$

1   a   3.142857142857..... recurring for ever   c ≈ 3.141592654
    b   3.14084507......

2   a   i   1   ii 2π iii ≈ 6.283185307
    b   i $\sqrt{2}$ ii $2\pi\sqrt{2}$ iii ≈ 8.885765876

3   a   i $\sqrt{3}$ ii $2\pi\sqrt{3}$ iii ≈ 10.88279619
    b   i   2   ii 4π iii ≈ 12.56637061

4   10 cm by 10π cm

5   a 320 $\left(= 2 \times \frac{4 \times 120}{3}\right)$ b $\frac{480}{\pi} \approx 153$

6   a   i   area$(\triangle OAB) = \frac{1}{2}(AB \times OX)$
      ii   area$(ABCD) = \frac{1}{2}$(perimeter of $ABCD$) $\times r = \pi_4 \times r^2$

    b   i   area$(\triangle OAB) = \frac{1}{2}(AB \times OX)$
      ii   area$(ABCDEF) = \frac{1}{2}$(perimeter of $ABCDEF$) $\times r = \pi_6 \times r^2$

    c   i   area$(\triangle OAB) = \frac{1}{2}(AB \times OX)$
      ii   area$(ABCDEFGH) = \frac{1}{2}$(perimeter of $ABCDEFGH$) $\times r = \pi_8 \times r^2$

7   $4(4 - \pi)$ square metres $(= 4^2 - \pi \times 2^2)$

8   a $220 + 74\pi$ metres   b $37(220 + 37\pi)$ m^2

9   a 12740π km $(= 2 \times \pi \times 6370$ km$)$ b 400π km $(= (2\pi \times 6570) - (2\pi \times 6370))$

10   a   40 000 m^2 $(= 200^2)$
     b $2\pi r = 800$; $\therefore r = \frac{400}{\pi}$;

$\therefore \pi r^2 = \pi \left(\frac{400}{\pi}\right)^2 = \frac{160\,000}{\pi} \approx 50929.58179$ (more than 25% greater than a)

γ: C9   Negative numbers   NC

This section should be straightforward. However, as Problem **0** may demonstrate, there is enormous scope for errors, which in themselves appear 'minor', but which undermine the reliability of all algebraic calculations. Hence, rather than neglecting such simple skills, it is worth explicitly setting pupils the challenge of completing these problems *quickly* and *accurately*.

Answers

> 0   −4

1	i	9	x	4	xix	16	xxviii	−4	xxxvii	25
	ii	−9	xi	−4	xx	−16	xxix	0	xxxviii	25
	iii	9	xii	4	xxi	16	xxx	−1	xxxix	16
	iv	−27	xiii	−243	xxii	32	xxxi	42	xl	2
	v	27	xiv	243	xxiii	−32	xxxii	252	xli	−1
	vi	27	xv	243	xxiv	−32	xxxiii	13	xlii	6
	vii	81	xvi	8	xxv	−24	xxxiv	1	xliii	0
	viii	−81	xvii	−8	xxvi	−4	xxxv	1	xliv	6
	ix	81	xviii	−8	xxvii	−96	xxxvi	−5		

2	i	$x = 6$	iv	No solutions	vii	$x = \pm 2$	x $x = -2$
	ii	$x = -6$	v	$x = 3$	viii	No solutions	
	iii	$x = \pm 3\sqrt{2}$	vi	$x = -3$	ix	$x = 2$	
3	i	−5	iii	−5	v	−3	
	ii	5	iv	−3	vi	3	

γ: C10 Angles in regular polygons

In primary school, definitions tend to be *encyclopaedic* – identifying each mathematical object with a list of all its properties. In secondary school this should change, so that each object is specified in terms of some *minimal* collection of formal properties that suffice to guarantee all the others. In this spirit a *regular polygon* is defined as having all sides equal and all angles equal; nothing is said in the definition to suggest that each regular polygon has a 'centre', or that it can be inscribed in a circle. Hence this 'property' of regular polygons has to be proved solely on the basis of the formal definition.

Answers

0 a 108°

 b i ∠EAB = 108°, ∠ABE = **36°**, ∠EBC = **72°**

  ii 180°

  iii EB∥DC (by ii); similarly AC∥ED

1 a AB = BC and ∠ABC = 90° (given); ∴∠BAC = ∠BCA = **45°**

 b ∠ABD = **45°**

 c ∴ △ABX is isosceles with XA = XB

 d Similarly one shows that XB = XC, and that XC = XD. Hence XA = XB = XC = XD.

2 a ∠ABC = **120°**

 b △BCD is isosceles, so ∠CBD = **30°**

 c ∠ABD = ∠ABC − ∠CBD = **90°**

 d Similarly ∠BDE = 90°, ∠BAE = 90°

 e ABDE is a rectangle (by d), and so is a parallelogram (e.g. by *Beta* C2, Problem 5). ∴ AD, BE bisect each other (e.g. by *Beta* C15, Problem 3). Let AD, BE meet at X. Similarly BE, CF bisect each other (at X, the midpoint X of BE)

 f ∴ XA = XB = XC = XD = XE = XF.

 g i SSS congruence criterion.

  ii ∠AXB = $\frac{1}{6} \times 360°$ = **60°**; ∴ △XAB is equilateral; ∴ XA = AB.

γ: C11 Ratios   NC

This section should serve as a useful review, and as an opportunity to apply ideas related to ratio.

Answers

0 $x = 6$

1 £6 : £10.50 : £13.50

2 750 blue, 1250 white

3 a 72   b 264

4 Length = 270 m, speed = 64.8 km/h

5 a increased   b 2×63

6 3 : 2

7 4 km, 12 km/h

> 8 4 days (initially each lays $\frac{1}{10}$ wall per day; latterly one lays $\frac{2}{10}$ wall a day while the other lays $\frac{1}{20}$ wall a day – and hence $\frac{5}{20}$ wall per day between them)
>
> 9 $\sqrt{2} : 1$ ($AC = CE$ = short diagonal; AE = long diagonal. $\therefore \triangle ACE$ isosceles with $\angle ACE = 90°$)
>
> 10 a $1 : 1$ $\left(\frac{x}{y} + 1 = 3\left(\frac{x}{y} - 1\right)\text{, so }\frac{x}{y} = r = 2; \therefore \frac{x + 3y}{3x - y} = \frac{r + 3}{3r - 1} = 1\right)$ b $4 : 25$
>
> 11 $\frac{3}{5}$
>
> 12 $(1 + \sqrt{2}) : 1$ $\left(\text{Speeds } u > v\text{, lengths } m \text{ and } n; \text{ then } r = u : v = \left(\frac{m + n}{u - v}\right) : \left(\frac{m + n}{u + v}\right) = \frac{u + v}{u - v} = \frac{r + 1}{r - 1}\text{, so } r^2 - 2r - 1 = 0\right)$

γ: C12 Power play C   NC

The common element in the problems in this section is *surprise*. Problem **0** and Problem **1** are accessible, but require care: more of these numbers can be constructed than one might at first expect. Problem **2** requires a degree of flexibility. Problem **3** is counterintuitive; whilst Problems **4–11** provide a glimpse into a world whose later exploration will require a significant fluency in algebra.

Answers

> 0 a 29 only   b $29 = 3^{(4-1)} - 2 = 2^{(4+1)} - 3$

1 Only $32 = 2 \times 4 \times (3 + 1)$ and $36 = (1 + 2) \times 3 \times 4$ can be achieved using the four rules alone.
   $31 = (1 + 2)^3 + 4$; $33 = 4^3 \div 2 + 1$; $35 = 3^2 \times 4 - 1$; $37 = 3^2 \times 4 + 1$; $40 = (3^4 - 1) \div 2$

2 a $x = 0$ ($2^x = 2^{3x}$; $\therefore x = 3x$)   c $x = 8$ ($3^{48} = 3^{6x}$; $\therefore 48 = 6x$)
   b $x = 20$ ($7^x = 7^{20}$)   d $x = 4$ ($x > 1$, so x^x is increasing; $\therefore$ one root)

3 a Yes: $1 + 2 + 2^2 + \ldots + 2^9 = 2^{10} - 1 = 1023\text{p} = £10.23$
   b 17 ($1^2 + 2^2 + 3^2 + \ldots + 17^2 = 1785 > 1700$)

4 b $1^3 + 2^3 + 3^3 + 4^3 = (1 + 2 + 3 + 4)^2 = 100$
   c The sum of the first n cubes is equal to the square of the nth triangular number (that is, the square of the sum of the first n positive integers).

5 Squares; (*) $1 + 3 + 5 + \ldots + (2n - 1) = n^2$ (proved by noticing that it is true for small values of $n = 1, 2, 3$ say; and then using $(n + 1)^2 = n^2 + (2n + 1)$ to move from formula (*) to the next).

> 6 a $x = \frac{16}{3}$ b $x = 1$ (if $x > 1$, then LHS < 1; if $x > 1$, then LHS > 1)
>
> 7 b $36^2 + 37^2 + 38^2 + 39^2 + 40^2 = 41^2 + 42^2 + 43^2 + 44^2$
>   c The sum of the n squares starting at the $2n^{\text{th}}$ triangular number is equal to the sum of the next $n - 1$ squares
>
> 8 b $(1^5 + 2^5 + 3^5 + 4^5) + (1^7 + 2^7 + 3^7 + 4^7) = 2 \times (1 + 2 + 3 + 4)^4$
>   c The sum of the first n 5th powers plus the sum of the first n 7th powers is equal to twice the 4th power of the sum of the first n positive integers.
>
> 9 Cubes
>
> 10 b $16 + 17 + 18 + 19 + 20 = 21 + 22 + 23 + 24 = 3 \times (1^2 + 2^2 + 3^2 + 4^2)$
>   c The sum of the $n + 1$ integers starting with n^2 is equal to the sum of the next n integers, and both are equal to $n - 1$ times the sum of the squares of the first n positive integers.
>
> 11 If F_n denotes the nth Fibonacci number, then $F_1^2 + F_2^2 + F_3^2 + F_4^2 = F_4 \times F_5$ etc.

γ: C13 Similar triangles B: The SAS similarity criterion

Similar triangles constitute perhaps the single most powerful technique in elementary mathematics. They bring together geometry and algebra, arithmetic and ratio, functions and linear dependence, scale factors and enlargement; they also lay the foundations for trigonometry (and later linear algebra). However, the first objective is to understand the SAS similarity criterion and to be able to use it to solve problems like Problems 5-8 here.

Answers

> **0** KLMN is similar to BCDE with scale factor $\frac{1}{2}$, and the plane of KLMN is parallel to BCDE.
> (In $\triangle ABC$, KL||BC and KL = $\frac{1}{2}$BC (by the *Midpoint theorem*);
> similarly, in $\triangle ACD$, LN||CD and LN = $\frac{1}{2}$CD, etc.)

1 Yes (since $\angle A = \angle D$ and $AB : DE = 5 : 3 = AC : DF$)
[Note: If $\angle B = 47°$ with $AB = 10$ cm and $AC = 8$ cm, then $\angle BAC$ could be $90° \pm 23.91°$.]

2 $BD = 262.5$ cm $\left(= \frac{168}{32} \times 50\right)$

3 a $A'C' : AC = A'B' : AB = 4$ and $\angle C'A'B' = \angle CAB$; $\therefore B'C' : BC = 4$
   b Let B'' be the midpoint of AB' and let C'' be the midpoint of AC'.
   By the *Midpoint theorem* (applied to $\triangle AB''C''$), $BC||B''C''$ and $B''C'' = 2 \times BC$, and by the *Midpoint theorem* (applied to $\triangle AB'C'$), $B''C''||B'C'$ and $B'C' = 2 \times B''C''$.

4 a $\angle XAB = 30°$ ($\triangle ABC$ is isosceles with $\angle ABC = 120°$);
   $\angle XBA = 30°$ ($\triangle ABF$ is isosceles with $\angle FAB = 120°$).
   b $\angle XFC = 30°$ (= $\angle AFC - \angle AFB = 60° - 30°$); similarly $\angle XCF = 30°$.
   c $FC = 2 \times AB$ (for example, by Section **C10**, Problem 2);
   so $\triangle FCX$ and $\triangle BAX$ are similar (by AAA similarity) with sides in the ratio 2 : 1;
   $\therefore CX : AX = 2 : 1$.

5 20.4 m (Let the height of the tower = h metres. The horizontal line through the boy's eye creates two similar right angled triangles: $\therefore \frac{472 \cdot 5}{22 \cdot 5} = \frac{h - 1 \cdot 5}{0 \cdot 9}$; $\therefore h - 1.5 = 18.9$.)

6 a 1.9 m   **b** 3.52 m   **c** $\left(1 + \frac{6x}{100}\right)$ m

7 a $LM = \sqrt{2}$, $MH = \sqrt{5}$, $MN = \sqrt{6}$, $NL = 2\sqrt{2}$
   b $LM : MN : NL = 1 : \sqrt{3} : 2$;
   $\therefore \triangle LMN$ is similar to half an equilateral triangle (by the SSS similarity criterion);
   $\therefore \angle LMN = 90°$, $\angle MLN = 60°$, $\angle MNL = 30°$

8 84 cm $\left(\text{Let the height of the cone from the base} = h \text{ cm.} \therefore \frac{h - 30}{h} = \frac{27}{42}.\right)$

> **9 a** $\triangle BAC$ is isosceles and $\angle ABC = 108°$;
> $\therefore \angle BAC = 36°$; $\therefore \angle CAE = 72° = 180° - \angle DEA$;
> $\therefore AC||ED$. Similarly $BD||AE$, so $AXDE$ is a parallelogram. Also $AE = ED$.
> **b** $x = \frac{1 + \sqrt{5}}{2}$ ($\triangle XAD$ and $\triangle XCB$ are similar, by AAA similarity; $\frac{x}{1} = \frac{AD}{BC} = \frac{AX}{CX} = \frac{1}{x-1}$.)
>
> **10** $\frac{1}{12}$
>
> **11** $\frac{45}{4}$ cm (Let the rectangle be WXYZ, with $WX = 12$. Suppose W folds onto Y.
> Then $WY = 15$ (by Pythagoras' theorem).
> Let the crease be AB, with A on WX and B on ZY; let AB and WY cross at O.
> $\therefore$ WO folds onto YO, so O is the midpoint of WY,
> $\therefore OY = \frac{15}{2}$.
> $\triangle OBY$ and $\triangle XYW$ are similar (by AAA);
> $\therefore \frac{OY}{WX} = \frac{OB}{XY}$; $\therefore OB = \frac{45}{8}$.)

γ: C14 Word problems   NC

As a pupil's range of available techniques develops, mixed collections of word problems help to ensure that these techniques can be selected and combined to solve genuinely challenging problems.

Problem **0** should clearly be a routine exercise: each step is as simple as could be. Yet many 18 year olds cannot coordinate the necessary steps in a reliable way. So rather than rushing on, use Problem **0** to bring out the need to break down each problem into simple steps, and then to link these steps reliably and accurately. It may then make sense to concentrate on a subset of five or six problems – chosen specifically to suit a particular class.

Answers

0 6.5 km/h

1 a 5 @ 50 p, 25 @ 10 p   c 20 @ 20 p (and 40 @ 10 p)
   b 10 @ 50 p, 10 @ 10 p   d 30 @ 10 p (and 30 @ 20 p)

2 $\frac{3}{4}$ km

3 $1\frac{1}{2}$ hours

4 42 cm $\left(=\frac{448}{8}\times\frac{3}{4}\right)$

5 10 kg ($4L + 6S = 45$, $3L + 7S = 40$; so $L - S = 5$. Now add first and third equations.)

6 a 8 miles
   b Between 3 and 3:20 (just after 3 if the hill is very small; just before 3:20 if the level walk is very short)

7 Dead heat; width of river = 300 m (Mole takes 6 minutes at 3 km/h)

8 10.5 m/sec, 9.5 m/sec

9 $\frac{40}{7}$ km/h (Combined speed covers $3 \times (8.5) = 25.5$ km in $\frac{7}{5}$ hours.

   First runner covers $\frac{7}{5}\times\frac{25}{2} = 17.5$ km in the same time;

   ∴ second runner covers 8 km in $\frac{7}{5}$ hours.)

10 Every **6 minutes** (Suppose I walk along the x-axis in the positive x-direction. Choose the distance I walk in 1 minute as the unit of distance.
   My actual position is irrelevant, so start measuring distance ($x = 0$) and time ($t = 0$) when two buses pass me – one in each direction.
   The next bus going in my direction is then at $x = -c$ and will pass me at $t = x = 12$;
   ∴ speed = $\frac{12+c}{12}$ units per minute.
   At time $t = 0$, the next bus in the opposite direction is at $x = c$ ("gaps same in each direction").
   ∴ speed = $\frac{c-4}{4}$ units per minute.
   Hence $\frac{c-4}{4} = \frac{12+c}{12}$, so $c = 12$ and speed = 2 units per minute.)

11 a 2:24 $\left(2\times\frac{60+m}{2}=m\times 6\right)$ b 3:36   c 1:12

12 **40** eggs $\left(\text{sold at }\frac{1}{4}\text{ kreuzer each}\right)$ and **60** eggs $\left(\text{sold at }\frac{1}{6}\text{ kreuzer each}\right)$

γ: C15 Volumes and surface areas of right prisms

Right prisms extend the notion of a cuboid. At this level they constitute the most general basic shape whose volume needs to be routinely calculated, and for which the standard formula can be genuinely proved.

Answers

> **0** 4 cubic units (= volume(ABCDEFGH) − volume(EKMHDA) − volume(FGCNLB) = 8 − 4)

1 a Volume = $\frac{1}{2}(3 \times 4 \times 5) = 30$ cm³   **b** = $\frac{1}{2}[3 \times 4] \times 5$

2 Surface area = **72 cm²** (= 3 × 5 + 5 × 5 + 4 × 5 + 3 × 4)

4 a 1980 m³ (area(end pentagon) = $7 \times 12 + \frac{1}{2}(12 \times 2.5) = 99$ m²; ∴ volume = 99 × 20 m³)
  b 260 m² (= 2 × 20 × 6.5)
  c 478 m² (= 2 × 20 × 7 + 2 × 99)

5 a 27.5 m³ (area(end pentagon) = 5.5 m²; ∴ volume = (5.5 × 5) m³)
  b ≈ 33.1 m² ≈ $2 \times 5.5 + 5 \times 1 + 5 \times \sqrt{2} + 5 \times 2 = 26 + 5\sqrt{2}$)

6 a 1948.6 cm³ (area(hexagon) = $6 \times \frac{1}{2}(5 \times 5\sqrt{3})$; ∴ volume = $30 \times \frac{75\sqrt{3}}{2} = 15 \times 75\sqrt{3}$)
  b $(900 + 75\sqrt{3})$ cm² ≈ 1029.9 cm²

7 a 375π cm³ (= 25π × 15)   **b** 200π cm² (= 50π + 10π × 15)

> **8 a** Length = $\frac{10^8}{9\pi}$ cm = $\frac{10^6}{9\pi}$ m = $\frac{10^3}{9\pi}$ km   **b** ≈ 35.368 km

γ: C16 From formula to function   NC

The step from using formulae to thinking in terms of functions is often left to "osmosis". This section takes the familiar formulae for the area and arc length of a sector of a circle and seeks to underline the way these quantities depend on the radius r and on the sector angle θ.

Answers

> **0 a** $\frac{\pi r^2}{4}$ **b i** $\frac{\pi r}{2}$ **ii** $2r + \frac{\pi r}{2} = \left(2 + \frac{\pi}{2}\right)r$

1 a i $\frac{\pi}{6}$ **ii** $\frac{25\pi}{6}$ **iii** $\frac{\pi r^2}{6}$

  b i $\frac{\pi}{2}$ **ii** $\frac{25\pi}{2}$ **iii** $\frac{\pi r^2}{2}$

  c i $\frac{3\pi}{4}$ **ii** $\frac{75\pi}{4}$ **iii** $\frac{3\pi r^2}{4}$

  d i $\left(\frac{\theta}{360}\right)\pi$ **ii** $\left(\frac{\theta}{360}\right)25\pi$ **iii** $\mathcal{A} = \left(\frac{\theta}{360}\right)\pi r^2$

  e i $\mathcal{A} = \left(\frac{\pi}{10}\right)\theta$ (straight line through the origin with gradient just less than $\frac{1}{3}$)

    ii $\mathcal{A} = \left(\frac{\pi}{3}\right)r^2$ (parabola with apex at the origin, just below the curve $\mathcal{A} = r^2$)

2 a i $\frac{\pi}{3}$ **ii** $\frac{5\pi}{3}$ **iii** $\left(\frac{\pi}{3}\right)r$

  b i π **ii** 5π **iii** πr

  c i $\frac{3\pi}{2}$ **ii** $\frac{15\pi}{2}$ **iii** $\left(\frac{3\pi}{2}\right)r$

  d i $\left(\frac{\theta}{180}\right)\pi$ **ii** $\left(\frac{\theta}{36}\right)\pi$ **iii** $\mathcal{L} = \left(\frac{\theta}{180}\right)\pi r$

  e i $\mathcal{L} = \left(\frac{\pi}{3}\right)\theta$ (straight line through the origin with gradient just less than 1)

    ii $\mathcal{L} = \left(\frac{\pi}{3}\right)r$ (same line as for i)

3 a i $2 + \frac{\pi}{3}$ ii $10 + \frac{5\pi}{3}$ iii $2r + \left(\frac{\pi}{3}\right)r$

    b i $2 + \pi$ ii $10 + 5\pi$ iii $2r + \pi r$

    c i $2 + \frac{3\pi}{2}$ ii $10 + \frac{15\pi}{2}$ iii $2r + \left(\frac{3\pi}{2}\right)r$

    d i $2 + \left(\frac{\theta}{180}\right)\pi$ ii $10 + \left(\frac{\theta}{36}\right)\pi$ iii $\mathcal{L} = 2r + \left(\frac{\theta}{180}\right)\pi r$

    e i $\mathcal{P} = 2 + \left(\frac{\pi}{180}\right)\theta$ (straight line through (0,2), gradient $\frac{\pi}{180} \approx 0.01745$; almost horizontal)

       ii $\mathcal{P} = \left(2 + \frac{\pi}{3}\right)r$ (straight line through origin, gradient $2 + \frac{\pi}{3} \approx 3.0472$)

4 a i Arc length also doubles   ii $\left(\frac{\theta}{360}\right)2\pi$

    b i Arc length also doubles   ii $\left(\frac{\pi}{180}\right)r$

5 a i Perimeter also doubles   ii $2 + \left(\frac{\theta}{180}\right)\pi$

    b i $\mathcal{P} - 2r$ doubles   ii $\frac{2r}{\theta} + \left(\frac{\pi}{180}\right)r$

6 a i Area multiplied by 4   ii $\left(\frac{\theta}{360}\right)\pi$

    b i Area also doubles   ii $\left(\frac{\pi}{360}\right)r^2$

7 a $r = 0$ or $r = 2 + \frac{12}{\pi} \approx 5.82$ b $\theta = \frac{360}{29}\pi \approx 3.95°$

γ: C17 Black hats and white hats

Though scarcely an explicit curricular theme, logic, and the challenge to think and to argue strictly logically, lies at the heart of all mathematics.

It is not easy to make these problems precise (see the comments in the text after Problem 0). The goal is to generate structured, constructive discussion: so Problem **0** may best be done 'practically' – with pupils standing at the front of the class (lined up facing from right to left) playing the roles of the students, with contributions (and reasons!) being invited from the class. For some classes it may suffice to suppress Problems **3** and **4**, to begin by treating Problem **0** collectively, and then get pupils to tackle Problems **1** and **2** in pairs – closing with a plenary analysis of just these two problems.

Answers

0 a *A* (A sees B's hat, and knows that his own colour is different)

    b First *B*; then *C* (A sees one hat of each colour, so cannot know his own colour; B "hears" A's silence and concludes that his hat must have a different colour from C)

1 a Since all three hands go up after the first drumbeat, everyone concludes that there is at most 1 white hat, but noone knows whether the number of white hats is 0 or 1. If someone could see a white hat, then he would know that his own hat was black. Since all three hands drop after the second drumbeat, it follows that all three hats are black.
So at the third drumbeat, all hands are raised.

    b Since all three hands go up after the first drumbeat, everyone concludes that there is at most 1 white hat, but no-one knows whether the number of white hats is 0 or 1. If after the second drumbeat some hand remains raised, it must be because someone can see a white hat; so there must be exactly one white hat and two people can see it, so two people keep their hands raised – knowing that their hats are black.

2 a Since all four hands go up after the first drumbeat, everyone concludes that there are at least 2 black hats (and so at most 2 white hats), but no-one knows how many. If someone could see just one black hat, then he would know that his own hat was black. Since all four hands drop after the second drumbeat, they all know that ≥3 hats are black.
Since all four hands stay down after the third drumbeat, they all know that noone can see a white hat, so they all know that all four hats are black.
So after the fourth drumbeat, all hands are raised.

b Since all four hands go up after the first drumbeat, everyone concludes that there are at least 2 black hats (and so at most 2 white hats), but no-one knows how many. If after the second drumbeat some hand remains raised, then someone must be able to see just one black hat, and so knows that his own hat is black; but then exactly 3 people see exactly one white hat and conclude the same, so 3 hands remain raised (all black).

---

3 There are two possibilities – one of which splits into two cases.
  a If A sees three white hats, he knows his own hat must be black and calls out immediately. B, C and D then conclude that their own hats must be white.
  b If A does not call out immediately, then B, C and D know they are not all the same colour.
    i If B sees 2 black or 2 white, B can identify his own colour; C then knows that $C = D$ and calls out; D then knows his colour. A never knows.
    ii If B sees 1 black and 1 white, then B remains silent. C then knows that B can't tell, so $C \neq D$, so C calls out; then D calls out. A never knows.

4 The only possible triple is: Fermat: **50**; Gauss: **20**; Hermite: **30**

γ: C18 The unitary method

The basic strategy for tackling 'rate' problems (what is here called the *unitary method*) requires lots of practice; it cannot be based on raw common sense, so it has to be explicitly taught. Front-led teacher input may be needed to bring out the underlying algebraic principles (e.g. Problem 3) before they can be used for subsequent problems. But be prepared to discover serious weaknesses: for example, pupils may consistently ignore the basic principle of all algebra – namely that *letters stand for ∗u∗∗e∗∗* – so that things like 'Tom and Dick take 2 hours' are translated as 'T + D = 2'.

Answers

---

0 a $\frac{6}{5}$ hours (In 1 hour Tom does $\frac{1}{2}$ job, Dick does $\frac{1}{3}$ job; together they complete $\frac{5}{6}$ job)

b $\frac{24}{13}$ hours (Let Tom complete t jobs in 1 hour and Dick complete d jobs; then together they complete $t + d$ jobs in 1 hour, so $t + d = \frac{1}{2}$.
Similarly $d + h = \frac{1}{3}$, $h + t = \frac{1}{4}$. ∴ $t + d + h = \frac{13}{24}$)

---

1 a i £$\frac{3}{4}$ = £0.75   **ii** $\frac{4}{3}$ m   **b** Product = 1

3 $\frac{1}{T} + \frac{1}{D}$ jobs in 1 hour.

5 $\frac{12}{13}$ hours (In 1 hour Tom, Dick and Harry together complete $\frac{1}{2} + \frac{1}{3} + \frac{1}{4} = \frac{13}{12}$ jobs)

---

6 a i $T \times t = 1$ **ii** t
  b i $t + d$; ∴ $t + d = \frac{1}{2}$ **iii** $h + t = \frac{1}{4}$
    ii $d + h = \frac{1}{3}$ **iv** $\frac{24}{13}$ hours ($t + d + h = \frac{13}{24}$)

γ: C19 Estimation C: Arithmetic meets geometry NC

Surds arise naturally in modelling geometry problems (thanks to Pythagoras' theorem and the need to translate information concerning areas or volumes into information about lengths). These problems challenge pupils to use arithmetical methods to derive reasonable estimates, or exact values, for simple surds.

Answers

0 $\sqrt[3]{2} \approx 1.28$

1 ≈ 3.25
2 a 2.1 m × 2.1 m   d ≈ 4.5 cm × 4.5 cm
   b ≈ 6.7 cm × 6.7 cm   e ≈ 14.1 m × 14.1 m (or 14 m × 14 m)
   c 2.3 m × 2.3 m
3 a 1.8 m × 1.8 m × 1.8 m   c ≈ 5.8 cm × 5.8 cm × 5.8 cm (or 5.9 × 5.9 × 5.9)
   b ≈ 2.7 cm × 2.7 cm × 2.7 cm   d ≈ 12.8 cm × 12.8 cm × 12.8 cm
4 a 1.8 m × 1.8 m   c 5.8 cm × 5.8 cm × 5.8 cm
   b ≈ 1.8 cm × 1.8 cm × 1.8 cm   d ≈ 18.25 cm × 18.25 cm × 18.25 cm

5 360 litres (= 400 × 25 × 36 cm^3)

γ: C20 Similar triangles C: Tan NC

Trigonometry encodes the fact of similarity in numerical form. These problems use carefully chosen angles to introduce the simplest trigonometric ratio *tan* and to explore simple applications.

Answers

0 b

Length of AB	6 cm	10 cm	12 cm	15 cm	18 cm	20 cm
Length of BC	4.2 cm	7 cm	8.4 cm	10.5 cm	12.6 cm	14 cm
Ratio $\frac{BC}{AB}$	0.7	0.7	0.7	0.7	0.7	0.7

   c All the right angled triangles ABC are similar, so $\frac{BC}{AB} = \lambda$ must be constant.

1 b

Length of AB	6 cm	10 cm	12 cm	15 cm	18 cm	20 cm
Length of BC	5.4 cm	9 cm	10.8 cm	13.5 cm	16.2 cm	18 cm
Ratio $\frac{BC}{AB}$	0.9	0.9	0.9	0.9	0.9	0.9

   c All the right angled triangles ABC are similar, so $\frac{BC}{AB} = \lambda$ must be constant.

2 b

Length of AB	6 cm	10 cm	12 cm	15 cm	18 cm	20 cm
Length of BC	9.6 cm	16 cm	19.2 cm	24 cm	28.8 cm	32 cm
Ratio $\frac{BC}{AB}$	1.6	1.6	1.6	1.6	1.6	1.6

   c All the right angled triangles ABC are similar, so $\frac{BC}{AB} = \lambda$ must be constant.

3 b

Length of AB	6 cm	10 cm	12 cm	15 cm	18 cm	20 cm
Length of BC	13.8 cm	23 cm	27.6 cm	34.5 cm	41.4 cm	46 cm
Ratio $\frac{BC}{AB}$	2.3	2.3	2.3	2.3	2.3	2.3

   c All the right angled triangles ABC are similar, so $\frac{BC}{AB} = \lambda$ must be constant.

5 a i 0.7 ii 0.9 iii 1.6 iv 2.3
  b i $\frac{1}{0.7} = \frac{10}{7}$ ii $\frac{1}{0.9} = \frac{10}{9}$ iii $\frac{1}{1.6} = \frac{5}{8}$ iv $\frac{1}{2.3} = \frac{10}{23}$

6 a $\frac{13}{14}$ c $\tan(\angle A) = \frac{B'C'}{AB'''}$; $10 \times \frac{13}{14} = \frac{65}{7}$

  b $\tan(\angle A) = \frac{B'C'}{AB'}$; $7 \times \frac{13}{14} = \frac{13}{2}$

7 a $\tan 45° = 1$ b $\tan 60° = \sqrt{3}$; $\tan 30° = \frac{1}{\sqrt{3}}$

8 $\tan \angle BAC = \frac{5.25}{7.5} = 0.7$; $\therefore \angle BAC = 2 \times 35° = \mathbf{70°}$

9 a $\angle CAB = 35°$, $\angle ABC = 90°$, $\angle BCA = 55°$
  b $\angle CAB = 45°$, $\angle BCA = 122°$, $\angle ABC = 13°$

> c Let the line $y = -11$ meet AC at X.
>   In $\triangle ABX$: $\angle ABX = 66\frac{1}{2}°$; in $\triangle CBX$: $\angle BCX = 42°$ and $\angle CBX = 48°$.
> $\therefore \angle ABC = 114\frac{1}{2}°$, $\angle CAB = 23\frac{1}{2}°$, $\angle ACB = 42°$.
>
> 10 height = 11.5 cm, area = 57.5 cm²
> 11 $BC = \tan(\angle BAC)$
> 12 $AP = 10$ cm, $OP = \sqrt{181}$ cm $\left(\tan 42° = \frac{9}{AP}; \therefore AP = 10\right)$

γ: C21 Integer problems   NC

Here is another set of problems which illustrate the wealth of interesting questions relating to the simplest of all mathematical objects – the positive integers. Problem **0** should indicate whether pupils' basic arithmetic is uncomfortably rusty or available 'on demand'.

Answers

> 0 **15** ($79 = 4 \times (7 + 9) + 15$; no larger remainder since digit-sum = 18 for 99 only and digit-sum = 17 for 89 and 98 only)

1 $n = 34$

2 364 $(= 1 + (2 + 1) + (3 + 2 + 1) + \ldots)$

3 a 2; 3; 4; 6   c 24 $\left(= \frac{100}{5} + \frac{100}{25}\right)$

   b 12 $\left(= \frac{50}{5} + \frac{50}{25}\right)$ d 31 $\left(= \frac{125}{5} + \frac{125}{25} + \frac{125}{125}\right)$

4 a 2 (Divisible by 8; $\therefore$ **760 or **768. Divisible by 9; $\therefore$ 86760 or 96768)
   b 2 (Divisible by 25; $\therefore$ *****25, or *****75. Divisible by 9; $\therefore$ 2723625 or 2763675)

5 1 solution: rows 1342; 2304; 9790; 6561 (7A = 6561; $\therefore$ 1D = 1296 since first digit of 5A ≠ 0)

6 24 ($799 = 31 \times (7 + 9 + 9) + 24$. The largest possible digit-sums are 27 (999: remainder 0); and 26 (998, 989 and 889: remainders 10, 1, 5). Digit-sum 25 arises for 997, 979, 799, 988, 898, 889: some pupils may grab the largest 997 which gives remainder 22.)

7 11 solutions – up to switching rows and columns (Bottom right corner = 0, 1, 4, 5, 6 or 9. If bottom right corner = 0, there are **3** solutions with last row = 100 and last column = 400, **1** solution with last row = 100 and last column = 900, and **2** solutions with bottom row = 400 and last column = 900. If bottom right corner = 1, there is **1** solution with bottom row = 441 and last column = 121 and **2** solutions with bottom row 441 and last column 961. If bottom right corner = 4, there is **1** solution with bottom row = 144 and last column = 484. If bottom right corner = 6, there is **1** solution with bottom row = 576 and last column = 676. There are no solutions with bottom right corner = 5 or 9.)

8 a 5   b 11   c 1   d 19?

> e $(n-1)n(n+1)(n+2) = (n^2 + n - 1)^2$

9 a 23, 41; 3, 241

   b 4 pairs (2 with 431; 3 with 241 or 421; 23 with 41)
10 a 16, 17   b $2^3 \times 3^3 \times 5^2 \times 7 \times 11 \times 13 \times 17 \times 19 \times 23 \times 29 \times 31$
11 3 (Let $n + 99 = m > n$.
   $\therefore (\sqrt{m} - \sqrt{n})(\sqrt{m} + \sqrt{n}) = m - n = 99 = 1 \times 99 = 3 \times 33 = 9 \times 11$.
   $\therefore (\sqrt{m}, \sqrt{n}) = (50,49)$, or $(18,15)$, or $(10,1)$;
   $\therefore (m, n) = (2500,2401)$, or $(324,225)$, or $(100,1)$.)
12 48 651

γ: C22 From fractions to decimals A   NC

Fractions with the same (prime) denominator are connected in two ways:

(i) two fractions may be *complementary* (i.e. have sum = 1, like $\frac{1}{7}$ and $\frac{6}{7}$), or

(ii) the recurring decimal block of one may be obtained by shifting the recurring block of the other one place to the left or to the right.

This section introduces these two basic relations, concentrating on decimals whose recurring blocks are conveniently *short*. Sadly, small cases sometimes mislead: in the simplest instance (namely *elevenths*, where the recurring block has length 2) these *two* relations *blur into one*! So be ready to disentangle things! The ideas will be developed further in Sections **C34** and **E2**.

Answers

0 a i $\frac{1}{7} = 0.\dot{1}4285\dot{7}$

      ii $\frac{3}{7} = 0.\dot{4}2857\dot{1}$: recurring block moves one place to the left

      iii $10 \times \frac{1}{7} - 1 = \frac{3}{7}$: multiplying by 10 moves the endless decimal one place to the left

   b i $\frac{1}{7} + \frac{6}{7} = 1$

      ii $\frac{6}{7} = 0.\dot{8}5714\dot{2}$: recurring block moves 3 places to the left

      iii $1 = \frac{1}{7} + \frac{6}{7} = 0.\dot{1}4285\dot{7} + 0.\dot{8}5714\dot{2} = 0.\dot{9}9999\dot{9}$

1 a $\frac{3}{11} = 0.\dot{2}\dot{7}$ b $\frac{8}{11} = 0.\dot{7}\dot{2}$
2 a $\frac{2}{11} = 0.\dot{1}\dot{8}$ b $\frac{9}{11} = 0.\dot{8}\dot{1}$
3 a $\frac{5}{11} = 0.\dot{4}\dot{5}$ b $\frac{6}{11} = 0.\dot{5}\dot{4}$
4 a $\frac{4}{11} = 0.\dot{3}\dot{6}$ b $\frac{7}{11} = 0.\dot{6}\dot{3}$
5 a i $10 \times \frac{3}{11} = 2 + \frac{8}{11}$;
      ii $10 \times 0.\dot{2}\dot{7} = 2 + 0.\dot{7}\dot{2}$;   iii recurring block moves 1 place left
   b i $10 \times \frac{2}{11} = 1 + \frac{9}{11}$;
      ii $10 \times 0.\dot{1}\dot{8} = 1 + 0.\dot{8}\dot{1}$;   iii recurring block moves 1 place left
   c i $10 \times \frac{5}{11} = 4 + \frac{6}{11}$;
      ii $10 \times 0.\dot{4}\dot{5} = 1 + 0.\dot{5}\dot{4}$;   iii recurring block moves 1 place left
   d i $10 \times \frac{4}{11} = 3 + \frac{7}{11}$;
      ii $10 \times 0.\dot{3}\dot{6} = 1 + 0.\dot{6}\dot{3}$;   iii recurring block moves 1 place left

6 a $\frac{4}{37} = 0.\dot{1}0\dot{8}$ b $\frac{3}{37} = 0.\dot{0}8\dot{1}$ c $\frac{30}{37} = 0.\dot{8}1\dot{0}$

7 a $\frac{5}{37} = 0.\dot{1}3\dot{5}$ b $\frac{13}{37} = 0.\dot{3}5\dot{1}$ c $\frac{19}{37} = 0.\dot{5}1\dot{3}$

8 a i $10 \times \frac{4}{37} = 1 + \frac{3}{37}$
      ii $10 \times 0.\dot{1}0\dot{8} = 1 + 0.\dot{0}8\dot{1}$;;   iii recurring block moves 1 place left
   b i $10 \times \frac{5}{37} = 1 + \frac{13}{37}$;
      ii $10 \times 0.\dot{1}3\dot{5} = 1 + 0.\dot{3}5\dot{1}$;   iii recurring block moves 1 place left
   c i $10 \times \frac{2}{37} = 0 + \frac{20}{37}$;
      ii $10 \times 0.\dot{0}5\dot{4} = 0.\dot{5}4\dot{0}$;   iii recurring block moves 1 place left

9 a $\frac{33}{37} = 0.\dot{8}9\dot{1}$ b $\frac{32}{37} = 0.\dot{8}6\dot{4}$ c $\frac{35}{37} = 0.\dot{9}4\dot{5}$

10 a i $\frac{4}{37} + \frac{33}{37} = 1$ iii $\frac{2}{37} + \frac{35}{37} = 1$;
      ii $\frac{5}{37} + \frac{32}{37} = 1$ Each pair of decimals add to $0.\dot{9}$
   b $0.\dot{2}7\dot{0}, 0.\dot{7}2\dot{9}$; $\frac{10}{37} + \frac{27}{37} = 1$; $0.\dot{2}7\dot{0} + 0.\dot{7}2\dot{9} = 0.\dot{9}$

γ: C23 Averages   NC

Averages are often thought to be a matter of simple arithmetic. In fact they are an excellent challenge precisely because the simplest examples force pupils to go back to first principles and to think about the underlying meaning of what is to be calculated. They therefore serve as an excellent medium for basic problem solving and for cultivating algebraic thinking.

Answers

0 5%

1 20%   4 2 : 1

2 15 mph   5 Car A $\left(\frac{257}{34} < \frac{31}{4} < \frac{109}{14} = \frac{436}{56}\right)$

3 200 m   6 4 km

7 217 (329 ÷ 47 = 7 numbers; 1 + 2 + 3 + 4 + 5 + 97 + x = 329)

8 Impossible (must descend in zero time)   9 1 : 2

10 14.7 minutes = 14 min 42 sec $\left(= 1 + \frac{6}{5} + \frac{6}{4} + \frac{6}{3} + \frac{6}{2} + \frac{6}{1} \text{ minutes}\right)$; speed = $24\frac{24}{49}$ mph

11 £12 per kg   12 35 days

γ: C24 Index laws B   NC

The quickest way to uncover basic arithmetical and algebraic weakness is by setting simple tasks involving *fractions* and *powers*. This is one of four short sections intended to test and to develop fluency in using the basic index laws.

Answers

0 a i $64 = 2^6$ ii $4096 = 2^{12}$ b $64^2 = (2^6)^2 = 2^{12} = 4096$

1 a i 2^6 ii 2^{12} iii 2^{20} b i 3^8 ii 3^{10} iii 3^{15}

2 a $\frac{1}{9}$ b $\frac{1}{4}$ c 1   d $\frac{1}{8}$ e 9   f 2

3 a i 2^{12} ii 2^{10} iii 2^{-6} iv 2^{-24} v 2^{8}
  b i 3^{6} ii 3^{6} iii 3^{-8} iv 3^{-12} v 3^{6}
  c i 10^{5} ii 10^{6} iii 10^{-8} iv 10^{6} v 10^{8}

4 a i 2^{9} ii 2^{7} iii 2^{5} iv 2^{10}
  b i 3^{6} ii 3^{7} iii 3^{5}
5 a 2nd term = 3rd term = $\sqrt{2}$ b (2nd term) × (3rd term) = 2

γ: C25 Missing digits   NC

These problems may look easy. But they should be used as an opportunity to develop logical thinking in the familiar context of the standard arithmetical algorithms. They may also reveal (and help to plug) some surprising gaps.

Answers

0 3 solutions (393 × 8, 493 × 8, 443 × 8)

1 2 solutions (83 × 3, 61 × 9)
2 See Problem 0. ("*ab*3" × *m* = 3∗44; *m* = 8; ∴ *b* = 4 or 9; etc.)
3 749 × 63   5 550 × 11
4 13 × 4 = 52   6 54 × 3 = 162

7 a Unique: 291 × 45 = 13095
  b 2 solutions: 95 × 11 = 1045; 19 × 55 = 1045
8 Unique: 269 × 47 = 12643 (The third line must read ∗∗83, and the units column must be 1 × 3, or 3 × 1, or 7 × 9, or 9 × 7. The first three of these don't work.)

γ: C26 Equations   NC

This mixed collection of problems vary considerably in difficulty. But they all share the important feature that once the relevant equation or expression has been identified and set up, the solution becomes straightforward.

Answers

0 80 g
   (Let one ball weigh *b* g and one cube weigh *c* g.
   ∴ *b* + *c* = 170 and 2*b* + 3*c* = 420.
   ∴ *c* = (2*b* + 3*c*) − 2(*b* + *c*).)

1 49 (Denote the number of rungs initially above the painter by *x*. ∴ 2*x* − 8 = *x* + 8)
2 No (Let the number be *x*. Then [(5(2*x* + 1) + 5) ÷ 10] − *x* = 1 for all *x*)
3 $j \times \frac{1}{m}\left(\frac{1}{m}\text{ litres per mile}\right)$ 5 32 kg (= 12 + 16 + 4)
4 2 lbs and 8 lbs   6 47
7 Cameron = 21, David = 28 (*d* = 2(2*c* − *d*) and *d* + (2*d* − *c*) = 63)

8 24 hours   9 16 or 48
10 30 and 18 (Let their ages in years "when William was three times as old as Mary" be
   3*m* and *m* – difference = 2*m*. When Mary is three times as old as William was [then], she will be 9*m*.
   When William is half as old, he will be $\frac{9m}{2}$ and Mary will then be $\frac{5m}{2}$.
   So William's age now is 5*m* and Mary's is 3*m*.)
11 £199.98

γ: C27 Sequences B   NC

This section moves on from the term-to-term rules of Section **T4** and seeks to establish the idea of a position-to-term rule (Problems **1, 2, 3**), culminating in a *closed formula* for the nth *triangular number* (Problem **4**).

Answers

> **0 a** 2   **b** 3   **c** 4   **d** 5
> **e** This may *suggest* that "the number of ways to make 6" = 6
> **f** 7 ways (3 + 3, 3 + 2 + 1, 3 + 1 + 1 + 1, 2 + 2 + 2, 2 + 2 + 1 + 1, 2 + 1 + 1 + 1 + 1, 1 + 1 + 1 + 1 + 1 + 1)

1 a 5, 7, 9   **b** 10, 13, 16   **c** 8, 15, 24

2 a 4, 7, 10, 13, 16; 10th term = $4 + 9 \times 3$ **b** 4, 8, 12, 16, 20; 10th term = 4×10
  c 1, 3, 6, 10, 15; 10th term = $1 + 2 + 3 + 4 + 5 + 6 + 7 + 8 + 9 + 10 = 55$

> **d** 1, 5, 13, 25, 41; 10th term = $9^2 + 10^2 = 199$

3 a i $1 \times 2 = 2, 2 \times 3 = 6, 3 \times 4 = 12$ **ii** 20, 30, 42, 56, 72, 90, 110
  b $8 = 2 \times 2^2, 18 = 2 \times 3^2, 32 = 2 \times 4^2$
  c i $(n-1)n; n(n+1)$ **ii** $(n-1)n + n(n+1) = n[(n-1) + (n+1)] = 2n^2$

> **4 a** 1, 3, 6, 10, 15
> **b** n^{th} term: add n to the previous term; 21, 28, 36, 45, 55
> **c i** $2 \times (n^{th} \text{ term}) = n(n+1); \therefore n^{th} \text{ term} = \frac{1}{2}n(n+1)$
> **d i** 10, 15, 21, 28, 36; $1 + 3 = 4, 3 + 6 = 9, 6 + 10 = 16: (n-1)^{th} \text{ term} + n^{th} \text{ term} = n^2$
>   **ii** $\frac{1}{2}(n-1)n + \frac{1}{2}n(n+1) = \frac{1}{2}n[(n-1) + (n+1)] = n^2$

γ: C28 Surd arithmetic B   NC

Surd arithmetic is an essential element of exact mathematical calculation. It also serves as a stepping stone on the path to simple algebra. In addition it allows pupils to experience at first hand how inner structure often gives rise unexpectedly to satisfyingly simple answers.

Answers

> **0 a i** 4   **ii** 3   **iii** $\frac{5}{6}$ **c** $\sqrt{5}(\sqrt{5} - \sqrt{3}) + \sqrt{3}(\sqrt{5} - \sqrt{3}) = 2$
> **b** $\sqrt{2}(\sqrt{2} - 1) + \sqrt{2} - 1 = 1$

1 a i 9   **ii** $3\sqrt[3]{3}$ **iii** $4\sqrt[3]{4}$ **iv** 16
  b i 16   **ii** $5\sqrt[3]{5}$ **iii** 36
2 a i 1   **ii** 2   **iii** 3   **iv** 4   **v** 5
  b i $\sqrt{2}$ **ii** $2\sqrt{3}$ **iii** $6 (= 3\sqrt{4})$ **iv** $4\sqrt{5}$ **v** $5\sqrt{6}$
3 a 1   **b** 1   **c** 1   **d** 1
4 a i $\sqrt{2}(1+\sqrt{2})$ **ii** $\sqrt{3}(1+\sqrt{3})$ **iii** $\sqrt{4}(1+\sqrt{4}) = 6$ **iv** $\sqrt{5}(1+\sqrt{5})$
  b i $\sqrt{6}+2$ **ii** $3+\sqrt{6}$ **iii** $\sqrt{6}-2$ **iv** $3-\sqrt{6}$
5 a i $11+6\sqrt{2}$ **ii** $14-6\sqrt{5}$ **iii** $6+4\sqrt{2}$ **iv** $4+2\sqrt{3}$ **v** $7-4\sqrt{3}$ **vi** 8
  b i $11+6\sqrt{2}$ **ii** $14-6\sqrt{5}$ **iii** $6+4\sqrt{2}$ **iv** $4+2\sqrt{3}$ **v** $7-4\sqrt{3}$ **vi** 8
6 a i 1   **ii** 2   **iii** 3   **iv** 4
  b i $2+\sqrt{6}-\sqrt{2}-\sqrt{3}$ **iii** $\sqrt{10}+\sqrt{6}-\sqrt{5}-\sqrt{3}$
   ii $2\sqrt{2}+\sqrt{6}-2-\sqrt{3}$ **iv** $\sqrt{3}$

> **7** Edge lengths $\sqrt{2}, 2\sqrt{2}, 4\sqrt{2}$; volume = $16\sqrt{2}$ cm^3

γ: C29 Adding and subtracting fractions — NC

Another dose of exercises to help develop crucial arithmetical and algebraic techniques.

Answers

0 $\dfrac{1}{99} + \dfrac{1}{264} = \dfrac{8}{99 \times 8} + \dfrac{3}{3 \times 264} = \dfrac{11}{99 \times 8} = \dfrac{1}{72}$

1 a $\dfrac{1}{35}$ b $\dfrac{3}{35}$ c $\dfrac{1}{72}$ d $\dfrac{1}{50}$

   e $\dfrac{4}{5 \times 49}$ f $\dfrac{1}{36 \times 7 \times 48}$ g $\dfrac{2}{17 \times 19}$ h $\dfrac{3}{11 \times 20}$

2 Three rows: $\dfrac{2}{3} - \dfrac{1}{6} = \dfrac{1}{2}$; $-\dfrac{1}{24} + \left(-\dfrac{9}{48}\right) = -\dfrac{11}{48}$; $\dfrac{17}{24} - \left(-\dfrac{1}{48}\right) = \dfrac{35}{48}$; final column $\dfrac{1}{2} - \left(-\dfrac{11}{48}\right)$

3 a $5a$ b $\dfrac{5a}{6}$ c $\dfrac{a}{2}$ d $\dfrac{3a}{4}$

4 a $\dfrac{5}{a}$ d $\dfrac{3b+4}{ab}$ g $\dfrac{3+a}{a}$ j $\dfrac{(9y^2 - 4z^2)}{42yz}$

   b $\dfrac{2a+b}{ab}$ e $\dfrac{2b+3}{b^2}$ h $\dfrac{8b-1}{2b}$ k $\dfrac{p(x-1)}{x^2}$

   c $\dfrac{2b+3a}{ab}$ f $\dfrac{3}{4a}$ i $\dfrac{3(b-a)}{ab}$ l $\dfrac{p(x-p)}{x^2}$

5 a $\dfrac{1}{10a}$ c $\dfrac{(2b-a)(b-a)}{a^2 b^2}$ e $\dfrac{xb - 2ya}{a^2 b}$

   b $\dfrac{y+z-x}{xy}$ d $\dfrac{(3a - 2x)(a+x)}{ax}$ f $\dfrac{5x - 4a}{x}$

6 a $\dfrac{2}{b}$ b $\dfrac{3}{a}$ c $\dfrac{2}{3x}$ d $\dfrac{8a}{15}$

γ: C30 Algorithms and strategies — NC

Don't expect pupils to tackle all 15 problems. Choose a subset that appeals to your own taste and that you enjoy using.

Problem **0** needs to be managed with care in order to reap the potential benefit. Every class quickly becomes convinced that 14 minutes is the quickest! Don't burst their bubble too soon: look quizzical and ask 'Are you sure?'. (If some bright sparks see the light, ask them quietly to keep it to themselves for the moment.)

Ignoring arithmetical errors, the standard logical error lies in grabbing at a 'greedy strategy' which is invalid – namely the assumption that 'taking the torch back wastes time and so is best done by the fastest person'. When most pupils are 'sure' that 14 minutes is the answer, you might simply declare that there is a quicker way (without cheating) and challenge them to find it.

When reviewing the whole episode start by asking: 'To keep the total time short, which two soldiers should ideally travel together?'. Then get them to see that their 'greedy' assumption forced these two soldiers to travel separately. If possible, close Problem **0** by indicating the simple proof that 13 is the shortest (see below).

Answers

0 13 minutes (There have to be at least three double crossings and two single crossings. Either (i) 4 and 6 cross separately, or (ii) 4 and 6 cross together. In case (i), the two crossings with 4 and 6 use up 4 + 6 minutes, so total time $\geq 4 + 6 + 2 + 1 + 1 = 14$; in case (ii), 4 and 6 should not travel first or last; so the fastest time is $\geq 2 + 1 + 6 + 2 + 2 = 13$. Moreover, 13 minutes is achievable.)

3C Gamma

2 **After supper.** Originally **41** men, **28** monkeys, **60** maggots

3 A draw involves two teams, so each draw is recorded twice in the table. Hence the total number of draws listed in the table must be even.

4 a $25 = 5 + 5 + 5 + 5 + 1 + 1 + 1 + 1 + 1$

   b **No** ("odd + odd = even"; ten odds is even)

5 Start at the bottom: (i) D and E play twice; E loses at least once and D wins at most once; hence 1 win for D and 1 draw. (ii) E loses all other games, so E loses twice to C, twice to B, twice to A. (iii) D loses all other games, so D loses twice to C, twice to B and twice to A. (iv) C wins no other games, so draws once with B and loses once, and loses twice to A. (v) Finally B beats A once and loses once.

6 a **Yes** (e.g. switch colours in rows 1, 3, 5, 7; then switch colours in columns 1, 3, 5, 7).

   b **Yes**; yes.

7 **11** points (12 points is clearly enough: one cannot have 5 teams each scoring ≥ 12 points. It is not hard to find an arrangement which shows that 10 points is not enough: e.g. A, B, C, D, E all beat F, G, H; F beats G, G beats H, H beats F, and A beats B and C, B beats C and D, C beats D and E, D beats E and A, E beats A and B. This gives the clue as to why 11 points is enough: suppose A, B, C, D, E finish as the top five teams; then F, G, H all play each other with 6 points at stake, so A, B, C, D, E must share at most $56 - 6 = 50$ points between them.)

8 a **Yes**; 2413 (2 and 3 must go on the two ends; 4 must be next to 2 and 1 must be next to 3)

   b **Yes**; 362514 (3 and 4 must go on the two ends; 6 must be next to 3 and 1 must be next to 4. 2 must be between 5 and 6 and 5 must be between 1 and 2.)

   c **Yes**. 50 and 51 must go on the two ends.
      Starting at 51: 51, 1, 52, 2, 53, 3, ..., 75, 25; starting at 50: 50, 100, 49, 99, 48, 98, ..., 26, 76; then join up the ends.

9 **4**

10 Each 2 by 2 sub-grid includes the centre square and one corner square; so each move increases the entry in the centre square by 1 and increases the entry in exactly one corner square by 1. So the sum of the four corner squares is always equal to the centre square.

11 **No.** (He starts and finishes with 100 cards;
    ∴ the number of 2-for-3 swaps must equal the number of 3-for-2 swaps;
    ∴ the total number of cards "given" must be a multiple of $2 + 3$.)

12 Teams A and D win 0 games – or they would each have $\geq 5 + 4$ points (5 for a win and 4 for goals, since to win you must score at least 2 goals); ∴ D can neither beat nor be beaten by A, so A and D must draw. B wins only 1 game – or would have $\geq 2 \times 5 + 5$ points; ∴ B beats D and does not lose to A, so A and B draw. A cannot draw all three games (or else A would score $\geq 3 \times 2 + 3$ points); ∴ A loses to C. C wins only 2 games (or else scores $\geq 3 \times 5 + 6$ points).
    Hence results: C2, A1; C2, D1; C1, B1; B1, A1; B2, D1; A2, D2.

13 a Leave 01111111110; leave 95617181920

    b Leave 00000123450; leave 99999785960

14 Consider the three possibilities: **i** C draws with B; **ii** C draws with D; **iii** C draws with E.

    i In this case, D and E must draw twice; ∴ C beats E twice, and has only one other victory and no other draws, so C beats D once and loses to D once. All that remains for C, D, E are defeats, so A, B beats C, D, E. ∴ A beats B once and B beats A once.

    ii In this case C beats E twice; D draws with E at most once; E does not beat D, and must draw with D at least once; ∴ D beats E once and draws with E once. ∴ E draws with B once and loses once; C beats D once; A and B beats C, D twice; A beats B once and loses once.

    iii Here C beats E once; E draws with D once and loses once; C beats D twice; D draws with B once and loses once; A, B each beat C, E twice; A beats B once and loses once.

γ: C31 Index laws C   NC

Another brief set of problems exercising the index laws.

Answers

| 0 | a | 2 | b | $\sqrt{2}$ | | | | | | | | | | | | | |

1	a	200	b	150													
2	a	3	b	2	c	$\frac{2}{3}$	d	$\frac{3}{2}$	e	$\frac{1}{2}$	f	3	g	$\frac{3}{2}$		
3	a	4	b	$\frac{1}{3}$	c	$\frac{1}{4}$	d	4	e	$\frac{1}{2}$	f	$\frac{1}{3}$	g	$\frac{1}{4}$	h	$\sqrt{2}$	i	3

| 4 | a | 5 | c | 10 | e | 9 | g | 27 | i | 10 000 | k | $\frac{1}{2}$ |
| | b | $\sqrt{3}$ | d | 100 | f | 32 | h | 16 | j | 16 | l | 4 |

γ: C32 Approximate calculation: Multiplication and division   NC

There is much more to the art of 'estimation' and to 'approximation' than is generally acknowledged. These exercises concentrate on deriving guaranteed upper and lower bounds for products and quotients.

Answers

| 0 | a | ii $75 \times 32 = 2400$ | c | ii $23456 \div 779 \approx 30.11$ |
| | b | vi $12345 \div 616 \approx 20.04$ | | |

1 xi $169 \times 32 = 5408$

2 i $2100 < 75 \times 32 < 3200$ iv $7500 < 153 \times 52 < 9600$
   ii $5100 < 174 \times 32 < 7200$ v $42\,000 < 754 \times 67 < 56\,000$
   iii $3600 < 97 \times 43 < 5000$

3 a i   400   iii 2000   v 10 000
      ii 1200   iv   5000
   b i   100   iii 1200   v 8100
      ii 500   iv   3600
   c i   300   iii 800   v 1900
      ii 700   iv   1400

4 a 1900 $((10a + 10)(10b + 10) - 10a \times 10b = 100(a + b) + 100$ is largest when $a = b = 9$)
   b 10 900
5 a $20 \times 4 = 80, 25 \times 4 = 100$ e $120 \times 8 = 960, 125 \times 8 = 1000$
   b $25 \times 16 = 400, 26 \times 20 = 520$ f $16 \times 625 = 10\,000, 20 \times 630 = 12\,600$
   c $20 \times 75 = 1500, 25 \times 80 = 2000$ g $1200 \times 75 = 90\,000, 1250 \times 8 = 100\,000$
   d $37 \times 20 = 740, 40 \times 25 = 1000$ h $1250 \times 40 = 50\,000, 1280 \times 50 = 64\,000$
6 1 000 000 hours (100 years = $100 \times 365 \times 24$ hours < $100 \times 400 \times 25$ = 1 000 000 hours)
7 1 tonne ($407 \times 273 = 111111$; ∴ 111111 m² @ 9 g per square metre = 999.999 kg)
8 Upper bound: 206.5 m²; lower bound: 166.5 m²

9 vi $24680 \div 3579 \approx 8.015$
10 vi $86420 \div 7931 \approx 10.896$

11 i $1.75 = 70 \div 40 < 75 \div 32 < 80 \div 30 = 2.666\ldots$
    ii $4.25 = 170 \div 40 < 174 \div 32 < 180 \div 30 = 6$
    iii $2 = 90 \div 45 < 97 \div 43 < 100 \div 40 = 2.5$
    iv $2.5 = 150 \div 60 < 153 \div 52 < 160 \div 50 = 3.2$
    v $10 = 700 \div 70 < 754 \div 67 < 800 \div 60 = 13.333\ldots$

12 Just over 10 days (in fact 11.57 days; 1 day = $24 \times 60 \times 60$ sec $< 25 \times 4000 = 100\,000$ sec)

γ: C33 Similar triangles D: Sin and cos NC

This sequence of problems seeks to cement the basic link between similarity and the sin and cosin functions, and to provide some simple applications which illustrate how these trig functions allow one to 'solve triangles'. The approach mimics that adopted for tan in Section C20, but in a compressed form.

Answers

0 b, c

Length of AB	13 cm	18 cm	22 cm
Length of BC	7.5 cm	10.4 cm	12.7 cm
Length of AC	15 cm	20.8 cm	25.4 cm
Ratio $\frac{BC}{AC}$	0.5	0.5	0.5

   d All the right angled triangles ABC are similar, so $\frac{BC}{AC}$ = sin 30° = 0.5 must be constant.

1 b, c

Length of AB	8 cm	12 cm	16 cm
Length of BC	6 cm	9 cm	12 cm
Length of AC	10 cm	15 cm	20 cm
Ratio $\frac{BC}{AC}$	0.6	0.6	0.6

   d All the right angled triangles ABC are similar, so $\frac{BC}{AC}$ = sin 37° = 0.6 must be constant.

4 a i sin 30° ≈ 0.5   ii sin 37° ≈ 0.6
   b i cos 60° ≈ 0.5   ii cos 53° ≈ 0.6

5 24 cm

6 i $\frac{5}{12}$ ii $\frac{5}{13}$ iii $\frac{12}{13}$ iv $\frac{12}{5}$ v $\frac{12}{13}$ vi $\frac{5}{13}$

7 a i $\frac{1}{\sqrt{2}}$ ii $\frac{1}{\sqrt{2}}$ b i $\frac{\sqrt{3}}{2}$ ii $\frac{\sqrt{3}}{2}$

8 74°

9 ∠ABC = 180° − 37° = 143°, ∠BAC = ∠BCA = $18\frac{1}{2}°$ (since BA = BC = 5)

10 3 m

11 60°

12 12 cm

13 9 cm (Apex A, point of contact B between the ball and the cone, and centre C of the ball form a right angled triangle with right angle at B, with hypotenuse AC = 15 cm and ∠BAC = 37°.)

14 a cos θ   c $\cos^2 \theta + \sin^2 \theta = 1$
    b sin θ   d area(△AXC) = $\frac{1}{2}\sin \theta$, area(△ABC) = $\frac{1}{2}\cos \theta \sin \theta$

γ: C34 From fractions to decimals B   NC

This section underlines the two ideas introduced in Section C22. First we explore the way two fractions with a given denominator may be linked in that the recurring block of one may be obtained by moving the recurring block of the other one place to the left or right (which is the result of multiplying by 10 and discarding the integer part). Second we confront the awkward fact – which needs open discussion – that when two such fractions clearly add to 1, their recurring decimals add to '0.999......... for ever' (a phenomenon which should already be familiar, since $\frac{1}{3}$ = 0.333... , so 1 = 3 × $\frac{1}{3}$ = 0.999...).

Answers

> 0 a 0.$\dot{1}4285\dot{7}$ b 0.$\dot{8}5714\dot{2}$ c 0.$\dot{9}$

1 a 0.$\dot{4}2857\dot{1}$ d 0.$\dot{8}5714\dot{2}$ f 0.$\dot{7}1428\dot{5}$
   c 0.$\dot{2}8571\dot{4}$ e 0.$\dot{5}7142\dot{8}$ g 0.$\dot{1}4285\dot{7}$

2 a Recurring block moves one place to the left: $10 \times \frac{3}{7} = 4 + \frac{2}{7}$
   b Recurring block moves one place to the left: $10 \times \frac{2}{7} = 1 + \frac{6}{7}$
   c Recurring block moves one place to the left: $10 \times \frac{6}{7} = 8 + \frac{4}{7}$
   d Recurring block moves one place to the left: $10 \times \frac{4}{7} = 5 + \frac{5}{7}$
   e Recurring block moves one place to the left: $10 \times \frac{5}{7} = 7 + \frac{1}{7}$

3 See Problem **2** above.
4 a 0.$\dot{1}4285\dot{7}$ + 0.$\dot{8}5714\dot{2}$ = 0.$\dot{9}$ c 0.$\dot{4}2857\dot{1}$ + 0.$\dot{5}7142\dot{8}$ = 0.$\dot{9}$
   b 0.$\dot{2}8571\dot{4}$ + 0.$\dot{7}1428\dot{5}$ = 0.$\dot{9}$
5 a 0.$\dot{2}\dot{7}$ + 0.$\dot{7}\dot{2}$ = 0.$\dot{9}$ c 0.$\dot{4}2857\dot{1}$ + 0.$\dot{5}7142\dot{8}$ = 0.$\dot{9}$
   b 0.$\dot{1}0\dot{8}$ + 0.$\dot{8}9\dot{1}$ = 0.$\dot{9}$

γ: C35 Pythagoras' theorem B   NC

Three-dimensional problems have to be analysed by combining a fluency in two-dimensional geometrical techniques with the (learned) ability to identify two-dimensional cross-sections in three-dimensional configurations. In particular, pupils need to learn to use Pythagoras' theorem to calculate exact lengths in three-dimensions. If the idea in Problem **0** of looking for a triangle to act as a stepping-stone (see the commentary in the text of Section C35) is unfamiliar, be prepared to let pupils struggle for a good while before using the commentary in the text to bring out the general underlying principle.

Answers

> 0 3

1 a $8\sqrt{2}$ b 12   c 12, 12, 12
2 a EB = BD = DE   b 60°
3 a $8\sqrt{2}$ cm   b 15 cm

> 4 a $\sqrt{6}, \sqrt{6}, \sqrt{6}$ b 60°
> 5 2 cm (= 17 – 15 as in Problem **3b**)

γ: C36 Algebra review   NC

A *pot-pourri* of basic algebra, which will either serve as a useful review, or indicate where more basic work is needed.

Answers

> 0 a $\sqrt{3} - \sqrt{2}$
>   b True for all x
>   c $(b-x)(a-x)$

1 a 2
   b $17\sqrt{2}$

2 a $3y^2(x-y)$
   b $7y(x-y)(x+y)$
   c $(x-1)(x+1)$
   d $(x-2)(x+2)$
   e $(2x-3)(2x+3)$
   f $(5x+4)(x-1)$
   g $2(x-2)^2$
   h $(2x-3y)(2x+3y)$
   i $(x-15)(x+8)$
   j $(x+2b)(2x-a)$
   k $(2x-1)^2(2x-6)$
   l $(3x-4)(3x+6)$

3 a $x = -28$
   b $x = -\frac{1}{8}$
   c $x = \pm 6$
   d $x = \pm 4$
   e $x = -1$ or $x = 4$
   f $x = -\frac{1}{2}$ or $x = 1$
   g $x = -\frac{8}{3}$ or $x = \frac{10}{3}$
   h $x = 0$ or $x = \frac{2}{3}$

4 a $x = 10.5$
   b $x = 25$ ($x = 1$ is physically impossible)

5 a $\frac{6+x}{4x^2}$
   b $\frac{3x-10}{2x(x+2)}$

6 74 $(= 5^2 + 7^2)$

7 a $(2x+3)(x+2)$
   b $203 \times 102 = 7 \times 29 \times 2 \times 3 \times 17$ ($x = 100$)

8 a $\frac{\pi}{2}$ ($4x = 2\pi$)
   b $\sqrt{\pi}$ ($x^2 = \pi$)
   c $\frac{c}{2\pi}$
   d $2\sqrt{\frac{A}{\pi}}$

9 a $3x = 5y$
   b $\frac{4}{5}$ hours (= 48 minutes)

10 a $x = y^2 + 2$
    b $x = (y+2)^2$
    c $x = \frac{1-2y}{3y}$
    d $x = \pm\sqrt{\frac{a^2 y - b}{y}}$

11 a $2x^3 - 5x^2 + 7x + 5$
    b $x^3 - 8$
    c $3x^3 + 11x^2 + 8x - 4$
    d $4x^3 - 3a^2 x + a^3$

12 a $\frac{5}{9}(F - 32)$
    b $\frac{b}{2a}$

>   c $x = \frac{2b}{1+3a}$
>   d $\frac{c}{2a-b}$

13 a $x = 6$
    b $x = -3$

>   c $x = 6$
>   d $x = -6$

γ: C37 Sequences C   NC

A mixed collection of problems that challenge pupils to find (and to justify) a closed formula for the nth term of certain geometrically defined sequences. In Problem **0c** it is important to insist that the justification must be based on the way the sequence is defined, and not on presumptuous extrapolation from the familiar-looking sequence of entries in the table in part **a**. Problems 6-8 should perhaps be used sparingly.

Answers

0 a (3,) 5, 7, 9, 11
   b $1 + 2n$
   c First term = $3 = 1 + 2$; then add 2 matches each time.

1 $1 + 3n$
2 $n^2 \ (= 1 + 3 + 5 + \ldots + (2n - 1))$
3 $2n - 1$ (first term = 1; add 2 squares each time)
4 $\frac{1}{2}n(n + 1)$ (see **C27** *Sequences B*)

5 $(n-1)^2 + n^2$ (Colour the squares alternately black and white; then turn the figure through 45° to see $(n - 1)^2$ squares of one colour and n^2 squares of the other colour)

6 a $4n^2 - \frac{1}{2}(2n - 1)(2n - 2) = 2n^2 + 3n - 1$. (Each square contributes 4 matches, except that neighbouring squares can share a match, or edge.
      Horizontal shared edges contribute 1 (top) $+ 3 + \ldots + (2n - 3)$; and vertical shared edges contribute 2 (top) $+ 4 + \ldots + (2n - 2)$;
      ∴ total number of redundant matches $= 1 + 2 + 3 + \ldots + (2n - 2) = \frac{1}{2}(2n - 1)(2n - 2)$.

   b $6n - 2$ (first term = 4; add 6 matches each time)

   c $4 \times \frac{1}{2}n(n + 1) - n(n - 1) = n(n + 3)$. (Each square contributes 4 matches to the total; but $1 + 2 + \ldots + (n - 1) = \frac{1}{2}n(n - 1)$ vertical edges are duplicated and the same number of horizontal edges are duplicated;
      ∴ total number of redundant matches $= n(n - 1)$.)

   d $4n^2$. (Start by using the same idea as in **a** to count separately the duplicated edges
      i   for the middle row and above, and
      ii for the rows below the middle row.
      But when the answer turns out nicely, stop and look for a better way!)

7 $3 + \frac{3}{2}n(n - 1)$
8 $1 + \frac{3}{2}n(n - 1)$

γ: C38 Index laws *D*   NC

A final brief set of problems exercising the index law $a^m b^m = (ab)^m$.

Answers

0 a $\frac{4}{9}$ b 1

1 6
2 a $\left(\frac{1}{3}\right)^2$ b $\left(\frac{1}{5}\right)^2$ c $\left(\frac{1}{6}\right)^2$ d $\left(\frac{1}{2}\right)^2$ e $\left(\frac{1}{6}\right)^2$
3 a $\left(\frac{1}{3}\right)^3$ b $\left(\frac{1}{5}\right)^3$ c $\left(\frac{2}{3}\right)^3$
4 a 2^2 b 4^2 c 1^2 d 1^2 e 1^2
5 a 2^2 b 6^2 c 20^2 d 1^2
6 a 1^2 b 3^2 c 2^2 d 4^2
7 a 1^3 b 2^3 c 2^3

γ: C39 Geometry problems *B*   NC

These problems are labelled 'geometry'. But geometry here provides the setting in which techniques from all parts of elementary mathematics are exercised to create a curious unity: counting, arithmetic, interpreting a written problem, fractions, ratio, visualising, surds, simple algebra, and practical problem solving, as well as angles, perimeters, areas, circles, rectangles, isosceles triangles, etc. . Geometry is the part of mathematics that offers the most intuitive and accessible activities (from making sense of everyday three-dimensional configurations to accurate drawings), the most powerful calculational machinery (Pythagoras, similarity and trigonometry), and the most natural vehicle for formal reasoning (ruler and compass constructions, isosceles triangles, congruence and similarity). That is why geometry should take centre stage in any humane curriculum.

Answers

> 0 6 angles of 90° and two reflex angles (for example, two angles of 270°)

1 80 cm (edges alternately 5 cm and 10 cm)

2 10 : 3 $\left(\text{Let radii be } r \text{ and } R, \text{ with } r < R. \text{ Then } \frac{2}{5}\pi r^2 = \frac{1}{6}\pi R^2, \text{ so ratio } \frac{5}{6}R^2 : \frac{3}{5}r^2 = 10 : 3\right)$

3 $(135 - x)°$ ($\angle CDB = \angle ABD = x°$ (alternate angles); $\triangle ADN$ is isosceles, so $\angle DNA = 45°$)

4 $2(1 + \sqrt{3})^2 = 4(2 + \sqrt{3})$ $\left(PR = \sqrt{3} + 2 + \sqrt{3}, \text{ and } PR = \sqrt{PQ^2 + PR^2}. \therefore PQ = \sqrt{2}(1 + \sqrt{3})\right)$

5 a Use the SSS congruence criterion ((S) $AP = AQ$; (S) $BP = BQ$; (S) AB is common)
   b Use the SAS congruence criterion ($AP = AQ$; $\angle PAX = \angle QAX$ by part a ; AX is common. $\therefore \angle AXP = \angle AXQ = 90°$ and $PX = QX$.)

6 84° ($AP = AE$ and $\angle EAP = 48°$; $\therefore \angle APE = 66°$. DP produced bisects $\angle APB$; $\therefore \angle DPE = 180° - 66° - 30°$.)

7 a 3 : 4   b $\sqrt{3} : 2$

8 26 cm (Let $AW = a$, $WB = b$ and assume $a > b$; then $338 = a^2 + b^2$. Let the line through Y parallel to DA meet AB at V; then $YV = a + b$, $VW = a - b$, so $WY = 2(a^2 + b^2)$.)

9 a $\frac{5}{6}\left(= 1 - \frac{1}{12} - \frac{1}{12}\right)$ b $\frac{1}{3}\left(= \frac{5}{6} \div \frac{15}{6}\right)$

10 a Either use Pythagoras' theorem for suitable right angled triangles; or observe that $\triangle SAO$ and $\triangle ZAO$ are congruent ($SA = ZA$, $\angle SAO = \angle ZAO = 45°$, AO is common) and $\triangle SAO$ and $\triangle TBO$ are congruent ($SA = TB$, $\angle SAO = \angle TBO = 45°$, $AO = BO$); etc.)
   b The square (If $AB = 4s$, then $OS = s\sqrt{5}$; so the circle has area $5\pi s^2$ and the square has area $16s^2$)

> 11 13
> 12 Radius = 5 m
> 13 The covered part is larger.
> 14 17 cm (twice), 15 cm (twice)
> 15 $a = 11, b = 35$ or vice versa (area($ABCD$) = ab = 385 = 5 × 7 × 11, with $a + b$ minimal)

γ: C40 Estimation D: Big numbers   NC

The problems in this section illustrate the kind of questions you would like able pupils in Years 9-11 to tackle with a degree of confidence. Rather than expecting all pupils to grind through all 11 problems, it may be wise to concentrate on Problem **0** and two or three others (chosen to suit the teacher's taste). Problem **0** is deliberately challenging; but it is an excellent example of the way intelligent arithmetic can lead to unexpected insight.

Answers

> 0 4 minutes per day × 365 days per year ≈ 24 × 60 minutes per year = 1 day per year. So these figures suggest that 1 complete rotation is gained each year. This must be due to the rotation of the Earth around the Sun: if the Earth rotates clockwise around the Sun, then it also rotates clockwise on its own axis, so needs to make *slightly more than* 1 complete turn each day between noon and noon in order to point again directly at the Sun.

1 70 000 bees (= (7 000 000 × 10) ÷ 1000)
2 No (1 000 000 hours = 1 000 000 ÷ (24 × 365) years > 1 000 000 ÷ (25 × 400) = 100 years)
3 a ∠AOS = 7°   b ≈ 250 000 stades $\left(\frac{7}{360} \times \text{circumference} = 5000\right)$
4 A patch about 20 cm by 30 cm in size
5 Just over 10 days (1 000 000 seconds = 1 000 000 ÷ (60 × 60 × 24) days >
   1 000 000 ÷ (4000 × 25) days = 10 days)
6 a Something of diameter approximately 1 mm – say a grain of rice.
      (Let the orange have diameter ≈ 10 cm, and let the diameter of the model Earth = d cm. Then d : 10 = 12 740 : 1 392 000 ≈ 13 000 : 1 300 000 = 1 : 100, so d ≈ 0.1 cm.)
   b Nearly 12 metres away. (The diameter of the Earth is 12 740 km. If the model Earth should be placed r cm from the orange, then r : 0.1 = 150 000 000 : 12 740.)
7 ≈ 4 × 10^9 beats (In 100 years: 72 × 60 × 24 × 365 × 100 ≈ 4200 × 25 × 400 × 100 = 4.2 × 10^9)
8 1 200 000 km² (1 hectare = 10 000 m²; 1 km² = 1 000 000 m² = 100 hectares.
   54 acres ≈ 22 hectares.
   (22 hect/min) × (60 × 24 × 365 min/yr) ≈ 1200 × 10 000 hect/yr
                                          = 120 000 km²/yr
9 ≈ 1700 km/h $\left(\text{One orbit every 24 hours} = \pi \times 12\,740 \text{ km/day} \approx 40\,000 \text{ km/day}\right)$

10 Nothing definite can be concluded from a single experiment, and what can be concluded depends on knowing much more about the situation being sampled. So this is an invitation to think intelligently rather than to be dogmatic. All one knows for sure is that there are at least 40 fish (or 40 + 28 = 68 if all of the original 30 remain alive). However, since specimens from my original sample constitute 5% of the second sample, this suggests that my second sample of 40 may constitute roughly 5% of the total fish population, in which case there are around 20 × 40 = 800 fish altogether. But this is rough: it is easy to imagine that seconds later my second sample might have included only 1 (or even 0) or perhaps 3 fish from my first sample.

γ: C41 Scale factors B: Length, area and volume   NC
Geometrical and practical problems involving similarity and enlargement.

Answers

0 $3\sqrt{2}$ (Let the rectangles be 2 by x and y by 6. ∴ $\frac{6}{x} = \frac{y}{2}$. Also $6y = 2 \times (2x)$, so $3y = 2x$.)

1 20 cm (x : 24 = 45 : 54 = 5 : 6)
2 Less than half $\left(\text{area}(APQR) = \left(\frac{2}{3}\right)^2 = \frac{4}{9}\right)$
3 4³ × 25 kg = 1.6 tonnes
4 $\frac{1}{4}$ (△ALN, △NLB, △MCL and △MNL are congruent equilateral triangles)
5 24 cm (= $\sqrt[3]{216}$ × 4 cm)

6 a $RA = RB = 2$, $\angle RAP = \angle PBQ = 60°$, $AP = BQ = 1$;
      ∴ △RAP and △PBQ are congruent by SAS, so $RP = PQ$. Similarly $PQ = QR$.
   b 3 : 1 (△RAP is congruent to half an equilateral triangle of side 2, so $RP = \sqrt{3}$)
7 a ∠UAB = ∠UBA = 30°; ∴ ∠ZUV = ∠BUA = 120°, so all angles of UVWXYZ equal 120°.
      Also △UAB has equal base angles; ∴ UA = UB.
      △UAB and △VBC are congruent; ∴ BU = BV.
      ∠UBV = ∠ABC − ∠UBA − ∠VBC = 60°, so △BUV is equilateral.
      ∴ $UV = \frac{1}{3}AC$, so all sides of UVWXYZ are equal $\left(\text{to } \frac{1}{3}AC = \frac{AB}{\sqrt{3}}\right)$.
   b 3 : 1

> 8 a It is easy to show that △ACD, △ABW, △AVZ are all isosceles with apex angle = 36°.
>   b If DC = 1, then WB = DB = DW = τ − 1, and ZV = ZB − VB = 1 − (τ − 1) (C13, problem **9**)
> 9 0.963 kg and 1.941 kg

γ: C42 Sequences D: Guess my rule NC

This section builds on Sections C27 and C37. Problem **0b** should make it clear that, while a sequence may be defined in a way that allows you to generate successive terms, it is often hard even to guess the algebraic rule behind the terms which emerge. Before returning to solve this problem in Problem **3**, pupils are immersed in the valuable task of trying to formulate conjectured arithmetical patterns in algebraic terms: Problems **1** and **2** will constitute a serious challenge for many pupils and should not be hurried. Problems **1**, **2** and **3** all make use of the closed formula for the nth triangular number (section C27, Problem **4**).

Answers

> 0 a 7   b Probably unclear; see Problem **3**

> 1 a $2n$ e $4n$ i $4n - 1$ m $n(n + 1)$
>   b $3n$ f $-2n$ j $4n + 2$ n 3^n
>   c $2n + 1$ g $2(n - 1)$ k $n^2 - 1$ o $5(n - 1)$
>   d $2n - 1$ h $3n - 1$ l $3n + 1$ p $4n - 2$

> 2 a 2^n e $\frac{1}{2}n(n+1) + 2$ i $\frac{1}{2}n(n+1) + 1$ m $(n+1)^2 - 3$
>   b $\frac{1}{2}n(n+1)$ f $2^n - 1$ j 2×3^n
>   c $n(n+2) = (n+1)^2 - 1$ g $n(n-1) + 1$ k $3 \times 2^{n-1} + 2$
>   d 2^{n-1} h $3 \times 2^{n-1}$ l $\frac{1}{2}n(n+1) + 3$
>
> 3 a Number of regions created by 0 lines = 1
>   Let the maximum number of regions created by n lines be R_n. ∴ $R_0 = 1$ and $R_n = R_{n-1} + n$.
>   ∴ $R_n = R_{n-1} + n = [R_{n-2} + (n-1)] + n = \ldots = R_0 + (1 + 2 + 3 + \ldots + (n-1)) + n$
> $= 1 + \frac{1}{2}n(n+1)$

γ: C43 What's my number? NC

Although these problems are still formulated numerically, and so could be tackled purely by "searching", the range to be scanned is now deliberately larger, so encourage pupils to use a little algebra (as indicated in the text). Problem **0** is deliberately designed so that primitive searching suffices; but after it has been solved, it should be used to illustrate the algebraic approach – which is the only viable way to solve most of the other problems.

Answers

> 0 a 14, 44, 74 ("4 more than a multiple of 5" means the units digit = 4 or 9;
>   "2 more than a multiple of 6" means the number must be even.
>   So only need to try 14, 24, 34, ...)

1 3 (28, 91 or 154)

2 3 (121, 144, 169; or 6 if we include 1, 4, 9)

3 **2** (Must have the form $42t + 41$, so 41 or 83)
4 **Yes**; **3** (If $10a + b$ is a multiple of $a + b$, then $9a$ is a multiple of $a + b > a$; $\therefore a + b = 3$.)
5 **65 or 245** (Digit-sum 11 means 2 more than a multiple of 9; $\therefore$ must have the form $45t + 20$)
6 **7, 91, 175, or 259** (Must have the form $84t + 7$)
7 **2** (55 or 235. Must have the form $180t + 55$)
8 **2** (11 or 179. Must have the form $168t + 11$)
9 **59, 119, 179** (Must have the form $60t + 59$)

γ: E1 Integers, digits and algebra NC

Answers

1. 61 (Units digit of a 2-digit prime = 1, 3, 7 or 9. Only square with tens digit = 1 is 16; only square with tens digit 3 = 36; no squares with tens digit 7 or 9)

2. 11, 13, 17, 31, 37, 71, 73, 79, 97 (Tens digit must be 1, 3, 7 or 9)

3. 86 ($100a + 10b + 3 = 10a + b + 777$; $\therefore 90a + 9b = 774$)

4. a One of the integers must be even
   b i 4   ii 23, 29   iii 89, 97
   c 113 to 127

5. a Let each edge have sum s. Adding all four edges uses each of 1-12 once and the four corners twice: $\therefore 4s = (1 + 2 + 3 + \ldots + 12) + (1 + 2 + 3 + x) = 84 + x$;
   $\therefore x = 4$ ($s = 22$), or $x = 8$ ($s = 23$), or $x = 12$ ($s = 24$).
   If $x = 12$, top row = 1 + 10 + 11 + 2; then right edge cannot be completed.
   b $x = 3$ ($s = 31$) or $x = 7$ ($s = 32$). Neither actually works.

6. The answer is the tens digit of the original number: $(10a + b) - (a + b) = 9a$.

7. a "ab" + "ba" = $11(a + b)$; $\therefore$ "ab" = 10 is the only solution.
   b "ab" − "ba" = $9(a − b)$ is never prime.

8. Yes; 25 ($9(a − b)$ is a square precisely when $a − b = 0$ ("ab" = 11, 22, ..., 99), or $a − b = 1$ ("ab" = 10, 21, ..., 98), or $a − b = 4$ ("ab" = 40, 51, ..., 95), or $a − b = 9$ ("ab" = 90).)

9. 7744 = 88^2 ("$aabb$" = $11(100a + b)$; for a square, the bracket = $99a + [a + b]$ must be a multiple of 11, so $[a + b] = 11$ Now test $100a + b$ to see when it equals 11 times a square.)

10. a £199.98 (see **C26**, Problem 11)
    b £65.32

γ: E2 From fractions to decimals C NC

Answers

1. a $\frac{2}{3}$ b $\frac{1}{3}$ (with a loop)   c $\frac{2}{3}$ (with a loop)

2. a i $\frac{6}{7}$ ii $\frac{5}{7}$ iii $\frac{4}{7}$
   b i $\frac{3}{7}$ iii $\frac{6}{7}$ v $\frac{5}{7}$ vii a hexagon
      ii $\frac{2}{7}$ iv $\frac{4}{7}$ vi $\frac{1}{7}$

3. a i $\frac{10}{11}$ ii $\frac{9}{11}$ iii $\frac{8}{11}$ iv $\frac{7}{11}$ v $\frac{6}{11}$
   b i $\frac{10}{11}$ iii $\frac{9}{11}$ v $\frac{8}{11}$ vii $\frac{7}{11}$ ix $\frac{6}{11}$
      ii $\frac{1}{11}$ iv $\frac{2}{11}$ vi $\frac{3}{11}$ viii $\frac{4}{11}$ x $\frac{5}{11}$

4. a i $\frac{10}{13}$ iii $\frac{12}{13}$ v $\frac{4}{13}$ vii a hexagon
      ii $\frac{9}{13}$ iv $\frac{3}{13}$ vi $\frac{1}{13}$
   b i $\frac{7}{13}$ iii $\frac{11}{13}$ v $\frac{8}{13}$ vii a hexagon
      ii $\frac{5}{13}$ iv $\frac{6}{13}$ vi $\frac{2}{13}$
   c i $\frac{12}{13}$ iii $\frac{4}{13}$ v $\frac{6}{13}$
      ii $\frac{3}{13}$ iv $\frac{11}{13}$ vi $\frac{8}{13}$
      vii two separate (dotted) hexagons, each with three (solid black) diagonals

5 Six separate triangular prisms, with dotted triangular ends (e.g. $\frac{1}{37}, \frac{10}{37}, \frac{26}{37}$ and $\frac{36}{37}, \frac{27}{37}, \frac{11}{37}$) joined by three parallel solid black edges.

6 a $0.\dot{0}5882352941176\dot{4}7$
   b $0.\dot{0}5263157894736842\dot{1}$
   c $0.\dot{0}4347826086956521739\dot{1}3$
   d $0.\dot{0}344827586206896551724137793\dot{1}$
   e $0.\dot{0}3225806451612\dot{9}$

γ: E3 Consecutive integers   NC

Answers

1 a 1, 2, 3   b 3, 4, 5
   c i   Middle number even
      ii $(n-1) + n + (n+1) = 3n$ is even precisely when n is even.

2 a 3, 4, 5   b 7, 8, 9
   c i   Middle number a multiple of 4
      ii $(n-1) + n + (n+1) = 3n$ is a multiple of 4 precisely when n is a multiple of 4.

3 a 1, 2, 3   b 3, 4, 5
   c i   Middle number even
      ii $s = (n-1) + n + (n+1) = 3n$ is a multiple of 6 precisely when n is even.

4 a 2, 3, 4   b 5, 6, 7
   c i   Middle number a multiple of 3
      ii $s = (n-1) + n + (n+1) = 3n$ is a multiple of 9 precisely when n is a multiple of 3.

5 a Middle number a multiple of 4   b $s = (2n-2) + 2n + (2n+2) = 6n$
   c $s = 6n$ is a multiple of 4 precisely when n is even (i.e. when the middle number $2n$ is a multiple of 4)

6 a $s = 6n$ is a multiple of 5 precisely when n is is a multiple of 5 (i.e. when the middle number $2n$ is a multiple of 10)
   b $6n$ is a multiple of 7 precisely when n is a multiple of 7 (i.e. when the middle number $2n$ is a multiple of 14)

7 a Always! $s = 6n$ is always a multiple of 3
   b Always! $s = 6n$ is always a multiple of 6
   c When n is divisible by 3 (∴ $s = 6n$ is divisible by 9); i.e. when the middle number $2n$ is divisible by 3
   d When n is divisible by 2 (∴ $s = 6n$ is divisible by 12); i.e. when the middle number $2n$ is divisible by 4

8 a Middle number even; $s = (n-2) + (n-1) + n + (n+1) + (n+2) = 5n$ is even precisely when n is even
   b Middle number a multiple of 3; $s = (n-2) + (n-1) + n + (n+1) + (n+2) = 5n$ is divisible by 3 precisely when n is divisible by 3
   c Middle number a multiple of 4; $s = (n-2) + (n-1) + n + (n+1) + (n+2) = 5n$ is a multiple of 4 precisely when n is a multiple of 4
   d Always! $s = (n-2) + (n-1) + n + (n+1) + (n+2) = 5n$ is always divisible by 5

9 a Always! $s = n + (n+1) + (n+2) + (n+3) = 4n + 6 = 2(2n+3)$ is always even
   b When the first number is divisible by 3, since $n + (n+1) + (n+2) + (n+3) = 4n + 6$ is divisible by 3 precisely when n is divisible by 3
   c When the first number is one more than a multiple of 5, since $(n+1) + (n+2) + (n+3) + (n+4) = 4n + 10$ is divisible by 5 precisely when n is divisible by 5
   d Never! $s = n + (n+1) + (n+2) + (n+3) = 4n + 6 = 4(n+1) + 2$ always leaves remainder 2 on division by 4

3C Gamma

γ: E4 How many?

Answers

1. 14
2. 15
3. a 5   b 41
4. a 10   b 574 $\left(=\tfrac{1}{2}(41 \times 28)\right)$
5. a i 1   ii 1

   iii 4 (consider in turn each possible way of adding a tile to the unique shape with 3 tiles)

   b 6 (consider in turn each possible way of adding a tile to each of the 4 shapes with 4 tiles)
6. a 2893 $(= 4 + 900 \times 3 + 90 \times 2 + 9 \times 1)$

   b 8 888 888 899 $(= 10 + 9 \times (10^9 - 10^8) + 8 \times (10^8 - 10^7) + \ldots + 1 \times (10^1 - 10^0)$
   $= 10 + 9\,000\,000\,000 - 111\,111\,111)$
7. a 81 $(= 9 \times 9)$ b 19 $(= 100 - 9 \times 9)$ c 271 $(= 1000 - 9 \times 9 \times 9)$
8. a i 6 $(= 3 \times 2$; one bag must contain exactly 2 marbles and there are 3 ways to choose this pair, and then 2 ways to choose the bag they go in)

   ii 6 $(= 3 \times 2 \times 1$; 1 marble goes in each bag; there are 3 ways to choose the bag for the first marble to go in, then 2 ways to choose the bag for the second marble, and 1 way to choose the bag for the last marble)

   b i 14 $(= 4 \times 2 + 3 \times 2$; the marbles must be split either 3 + 1 or 2 + 2; in the first case, there are 4 ways to choose the 3 and then 2 ways to choose the bag they go in; in the second case there are 3 ways to split the 4 marbles into 2 + 2, and 2 ways to allocate each split to the two bags)

   ii 36 $(= 6 \times 3 \times 2$; the marbles must split as 2 + 1 + 1; there are 6 ways to choose the 2, 3 ways to decide which bag they go in; for each such choice there are then 2 ways to allocate the remaining 2 marbles to the other two bags)

   iii 24 $(= 4 \times 3 \times 2 \times 1$; the marbles must split 1 to a bag – so there are 4 ways to choose the bag for the first marble, then 3 ways to choose the bag for the second marble, then 2 ways to choose the bag for the third marble, and 1 way for the last marble)
9. a 125 $(= 5 \times 5 \times 5)$ b 100 $= (4 \times 5 \times 5)$
10. a 36   b 488
11. 72 $(= 4 \times 4 \times 3 + 2 \times 4 \times 3)$ solutions altogether.

    a R = 0   b O = 9 (with a carry of 1 from the tens column)

    c O + I must carry 1; 2F is even, so N is odd and ≥ 3; U + V cannot add to 17 or 19, so N can be 3 or 5

    d i If N = 3, F = 1;   ii if N = 5, F = 2

    e If i, U + V = 13 = 5 + 8, 8 + 5, 6 + 7, or 7 + 6;
    if ii, U + V = 15 = 7 + 8, or 8 + 7

    f 4 digits left for E; then 3 digits left for I

γ: E5 Primes in arithmetic progression   NC

Answers

> 0. a 3, 5, 7;   5, 11, 17;   7, 13, 19
>   b 5, 11, 17, 23
>   c i Must be even (two equal steps on from first term 2), so can't be prime
>   ii length ≤ 2

1. b Yes   c No   d Yes   e No   f No
2. a No   b No   c No   d Yes   e Yes   f No
3. a Yes   b Yes   c 19

4 No: if step length = n, the AP is "3, 3 + n, 3 + 2n, 3 + 3n", and the fourth term = 3(1 + n) can't be prime

5 a No (unless we extend it backwards)   b Yes   c 13

6 a Yes: for example, 5, 11, 17, 23

   b Yes: for example, 5, 11, 17, 23, 29; or 5, 17, 29, 41, 53

   c No: if step = n, we get "5, 5 + n, 5 + 2n, 5 + 3n, 5 + 4n, 5 + 5n", and the sixth term = 5(1 + n) can't be prime

7 a Yes: for example, 7, 19, 31, 43

   b i Yes: for example, 7, 37, 67, 97, 127

      ii Yes: for example, 7, 37, 67, 97, 127, 157

      iii Yes. If p has units digit 1, the third term must be a multiple of 5; if p has units digit 3, the fourth term must be a multiple of 5; if p has units digit 9, the fifth term must be a multiple of 5; so any such AP must have all terms ending in 7. 27 composite rules out step length 10 or 20; 57 composite rules out step length 50; 187 composite rules out step length 60, or 120 or 180; 77 composite rules out step length 70; 87 composite rules out step length 80; 207 composite rules out step length 100; 117 composite rules out step length 110; 247 composite rules out step length 120; 267 composite rules out step length 130; 147 composite rules out step length 140.
So try step length 150: 7, 157, 307, 457, 607, 757, 907.

      iv No: if step length = n, we get "7, 7 + n, 7 + 2n, 7 + 3n, 7 + 4n, 7 + 5n, 7 + 6n, 7 + 7n" and the eighth term = 7(1 + n) can't be prime

8 If the step length has units digit 2, 4, 6 or 8, we will hit a multiple of 5 as in **7biii**; hence the step length must be a multiple of 10. If the step length is not a multiple of 3, then each group of 3 successive terms contains a multiple of 3; hence the step length must be a multiple of 3. Similarly, the step length must be a multiple of 7 – as well as a multiple of 2 and 5, and so must be a multiple of 210.
For example, 881, 1091, 1301, 1511, 1721, 1931, 2141, 2351.

γ: E6 More missing digits   NC

Answers

1 154 + 76, 156 + 47, 325 + 76 each giving rise to 4 solutions (by interchanging tens and units digits)

2 287 × 89 (units column cannot be 1 × 3 or 3 × 1, so must be 7 × 9 or 9 × 7)

3 26 × 96

4 277 × 15, or 259 × 35

5 733 × 54

6 919 × 99, 929 × 99, ..., 999 × 99

7 805 × 73, or 523 × 55

γ: E7 Tiling

Answers

1 a Need 4 tiles; two – all tiles horizontal or all tiles vertical

   b i Cover $\leq$ 24 squares;   6 tiles   iii Seems to always be **in a corner**

      ii **Yes**; 1 square remains uncovered

2 a 62 squares; $\leq$ 31 tiles

   b **No** (Each tile covers 1 black and 1 white square; but there are 30 of one colour and 32 of the other colour, so a complete tiling is impossible)

3C Gamma

3 a 12 black squares and 13 white squares
  b Two black squares and two white
  c 6 tiles; 12 black, 12 white – leaving one uncovered *white* square
4 a The other three white squares positioned like *B* (diagonally adjacent to the centre square)
  b The other three white squares positioned like *C* (in the middle of an edge)
5 a Because the "colours" occur in sequence in each row and column
  b 6 "x", 6 "y", 6 "z" – but 7 with colour "w", so the uncovered square will be a "w"
  c The one centre square (type *A*), the four squares of type *C* (middle of an edge) and two of the squares of type *B* are coloured "y", so cannot be the one uncovered square

γ: E8 Identical portions   NC

Answers

1 a $4 \times \frac{1}{2}$ **b** $6 \times \frac{1}{3}$ **c** $8 \times \frac{1}{4}$

2 a No; one cake remains uncut, so one piece is $> \frac{2}{3}$
  b Yes; $4 \times \frac{1}{2}$
  c i No; one cake is cut into at most 2 pieces, so one piece is $> \frac{2}{5}$
    ii Yes; $5 \times \left(\frac{1}{5} + \frac{1}{5}\right)$, $5 \times \left(\frac{1}{3} + \frac{1}{15}\right)$, or $5 \times \left(\frac{1}{4} + \frac{3}{20}\right)$
  d i Yes; $6 \times \frac{1}{3}$ **ii** $6 \times \left(\frac{1}{6} + \frac{1}{6}\right)$, $6 \times \left(\frac{1}{4} + \frac{1}{12}\right)$

3 a 4 people, 4 identical portions – each with *r* pieces; ∴ 4*r* pieces altogether
  b $4 \times \left(\frac{1}{4} + \frac{1}{4}\right)$, $4 \times \left(\frac{1}{3} + \frac{1}{6}\right)$
  c $4 \times \left(\frac{1}{6} + \frac{1}{6} + \frac{1}{6}\right)$, $4 \times \left(\frac{1}{3} + \frac{1}{12} + \frac{1}{12}\right)$, or $4 \times \left(\frac{1}{4} + \frac{1}{8} + \frac{1}{8}\right)$

4 a i No (with identical portions for 3 people, the number of pieces must be a multiple of 3)
    ii No (same reason)
  b i No (same reason)   **ii** No (same reason)

5 a $3 \times \left(\frac{1}{3} + \frac{1}{3}\right)$, $3 \times \left(\frac{1}{2} + \frac{1}{6}\right)$ **b** $3 \times \left(\frac{1}{3} + \frac{1}{6} + \frac{1}{6}\right)$, $3 \times \left(\frac{1}{4} + \frac{1}{4} + \frac{1}{6}\right)$

6 a $5 \times \left(\frac{1}{5} + \frac{1}{5}\right)$, $5 \times \left(\frac{1}{3} + \frac{1}{15}\right)$ **b** $5 \times \left(\frac{1}{6} + \frac{1}{6} + \frac{1}{15}\right)$, $5 \times \left(\frac{1}{4} + \frac{1}{10} + \frac{1}{20}\right)$

7

Number of people *p*	1	2	3	4	5	6	7	8	9	10
Minimum number of pieces required *N*	2	2	6	4	10	6	14	8	18	10

8 a *p* pieces (The number of pieces has to be a multiple of *p*, so must be $\geq p$. If $p = 2m$, cut each cake into *m* equal pieces and give each person 1 piece.)
  b i **2*p***. 2*p* pieces is possible: cut each cake into *p* equal pieces and give each person 2 pieces. The number of pieces must be a multiple of *p*; and with just $p = 2n + 1$ pieces, one cake must be cut into at most *n* pieces, so the largest piece has size $\geq \frac{1}{n} > \frac{2}{p}$.
    ii $3 \times \left(\frac{1}{3} + \frac{1}{3}\right)$, $3 \times \left(\frac{1}{2} + \frac{1}{6}\right)$
    iii $5 \times \left(\frac{1}{5} + \frac{1}{5}\right)$, $5 \times \left(\frac{1}{3} + \frac{1}{15}\right)$, $5 \times \left(\frac{1}{4} + \frac{3}{20}\right)$
    iv $7 \times \left(\frac{1}{7} + \frac{1}{7}\right)$, $7 \times \left(\frac{1}{4} + \frac{1}{28}\right)$, $7 \times \left(\frac{1}{6} + \frac{5}{42}\right)$, $7 \times \left(\frac{1}{5} + \frac{3}{35}\right)$
    v $9 \times \left(\frac{1}{9} + \frac{1}{9}\right)$, $9 \times \left(\frac{1}{5} + \frac{1}{45}\right)$, $9 \times \left(\frac{1}{6} + \frac{1}{18}\right)$, $9 \times \left(\frac{1}{9} + \frac{1}{63}\right)$

9 a $3 \times \left(\frac{1}{3} + \frac{1}{6} + \frac{1}{6}\right), 3 \times \left(\frac{1}{2} + \frac{1}{12} + \frac{1}{12}\right), 3 \times \left(\frac{1}{4} + \frac{1}{4} + \frac{1}{6}\right)$

b $4 \times \left(\frac{1}{4} + \frac{1}{4}\right), 4 \times \left(\frac{1}{3} + \frac{1}{6}\right), 4 \times \left(\frac{5}{12} + \frac{1}{12}\right)$

c $5 \times \left(\frac{1}{5} + \frac{1}{10} + \frac{1}{10}\right), 5 \times \left(\frac{1}{4} + \frac{1}{10} + \frac{1}{20}\right), 5 \times \left(\frac{1}{3} + \frac{1}{30} + \frac{1}{30}\right)$

d $6 \times \left(\frac{1}{6} + \frac{1}{6}\right), 6 \times \left(\frac{1}{5} + \frac{2}{15}\right), 6 \times \left(\frac{1}{4} + \frac{1}{12}\right)$

10 a i No (two of the cakes remain completely uncut, so two pieces are $> \frac{3}{4}$).

    ii $4 \times \left(\frac{1}{2} + \frac{1}{4}\right)$ (Unique! With 8 pieces, one of the three cakes is cut into at most 2 pieces, so the largest piece is $\geq \frac{1}{2}$.)

b i No (one of the three cakes remain completely uncut, so one piece has size $1 > \frac{3}{5}$)

    ii $5 \times \left(\frac{2}{5} + \frac{1}{5}\right), 5 \times \left(\frac{1}{2} + \frac{1}{10}\right)$

c i Yes; $6 \times \frac{1}{2}$

    ii $6 \times \left(\frac{1}{4} + \frac{1}{4}\right), 6 \times \left(\frac{1}{3} + \frac{1}{6}\right), 6 \times \left(\frac{2}{5} + \frac{1}{10}\right)$

11 $4 \times \left(\frac{1}{4} + \frac{1}{4} + \frac{1}{4}\right), 4 \times \left(\frac{1}{2} + \frac{1}{8} + \frac{1}{8}\right), 4 \times \left(\frac{1}{4} + \frac{1}{3} + \frac{1}{6}\right)$

12 $6 \times \left(\frac{1}{4} + \frac{1}{4}\right), 6 \times \left(\frac{1}{3} + \frac{1}{6}\right), 6 \times \left(\frac{2}{5} + \frac{1}{10}\right)$

13 $6 \times \left(\frac{1}{2} + \frac{1}{3}\right)$ (Unique! Three of the five cakes are cut into at most 2 pieces, so the largest piece is $\geq \frac{1}{2}$)

14 $12 \times \left(\frac{1}{3} + \frac{1}{12}\right), 12 \times \left(\frac{1}{4} + \frac{1}{6}\right), 12 \times \left(\frac{1}{8} + \frac{7}{24}\right)$

15 $12 \times \left(\frac{1}{2} + \frac{1}{12}\right), 12 \times \left(\frac{1}{3} + \frac{1}{4}\right), 12 \times \left(\frac{5}{12} + \frac{1}{6}\right)$

Glossary

A definition (according to Pirandello) is like a sack: it refuses to stand up until you put something in it! Rather than try to give a string of succinct formal definitions, this list is more like an 'index'. To convey the formal mathematical meaning of each term we simply refer the reader to the section(s) where each term first appears, or where its meaning or significance is elucidated. Where this seems inadequate, we give a rough definition.

algebraically identical Two algebraic expressions are algebraically identical if one can be transformed into the other using the permissible rules of elementary algebra. (At lower secondary school level we tend to ignore the difficulty that the formal domains of definition of the two expressions may differ – as with 'x' and '$\frac{x^2}{x}$', where the second is not strictly defined when $x = 0$.)

algorithm A procedure for solving *any* problem of a specified type (often consisting of a sequence of precisely described steps). A valid algorithm should come with a *proof* showing that it 'does exactly what it says on the tin'.

alternate angles Beta C2
apex (base) Beta T20
arithmetic progression (AP) Gamma E5
average (mean) Beta C1; Beta C32

base 10 Alpha E10
bisector Alpha C7, Beta C5

composite Gamma C2
congruent (Alpha T11) Beta T11
congruence criteria for triangles (SSS, SAS, ASA) (Alpha C17) Beta C4, Beta C7, Beta C15
consecutive Beta C23
contradiction Beta C10
corresponding angles Alpha T10
cuboid (Alpha C18) Alpha E14, Gamma C15
cylinder Gamma C15

decimal fraction Beta C9
denominator Alpha C14
digits Alpha T8
distributive law (Gamma T7) Gamma C5
divisible/factor/multiple Alpha C11

enlargement Beta T8
equilateral triangle Beta T20
estimate: lower; upper Beta C13, Gamma C32
exponent Gamma T14
exterior angle of a triangle (or polygon) Beta C11

factor/divisible/multiple Alpha C11
formula Beta T9
fraction: numerator/denominator; lowest terms Alpha C14
function Gamma C16

index Gamma T14
interior angle of a triangle (or polygon) Beta C11
isosceles triangle Beta T11

kite Beta T11

line, line segment Alpha T11
linear Gamma C7
locus Gamma T24

mean Beta C1
midpoint Alpha C17
multiple/divisible/factor Alpha C11

numerals Alpha T26
numerator Alpha C14

operators Alpha T14

parallel (||) Beta T2, Beta C2
parallelogram Alpha T11
perpendicular (⊥) Alpha C17, Beta T2, Beta C5
polygon Alpha E16, Gamma C10
polyhedron Alpha E16
position-to-term Beta T9
prime number Beta T24
prime factorisation Beta T13
prism Gamma C15
produced Beta C11
product Beta T4
proportion Beta C20
pyramid Gamma C35

QED These are the first letters of the latin phrase 'Quod Erat Demonstrandum' (= that which was to be

proved). The letters are often inserted to mark the end of a proof.
quadratics Alpha T19
quadrilateral Beta C2

ratio: part-to-part; part-to-whole Beta C20
reciprocal Beta C22
rectangle (Alpha C19) Beta T11
regular polygon Gamma C10
rhombus Beta T11
right angle Alpha C17
right angled triangle (Alpha C17) Beta T20
ruler and compass constructions Beta C5

sector Alpha E5
sequence Beta T9
similar triangles Gamma T13, Gamma C13

similarity criteria for triangles Gamma T13, Gamma C13
straight angle Beta C11
simplify/simplification Beta T16, Beta C25, Gamma T5, Gamma C13
surd Gamma T15

term-to-term Beta T9
trapezium Gamma C3

unit Alpha T21, Beta T22, Beta C18
unitary method Beta C20, Gamma C18

vertices Alpha E16

word problems Alpha C12